# OXFORD STUDIES IN AFRICAN AFFAIRS

*General Editors*
John D. Hargreaves, Michael Twaddle,
Terence Ranger

# THE MAKING OF APARTHEID
# 1948–1961

# The Making of Apartheid 1948–1961

## Conflict and Compromise

DEBORAH POSEL

CLARENDON PRESS · OXFORD

OXFORD UNIVERSITY PRESS

Walton Street, Oxford OX2 6DP

*Offices in*
Oxford, New York
Athens, Bangkok, Calcutta, Cape Town, Chennai,
Dar es Salaam, Delhi, Florence, Hong Kong, Istanbul, Karachi,
Kuala Lumpur, Madrid, Melbourne, Mexico City, Mumbai,
Nairobi, Paris, Singapore, Taipei, Tokyo, Toronto

*and associated companies in*
Berlin, Ibadan

*Oxford* is a trademark of Oxford University Press

THE MAKING OF APARTHEID
1948–1961

ISBN 0 19 571515 2

© Deborah Posel 1991, 1997

This edition of *The Making of Apartheid 1948–1961* is published by arrangement with Oxford University Press, Oxford. Originally published in 1991 by Oxford University Press, Oxford.

Published by Oxford University Press Southern Africa,
Harrington House, 37 Barrack Street, Cape Town 8001,
South Africa

Typeset by Best-set Typesetter Ltd, Hong Kong
Printed and bound by ABC Press, Cape Town

*To*
*Max and Jessica*

# PREFACE

THIS book has two principal concerns. On one level, it is a study of the policy and practice of influx control during what is conceived as the first phase of Apartheid, from 1948 to 1961. ('Influx control' is taken to refer to the system of laws and regulations which governed Africans' residence and employment in so-called 'white' urban areas of the country.) On another level, this case study is the vehicle for a more wide-ranging discussion of the political processes and struggles which shaped Apartheid, their relationship to various capitalist interests, and the nature of the Apartheid state. Three principal, interrelated arguments are advanced. First, the book challenges the dominant view of Apartheid as the enactment of a single, long-term 'grand plan'. Although guided by broad National Party principles, the making of Apartheid is shown to have taken an often reactive course, buffeted by a series of conflicts, negotiations, and compromises. Secondly, the book argues that capitalist interests were fundamentally important in shaping both the design and the practice of Apartheid; but this relationship was fraught with tensions, contradictions, and changes, making for greater unevenness and complexity than is generally claimed in the literature. Thirdly, implicit in this analysis is a non-instrumentalist account of the workings of the South African state. The state is revealed to be an actor in its own right, engaged in ceaseless processes of struggle and accommodation, both internally and with subordinate as well as dominant classes.

As far as terminology is concerned, influx control laws were referred to popularly as 'pass laws', because Africans' (legal) access to the 'white' urban areas depended on acquiring the necessary passes. I have used the popular terminology when appropriate. Since most of the discussion concerns Africans in particular (i.e. members of the Bantu-speaking groups), I have differentiated between Africans and blacks (i.e. Africans, so-called 'Coloureds', and Indians).

For the sake of convenience, I have translated all quotations from Afrikaans sources into English.

This book is based substantially on my doctoral dissertation, 'Influx Control and the Construction of Apartheid, 1948–1961', which was submitted to the University of Oxford in 1987. I owe much to the many people who assisted me, both during my doctoral research and during its transformation into this book. While in England, I gained much from discussions with my supervisors, Stanley Trapido and John Goldthorpe, and colleagues and friends, particularly Saul Dubow, Shaun Johnson, John Lazar, Steven Lukes, Shula Marks, Iona Mayer, Terence Moll, Kate O'Regan, and Gavin Williams. I am also grateful for substantial financial help during this period, in the form of scholarships from the University of Witwatersrand, the University of Natal (Durban), and the Committee of University Vice-Chancellors and Principals, and a grant from the Ernest Oppenheimer Memorial Trust. Nuffield College also contributed generously towards my research expenses, and a two-year research fellowship there provided a comfortable and well-equipped environment in which the thesis was written up. Work on the book was done at the African Studies Institute, University of Witwatersrand. I am immensely grateful to the Institute's director, Charles van Onselen, both for having given me the space and time in which to complete this project, and for his careful and acute reading of my doctoral thesis. Informed comments from Philip Bonner and Peter Delius were also extremely helpful, as were editorial suggestions from Belinda Bozzoli, Luli Callinicos, Isabel Hofmeyer, Jon Hyslop, and Eddie Webster. Thanks, too, to Ben Mazower for drawing my attention to useful archival sources, and to Santu Mofokeng for help with the jacket.

My greatest debt is to Max Price, on whom I could always rely for perceptive comment and intelligent suggestions. And his unstinting support allowed me to juggle the pleasures and pains of child care with the labour of producing this book.

Deborah Posel

*University of Witwatersrand*
*Johannesburg*

# CONTENTS

# TABLES

# ABBREVIATIONS

| | |
|---|---|
| AHI | Afrikaanse Handelsinstituut |
| ANC | African National Congress |
| ASSOCOM | Association of Chambers of Commerce |
| BAD | Department of Bantu Administration and Development |
| BCC | Brakpan City Council |
| BMR | Brakpan Municipal Records |
| CAD | Central Archives Depot |
| CLPP | Coloured Labour Preference Policy |
| CPSA | Communist Party of South Africa |
| DMR | Durban Municipal Records |
| DRC | Dutch Reformed Church |
| FAK | Federasie van Afrikaanse Kultuurverenigings |
| FCE | Fagan Commission Evidence |
| FCH | Fagan Commission Hearings |
| FCI | Federated Chamber of Industries |
| *HAD* | *House of Assembly Debates* |
| HNP | Herenigde Nasionale Party |
| IANA | Institute of Administrators of Non-European Affairs |
| ISCOR | Iron and Steel Corporation |
| IV | Instituut vir Volkswelstand |
| *JSAS* | *Journal of Southern African Studies* |
| JMR | Johannesburg Municipal Records |
| KCL | Killie Campbell Library |
| LABC | Location Advisory Boards' Congress |
| NAC | Native Affairs Commissioner |
| NAD | Native Affairs Department |
| NEAD | Non-European Affairs Department |

| NEAF | Non-European Affairs Files |
| NLA Bill | Native Laws Amendment Bill |
| NP | National Party |
| NTS | Native Affairs Files |
| REC | Regional Employment Commissioner |
| SA | South Africa |
| SAAU | South African Agricultural Union |
| SABRA | South African Bureau of Racial Affairs |
| SACTU | South African Congress of Trade Unions |
| SAJE | *South African Journal of Economics* |
| SAIRR | South African Institute of Race Relations |
| SAP | South African Police |
| SNA | Secretary for Native Affairs |
| TCE | Tomlinson Commission Evidence |
| TCH | Tomlinson Commission Hearings |
| TCM | Transvaal Chamber of Mines |
| ULPP | Urban Labour Preference Policy |
| UNISA | University of South Africa |
| UP | United Party |
| UW | University of Witwatersrand |
| WRAB | West Rand Administration Board Archives |

# 1

# Introduction

## The Myth of a 'Grand Design'

BUILDING on the foundations laid by previous segregationist regimes, the National Party (NP) government built Apartheid into a monstrously labyrinthine system which dominated every facet of life in South Africa. From its election victory in 1948, the NP steadily consolidated its hold on the state, with a greater degree of ideological fervour than any previous ruling party. Long-standing state controls over the African labour market were restructured and greatly intensified. A national system of labour bureaux, introduced in the 1950s to monitor and control African employment, placed increasingly severe constraints on Africans' freedom of movement and occupational choice. The Population Registration Act (1950), Group Areas Act (1950), Bantu Education Act (1953), Reservation of Separate Amenities Act (1953), and others laid the groundwork for a more rigid and thoroughgoing system of racial domination than had existed to date. Buttressed by a large and powerful arsenal of security laws, the Nationalists also mounted an unprecedented assault on their political enemies. By the early 1960s organised black opposition had been smashed, and would take over a decade to recover. The 1960s then saw the launch of an ambitious and ruthless programme of social engineering, which stripped the majority of Africans of their South African citizenship, and forcibly removed over three and a half million from allegedly 'white' areas of the country to putative ethnic 'homelands'.

Confronted by the formidable pace and breadth of the Nationalists' achievement, many a commentator has turned to the notion of an all-embracing 'grand plan' to explain the making of Apartheid (prior to the onset of 'reform' in the mid-1970s). The Afrikaner nationalist vanguard in the state is seen as having built the Apartheid edifice brick by brick, according to the dictates of a single, systematic long-term blueprint, the essence of which was already conceived in the minds of NP leaders on the eve of their election victory in 1948.

For Afrikaner nationalist scholars, this notion of a comprehensive master plan was a eulogy to the tenacity and vision of the Afrikaner *volk* (nation). In the words of Willem de Klerk, for example, 'never in history have so few legislated so programmatically, thoroughly and religiously, in such a short time . . . than the nationalist Afrikaners of the second half of the twentieth century'.[1] But the appeal of the 'grand plan' view has in fact spanned the political spectrum. According to Brian Bunting (former editor of the Communist Party newspaper *The Guardian* and then *New Age*), in his influential study of Apartheid (written in 1969),

there has been nothing haphazard or *laissez-faire* about Nationalist rule, in striking contrast to previous regimes. Operating on the basis of a preconceived ideology which has undergone very little change in the last fifteen years, the Nationalists have planned their strategy with care and worked step by step towards their goal. Nothing has been left to chance.[2]

Noted liberal scholar Pierre van den Berghe (writing in 1967) characterised Apartheid similarly, as 'a systematic, premeditated plan that has been meticulously perfected since the Afrikaner nationalists came into office in 1948'.[3]

The successful pursuit of this project, it is claimed, owed much to the authority and vision of Hendrik Verwoerd (first a Senator, then also Minister of Native Affairs, and ultimately Prime Minister). In de Klerk's words,

for the next eighteen years, Verwoerd would variously enlarge upon the themes of his speech to the Senate of September 1948. Certain emphases would shift and refinements would take place . . . These, however, would by no means be new to the *apartheidsgedagte* [apartheid idea] . . . On the whole, Verwoerd would not deviate in the slightest degree from the concept he had analysed, and the design he had sketched in his first major speech as a parliamentarian. He would revise nothing.[4]

This Promethean sense of Verwoerd's role, which abounds in the academic literature on Apartheid,[5] is also a commonplace in the

[1] W. A. de Klerk, *The Puritans in Africa: A History of Afrikanerdom* (1975; repr. Harmondsworth, 1976), p. 241.
[2] B. Bunting, *The Rise of the South African Reich* (Harmondsworth, 1969), p. 132.
[3] P. van den Berghe, *Race and Racism: A Comparative Perspective* (New York, London, and Sydney, 1967), p. 108.
[4] de Klerk, *The Puritans in Africa*, p. 239.
[5] See, e.g., F. A. van Jaarsveld, *From Van Riebeeck to Vorster, 1652–1974* (Johannesburg, 1975), and T. R. Davenport, *South Africa: A Modern History*

recent spate of journalistic depictions of Apartheid, which do much to shape popular thinking on the subject.[6] Many a television documentary, for example, has been preoccupied with Verwoerd's authoritarian personality and unbending dedication to the Afrikaner cause, as the key to understanding how Apartheid developed after 1948.

The 'grand plan' view is not often stated quite as baldly as by Bunting, van den Berghe, or de Klerk. Many acknowledge, at least in principle, that the tenets of Apartheid were refined as the system developed, and that several of the state's plans were hampered by temporary setbacks. But the idea of a master plan remains intact, in that the making of Apartheid is seen as having been an essentially systematic, cumulative process, which proceeded largely according to a single pre-existing plan. This view can be recognised in various familiar claims about Nationalist rule prior to the onset of 'reform' in the late 1970s. First, the idea of a master plan for Apartheid originates in the misconception that, by the late 1940s, the NP—and Afrikanerdom at large—had thrown its weight behind a single, uncontested conception of Apartheid. Many have been persuaded by Dan O'Meara, for example, who regarded a single, hegemonic 'Apartheid-idea' as the ideological cement binding the Afrikaner nationalist class alliance together from the late 1940s.[7] It is commonly claimed, moreover, that the key tenets of this 'Apartheid-idea' were set out in the Sauer Report, a confidential report produced internally for the NP in 1947. The Nationalist government thrust into power in 1948 is thus seen as having been equipped from the start with a ready-made, if rudimentary, blueprint for the future.[8] As David Welsh put it, 'the Nationalists had appealed to the electorate with the slogan "Apartheid", the tag given to a race policy

(London, 1977; repr. 1987); A. Hepple, *Verwoerd* (Harmondsworth, 1967); H. Adam and H. Giliomee, *Ethnic Power Mobilised: Can South Africa Change?* (New Haven, 1979); A. Keppel-Jones, *South Africa: A Short History* (London, 1949; repr. 1975); R. Horwitz, *The Political Economy of South Africa* (London, 1967).

[6] See, e.g., D. Harrison, *The White Tribe of Africa* (Berkeley, 1981); M. Attwell, *South Africa: Background to the Crisis* (London, 1986); B. Lapping, *Apartheid: A History* (London, 1987). Also, the Granada/Channel 4 TV series on 'Apartheid' (1986).

[7] D. O'Meara, *Volkskapitalisme* (Cambridge, 1983), p. 175. For more detail, see Ch. 3.

[8] See, e.g., B. Bunting, 'The Origins of Apartheid' in A. la Guma (ed.), *Apartheid: A Collection of Writings on South African Racism by South Africans* (London, 1972), pp. 24–5; G. Carter, *Which Way is South Africa Going?* (Bloomington, 1980), p. 22;

that had been drawn up by an internal commission and to which the new regime would faithfully adhere'.[9]

Notions of a 'grand plan' are also implied in studies which treat the development of Apartheid as having been fundamentally linear and cumulative, each step building on the successes of the last. A variety of works on South Africa regard the prominent Apartheid policies of the late 1960s—such as industrial decentralisation, population removals, restrictions on the scale of African employment in certain urban areas, and homeland development—as having been central to the design of Apartheid from the start (even if historical circumstances did not permit their immediate implementation).[10] And implicit in such representations of the development of Apartheid is the assumption that resistance (within and beyond the state) to the strategies of Apartheid's planners played little role in fashioning the contours of state policy. Rather, the effect of opposition is treated as having been largely limited to delaying or complicating the implementation of policies already prescribed by 'the grand design'.

As suggested at the outset, 'grand plan' views of the construction of Apartheid are understandably seductive. During the 1950s and 1960s the Apartheid state did indeed advance from strength to strength. As the NP's grip on the state tightened, so the Apartheid system grew more vicious and all-encompassing, reaching awesome proportions by the late 1960s. It is true, too, that Verwoerd

Davenport, *South Africa: A Modern History*, ch. 14; D. Hindson, 'The Pass System and the Formation of an Urban African Proletariat' (Ph.D. thesis, University of Sussex, 1983), p. 162; Horwitz, *The Political Economy of South Africa*, p. 2; J. Robertson, *Liberalism in South Africa, 1948–1963* (Oxford, 1971), p. 12; F. Troup, *South Africa: An Historical Introduction* (Harmondsworth, 1975), ch. 6; Lapping, *Apartheid: A History*, p. 73.

[9] D. Welsh, 'The Growth of Towns', in M. Wilson and L. Thompson (eds.), *Oxford History of South Africa*, ii (Oxford, 1971), p. 191.

[10] e.g. Carter, *Which Way is South Africa Going?*, p. 21; Commonwealth Eminent Persons' Group, *Mission to South Africa: The Commonwealth Report* (Harmondsworth, 1986), p. 48; T. Dunbar Moodie, *The Rise of Afrikanerdom* (Berkeley, Los Angeles, and London, 1975), pp. 263–4; G. Frederikson, *White Supremacy* (New York and Oxford, 1981), p. 240; H. Giliomee and L. Schlemmer (eds.), *Up Against the Fences: Poverty, Passes and Privilege in South Africa* (Cape Town and Johannesburg, 1985), p. 3; L. Platzky and C. Walker, *The Surplus People: Forced Removals in South Africa* (Johannesburg, 1985), pp. 109–13; R. Rotberg, *Suffer the Future* (Cambridge and London, 1980), p. 41; A. W. Stadler, *The Political Economy of Modern South Africa* (Cape Town and Johannesburg, 1987), pp. 80–1, 75; Troup, *South Africa: An Historical Introduction*, ch. 6.

was a leading, and an extremely powerful, actor in this process. The Nationalist regime was also ideologically far more fervent and cohesive than any of its predecessors, and implemented many of its policies with patent determination, sometimes bordering on fanatical zeal. There was clearly some method in the madness of Apartheid. Moreover, the notion of a single grand plan might well describe the development of a few features of Apartheid which were systematically and unfalteringly pursued from 1948 to the late 1970s, such as the prohibition of interracial sex and marriage.

Whatever its superficial appeal, however, the notion of a single master plan fundamentally misrepresents the political processes whereby Apartheid was built, greatly exaggerating the extent of the continuity, control, and long-term planning involved. The source of these distortions is a limited, often crude, analysis of the workings of the state. The notion of a 'grand plan' suppresses interest in the internal workings of state departments, because policy decisions and administrative practices seem merely to have been transcribed from a ready-made blueprint with little further ado. This book probes more deeply within the state, examining the processes whereby a particular set of Apartheid policies was made, implemented, and contested. In so doing, an alternative picture is painted of the making of Apartheid, as having been forged through a series of struggles within and beyond the state, which forced the architects of state policy to adapt and revise many of their original strategies. Uncertainties, conflicts, failures, and deviations, although often less visible than the continuities and triumphs of Apartheid, were fundamental to its development.

This case is made in several ways. In contrast to the orthodoxy in the literature, this book shows that, on the eve of the 1948 election, Afrikanerdom was divided over the very substance of Apartheid. The opposing factions, constituted largely (although not exclusively) along class lines, disputed the extent to which white economic prosperity should and need depend on African labour. This led, in turn, to basic disagreements over the appropriate manner of state control over African urbanisation. The Sauer Report, on which the NP based its election campaign, reproduced rather than resolved these divergences, and therefore cannot have provided a single master plan for the building of Apartheid (see Chapter 3). An alternative explanation is necessary, evaluating which version of Apartheid was the more influential, and the extent to which it determined the shape of state policy. This book also shows, however, that the conception of Apartheid which predominated in the state during the 1950s was itself only a rough guide, rather than a master plan, for the state's actions. Apartheid policy was partly a reaction to the immediate pressures and priorities of the historical moment. Uncertain of its re-election in 1953, the newly elected Nationalist government was anxious to consolidate its power base within the state and the electorate at large. Upholding shared Nationalist principles went some of the way towards reaffirming its support in Afrikaner circles. But the policy-making process also kept a keen eye on the inter-ests of powerful non-Nationalist constituencies, such as 'English-speaking' capital, and the large local authorities all dominated by the opposition United Party (UP). The objectives of state policy in the early 1950s were fashioned, too, by the threat of African mass re-sistance which had not yet been quashed (see Chapters 4 and 5).

Finally, this book shows that, despite marked continuities in the development of Apartheid, it underwent an important change of direction at the onset of the 1960s, which ushered in a discrete second phase of policy-making. By the late 1950s the escalation of urban African resistance had exposed serious gaps in the state's control over the urban proletariat. A fundamental reassessment of the methods and objectives of the state's policies on African pro-letarianisation was called for (see Chapter 9). But, once again, Afrikanerdom was divided over which new direction to take. The long-controversial issues of white dependence on African labour (economic integration) and African urbanisation were once more the principal source of disagreement. But the positions which had been formulated on these issues during the late 1940s were now revised, and the competing factions reconstituted. These realignments within Afrikanerdom had a direct effect within the then-renamed Depart-ment of Bantu Administration and Development (BAD) (the vanguard of Apartheid policy-making within the state), which abandoned many of the premises and objectives which had guided its policies during the 1950s. This change of tack was not prefigured in any master plan, however. Had the second phase of Apartheid been preplanned, it would have begun once the objectives of the first phase had been successfully realised. In fact, however, the inaugura-tion of the second phase represented the state's attempt to undo what it then perceived to be the errors of its previous policies. These policy shifts were made possible by the extent to which the NP had consolidated its hold on power and restructured the state during the 1950s; but it was not with the policy shifts of the 1960s in sight that the strategies of the 1950s were pursued.

This is by no means an exhaustive analysis of either the workings of the Apartheid state or the building of Apartheid. The principal focus of attention is on the period 1948–61, conceived as the first phase of Apartheid. Influx control—the policy area studied—is but one feature of the Apartheid system. Moreover, the discussion of the state is largely limited to those state institutions involved in the making and application of influx control policy—in particular, the Native Affairs Department (NAD), labour bureaux, and local authorities. Focusing on the workings of the NAD, and not other state departments, obviously produces an incomplete understanding of the state as a whole. However, it was the NAD which spearheaded the formulation of Apartheid policy during the 1950s. There is little to suggest that this policy-making process depended in major ways on negotiation or conflict with other state departments. Indeed, the NAD became increasingly a 'state within a state', creating its own subdepartments of Labour and Housing, and marginalising the Department of Economic Affairs in the control of the reserves (see Chapter 3). Also, although the book does not provide a full investigation of all aspects of Apartheid policy, influx control had a critical role to play within the wider Apartheid project. An examination of the design and implementation of influx control in the 1950s, and its restructuring during the 1960s, will reveal much, therefore, about the objectives and methods of the Apartheid system more generally during this period.[11]

The NP took office in 1948 in the midst of what its policy-makers considered economically irrational trends. Many urban areas enjoyed a large reservoir of African labour, while white farmers complained incessantly about labour shortages. Addressing the labour needs of white commercial agriculture was central to the design of Apartheid. Had white farmers been forced to compete for African labour in an open market with manufacturing and commerce, agricultural costs would have had to increase markedly

---

[11] This study has a broad national focus but draws on regionally specific material to assess the uneven nature and effects of influx control. In this respect there is something of a metropolitan bias. This is less of a limitation than it might seem, because the metropolitan areas loomed far larger than others in shaping the state's and business's policy decisions and administrative assessments.

through the payment of competitive wages. Influx control was devised in part to prevent such a situation. The supposedly irrational distribution of labour between rural and urban areas would be remedied by legal and administrative fiat. This project was not entirely new; before 1948 successive governments had attempted, largely unsuccessfully, to use influx control measures to curb the exodus of farm-workers to the cities. But the Nationalist government's commitment to influx control was far more systematic and wide-ranging than any of its predecessors'.

The imperatives of Apartheid were not simply economic, however. The Apartheid system, like its segregationist predecessor, was geared towards the simultaneous pursuit of white political supremacy and white economic prosperity. These joint goals straddled a basic tension: white reliance on African labour was simultaneously a source of strength and weakness. This dilemma was most vividly exemplified in the cities, where the manufacturing sector, the largest contributor to the country's gross national product since 1943, was concentrated. The growth of manufacturing was fuelled by an abundant supply of African labour, at wages typically well below the breadline. Industrial prosperity, therefore, went hand in hand with the expansion of an impoverished urban African proletariat, the very process which generated the most serious challenges to the preservation of white political supremacy. The massing of a large African, Indian, and Coloured proletariat in urban centres nurtured the threat of united black resistance to white domination, resistance provoked by exploitation and disfranchisement and empowered by rising levels of education, skill, and politicisation. The architects of Apartheid, therefore, grappled with ways of curtailing the growth of the urban African population, without thereby undermining the economic benefits of African labour. Until its abolition in 1986, influx control policy was an indispensable part of this project, being expressly designed to link the state's control over African urbanisation to its control over the distribution of African labour between urban and rural areas.

### Influx Control and the Liberal–Revisionist Debate

There are many roads to capitalist development. One of the distinguishing features of the South African route has been the extent to which the state intervened directly in controlling the movement of African labour, by means of influx control. Influx control, then, was built at the interface of Apartheid and capitalism in the country. It is not accidental, therefore, that much of the analysis of influx control in the literature has been conducted within a framework of debate about the relationship between Apartheid and capitalism.[12]

Controversy over this issue is as long-standing as Apartheid itself. However, students of South African history are generally introduced to it by way of the so-called 'liberal–revisionist debate', which has its origins in the revisionist critique of liberal historiography in the early 1970s. Although it is generally characterised as a single debate, there are in fact at least two separate issues at stake, which ought to be disaggregated. The first concerns the impact of capitalist development, and dominant class interests, on the design and objectives of Apartheid. Have Apartheid policies been designed to serve capitalist interests? What sorts of political powers have capitalist lobbies exercised over the policy-making process? The second issue debated concerns the degree of compatibility between capitalism and the ways in which Apartheid policies are administered in practice. Has the implementation of Apartheid policies advanced or hindered capitalist interests, whether originally intended to do so or not?

What is usually called the 'liberal' position on these issues is not wholly uniform;[13] but, as conceived by its revisionist opponents, it has one of three distinguishing features. First, a liberal analysis of Apartheid explains either its origins and/or its functions in terms of political and ideological factors, rather than the imperatives of capital accumulation or dominant class interests. Secondly, liberals have stressed the economic irrationality of Apartheid. Capitalist interests are thus not simply secondary to political and ideological variables, but at odds with them too. Thirdly, the liberal position expresses a profound confidence in the liberalising power of economic growth gradually but ineluctably to erode its racist fetters.

---

[12] What follows is not intended to be a comprehensive survey of either the Apartheid–capitalism debate or the literature on influx control. I am principally concerned with the terms of debate and the restrictive effects they have had on some of the more influential analyses of influx control. The alternative analysis of influx control developed in this book is also an argument for the reformulation of the issues at stake in the Apartheid–capitalism debate.

[13] For amplification of this point, see D. B. Posel, 'Rethinking the "Race–Class Debate" in South African Historiography', *Social Dynamics*, 9/1 (1983), 60.

Ralph Horwitz's analysis of influx control during the 1950s illustrates all three distinguishing features of the liberal position. The policy is seen as the work of an economically ignorant and indifferent Nationalist vanguard, whose primary purpose was the pursuit of political power irrespective of the economic costs. Nor was the practice of influx control flexible enough to lessen the economic damage. Industrialists were burdened with 'a hopelessly wasteful and cripplingly costly system of labour use'.[14] In order for the country's industries to 'expand', Horwitz claimed, they would therefore have to 'explode' the constraints of Apartheid labour policies.

The original revisionist position[15] developed as a challenge to the limitations of this liberal view. Revisionists saw the design of Apartheid as an expression of capitalist imperatives or particular dominant class interests. The functional compatibility between capitalism and the practice of Apartheid was also stressed. As Johnstone put it, 'this racial system may be most adequately explained as a class system—as a system of class instruments . . . generated, and determined in its specific nature and functions, by the specific system of production and class structure of which it formed a part'.[16]

Discussion of the economic effects of the influx control system occupied a central place in the elaboration of this revisionist critique. According to one of the leading revisionist figures, Martin Legassick, the distinctive feature of the Apartheid system (as compared with its segregationist predecessor) was the use of influx control to extend the migrant labour system, already institutionalised on the mines, to secondary industries in the towns. The primary purpose of Apartheid, in his view, was the reproduction of a supply of cheap African labour for urban industries.[17] And, he argued, influx control policy was the state's chief instrument to that end. By entrenching

---

[14] Horwitz, *The Political Economy of South Africa*, p. 13.

[15] This was first declared and developed in the early work of H. Wolpe, M. Legassick, and F. Johnstone. It was then extended and modified in the light of Poulantzian Marxism, in the work of, e.g., R. Davies, D. Kaplan, and D. O'Meara. An important critique of liberal assumptions has also been levelled by the work of Marxist social historians; but the discussion here refers specifically to those who articulated theoretical positions in terms of a critique of a 'liberal' stance on 'race' and 'class'.

[16] F. Johnstone, *Class, Race, and Gold* (London, 1976), p. 4.

[17] M. Legassick, 'Legislation, Ideology, and Economy in Post-1948 South Africa', *Journal of Southern African Studies* (*JSAS*) 1/1 (1974), 9.

the migrant labour system, influx control regulations cheapened the price of labour by creating a mass of workers who had 'a limited time to get a job, [and were] faced with exclusion from urban employment altogether should [they] get fired'.[18]

Harold Wolpe's analysis of Apartheid also stressed the importance of influx control mechanisms as the Apartheid state's strategy for depressing urban African wages in line with the interests of manufacturing capital. During the segregationist period (before 1948), Wolpe argued, agricultural production in the reserves partly subsidised migrant workers' reproduction. By the late 1940s, however, he claimed, agricultural productivity in the reserves had declined sharply. He therefore characterised Apartheid as the 'mechanism' devised to 'guarantee a cheap and controlled work-force under circumstances in which the conditions of reproduction (the redistributive African economy in the Reserves) of that labour force are rapidly disintegrating'.[19] Influx control was central to this strategy, he argued, in reducing workers' freedom of choice and bargaining power in the labour market.

Much has been written evaluating the relative merits of particular contributions to the debate; far less attention has been paid to the problems generated by the terms of debate themselves. Yet the form in which a question is posed has a decisive bearing on the content of the answer provided. The liberal–revisionist debate was originally constituted in a simple 'either/or' form: *either* the design and practice of Apartheid were instrumental in furthering the capitalist cause, *or* they were not. This starkly polarised formulation of the issue inhibited the declaration of a position which was sensitive to both the tensions and the affinities between Apartheid and capitalism, and to the fluctuations in this relationship over time and at various points in the political process.[20] Legassick's and Wolpe's highly influential analyses of influx control thus saw only its positive contributions to the processes of capital accumulation. Leading liberal thinkers, on the other hand, could only identify the economically harmful effects of the migrant labour system.

---

[18] M. Legassick, 'South Africa: Capital Accumulation and Violence', *Economy and Society*, 3/3 (1974), 276.

[19] H. Wolpe, 'Capitalism and Cheap Labour-Power in South Africa: From Segregation to Apartheid, *Economy and Society*, 1/4 (1972), 430–1.

[20] For a more detailed argument on this point, see Posel, 'Rethinking the "Race–Class Debate"', 50–1.

As a result, neither party to the debate is equipped to recognise or explain the historical paradox which marked the institution of influx control during the 1950s, and which features prominently in this book. On the one hand, organised commerce and industry took strong exception to the migrant labour system, adjudged to be the root of the high labour turnover and low labour productivity which beset the manufacturing sector. Throughout the 1950s the journals of organised urban business therefore regularly denounced methods of influx control which entrenched the migrant labour system. Yet, on the other hand, municipal administrators country-wide reported a widespread *preference* within the urban business community for migrant labour,[21] on the grounds that it was cheaper, more disciplined, and more docile than urbanised labour (see Chapters 6 and 7). This paradox immediately signals a more complex relationship between influx control and capitalist interests than the simple 'either/or' terms of debate can accommodate.

The 'either/or' formulation of the issue also blunted the debate to the possibility that the *policy* and *practice* of Apartheid had discrepant implications for capitalist interests. Horwitz, for example, seized on the economic costs incurred by the Nationalists' influx control policy as evidence of the state's disinterest in promoting the cause of manufacturing during the 1950s. Legassick's and Wolpe's case—that influx control in this period advanced the interests of industrial capital by lowering the price of African labour—also failed to distinguish between the state's intentions and the practical effects of influx control. Their analyses concentrated on how influx control functioned in practice and, in characteristically functionalist vein, assumed that this reflected what the state had intended. This book shows, however, that the state proposed to base its influx control policy on an urban labour preference principle, in terms of which urban employers would be *denied* access to migrant labour if urbanised African labour was available on their doorstep. This policy was intended to reduce the size of the urban labour reservoir and foster a situation of near full African employment in urban areas. The policy was not designed, then, to cheapen labour. Indeed, had this policy been implemented as planned, the price of African labour in urban

---

[21] What employers meant by 'migrant labour' was ambiguous, usually straddling two categories of workers: so-called 'raw' labour, newly arrived or directly recruited from rural areas, and migrants who retained a permanent base in a rural area, irrespective of the number of years spent working in the cities.

areas would have gone up, as competition for urban jobs declined. It was because the urban labour preference policy (ULPP) failed that employers were able fully to exploit the vulnerability of migrant workers.[22]

Lastly, because the nature of Apartheid was debated by way of its relationship to capitalism and dominant class interests, the terms of the original liberal–revisionist debate tacitly downgraded the importance of 'struggles from below' for an understanding of Apartheid. It is principally the South Africanist social historians[23] who, without explicitly intervening in the debate itself, have provided the definitive critique of exclusively 'top down' explanations. Their work has brought the subordinate classes to the foreground as actors, engaged in multi-faceted processes of struggle against the weight of the state and capital bearing down on them. Drawing on studies of migrancy by William Beinart, Philip Bonner, and Peter Delius, this book argues, too, that the realities of influx control and migrancy cannot be understood simply in terms of the relationship between the state and capital; equally fundamental were the preferences and priorities of male and female African migrants and city-dwellers trying to maximise their room for manœuvre in an increasingly constrained and repressive world (see Chapters 5, 6, 7, and 8).

For all its limitations, the original liberal–revisionist debate has, nevertheless, had a major impact on subsequent historical and sociological analysis, opening up a range of inquiries into areas which had hitherto been underresearched—such as, the nature of the white working class, the class underpinnings of Afrikaner nationalism, etc. Also, many of the ensuing studies were inspired by the original debate and articulated their positions in terms of a critique or elaboration of a liberal or revisionist stance. Two recent studies of influx control—Merle Lipton's book, *Capitalism and Apartheid: South Africa, 1910–1986*, and Douglas Hindson's *Pass Controls and the Urban African Proletariat in South Africa* (based on a more

---

[22] Wolpe's argument has an added problem. The motives which he attributes to the state make little sense: it is not at all clear why the state needed influx control to keep labour cheap in the midst of deteriorating agricultural production in the reserves. After all, the more desperate the poverty a migrant worker seeks to escape, the more likely he or she is to accept poorly paid work.

[23] e.g. William Beinart, Philip Bonner, Helen Bradford, Peter Delius, and Charles van Onselen, amongst others. See also Alf Stadler's important study of squatter movements in the 1940s, 'Birds in the Cornfield: Squatter Movements in Johannesburg, 1944–47', *JSAS* 6/1 (1979).

substantial doctoral thesis)—are cases in point. Taking their cue from the original debate, both try to move beyond its starkest formulations.

Criticising 'much of the analysis of South Africa' for producing an overly static and simplistic account of the relationship between Apartheid and capitalism,[24] Lipton adjusts the original liberal case. In contrast to Horwitz, she stresses the importance of agricultural class interests in shaping the design of influx control policy in the 1950s. But her position on the relationship between influx control policy and the interests of manufacturing and commercial capital is in line with Horwitz on two counts. Both the design and the practice of influx control are seen as fundamentally at odds with industrial and commercial interests. Although Lipton recognises at one point that the 'owners of the small, inefficient factories set up during the war'[25] had different priorities, the thrust of her argument is that industrial and commercial employers 'generally favoured higher wage levels',[26] linked to improvements in labour productivity, made possible by substituting 'stable' urbanised labour for migrant labour. In Lipton's view, therefore, 'manufacturing and commercial capital did not need, and indeed opposed, most apartheid labour policies'.[27]

To support her argument, Lipton points to the fact that organised commerce and industry complained bitterly about the Nationalists' influx control policy because it entrenched the migrant labour system, blamed for boosting labour turnover and depressing labour productivity. But this claim is itself open to the charge of over-simplification which Lipton levels against others. Reproducing the omission of earlier liberal historians, she does not explore the implications of the fact that the protestations of organised commerce and industry were out of step with the daily economic behaviour of the majority of business people during the 1950s. Yet both need to be taken into account to explain fully the manufacturing sector's response to influx control. Organisations such as the Association of Chambers of Commerce (ASSOCOM) and the Federated Chamber of Industries (FCI) took a long-term view of the interests of commerce and industry (particularly the larger, well-established

[24] M. Lipton, *Capitalism and Apartheid: South Africa, 1910–1986* (London, 1985), p. 6.
[25] Ibid. 161; see also p. 163.
[26] Ibid. 139.
[27] Ibid.

concerns), in terms of which continued reliance on migrant labour inhibited labour productivity, while low wages limited the growth of African consumer markets. But individual employers acted in the light of their own immediate interests, which were structured by the existence of the migrant labour system and influx control legislation and their effects on workers' options and preferences. Many industrialists at the helm of increasingly capital-intensive concerns, in which maintaining a stable, semi-skilled work-force took priority over keeping wages as low as possible, did choose urbanised workers in preference to migrants. But during the 1950s the trend towards increasing capital intensity was confined to a minority of urban employers.[28] The majority of urban business people drew on African labour principally for unskilled work, and asserted a strong preference for so-called 'tribal' labour, even when what Lipton calls 'stable' urbanised labour was available on their doorstep. One of the principal reasons for this preference, moreover, was the perception amongst employers that 'tribal' labour was cheaper, as well as more pliable and disciplined, than urbanised labour—a trend which belies Lipton's claim that employers 'generally favoured higher wage levels' (see Chapters 5 and 6).

Hindson's argument is presented as a critique of the original revisionist position. Criticising Legassick for inappropriately treating the African industrial work-force as uniformly cheap, Hindson stresses that the industrial demand for African labour was differentiated. In the aftermath of the Second World War, as the capital intensification of manufacturing accelerated, industrial employers experienced a growing need for a stable and semi-skilled African work-force, in addition to their long-standing dependence on cheap, unskilled African labour. His discussion of the Apartheid era therefore examines

how and why pass controls were redesigned to secure the reproduction of two dominant forms of African labour power: urban proletarians and temporary migrant workers. [It] . . . sets out to explain the development of the urban pass system in terms of the emergence of segmented African labour markets and the reproduction of differentiated forms of African labour power in the cities of South Africa . . . after World War Two.[29]

[28] I am referring here to all urban employers, not simply manufacturers.
[29] D. Hindson, *Pass Controls and the Urban African Proletariat in South Africa* (Johannesburg, 1987), p. x.

The very terms in which Hindson poses his central question un-wittingly reproduce the strictures of the early revisionist debate against the liberal case. He sets out to explain the influx control policy of the 1950s in terms of its economic functions; influx control policy is treated from the start as designed to accommodate urban industrialists' interest in a differentiated labour market. The Nationalists' influx control policy drew a sharp distinction between 'temporary migrants' and 'urbanised' Africans, as the basis for dif-ferential liabilities and privileges. In Hindson's view, the purpose of this legal and administrative differentiation was to mimic and repro-duce the differentiation in the African work-force between unskilled and semi-skilled. As he explains in the unpublished thesis on which his book is based,

cheap labour power was giving way to differentiated labour power, and the reconstruction and extension of influx control barriers under the Urban Areas Act [of 1952] were a means of securing the reproduction of dif-ferentiated forms of labour power in the cities in the face of the incoming tide of surplus population from the rural areas.[30]

Like Legassick and Wolpe, Hindson conflates the state's purpose with the unintended ways in which the influx control policy of the 1950s functioned in practice. The result is a misrepresentation of the state's objectives in the early 1950s. The urban labour preference principle lay at the heart of the Nationalists' influx control strategy; yet its significance is missing from Hindson's account (along with Legassick's and Wolpe's before him). The urban labour preference policy (ULPP) was intended to restructure urban employment patterns, so that unskilled work was no longer dominated by migrant workers. Urbanised work-seekers were to have been channelled into all available jobs ahead of labour recruited from rural areas, in a bid to reduce the size of urban labour 'surpluses'. It was only because the state failed to put the ULPP into operation that industrialists' preference for migrant labour for unskilled work was not thwarted by influx control (see Chapter 7).

In practice, then, the legal differentiation between 'migrant' and 'urbanised' Africans in the cities did tend to reproduce and satisfy the differentiated industrial labour demand. But this was an un-intended consequence of the state's influx control policy. Moreover,

[30] Hindson, 'The Pass System and the Formation of an Urban African Proletariat', p. 166.

the factors segmenting the urban labour market were considerably more complex and multi-faceted than Hindson recognises. He characterises the urban labour market baldly in terms of a differentiation between 'urban proletarians' and 'temporary migrants'.[31] This book argues, however, that a range of factors—including workers' age, level of education, gender, experience, ethnicity, informal networks, fluency in English or Afrikaans, as well as employers' preferences and prejudices—all came into play (see Chapter 6, 7, and 8).

The over-simplification in Hindson's analysis is a symptom of his having explained the differentiated labour market solely in terms of the interests of manufacturing capital and state institutions, treating workers as passive victims of the system. This book argues, however, that workers' preferences and priorities (themselves complexly structured) played a decisive role in reproducing the employment patterns which steered the Nationalists' influx control policy off its intended course. Employers' disdainful rejection of urbanised labour as 'cheeky' and 'unreliable' was partly a reaction to the fact that Africans already entrenched in the cities often refused to take poorly paid menial work. With well-established access to local informal township economies, many urbanised men and women found petty entrepreneurship a more attractive option, even if, in some cases, it was an economic safety net which allowed them to wait for better paid employment. And, ironically, the Nationalists' influx control legislation heightened, rather than undermined, this room for manœuvre. Obversely, the widespread preference amongst urban employers for 'tribal' labour as cheaper, more disciplined, and more loyal than urbanised workers was shaped partly by the effects within the workplace of particular migrant cultures, nurtured by informal migrant associations. Migrant workers, particularly those newly arrived from rural areas, were typically desperate to establish a foothold in an urban area. In terms of the influx control laws, this depended on securing and retaining a job. Compelled to seek work to escape often desperate rural poverty, 'tribal' labour was, therefore, generally cheaper than urbanised labour. But migrants' priorities were not merely economic. Migrant workers from particular areas and clans tended to find work through migrant associations

---

[31] Note that the sense in which Hindson uses the term 'migrant' is not defined, so that it is unclear whether workers newly arrived from rural areas with the intention of settling in town are included in the 'migrant' category.

which colonised particular jobs and work-forces for their members.[32] Building relationships and a sense of solidarity with like-minded people, similarly immersed in rural traditions and norms, offered migrants an alternative to the cultural milieu of city life. And, in so doing, the migrant associations drew their members into hierarchies of authority which were then transplanted into the workplace as self-imposed forms of control.

In short, then, the failure to differentiate between the *design* and the *practice* of influx control, and their distinct implications for capitalist interests, has characterised the liberal–revisionist debate about influx control across the board. Drawing attention to the discrepancies between the purposes and unintended consequences of influx control does more than simply correct the historical record. It recasts the explanatory framework in terms of which influx control, and Apartheid more generally, can be understood. Explaining how and why these discrepancies between policy and practice arose becomes centrally important, and this in turn opens the space for a matrix of factors hitherto largely excluded or marginalised to enter the explanatory arena. It will be shown that the powers and interests of central and local state institutions, individual African workers as well as mass organisations, individual employers as well as organised commerce and industry, must all be taken into account in explaining how Apartheid took shape. Instead of characterising Apartheid in stark terms as an instrument of, or obstacle to, capitalist interests, the explanation devolves on the many and varied ways in which state policy was contested.

### The Nature of the South African State

Implicit throughout this study is an inquiry into the workings of the South African state. Much has been written on the subject, but this is not the place for a comprehensive literature review. However, as Harold Wolpe[33] and John Lonsdale[34] have argued in the past, a

---

[32] e.g. P. Delius, 'Sebatakgomo: Migrant Organisation, the ANC and the Sekhukhuneland Revolt', *JSAS* 15/4 (1989).

[33] H. Wolpe, 'Towards an Analysis of the South African State', *International Journal of the Sociology of Law*, 7/4 (1980).

[34] J. Lonsdale, 'States and Social Processes in Africa: A Historiographical Survey', *African Studies Review*, 24/2–3 (1981).

strong tendency in much of this literature has been to conceptualise the state as first and foremost an instrument of capitalist interests. This instrumentalism is largely a legacy of the 'either/or' formulation of the debate about Apartheid and capitalism. In rebutting liberal accusations that the Apartheid state impeded the path of economic growth, the early revisionists set out to demonstrate the ways in which the state had advanced capitalist interests. Questions about the state were posed from the start in instrumentalist terms, by excluding from the scope of discussion the prospect of more complex workings of the state. Legassick, for example, set out 'to show that the specific structures of labour control which have been developed in post-war South Africa are increasingly functional to capital'.[35]

Most writers have since rejected the crudest formulations of an instrumentalist position, making Poulantzas's point that internal fractures within the ruling class introduce a necessary distance between the state and particular bourgeois interests. Robert Davies, for example, stressed the fact that 'the state has necessarily to assume a degree of relative autonomy from the dominant classes and all fractions thereof'.[36] And Dan O'Meara dismissed the view that the state can be analysed 'as an undifferentiated instrument in the hands of a political party representing specific and purely economic interests'.[37] Nevertheless, their writings still bore the hallmark of a class-instrumentalist view, namely, its limited notion of the autonomy of the state: ' "independence" is exercised only to the extent that conflicts must be settled between different sections of capital (industrialists and financiers for example) and between "domestic" capitalism and pressures generated by international capitalist markets'.[38] Thus, although the South African state was recognised as a 'differentiated and contradictory unity', its differentiations and contradictions were themselves explained in terms of the nature of class struggle.[39] Little attention was paid to the institutional workings and composition of the state, as a result of which the policy-making process remained something of a 'black box'. In the main, policies seemed simply to

[35] Legassick, 'South Africa: Capital Accumulation and Violence', p. 269. See also Johnstone, *Class, Race, and Gold*, p. 4.
[36] R. Davies, *Capital, State and White Labour in South Africa* (London, 1979), p. 27.
[37] D. O'Meara, ' "Muldergate" and the Politics of Afrikaner Nationalism', *Work in Progress*, 22 (1983), 2.
[38] D. Held (ed.), *States and Societies* (Oxford, 1983), p. 29.
[39] O'Meara, ' "Muldergate" ', p. 2.

20                          1. Introduction

emerge, in response to the exigencies of dominant class struggles.
The consequence, as Wolpe noted, was 'a paradoxical neglect . . . of
state structures and the political terrain in work concerned with the
state'.[40]

The analysis of the South African state in this book springs
theoretically from a dissatisfaction with the shortcomings of class-
instrumentalist accounts. Whereas class-instrumentalists settle the
issue of the state's relationship to various capitalist interests as a
matter of theoretical stipulation, this study starts out with 'a set of
what may be termed axiomatic uncertainties, each dependent on the
initial premise that for any reasonably significant historical development, monocausal explanation is *ipso facto* wrong'.[41] In any analysis
which locates the state at the nexus of economic and political forces,
as this study does, questions about the political power of capitalist
interests are crucial. But the methodological centrality of these questions does not mean that dominant class interests must necessarily
take precedence in explaining the way the state works. As Theda
Skocpol argues, state institutions are 'at least potentially autonomous from direct dominant class control. The extent to which they
actually are autonomous . . . varies from case to case.'[42] The account
of the state presented here, therefore, does not assume *a priori* that
the variable of class is necessarily and inevitably the fundamental
determinant of any and every facet of state structure and policy.

The capitalist state's interest in nurturing the growth and stability
of the capitalist economy more generally, however, is not merely an
historical contingency. Following Claus Offe, the analysis of the
state in this book accepts as a basic theoretical premiss that the
capitalist state has its own 'institutional self-interest' in furthering
the accumulation process. As Offe explains, in capitalist societies

the institutional separation of state and economy means that the state is
dependent upon the flow of resources from the organisation of profitable
production, through taxation and finance from capital markets. Since in the
main the resources from the accumulation process are 'beyond its power to
organise', there is an 'institutional self-interest of the state' and an interest of
those with state power to safeguard the vitality of the capitalist economy.[43]

[40] H. Wolpe, *Race, Class and the Apartheid State* (London, 1988), p. 39.
[41] Lonsdale, 'States and Social Processes', p. 140.
[42] T. Skocpol, *States and Social Revolutions* (Cambridge, 1979), p. 29.
[43] D. Held and J. Krieger, 'Accumulation, Legitimation and the State: The Ideas
of Claus Offe and Jurgen Habermas', in Held (ed.), *States and Societies*, p. 488.

The nature of the capitalist state is not fully captured by its interest and role in furthering accumulation. The capitalist state, like any other form of state, is fundamentally engaged in the protection and preservation of its rule. Nurturing a stable and prosperous economy is one of the ways in which this power is maintained. Another, as Max Weber pointed out, is through its monopoly of the legitimate use of force.[44] While 'every state is founded on force', the stability of the state depends on its being able to secure the 'sole "right" to use violence'.[45] One of the distinguishing features of the state, therefore, is its quest for legitimacy amongst (at least some of) its subject peoples, buttressed and complemented by the institutionalised use of coercion to retain power.

A state is never entirely outward-looking, however. While not losing sight of the state's unifying 'institutional self-interest', this study also stresses the state's internal institutional cleavages and conflicts, which play a major role within policy-making and administrative processes. Especially significant, certainly for the purposes of this study, is the power struggle between the executive and state bureaucracy. The bureaucracy's bid for supremacy within the state stems partly from bureaucrats' control of information, and their technical expertise. The complexity and breadth of the executive's task is such that political decision-makers may have to draw heavily on the specialised knowledge and accumulated experience of state administrators.[46] This gives the bureaucrats considerable leverage in advising policy-makers, and in defining and weighting the options between which the policy-makers choose.

These theoretical premises have several important methodological implications, which inform this study. First, if the state's 'self-interest' in accumulation does not imply that dominant class interests necessarily harmonise with state policies, nor that these interests are invariably the most important variable accounting for state policies, then the relationship between the state and particular capitalist interests must be addressed as an empirical, rather than a theoretical, question. And the state must be treated as an actor in its own right.

Secondly, the state must also be analysed internally, as a 'set of

[44] M. Weber, 'Politics as a Vocation', in H. H. Gerth and C. Wright Mills (eds.), *From Max Weber: Essays in Sociology* (London, 1948; repr. 1977), p. 78.

[45] Ibid.

[46] M. Weber, 'Bureaucracy', in Gerth and Mills (eds.), *From Max Weber*, p. 232.

administrative, policing and military organizations headed, and
more or less well co-ordinated by, an executive authority'.[47] Some of
the more recent studies on the South African state have stressed, too,
this need to examine internal state structures and processes, but in a
way which loses sight of the revisionist legacy altogether. The state is
treated as an autonomous—if differentiated—actor, apparently un-
constrained by class factors.[48] This study, however, attempts to
locate and explore institutional conflicts within the state in relation
to the broader economic and political forces impinging upon it.
Indeed, one of the ways in which the unevenness in the relationship
between state and dominant class interests is identified is by examining the divisions within and between state institutions.

Thirdly, taking theoretical cognisance of the state's drive for legitimacy (in at least some quarters) revives a methodological interest in
the logic of electoral politics and its relationship to the accumulation
process, which instrumentalist Marxists have tended to underplay or
ignore.

Fourthly, the policies and administrative practices of the state
cannot be understood fully without identifying the impact of 'struggles from below'. Ever intent on buttressing its power, the state is
constantly on the defensive against the threat of destabilisation
through popular unrest. This means that an analysis of any particular state must incorporate an investigation into the various ways in
which it reacts to such dangers. Moreover, the state's subjects are
not simply passive victims; state power is contested in organised and
unorganised ways, which play havoc with the state's capacity to
control its destiny.

[47] Skocpol, *States and Social Revolutions*, p. 29.
[48] See, e.g., S. Bekker and R. Humphries, *From Control to Confusion: The
Changing Role of Administration Boards in South Africa* (Pietermaritzburg, 1985);
A. Seegers, 'The South African State with Special Reference to the Military' (unpub-
lished mimeo, 1987); M. Swilling and M. Phillips, 'The Power and Limits of the
Emergency State' (Seminar Paper no. 258; African Studies Institute, Univ. of
Witwatersrand, August 1989). A noteworthy exception to this trend is H. Sapire,
'African Urbanisation and Struggles against Municipal Control in Brakpan, 1920–
1958' (Ph.D. thesis, Univ. of Witwatersrand, 1989), but the focus of this study is
largely confined to the local state.

# 2
# *The Legacy of the 1940s*

AFRICAN urbanisation in so-called 'white' South Africa has presented the state with a perennial dilemma, which successive influx control policies have attempted to resolve. Continued African migration to 'white' urban areas has been a mainstay of economic prosperity, supplying urban industries with an abundance of relatively cheap labour. But these economic gains have been tempered by concomitant political and economic costs. Urban poverty produced by low wages, the state's neglect of urban social services, coupled with disfranchisement and repression, have nurtured the seeds of political and industrial discontent. The expansion of urban African communities has also gone hand in hand with recurring complaints from various groups of white farmers about rural labour shortages. Since wages in manufacturing have been higher than those on the farms or mines, the supply of African labour to the cities has generally been more plentiful than to elsewhere in the country.

These problems engendered by the growth of the urban African proletariat loomed particularly large on the white political agenda in the late 1940s. With urban townships racked by successive outbursts of protest, and the South African Agricultural Union (SAAU; principal mouthpiece of white commercial agriculture) clamouring for an effective solution to the farm labour problem, the white polity was unanimous in calling for a new onslaught on 'the urban problem'. This chapter examines the contours of this 'problem' on the eve of the 1948 election which brought the NP to power, and the failure of existing influx control policies to have provided effective solutions. It then assesses the competing solutions proffered by the principal contenders in that election, the UP and the NP.

## Economic, Social, and Political Conditions in the 1940s

The 1946 Population Census was the first to reveal the presence of an

African majority in the urban areas.[1] In 1936 the white population of the urban areas was 1,307,386, which was 165,744 more than the urban African population. Between 1936 and 1946 the urban African population grew by 57.2 per cent, from 1,141,642 to 1,794,212, outstripping the urban white population, which increased by 31.5 per cent from 1,307,386 to 1,719,338.[2] In addition, the numbers of Africans squatting on the peripheries of the cities had grown substantially during the war years.[3]

An increasing proportion of the African population was settling permanently in the urban (and peri-urban) areas, rather than migrating there temporarily for the duration of an employment contract. Between 1936 and 1946 the proportion of Africans in the metropolitan areas[4] living in family circumstances increased from 30 per cent to 38 per cent.[5] Also, the proportion of African women in the urban areas was increasing faster than that of men. Between 1936 and 1946 the number of urban women grew by 79.95 per cent, compared with an increase of 46.80 per cent in the number of men.[6]

These demographic changes had two principal economic determinants: expanding avenues of urban African employment (largely due to the growth of manufacturing), and widespread rural impoverishment.

South Africa had been enjoying a period of unprecedented industrial expansion since the mid-1930s. Between 1934/5 and 1948/9 the number of private manufacturing establishments increased by 59.96 per cent and the value of their gross output shot up by 425 per cent

---

[1] The 1946 Census, along with all preceding ones, defined an 'urban area' as a 'city, town or village . . . which has some form of legally constituted urban local authority' (Union of South Africa (SA), Bureau for Census and Statistics, *Classification and Status of Urban and Rural Areas* (Pretoria, 1953–4), p. 2).

[2] Union of SA, *Report of the Native Laws Commission, 1946–48* (hereafter *Fagan Commission*), UG 28/1948, p. 6.

[3] Exact figures are unavailable.

[4] Metropolitan areas were defined as 'units of urban concentration' which extended beyond the boundaries of one local authority area, and which may in some cases have comprised 'more than one legally constituted local authority area'—e.g. the Witwatersrand, or Durban–Pinetown (Union of SA, *Classification and Status of Urban and Rural Areas*, p. 4).

[5] C. Simkins, *Four Essays on the Past, Present, and Possible Future of the Distribution of the Black Population of South Africa* (Cape Town, 1983), p. 22.

[6] University of South Africa (UNISA), Tomlinson Commission Evidence (TCE), Item 206, South African Bureau of Racial Affairs (SABRA), 'Memorandum ter Voorlegging aan die Beplanningskommissie vir die Sosio-Ekonomiese Ontwikkeling van die Naturellegebiede', 5 Jan. 1953, p. 2.

TABLE 1. *Growth of manufacturing (private sector), 1924/5–1948/9*

|  | 1924/5 | 1934/5 | 1939/40 | 1944/5 | 1948/9 |
|---|---|---|---|---|---|
| Number of establishments | 6,866 | 8,689 | 9,624 | 10,405 | 13,899 |
| Fixed capital (£000,000) | 41 | 61 | 91 | 133 | 239 |
| Fixed capital per establishment (£000) | 6 | 7 | 9 | 13 | 17 |
| Value of gross output (£000,000) | 70 | 116 | 194 | 341 | 610 |
| Gross output per establishment (£000) | 10 | 13 | 20 | 33 | 44 |
| Value of net output (£000,000) | 31 | 53 | 87 | 158 | 266 |

*Source*: A. J. Norval, *A Quarter of a Century of Industrial Progress in South Africa* (Cape Town, 1962), p. 3.

(see Table 1). State-owned industries received a fillip too, with the commissioning of the Iron and Steel Corporation (ISCOR) in 1934. This period of sustained growth was triggered initially by the increase in the price of gold following the abandonment of the gold standard in 1932. The consequent expansion of the gold-mining industry sponsored higher levels of investment in manufacturing, and an increasing demand for manufactured goods. The country's war effort then gave a second, massive boost to the manufacturing sector. With import costs inflated by the war, the scale and range of local manufacturing expanded to the extent that, by the end of the war, the country was able to export a number of products previously wholly or partially imported—such as clothing, footwear, electrical equipment, and a greater range of food exports.[7] By 1943 manufacturing's contribution to the country's gross national product exceeded that of mining (having surpassed that of agriculture by 1930). After the war the impressive growth of manufacturing continued, aided by a government policy of aggressive customs tariff protection.[8]

[7] A. J. Norval, *A Quarter of a Century of Industrial Progress in South Africa* (Cape Town, 1962), p. viii.
[8] Ibid. 2.

Secondary industries were heavily concentrated in the larger urban areas of the Transvaal, Cape, and Natal. (Industries were few and far between in the Orange Free State.) The Southern Transvaal alone was responsible for 44.5 per cent of the total net industrial output in 1944/5, as compared with 16.9 per cent in the Western Cape, 5.0 per cent in the Port Elizabeth–Uitenhage industrial area, and 13.5 per cent in the Durban–Pinetown area.[9] Although the UP government of the 1940s proclaimed the importance of industrial decentralisation as a means of stemming the accelerating African exodus from the reserves,[10] its efforts to establish the process failed.[11] With little if any infrastructure in the reserves and border areas, decentralisation remained a needlessly expensive undertaking for most industrialists. The only incentive to decentralise was the prospect of a lower African wage bill than that paid in the cities. But, as a result, the few decentralised industries which were established had to import workers from outside the country, since Union-born Africans refused work at such low wages.[12] Decentralisation under these conditions therefore offered little prospect of retarding the growth of the urban population.

The expansion of manufacturing, coupled with the temporary departure of many white workers into the army during the war, drew rapidly increasing numbers of Africans into the urban industrial work-force. Between 1935 and 1945 the number of Africans employed in manufacturing rose by 119.1 per cent, from 112,091 (which constituted 46.3 per cent of the manufacturing work-force) to 245,538 (54.6 per cent of the work-force).[13] By 1945 the large majority of these workers were still unskilled. But the variety of jobs open to Africans in manufacturing had widened, as a result of fundamental changes in the structure of manufacturing. In 1939 few if any of South Africa's secondary industries could be classed as

[9] Norval, *A Quarter of a Century of Industrial Progress*, table 6, p. 10.

[10] See, e.g., Union of SA, *Report of Board of Trade and Industries, no. 282: Investigation into Manufacturing Industries in the Union of South Africa* (Pretoria, 1945), paras. 128–35; also United Party (UP), *The Native and Coloured Peoples Policy of the United Party* (Johannesburg, 1948).

[11] See N. Clarke, 'From Dependence to Defiance: South African State Corporations, 1920–1960' (Ph.D. thesis, Yale Univ., 1988), ch. 5.

[12] UNISA Ziervogel Collection, Native Affairs Department (NAD) Research Dept., 'Die Probleme van 'n Aantal Bestaande Nywerhede naby Naturelle Arbeid', 3 June 1954.

[13] South African Institute of Race Relations (SAIRR), 'The Logic of Economic Integration', RR 76/1952, p. 5.

capital intensive. However, during the 1940s the manufacturing sector received a massive injection of capital, which sponsored an unprecedented degree of modernisation and mechanisation.[14] Some established pre-war industries earned sufficiently high profits during the war to invest in more sophisticated machinery, while the scale of capital investment in new factories during and after the war—such as engineering, metal, and chemical concerns—often allowed for highly mechanised production from the start. The result was a growing demand for semi-skilled labour to operate the new machines. The 1940s thus saw growing numbers of Africans moving into operative positions alongside smaller numbers drawn into more skilled work.[15] By 1948, according to the state's Wage Board, Africans comprised 5.8 per cent of the skilled, and 34.2 per cent of the semi-skilled, work-force in manufacturing.[16]

While employment opportunities for Africans in many urban areas expanded during the 1940s (albeit in the form of predominantly poorly paid, unskilled, and often casual jobs), economic prospects for the majority of Africans in the reserves declined sharply. Since the 1920s successive government commissions and committees[17] had documented appalling conditions in the reserves: malnutrition, stark poverty, overstocking, denuding of the land. The root of these problems was a serious land shortage. The 1913 Land Act had restricted Africans' land leasing and buying rights to the existing reserves, which comprised a mere 7 per cent of the country's land (approximately 9 million hectares). Despite the appointment of the Beaumont Commission in 1916 to investigate

[14] Norval, *A Quarter of a Century of Industrial Progress*, pp. 52–3. Note that during the war years, although manufacturing output increased (particularly in iron and steel), capital stock per worker fell, largely because the war hindered the importation of machinery. (Thanks to Terence Moll for this information.)

[15] The definition of skill is a matter of convention and, as such, is highly contested. The nature of these debates is beyond the scope of the present discussion, for which purpose it suffices to use the terms 'skilled', 'semi-skilled', and 'unskilled' in the sense in which they were used by the business community of the day. An operation is said to be 'skilled when the process involves a free use of tools requiring judgement and appraisal in carrying out the sequence of the operation'; and 'semi-skilled when the process is pre-set by the nature of the machine and requires only lever-pressing or button-pressing' (Y. Glass, *The Black Industrial Worker: A Social Psychological Study* (Johannesburg, 1960), p. 8).

[16] Union of SA, *Report of the Wage Board, 1948*, UG 50/1950.

[17] e.g. Union of SA, *Report of the Economic and Wage Commission*, UG 14/1926; *Report of the Native Economic Commission*, UG 22/1932; *Interim Report of the Industrial and Agricultural Requirements Commission*, UG 40/1941.

ways of enlarging the reserves, the position remained static until the 1936 Native Trust and Land Act recognised a number of 'released areas'—6.2 million hectares in all—to be added to the already 'scheduled' reserves. But little of this proposed extension material-ised, largely because of fierce opposition from white farmers.[18] By the 1940s, then, conditions in the reserves were appallingly con-gested. As the Secretary for Native Affairs acknowledged, 'in many areas the density of the population is very high and there are thousands of families who have . . . no arable allotments'.[19]

For the landless, there were few avenues of industrial or other employment within the reserves. And for most peasant farmers who owned small plots of land agricultural production was insufficient to feed their families. So, apart from a relatively small prosperous peasantry,[20] the vast majority of families in the reserves depended for their survival on remittances from family members who had become migrant workers, usually in urban areas or on the mines. The year 1942 was one of severe drought, which exacerbated what was for most an already desperate situation. The decade thus saw an accelerating exodus from the reserves to the urban and peri-urban areas of the country. Evidence to the 1946 Native Laws Commission (hereafter the Fagan Commission) revealed various patterns of migration criss-crossing the country between the reserves, small urban areas, large cities, and peri-urban areas. Many of those heading for the towns were single male bread-winners, who made the journey repeatedly, staying in urban areas for a few months at a time and then returning home for the ploughing or harvesting seasons. Others abandoned their rural ties and were absorbed into the settled urban population. Increasing numbers of women and children also left the reserves permanently, fleeing the rigours of tribal patriarchy and the stresses inflicted by the migrant labour system (such as desertion by, or inadequate remittances from, migrant husbands). All in all, between 1936 and 1946 the proportion

[18] Central Archives Depot (CAD), Department of Native Affairs Files (NTS), Vol. 9258 File 4/371, Secretary for Native Affairs (SNA) to Sec. of South African Agricultural Union (SAAU), re 'Native Labour', 7 Aug. 1948, p. 7.

[19] CAD NTS 9258 4/371, SNA to Sec. of SAAU, 7 Aug. 1948, p. 7.

[20] According to the *Summary of the Report of the Commission for the Socio-Economic Development of the Bantu Areas within the Union of South Africa* (hereafter *Tomlinson Commission*), by 1951 46.3% of the income earned in the reserves was concentrated in the hands of 12.7% of the population (Union of SA, *Tomlinson Commission*, UG. 61/1955, p. 98).

of the African population living in the reserves fell from 44.91 per cent to 37.79 per cent.[21]

The greatest migration to the urban areas, however, came from white-owned farms. According to the Commission for the Socio-Economic Development of the Bantu Areas within the Union of South Africa (hereafter the Tomlinson Commission), 40 per cent of the increase in the urban African population between 1936 and 1951 came from 'the European farms and other rural areas', as opposed to 8 per cent from the reserves.[22]

By the 1940s white commercial farmers typically drew their African labour from four groups: labour tenants, who generally worked for twelve to twenty-four weeks per year in return for the right to plant crops and graze cattle on a portion of the farm; full-time labourers; squatters, maintained by certain farmers on parts of their estates as labour pools;[23] and migrant labourers, usually hired on a seasonal or casual basis. The working conditions of each group varied, but grinding poverty and malnutrition were suffered across the board. Labour tenancy had become the dominant source of agricultural labour since the 1920s, particularly in the Orange Free State, Central and Northern Natal, and a large part of the Transvaal. The late 1920s, 1930s, and 1940s saw an unrelenting deterioration in the conditions of labour tenancy. Although a relatively small number of labour tenants fared well and owned sizable numbers of cattle, the majority were squeezed on to ever smaller and more inferior plots of land, their numbers of cattle increasingly restricted.[24] By the late 1940s it was common practice for white farmers to concentrate labour tenants on so-called 'labour farms', deliberately relegated to the least fertile portion of the farmers' lands.[25] The more unproductive the labour tenant's plot, the less its contribution to his family's subsistence, and therefore the more reliant he became on a cash

---

[21] Union of SA, *Fagan Commission*, p. 8.

[22] Union of SA, *Tomlinson Commission*, p. 28.

[23] CAD NTS 2229 463/280, 'Notas van vergadering tussen die Department van Naturellesake en die Skakelkommittee, 1 November 1948'. Note that the 1936 Native Trust and Land Act attempted to eliminate squatting by forcing farmers to register squatters at a fee. But the Act was rarely enforced, because it also put the onus on the government to find alternative land for the squatters.

[24] T. Marcus, *Restructuring in Commercial Agriculture in South Africa* (Amsterdam, 1986), 87; M. Morris, 'The Development of Capitalism in South African Agriculture: Class Struggle in the Countryside', *Economy and Society*, 5/3 (1976), p. 319.

[25] SAAU, *Report of the General Council for the Year 1959 for Submission to the Annual Congress* (Pretoria, 1959), p. 52.

wage. His obligatory service to the white farmer typically earned him very little, so that his family's survival depended on securing an additional cash income, usually on the mines or in the towns.

The lot of full-time and seasonal farm-workers was similarly meagre. In 1947 the average annual wage on white farms, including the cash value of food, was a mere £32 for African males, even less for women. (The comparable wage in manufacturing in 1949 was £128.)[26] But farm wages fluctuated widely, so that, in many instances, conditions were more desperate still. For example, in the Postmasburg district of the Northern Cape, cattle farmers paid cash wages of a mere £1 10s. 0d. per month or less.[27] To make matters worse, during the war years high food prices prompted farmers to cut labourers' food rations, which further depressed the net value of farm wages. During 1945, for example, rations fell by over two-thirds.[28]

White farmers had been complaining of both seasonal and permanent labour shortages since the late 1920s.[29] By 1939 the Native Farm Labour Committee, established by the NAD to investigate the problem, revealed a 'unanimous response of labour shortage' in all the regions surveyed.[30] The position worsened during the war years. Africans' prospects of urban employment were boosted by the exceptional demand for labour in secondary industries. And openings for Union-born Africans also proliferated on the mines, because the war curtailed the mines' customary labour-recruitment drives in Nyasaland and the Protectorates.[31] Unable or unwilling to increase regular wages, many farmers (particularly in the Transvaal and the Orange Free State) resorted to substantial long-term loans (often as much as £60 or £70) to lure workers into their service.[32] But, as long as wages remained pitifully low, the exodus of farm-workers to the

[26] M. Horrell, *Non-European Policies in the Union and the Measure of their Success* (Johannesburg, 1953), p. 8.

[27] CAD NTS 2230 463/280, NAD Memorandum on 'Beweerde Wegtrekkery van Plaasarbeid: Postmasburg Distrik' (n.d., *c*.1952).

[28] T. Lodge, *Black Politics in South Africa since 1945* (London and New York, 1983), p. 12.

[29] Morris, 'The Development of Capitalism', p. 314.

[30] Union of SA, *Report of the Native Farm Labour Committee, 1937–9*, GP S 3396–1939–102, p. 7.

[31] Union of SA, *Review of the Activities of the Department of Native Affairs for the Year 1942–3*, GP S 8618, p. 8.

[32] CAD NTS 2230 463/280, 'Notule van Vergadering van die Skakelkommittee, 15 November 1952'.

towns and mines persisted. During the war years the number of African farm-workers in fact increased.[33] However, this increase comprised mainly women; most of the Africans leaving the white farms were young or middle-aged males.[34] The loss of able-bodied male workers, particularly youths, to the towns therefore remained a pressing grievance amongst white farmers. As the Fagan Commission was told, 'it is only the old crocks, the older women, and children who stay on the farms'.[35]

Finally, economic pressures also drove thousands of foreign-born Africans across South Africa's borders, temporarily or permanently, in search of work. The majority of foreign-born men in the country were employed on the mines and farms. But higher wages in manufacturing attracted increasing numbers of foreigners, approximately 215,000 by 1951.[36] The Tomlinson Commission calculated that foreigners constituted 23 per cent of the increase in the resident urban African population between 1936 and 1951.[37] The Commission did not report on how many of the foreigners in the cities were women; but their numbers must have been significant. In the Transvaal, for example, a stream of single women migrants from Mozambique and Basutoland to towns of the Eastern Transvaal and the Rand had been reported from the 1920s.[38] Female migration from Basutoland then accelerated in the late 1930s, when Johannesburg and several other towns on the Rand 'experienced an unprecedented influx of Sotho women'.[39]

As the urban African proletariat continued rapidly to expand, the tensions between white industrial dependence on African labour and the protection of white supremacy were thrown into sharp relief. On the one hand, as has been shown, the growth of this proletariat was a condition of the spectacular economic successes of the late 1930s and 1940s, reflecting the growing white demand for African labour in an increasing variety of jobs. Yet, as the following discussion shows, as

[33] Horrell, *Non-European Policies*, p. 8.
[34] Union of SA, *Fagan Commission*, p. 10.
[35] University of Witwatersrand (UW), SAIRR Unsorted Papers, Fagan Commission Hearings (FCH), vol. 31, 26 Nov. 1946 at Ficksburg, Orange Free State, Evidence from the Farmers' Association of Hobhouse, p. 2167.
[36] Union of SA, *Tomlinson Commission*, p. 41.
[37] Ibid. 28.
[38] P. Bonner, '"Desirable or Undesirable Sotho Women?": Liquor, Prostitution and the Migration of Sotho Women to the Rand, 1920–1945' (Seminar Paper no. 232; African Studies Institute, Univ. of Witwatersrand, 1988), p. 10.
[39] Ibid. 15.

industrial dependence on African labour deepened, so too did the white electorate's alarm at the growing militancy and volatility of the urban African proletariat. In contrast to the relative quiescence of the 1930s, the war years ushered in a decade of political turbulence, stirred up by desperate social and economic conditions coupled with rising political expectations and assertiveness.

Severe poverty was rife in the cities, due less to unemployment than low wages. As the Fagan Commission pointed out, the 'popular view' that widespread squatting was proof of mass unemployment was mistaken. In Johannesburg, for example, a municipal survey of the Moroka squatter camp found that 95 per cent of its inhabitants had been in employment for six months or more.[40] A similar picture seems to have applied to the metropolitan areas as a whole: during 1946 95 per cent of the African male population and 55 per cent of the female population had been employed,[41] although an extremely large labour turnover produced a high rate of underemployment.

Employment, however, was no bulwark against poverty, since average urban wages for Africans remained well below the breadline throughout the decade. As the 1944 Commission of Inquiry into the Operation of Bus Services for Non-Europeans discovered,

the vast bulk of African workers . . . were in 1940 unable . . . to meet even the minimum requirements for subsistence, health and decency . . . Notwithstanding improvements in wage rates and the introduction of cost-of-living allowances since 1940, the gap between family income and the cost of living has widened considerably, owing to higher prices.[42]

With staple food prices alone increasing by 91 per cent between 1939 and 1944,[43] the average monthly deficit in the income of urban African families was £3 0s. 5d. in 1944 (widening to £4 17s. 10d. by 1950).[44]

Economic hardships were particularly severe for growing numbers of female-headed urban households, symptomatic to a large extent of the stresses imposed on women by the migrant labour system. It was

[40] Union of SA, *Fagan Commission*, p. 18.

[41] C. Simkins, 'African Urbanisation at the Time of the Last Smuts Government' (paper presented to Economic History Conference, Univ. of Cape Town, 1982), table 1.

[42] Cited in R. First, 'The Bus Boycott', *Africa South*, 1/4 (1957), 57.

[43] C. Walker, *Women and Resistance in South Africa* (London, 1982), p. 170.

[44] First, 'The Bus Boycott', 58.

widely reported during the 1930s and 1940s that the institution of marriage was 'noticeably unstable',[45] particularly in urban areas with a large proportion of male migrants.[46] A woman who came to town in search of her migrant husband frequently found that he had set up home with a second spouse, either through marriage or in an informal, so-called 'vat en sit' union. Such relationships, moreover, often offered little emotional or financial security to urban women. Research conducted in East London townships in 1949, for example, where the rate of migrancy was high, found that male migrants 'who come unaccompanied often pick up women for the time they are in the urban area and discard them at the end of the work period'.[47] Comprehensive data are unavailable and marriage patterns varied regionally.[48] Still, state reports during the 1930s and 1940s conveyed the impression of a growing proportion of such informal unions, with correspondingly mounting pressures on women to run their households and support their children largely single-handed.[49]

Impoverishment and malnutrition were compounded by a dire shortage of serviced municipal accommodation. In terms of the 1923 Natives (Urban Areas) Act, municipalities were obliged to supply accommodation to all Africans legally resident in their areas. This provision had not been enforced, however, and municipal housing was drastically undersupplied. Durban, for example, had an estimated African population of 109,141 in 1947 (almost certainly an underestimate, given a high percentage of illegal residents who eluded population counts), of whom a mere 9,817 had municipal housing. White employers housed another 9,685, and a few occupied

---

[45] UW SAIRR AD843 B100.13, Grahamstown Joint Council, 'Memorandum on African Marriage' (n.d., c.1949), p. 3; A. Steyn and C. Rip, 'The Changing Bantu Family', *Journal of Marriage and the Family*, 30/3 (1968), 512; J. F. Eloff, 'Die Verandering en Verval van die Gesinslewe van die Stedelike Bantoe', *Journal of Racial Affairs*, 4/3 (1953), 32.

[46] UW SAIRR AD843 B100.13, D. Bettison (Rhodes Univ.), 'Enquiry into African Marriage' (1949), p. 1.

[47] Ibid.

[48] e.g. Steyn and Rip ('The Changing Bantu Family') collating various studies of the urban African family, found that, in Johannesburg in 1941, approximately 50% of African couples were living together informally, as compared to only 21% in Pretoria in 1936.

[49] e.g. UW SAIRR AD843 B100.13, D. L. Smit to Rheinnalt Jones, re 'Native Marriage and Customary Unions', 8 Mar. 1938; SAIRR, 'Memorandum on Native Marriage Laws', 9 Sept. 1943; CAD NTS 7725 166/333, Office of Station Commander, Vereeniging, to Additional Native Commissioner, re 'Undesirable Women', 22 Sept. 1937.

self-built houses.[50] But the rest crowded into backyard shacks in the municipal townships and dense shack settlements scattered amongst the 'white' residential areas or lining the municipal boundary. By 1947 the immediate accommodation shortage in urban areas nation-wide was officially estimated at 154,185 houses and 106,877 hostel beds.[51] But official figures seriously underestimated the extent of the real accommodation problem, since they took no account of illegal inhabitants of the cities. Still, assuming (conservatively) an average occupancy of six persons per house, even the official figures implied that in 1947 as many as 1,031,987 Africans—at least 57.5 per cent of the urban African population—were squatters lacking approved, serviced accommodation. The existence of large squatter communities had become an essential condition of expanding urban African employment and renewed industrial prosperity.

Consigned to conditions of poverty, overcrowding, and ill health, Africans in the cities had no effective voice within the state. The institutions purporting to deal with their grievances were mostly ineffectual. The 1923 Natives (Urban Areas) Act had authorised the creation of African Advisory Boards in each municipal area, to present the residents' day-to-day problems to the local authority. But these Boards were often denied a serious hearing by the local authorities, and, even if they were heard, their role was a purely advisory one. Dashed hopes of a liberalisation of government policy, excited by the temporary suspension of the pass laws in 1942, made the state's implacable indifference to Africans' plight all the more injurious and provocative.

This mixture of desperation and disaffection proved explosive. Noting 'the increase of political agitation in locations'[52] in the early 1940s, municipal administrators conferred anxiously on the prolif-eration of 'subversive propaganda',[53] accompanying 'a growing tendency on the part of Natives to organise concerted resistance on any question which they consider affects them adversely, and at such

---

[50] Durban City Council, *Memorandum for Judicial Commission on Native Affairs in Durban* (Durban, 1947), pp. 2–6.

[51] Union of SA, *Report of the Department of Native Affairs*, UG 14/1948, p. 12.

[52] Brakpan City Council (BCC), Brakpan Municipal Records (BMR), 14/1/30, 'Minutes of Monthly Meeting of Reef Managers, Superintendents of Urban Native Administration and Native Commissioners, 20 July 1944', p. 4.

[53] BCC BMR 14/1/30, 'Minutes of Monthly Meeting of Reef Managers . . . 21 November 1946'.

gatherings to speak extravagantly and defiantly of authority'.[54] As Cherryl Walker comments,

the war years were a time of enormous social ferment and unrest, which found expression in numerous local campaigns and protests in all the major cities. Much was informal and spontaneous—particular local difficulties would reach a point at which they could no longer be tolerated and would provoke a reaction by township residents—meetings, election of local committees, boycotts, etc. Grassroots leaders emerged to direct local campaigns; sometimes other political organisations intervened to assist or direct the course of action.[55]

These grass-roots protests concentrated on bread-and-butter issues. Rising food prices prompted street marches and demonstrations in several cities. Increases in bus fares provoked three successive bus boycotts in Alexandra (outside Johannesburg), the third marshalling the support of about twenty thousand people. Squatter movements were also extremely active during the war years, resisting the appallingly overcrowded living conditions in municipal townships.[56] In Cape Town, for example, squatters at Blouvlei (near the suburb of Retreat) defeated the municipality's attempts in the early 1940s to flatten their settlement.[57] But the defiant creation of 'Shanty Town' near Orlando, Soweto, was perhaps the most well-publicised instance of squatter resistance. In 1944 James Mpanza led thousands of families who had been sub-tenants in cramped Orlando rooms where 'observance of any reasonable living standard was impossible'[58] on to nearby vacant land, in defiance of municipal regulations. Sub-tenants from Pimville township, Soweto, followed suit in 1946, their ranks swelled by squatters from Pretoria and East Rand towns.[59] The Johannesburg City Council responded by forcibly resettling squatters in Moroka emergency camp (an area set aside for controlled squatting) and arresting or deporting squatter leaders. With tensions running high, a police

[54] BCC BMR 14/1/30, 'Minutes of Monthly Meeting of Reef Managers . . . 19 October 1944'.
[55] Walker, *Women and Resistance*, p. 74.
[56] See, e.g., Stadler, 'Birds in the Cornfield'.
[57] Walker, *Women and Resistance*, p. 76.
[58] George Xorile's Personal Papers, 'Record of Proceedings at Joint Meeting of General Purposes, Non-European Affairs and Special Housing Committees . . . 26 January 1946', p. 2.
[59] *The Star*, 2 Apr. 1946.

raid on Moroka proved the last straw, and the ensuing riot resulted in the death of three policemen.

The surge of grass-roots militancy in the 1940s gave new momentum to the Communist Party of South Africa (CPSA). Pursuing a strategy of direct involvement with local popular struggles, the CPSA succeeded in 'establishing footholds in location communities',[60] particularly in areas on the Witwatersrand, the East Rand, Port Elizabeth, and East London. By 1945 the CPSA had established branches or groups in the African areas of most industrial towns.[61] Elias Motsoaledi (who joined both the CPSA and African National Congress (ANC)) remarked in later years that it was the CPSA more than the ANC which 'interpreted the aspirations of the masses' during the 1940s.[62] CPSA members sat on the Alexandra Shanty Town Committee, for example. And although initially wary of joining forces with Mpanza, the CPSA adopted the Orlando squatters' cause in 1947, setting up a Shanty Town Co-ordination Committee which incorporated some of the squatter leaders.[63] On the East Rand the political participation and successes of the CPSA were especially striking. As Hilary Sapire has argued, the sensitivity of CPSA activists on the East Rand such as David Bopape and Gideon Ngake to immediate local grievances established the CPSA as the leading political force in the region.[64]

Although the ANC capitalised far less on the energy and militancy of local community struggles, the post-war years saw a significant strengthening of the organisation, due largely to the efforts of its Youth League. Formed in 1944, the Youth League soon came to dominate the formulation of Congress ideology and strategy.[65] Committed to transforming the ANC from a moderate political élite into a more militant, populist movement, the Youth League stressed the need for 'a strategy of mass action'[66] which would mobilise

[60] H. Sapire, 'African Political Mobilisation in Brakpan in the 1950s' (Seminar Paper no. 250; African Studies Institute, Univ. of Witwatersrand, 1989), p. 6.

[61] T. Lodge, 'Class Conflict, Communal Struggle and Patriotic Unity: The Communist Party of South Africa during the Second World War' (Seminar Paper no. 180; African Studies Institute, Univ. of Witwatersrand, 1985), p. 12.

[62] *New Nation*, Supplement, 27 Oct.–2 Nov. 1989, p. 7.

[63] *Inkululeko*, no. 107, June 1947.

[64] Sapire, 'African Political Mobilisation', p. 6.

[65] For an account of the impact of the Youth League on the African National Congress (ANC) 'Old Guard', see D. Everatt, 'The Origins of Multiracialism' (Seminar Paper no. 270; African Studies Institute, Univ. of Witwatersrand, 1990).

[66] Lodge, *Black Politics*, p. 22.

popular support by means of a militant African nationalism.[67] These efforts were rewarded with a striking increase in the ANC's membership. Between 1944–5 and 1947 the number of paid-up members alone more than doubled, rising from just under 2,000 to 5,179.[68]

The ANC, but more especially the CPSA, also looked to Advisory Board politics as a means of extending the organisations' local influence and support. In the ANC's case, this strategy was initiated by the organisation's 'old guard' in the 1930s, but it continued well into the 1950s (despite strong opposition from Youth Leaguers, who condemned the Advisory Boards as collaborationist institutions). Aware of the severe limitations of the Advisory Board system, the ANC leadership nevertheless saw participation in it as a means of establishing a platform in local politics and exerting pressure on local authorities. As A. B. Xuma (President-General of the ANC from 1940 to 1949) put it in letters to various community politicians,

in the name of the African National Congress, I call upon you to get together the leaders of your area; members of Advisory Boards, Vigilance Associations and others into the banner of Congress so that we can speak with one voice before the authorities and have every right to claim recognition and attention to our grievances thereby.[69]

The CPSA pursued a similar strategy (interrupted by a temporary boycott during 1947[70]), using the 'fight for more power for advisory board(s)'[71] to boost the party's local influence and profile. Participation in Advisory Board politics was particularly active on the Rand. For example, during the early 1940s three CPSA members sat on the Orlando Advisory Board, including Edwin Mofutsanyana, editor of the CPSA paper *Inkululeko*.

In the Transvaal particularly, such collaboration between the ANC, CPSA, and Advisory Boards thrust many Boards into overtly political campaigns and confrontations with local authorities. For example, in 1946 Advisory Boards in the Transvaal resolved to challenge the pass system 'under the direction of . . . the National

---

[67] Everatt, 'The Origins of Multiracialism', p. 6.

[68] Walker, *Women and Resistance*, p. 87.

[69] UW Xuma Papers, ABX 431125, A. B. Xuma to J. M. Nthakha, 25 Nov. 1943.

[70] *Inkululeko*, no. 116, June 1947, and no. 117, July 1947.

[71] George Xorile's Papers, Communist Candidates' Pamphlet for Orlando Advisory Board Elections, 1945.

Anti-Pass Council',[72] which had been set up jointly by the ANC and
CPSA in 1943. Such politicisation of Board activities thoroughly disconcerted local authorities. Municipal administrators on the Reef
'pointed out that recent events showed that ... Native Advisory
Boards and other Native leaders were adopting a general attitude of
hostility towards constituted authority ... Unless the situation is
carefully handled, civil disorders might easily develop.'[73]

The political challenge levelled by Advisory Boards was limited,
in the sense that their powers remained purely advisory (see earlier).
But their protests underlined the breadth and intensity of African
dissent. The very bodies created by the state for the purposes of co-
opting support from moderate Africans were joining the throngs of
the disaffected.

African trade unions also grew in strength and size during the
1940s. By 1945 over 100,000 workers (approximately 40 per cent of
the African industrial work-force) were unionised, as compared with
37,000 in 1939.[74] This matched the size of the Industrial Commercial Union (the first mass African workers' movement) at the height
of its strength in 1927.[75] The years 1939–1945 also saw a record
number of 304 strikes, involving 58,000 Africans, Coloureds, and
Indians.[76] Over 70,000 African miners then went on strike in 1946.

The state viewed these developments with alarm, feeling particularly threatened by the prospect of a united, cohesive African working class in the cities, where 'tribal' differences and cleavages were
fast eroding. As the Board of Trade and Industries warned in 1948,

racial and class differences will create a homogenous proletariat which will
eventually lose all its earlier ties with rural community groupings which
previously had influence and meaning in their lives. The detribalisation of
large numbers of Natives .... rootless masses concentrated in the large
industrial centres, is a matter which no government can sit back and watch.
Unless these masses of detribalised Natives are effectively and carefully

[72] UW Xuma Papers, ABX 4602170, Minutes of 'Transvaal Location Advisory
Boards and Other Organisations Conference, ... 17 February 1946', p. 5.

[73] BCC BMR 14/1/30, 'Minutes of Monthly Meeting of Reef Managers, Superintendents of Urban Native Administration and Native Commissioners', 12 Dec.
1946.

[74] Walker, *Women and Resistance*, p. 113.

[75] K. Luckhardt and B. Wall, *Organize or Starve: The History of the South African
Congress of Trade Unions* (London, 1980), p. 40.

[76] H. J. Simons and R. E. Simons, *Class and Colour in South Africa, 1850–1950*
(Baltimore, 1969), p. 555.

controlled, they will become more of a burden than a constructive factor in industry.[77]

In sum, then, by the 1948 election the contours of the problem of influx control facing the state were starkly defined. The election took place in the midst of an economic upswing, marked by rapid industrial expansion which depended increasingly on African labour. Yet, at the same time, white farmers were complaining bitterly about worsening labour shortages, and the proliferation of black protests in the cities had exploded the political calm of the preceding decade.

### Failures of Pre-existing Influx Control Policies

The magnitude of the state's problem was also a reflection of the many glaring failures of the influx control system to date. From the start the question of an appropriate influx control strategy to deal with 'the urban problem' was a source of deep division within the state. The need for a law to impose uniform state controls over Africans in the urban areas was agreed as early as 1912. But protracted controversy over the formula for such control delayed legislation until 1923. By the early 1920s the issues at stake in these conflicts had been clearly stamped by various post-war developments. The size of the urban African population had soared by 71.4 per cent between 1904 and 1921, as compared with a growth of 50.9 per cent in the urban white population.[78] At the same time African proletarianisation had brought mounting discontent in its wake, most conspicuous in a spate of post-war strikes (such as the sanitary workers' strike of 1918 and a miners' strike in 1920). An influenza epidemic in 1918, which focused public attention on the appalling living conditions in urban African communities, thereby also underlined their political inflammability.

Two competing strategies for attacking 'the urban problem' were tendered within the state. The one was based directly on the recommendations of the Transvaal Local Government Commission of 1921, chaired by Colonel Stallard. Stallard's basic principle was that the urban African population should be treated as principally a

---

[77] Union of SA, *Report of Board of Trade and Industries, no. 282*, para. 35.

[78] P. Rich, 'Ministering to the White Man's Needs: The Development of Urban Segregation in South Africa, 1913–1923', *African Studies*, 37/2 (1978), 180.

labour reservoir at the disposal of whites. In the words of the Commission, 'the Native should only be allowed to enter urban areas, which are essentially the white man's creation, when he is willing to enter and to minister to the needs of the white man, and should depart therefore when he ceases so to minister'.[79] Africans in urban areas should have no unconditional rights to live there as permanent residents, not even if they had become fully urbanised and 'detribalised'. For Stallard, all Africans would always be merely 'temporary sojourners' in the urban areas.

The alternative approach started from a different premiss, accepting that Africans living continuously in the cities could take their place as permanent urban residents alongside whites. In acknowledging the presence of a permanent, urbanised African population, the state should undertake to improve urban living conditions and give Africans more of a stake in the locations through the allocation of freehold rights. On this view, the way for the state to achieve effective urban control was not simply through coercion (as Stallard's position implied), but also through the co-option of the more affluent section of the urbanised community.

The contest between these two approaches to influx control continued within the state throughout the next three decades. In 1923 it was the Stallardist approach which prevailed, dominating the substance of the first Natives (Urban Areas) Act. This was partly a reflection of the political power of particular class interests. White working-class lobbies favoured Stallard's line because, in undermining the security of urban Africans, it protected the cause of white workers in the cities. The urban commercial bourgeoisie backed Stallard because the prospect of a growing propertied urban African middle class posed a direct economic threat.[80] But the approach adopted by the Urban Areas Act also derived from a more generalised white fear that freehold rights would lead inexorably to the municipal enfranchisement of Africans.[81]

The 1923 Urban Areas Act laid the foundation for influx control for the following two and a half decades. Its core principle, *à la*

---

[79] Transvaal Province, *Transvaal Local Government Commission, 1921*, TP 1/1922, para. 42.

[80] Rich, 'Ministering to the White Man's Needs', 188–9.

[81] T. R. H. Davenport, 'The Beginnings of Urban Segregation in South Africa: The Natives (Urban Areas) Act of 1923 and its Background' (Occasional Paper no. 15; Institute for Social and Economic Research, Rhodes Univ. 1971), p. 19.

Stallard, was that the size of the urban African population should be restricted primarily according to the labour demands of the resident white population. Moreover, apart from certain categories of exempted persons,[82] Africans in the cities would be liable to expulsion if unemployed. The mechanism for exercising this control was to be the registration of all service contracts with the NAD. The NAD would approve and register the employment of all African men,[83] and issue a registration document which had to be produced on demand to police or state officials checking the men's right to be in urban areas.

From the start the implementation of these influx control provisions proved problematic. In terms of the 1923 Act influx control was not mandatory. Local authorities could elect to have their areas of jurisdiction proclaimed in terms of the Act, or not. Many did not, often because they lacked the resources to police the influx control restrictions. Others opposed the Stallardist premises of the Act. Even those local authorities that did invoke the Act had to endure long delays before the relevant proclamation was issued and applied. More serious obstacles to effective influx control were created by loopholes in the substance of the legislation itself. In terms of the 1923 Act, there was no prohibition on the entry of Africans to urban areas. All had the right to be issued with a work-seeker's permit; it was only if they failed to find work within fourteen days that their presence in the area became illegal. The efficacy of the influx control system therefore depended on ubiquitous policing, to locate all those whose work-seekers' permits had expired without their finding work—for most municipalities an impossibly onerous task. Also, the Urban Areas Act permitted work-seekers to bring their families to town with them, whether or not the family members took work. The Act thus compromised the very principle underpinning it, that Africans 'surplus' to white economic needs should not be permitted into the urban areas.

Subsequent amendments to the Urban Areas Act attempted to close these loopholes. The 1930 amendment coincided with the tightening of the state's so-called 'civilised-labour' policy. The onset of the Depression had accelerated the influx of all population groups

---

[82] These included registered parliamentary voters, property owners in urban areas, and professionals in government employ.
[83] African women were excluded from this provision.

to the cities. To cope with the resultant problem of white urban unemployment, the state insisted that white, 'civilised', labour should be substituted for black workers as widely as possible. Tighter influx control provisions, affording increased powers to remove 'surplus' Africans, were then introduced to cope with the consequent growth in black urban unemployment.

The effects of the 1930 legislation were uneven, however. A memorandum from the South African Institute of Race Relations (SAIRR) in 1932 noted 'the return of many unemployed Natives from the towns . . . to the rural areas'.[84] But this was not the rule. The imposition of influx control was still in the hands of the local authorities, and by 1937, as Smuts complained, 'there are only eleven towns in South Africa who have so far availed themselves of the power to limit and control the entry of Natives into their locations'.[85]

The government, meanwhile, had continued to ponder the influx control problem. No sooner was the 1930 Urban Areas Amendment Act passed than the process of introducing further amendments to tighten influx control was initiated. It culminated seven years later in the 1937 Native Laws Amendment Act, the legislative process once again having been buffeted by intra-state conflicts over the proper methods of influx control. After five years of debate and indecision, a departmental committee (the Young–Barrett committee) had been appointed in 1935 to investigate methods whereby Stallardist principles could be effectively applied. But the committee renounced Stallardism altogether. Urbanised Africans, the committee argued, could not simply be expelled from urban areas once economically 'redundant'.[86] They had become 'permanent town dwellers' and should be accepted as such. Indeed, the committee called on the state to encourage the growth of a stabilised urban African population with full security of tenure. Echoing the 1932 Native Economic Commission, Young and Barrett argued that 'in the interests of the efficiency of urban industries it is better to have a fixed urban Native

[84] UW Rheinnalt Jones Papers, B71, SAIRR, 'Distress and Unemployment Among Natives', 1932.

[85] Union of SA, *Notes on Conference between Municipalities and the Native Affairs Department . . . on 28 and 29 September 1937, to discuss the provisions of Native Laws Amendment Act (No. 46 of 1937)*, UG 56/1937, p. 3.

[86] Union of SA, *Report of the Departmental Committee . . . of the Residence of Natives in Urban Areas and Certain Proposed Amendments of the Natives (Urban Areas) Act No. 21 of 1923* (hereafter *Young–Barrett Report*) (1935), para. 49, 50.

population to the extent to which such a population is necessary, than the present casual drifting population'.[87] The committee agreed that migration to urban areas should be controlled, but primarily by 'improving the amenities of the country[side]'.[88]

Young and Barrett had ranked what they saw as the interests of the burgeoning industrial sector very highly in dismissing Stallardist principles. But by 1937 the opposing, and more powerful, faction within the state was more concerned to find a formula for urban control which served the cause of white commercial agriculture. Legislation which overrode the Young–Barrett recommendations was introduced and passed, in an effort to address the problem of agricultural labour shortages.[89]

This law, the 1937 Native Laws Amendment Act, took a far more aggressively Stallardist line than the original 1923 Act had done. The Minister of Native Affairs was empowered to remove Africans from an urban area if they were deemed 'surplus' to the 'reasonable labour requirements' of the area. Moreover, as long as an urban labour 'surplus' persisted, local authorities could impose a total ban on all further entry to the area by Africans. To keep track of the size of any 'surplus', local authorities were compelled to take a biennial census of the resident African population. And town councils in areas with populations over 15,000 had to furnish the NAD with monthly returns showing the current employment position and likely labour requirements.

These were formidable powers of influx control on paper. But, in practice, the system still proved defective in most cases. There were two principal reasons for its failures. The first was a problem of 'deficient co-ordination'[90] in the administration of influx control. In

---

[87] Ibid., para. 17.

[88] Ibid., para. 46.

[89] In defending the Native Laws Amendment (NLA) Bill, Smuts alleged that it was also intended to combat 'surpluses' of urban labour (Union of SA, *Notes on Conference between Municipalities and the Native Affairs Department*, p. 2. But this was a period of rapid industrial expansion, in which there were no convincing signs of widespread unemployment. Indeed, in concurrent parliamentary debates on the Immigration Amendment Bill, the same MPs who supported Smuts were worried not about African unemployment in the cities, but by the fact that 'the obtaining of work by them [Africans in the cities] means that they will squeeze out and put out of work another class of the population (i.e. white workers) (Union of SA, *House of Assembly Debates (HAD)* (1937), vol. 30, col. 5027).

[90] BCC BMR 14/1/30, 'Minutes of Special Meeting of Association of Administrators of Non-European Affairs . . . 15 June 1944'.

true Stallardist vein, the law emphasised the need to link Africans'
right to be in urban areas (regulated by the issue of a pass) to their
ministering to white economic needs (regulated by the registration of
service contracts). Yet, administratively, this linkage was subverted.
The NAD controlled the pace of (legal) urban African employment
by registering workers' service contracts. But this control was
exercised independently of the issue of passes by municipalities.

Secondly, the NAD was itself deeply divided over the merits of
the 1937 Act, and therefore failed to oversee its implementation in
any consistent way. The extraordinary wartime demand for labour
brought long-standing conflicts between pro- and anti-Stallardist
factions within the NAD to a head, plunging the department's policy
into ambiguity and incoherence. In 1940 Deneys Reitz, then Minister of Native Affairs, deviated from the NAD's dominant Stallardist
tradition by announcing that he opposed the pass system.[91] Reitz's
move was contested by the Native Affairs Commission (an influential
body set up to advise the NAD in its policies regarding the reserves),
but was firmly endorsed by an interdepartmental inquiry into the
Social, Health and Economic Conditions of Urban Natives (1942),
chaired by the Secretary of Native Affairs, D. L. Smit. Smit's call
for the abolition of pass laws was well timed. Industrial labour
requirements having expanded dramatically during 1941, particularly in the Western Cape, the NAD agreed to suspend the pass laws
temporarily in the country's major industrial centres during 1942.[92]
The NAD's response to this experiment, however, typified its indecision and vacillation. The NAD acted swiftly to reinstate
draconian influx control measures in the Cape Peninsula. By 1943
local authorities in this region reported that the labour market was
'saturated', at which point the NAD immediately intervened, order-
ing that Proclamation 105 of 1939, which imposed strict conditions
on Africans' access to Cape Town,[93] be 'reapplied with full
severity'.[94] Yet the NAD did little to deter the huge numbers of

[91] E. Kahn, 'Whither our War-Time Policy', *South African Journal of Economics*
(*SAJE*), 10/2 (1942), 142.

[92] *The Star*, 12 May 1942.

[93] In terms of this Proclamation, Africans were prohibited from entering Cape
Town unless they were *bona fide* visitors, or returning to a previous employer, or
allocated to a specific job for which labour was in demand.

[94] UW Ballinger Papers, A410 B2.14.3, Memorandum of Langa Advisory Board
and Vigilance Committee.

Africans streaming into many other urban centres, despite complaints about burgeoning 'Native surpluses' from local authorities. The influx was particularly dramatic in the main industrial centres outside Cape Town: the East London—Port Elizabeth region, Durban, Johannesburg, and other Witwatersrand towns.[95] The Fagan Commission heard evidence from Africans across the country that there was 'no question of prohibiting people from going to Johannesburg'.[96] Local authorities on the Witwatersrand were particularly disconcerted by the influx of 'thousands of [Basuto] women in Johannesburg and on the Reef . . . [over whom] there was no control whatsoever'.[97] Durban, too, was similarly inundated with illegal residents. By 1946 80 per cent of the Africans registering service contracts had secured jobs without first obtaining work-seekers' permits, which meant that they had infiltrated the city illegally.[98] And there was little the Durban municipality could do about it.

Alarmed at their impotence, municipalities on the Witwatersrand, represented by the Association of Administrators of Non-European Affairs, repeatedly petitioned the NAD for the introduction of more effective influx controls.[99] By September 1944 the magnitude of the problem, coupled with the NAD's lethargy, prompted the Association (the largest and most influential organisation of municipal administrators) to call for a conference with the NAD as a matter of 'considerable urgency'.[100]

The NAD met local authorities in December 1945. The Association of Administrators of Non-European Affairs used the opportunity to present the NAD with a series of recommendations

[95] See UW SAIRR Unsorted Papers, FCH, vol. 7, p. 476; vol. 17, p. 1237; vol. 23, p. 1607; vol. 39, p. 2681, vol. 46, p. 3145.

[96] Ibid., vol. 16, p. 1190.

[97] BCC BMR 14/1/30, 'Minutes of Meeting of Native Affairs Advisory Committee . . . Consisting of Representatives of All Reef Municipalities, 26 June 1942', p. 4.

[98] UW SAIRR Unsorted Papers, Fagan Commission Evidence (FCE), 'Memorandum of Evidence Submitted by the Department of Economics, Natal University College, Durban', p. 18.

[99] BCC BMR 14/1/30, 'Minutes of Meeting of Native Advisory Committee . . . 26 June 1942', p. 4; 'Minutes of Monthly Meeting of Reef Managers and Superintendents of Urban Native Administration . . . 17 February 1944', p. 4; 'Minutes of Monthly Meeting of Reef Managers . . . 16 June 1944', p. 2.

[100] BCC BMR 14/1/30, 'Minutes of Monthly Meeting of Association of Administrators of Non-European Affairs . . . 21 September 1944', p. 3.

designed to restructure the influx control system.[101] The NAD was urged to transfer the registration of service contracts, and the revenue accruing from it, to local authorities. African women, the Association claimed, should be subjected to the registration regulations. 'As an important corollary to the registration system', the NAD was called upon to establish a national system of compulsory 'labour exchanges', to control the allocation of African labour within urban areas.[102] These labour exchanges, it was argued, should operate according to a principle of urban labour preference: 'the regulations should give the local authority the power to refuse to register natives from outside until every native in its area had been given employment'.[103]

The NAD agreed in principle to surrender its control over the registration of service contracts, but its response to the other proposals was predictably vague and indecisive. Departmental officials revealed that they had been 'thinking along the lines' of establishing labour exchanges, but with little of the urgency or clarity demanded by local authorities.[104] The NAD's attitude towards subjecting African women to influx control was fundamentally ambiguous. While inviting representations from local authorities 'regarding the restrictions they required over Native females',[105] the NAD was also adamant that there was no 'intention of imposing undue restrictions on the movement of women'.[106] But most disconcerting of all to the local authorities was the NAD's equivocation regarding the future of pass laws. Confronted on this issue during the 1945 meeting, NAD representatives were evasive: 'no government can bind itself indefinitely. The Minister stated . . . that he could not say what the Government's future policy would be in this regard'.[107] It was clear, however, that the Minister of Native

---

[101] These proposals were then more elaborately and systematically stated in the Association's evidence to the Fagan Commission in 1946.

[102] BCC BMR 14/1/30, 'Notes of Conference . . . December 1945 between Urban Local Authorities and Representatives of Native Affairs and Other Government Departments', p. 17.

[103] BCC BMR 14/1/30, 'Minutes of Special Meeting of Association of Administrators of Non-European Affairs . . . 27 December 1945', p. 3.

[104] BCC BMR 14/1/30, 'Notes on Conference . . . December 1945', p. 2.

[105] Ibid. 30.

[106] BCC BMR 14/1/30, 'Matters for Discussion at Conference between Urban Local Authorities and Representatives of the Native Affairs and Other Government Departments', Dec. 1945, pp. 9–10.

[107] BCC BMR 14/1/30, 'Notes of Conference . . . December 1945', p. 6.

Affairs had no intention of embarking on the immediate and vigorous reappraisal of influx control policy advocated by the local authorities. For, in his eyes, the current problems had been produced by abnormal wartime conditions, and would settle automatically with time.[108] The NAD thus failed completely to recognise and address the sense of crisis expressed by local authorities.

On the eve of the 1948 election, then, it was abundantly clear to both the UP and the NP that a thoroughgoing reassessment of the issue of influx control was needed. Not only were the problems which influx control policy was intended to address looming larger than ever, but the state's existing capacity to tackle these problems was manifestly inadequate.

The differences between the influx control strategies proposed by the UP and the NP reiterated some of the long-standing divisions within the state over the appropriate principles and methods of influx control. The NP's approach was ideologically the heir of Stallardism, whereas the UP's line inherited many of the principles upheld by the anti-Stallardist faction. These ideological divergences over influx control were underlined by their being articulated as part of competing, all-encompassing blueprints for 'native policy' as a whole. The UP heralded its position as a 'middle way' between 'segregation' and 'integration', whereas the NP insisted that 'any middle way or compromise is at best temporary and mere patch work'[109] and declared its programme for Apartheid the only feasible alternative to 'integration'.

Such rhetoric presented the two blueprints, and their influx control components, as diametrically opposed. In fact, however, the NP vacillated between two conflicting conceptions of Apartheid and two correspondingly different solutions to the problem of influx control, one of which bore some striking resemblances to the UP's position on the issue. The following discussion briefly examines the UP's position on influx control, and then exposes the controversy and conflict within the Afrikaner nationalist alliance, and its implications for an understanding of the policies of the first Nationalist government.

---

[108] *HAD* (1945), vol. 52, col. 4305.

[109] P. Sauer, 'Verslag van die Kleurvraagstuk Kommissie van die Herenigde Nasionale Party' (hereafter 'Sauer Report'), (1947), p. 2.

## The United Party Solution to the Influx Control Problem

The UP based its strategy for the urban areas on the recommendations of the 1946 Native Laws Commission, chaired by Justice Fagan. Many of Fagan's findings in turn reiterated the views of several anti-Stallardist commissions and committees to date. Having conducted a detailed examination of the economic and social dimensions of African proletarianisation in the cities, the report concluded that the continuing expansion of urban industries, and the growth of the permanent urban African population, were 'simply facts which we have to face as such'.[110] 'Total segregation' was simply not feasible. The reserves were already overpopulated and overstocked, Fagan argued, so that even the most ambitious development programmes could never facilitate the complete rural reabsorption of existing urban communities. Indeed, since industrial development necessitated the presence of a reservoir of African labour in the cities, renewed economic growth would depend on drawing growing numbers of Africans from the rural to the urban areas.

The Fagan Commission stressed, however, that the continuing integration of Africans into urban areas and industries need not inevitably lead to their political enfranchisement. The Commission recognised that the political turbulence of the decade had placed the issue of African political rights prominently on the state's agenda. But, remaining thoroughly committed to white political supremacy, Fagan recommended that these rights be allocated at a municipal level only, and in separate bodies from those run by whites. Thoroughgoing political 'integration' was thus not the only alternative to 'total segregation'.

Satisfied, then, that continuing African proletarianisation need not threaten the foundations of white supremacy, Fagan urged that rural Africans taking up urban jobs be permitted to settle permanently in the cities, together with their families. Although against the enforced termination of the migrant labour system, the Commission heeded industrialists' calls for an increasingly stabilised African work-force, borne of continuing urbanisation.

This was not a case for unrestricted access to the urban areas. The numbers of urban Africans had to be limited according to industrial requirements, and restricted to racially segregated residential areas.

---

[110] Union of SA, *Fagan Commission*, p. 19.

The principle of influx control was thus endorsed. But the Commission's recommendations on the substance of an influx control policy were fundamentally ambiguous. On the one hand, Fagan concluded that, in view of deepening African resentment of enforced influx control barriers, 'the emphasis must shift from compulsory measures and from restrictive laws to machinery for advice, guidance and voluntary regulation'.[111] The two principal tools of influx control—a national system of labour bureaux to channel work-seekers to available jobs, and a new system of identification documents—were thus 'ideally' voluntary.

On the other hand, the Commission also called for a national system of compulsory state control over the movement of Africans in and out of the towns, which was necessary 'in order to take steps . . . to ensure that everybody has some fit place to which he is entitled to go'.[112]

Inheriting this ambiguity, the UP's position on influx control prevaricated between calls for overall state control over population movement on the one hand, and the institution of voluntary influx control procedures on the other.

### The National Party's Position on Influx Control

The NP's stance on the problem of influx control was declared by the unpublished Sauer Report, commissioned in 1947 to develop the outlines of an Afrikaner Nationalist blueprint for a 'white' future under an 'Apartheid' system. As O'Meara has argued, the NP provided a party political platform for the Afrikaner nationalist alliance, which encompassed 'Transvaal, Cape and Orange Free State farmers, specific categories of white labour, and the Afrikaner petty-bourgeoisie'.[113] By 1948 the notion of Apartheid had become one of the central slogans ideologically cementing this alliance. Yet the *meaning* of Apartheid was contested, largely along class lines. While stressing the class differences within the Afrikaner alliance, O'Meara did not recognise that these class divisions were generally associated with conflicting attitudes towards white dependence on African

---

[111] Ibid. 27.
[112] Ibid.
[113] O'Meara, *Volkskapitalisme*, p. 243.

labour, which in turn generated incompatible blueprints for Apartheid. Afrikaner capital generally supported a 'practical' conception of Apartheid premissed on continuing white access to African labour. But Afrikaner workers, professionals, civil servants, and intellectuals tended to endorse the competing version of Apartheid as 'total segregation', including the systematic extrication of African labour from the supposedly 'white' areas of the country. The Sauer Report then emerged as a contradictory combination of both competing conceptions of Apartheid. What follows is a brief examination of these competing versions of Apartheid, and their inconsistent synthesis within the Sauer Report.

### Apartheid as Total Segregation

This conception of Apartheid was widely espoused amongst Afrikaner intellectuals, teachers, lawyers, and workers, and the organisations dominated by them, notably the Afrikaner Broederbond,[114] South African Bureau of Racial Affairs (SABRA), and affiliates of the Federasie van Afrikaanse Kultuurverenigings (FAK), such as the Instituut vir Volkswelstand (IV).[115] The notion of 'total segregation' was also widely vaunted within the Dutch Reformed Church (DRC), and attracted support within some Afrikaner business circles, such as the Stellenbosch Chamber of Commerce (partly a reflection of the fact that some leading Afrikaner intellectuals were themselves businesspeople).

One of the clearest and most vigorous defences of total segregation was made by SABRA, launched by the Broederbond in 1947 to 'investigate . . . and propagate' the basic 'Apartheid idea' which had been endorsed by the Broederbond Council in 1935.[116] Led by a group of prominent Afrikaner academics at Stellenbosch University, SABRA described its project as scrupulously 'scientific',[117] but its deliberations on 'racial policy' were nevertheless conducted within

---

[114] Established in 1918, the Afrikaner Broederbond (Afrikaner Brotherhood) was dedicated to promoting the Afrikaner nationalist cause. Initially an open organisation, it became a secret society in 1921.

[115] Translated into English, the names of these organisations are the Federation of Afrikaans Cultural Associations, and—translating literally—the Institute for the Well-Being of the Nation.

[116] Quoted in I. Wilkins and H. Strydom, *The Super-Afrikaners* (London, 1979; repr. 1980), p. 198.

[117] *Journal of Racial Affairs*, 1/1 (1949), 2–3.

the ideological and organisational framework of Afrikaner nationalism, and therefore accepted 'the right to White self-determination' as a fundamental starting-point.[118]

The commitment to the political disfranchisement of Africans, as an essential condition of renewed white political supremacy, was shared by all members of the Afrikaner nationalist alliance. SABRA's argument that Africans should be segregated into their own polity, based in the reserves, was therefore uncontentious. What distinguished the total segregation position was the conviction that 'white self-determination' was neither politically secure nor morally defensible in the midst of the renewed 'economic integration' of Africans in the 'white' areas of the country. SABRA argued that if the 'economic integration' of Africans persisted, a growing African presence in the 'white' areas was unavoidable. To continue to deny the vote to these people would not only be immoral, SABRA maintained; it would also become the target of increasingly vociferous and powerful African opposition. As more and more Africans gathered in the 'white' areas, and the cities in particular, their improving standards of living and levels of education would further boost their political expectations and powers. Sheer force of numbers would ensure that victory would ultimately be theirs.

Has not the rise to power of the labouring classes in nearly all industrialised countries, through the systematic extension of the franchise . . . taught . . . the inescapable lesson that even repeated recourse to *force majeure* is powerless in the end against the force of numbers? And do not the Native labouring classes in South Africa outnumber the Europeans by some 3 or 4 to 1?[119]

On this view, then, Apartheid, as a recipe for the protection of white supremacy, entailed the systematic progression towards complete segregation, 'the separation of White and Native into separate and self-sufficient socio-economic units'.[120] There could be no half measures in which whites enjoyed political supremacy without foregoing their access to an abundant supply of African labour.

SABRA was well aware, however, that white dependence on African labour had deepened dramatically during the course of the

---

[118] SABRA, *Integration or Separate Development* (Stellenbosch, 1952), p. 11.

[119] UW SAIRR Unsorted Papers, FCE, W. M. R. Malherbe *et al.*, 'Reply to Mr Justice Fagan's Defence', 10 May 1949, p. 3.

[120] W. M. Eiselen, 'The Meaning of Apartheid', *Race Relations*, 15/3 (1948), 80.

decade. The extrication of African labour from the 'white' areas would therefore be a difficult and slow process. Some measure of economic inconvenience would be inevitable, but SABRA insisted that this was a sacrifice worth making for the sake of a higher good.

It must be emphasised that it has never been claimed that the apartheid policy is one which can easily be carried out; the evidently powerful economic factors which hinder and retard the efficient applicaiton of the policy are fully recognised. But the opponents of this policy have made the economic factors their main trump card and dominating consideration, instead of viewing them as merely one facet of this tremendous problem.[121]

Nevertheless, the exponents of total segregation insisted that, whatever the short-term economic costs, it was possible to achieve their goal without bringing the economy to its knees. In the words of W. M. Eiselen, a prominent member of the SABRA executive (and later Secretary for Native Affairs), it was 'a major fallacy' to assume that, 'if Native labour were withdrawn from farms, industries and domestic service, the whole economy would be dislocated and the country would tumble to ruin.'[122] The importation of white immigrant labour, coupled with widespread mechanisation, would systematically diminish the need for African labour. Besides, he argued, African labour was less of an economic asset than was customarily claimed. Productivity was low, and the high labour turnover exacted a high price. Furthermore, the growing bargaining powers of African trade unions would ensure that African labour would not remain cheap indefinitely.[123] The total segregationists therefore envisaged Apartheid policies as (in part) instruments for the systematic reduction of white dependence on African labour, which would in turn enable the progressive removal of Africans settled in the 'white' areas, back to their rightful 'homes' in the reserves.

An influx control policy was to be one of the central instruments of this process. As the IV told the Fagan Commission,

the urbanisation of Africans conflicts with the accepted policy of segregation, and therefore the state must institute all possible controls on the influx of natives into the cities, until whites can satisfy the demand for labour

[121] SABRA, *Integration or Separate Development*, p. 4.
[122] Eiselen, 'The Meaning of Apartheid', 79.
[123] Ibid. 78.

from within their own ranks, after which complete segregation must be implemented.[124]

The process of African urbanisation would be summarily halted. 'Unproductive' African women and children would be barred from entering the cities. As far as possible only male migrant workers (in declining numbers) would be permitted into the cities, to meet the diminishing white needs for African labour during the transition to complete economic segregation.[125] The state would expedite the extrication of African labour from the cities by imposing successive labour quotas, which would progressively diminish the permissible ratio of African to white workers in the urban work-force.[126] Also, increasingly strict controls over the entry of Africans into the cities would be accompanied by the systematic removal of African families from the cities to the reserves, so as to dismantle the existing urbanised proletariat.[127]

### 'Practical' Apartheid

The notion of 'practical' Apartheid was coined by the Afrikaanse Handelsinstituut (AHI),[128] and concurred in many, although not all, respects with the programme for 'separate development' outlined by the South African Agricultural Union (SAAU).[129] Established in 1942, the AHI was part of the so-called 'Economic Movement' launched by the Broederbond to advance the prospects of Afrikaner industrial, financial, and commercial capital. The AHI was dominated by the more prosperous Afrikaner financiers and industrialists concentrated mainly in the Cape, whose interests did not always coincide with those of small-scale business more characteristic of the

[124] UW SAIRR Unsorted Papers, FCE, Instituut Vir Volkswelstand (IV), 'Getuienis voorgele aan die Kommissie van Ondersoek insake Wette op Naturelle in Stedelike Gebiede', Q.1, para 2(d).

[125] Ibid. Q.24(b) 3(h)(i).

[126] Ibid. Q.24(b) 3(b).

[127] UNISA TCE, Item 206, SABRA, 'Memorandum Ter Voorlegging aan die Beplanningskommissie vir die Sosio-Ekonomiese Ontwikkeling van die Naturellegebiede', p. 8.

[128] In English, the Afrikaans Chamber of Commerce.

[129] See UW SAIRR Unsorted Papers, FCE SAAU, 'Memorandum on Separate Development' (1944). Note that, although the SAAU (representing the interests of white commercial agriculture) was not directly implicated in the Afrikaner nationalist alliance, by the late 1940s the white farming community had begun to shift its previous allegiances from the UP's 'Fusion' government, to the NP.

northern provinces. But there was no disagreement over fundamental features of an Apartheid blueprint. For both, but especially the smaller and newer undertakings established under the auspices of the Economic Movement, profitability was inescapably dependent on uninterrupted access to an abundant supply of cheap African labour. The alternatives to African labour urged by the total segregationists, such as accelerated mechanisation and a proportionately larger (and more expensive) white work-force, were wholly unpalatable, since they entailed vastly increased capital and labour costs.

Farmers within the Afrikaner nationalist alliance likewise had strong economic interests in dismissing the total segregation blueprint, in favour of a more 'practical' conception of Apartheid. By the late 1940s the scale and success of Afrikaner commercial agriculture varied widely, spanning the spectrum from relatively small, uneconomic farms to larger, more highly capitalised enterprises. The interests and priorities of the Afrikaans farming community were, therefore, not wholly uniform. Nor was the SAAU, a national body representing the four provincial agricultural unions, entirely homogenous.[130] But the SAAU spoke for the farming community at large in respect of perhaps the single most debilitating problem suffered across the board: recurring labour shortages, aggravated by the war. With the passing of the 1937 Native Laws Amendment Act, Smuts had acknowledged the severity of the agricultural labour problem. But in practice the new legislation had provided little remedy. Indeed, during the war years farmers' problems had worsened as urban labour demands had rocketed. Thoroughly disillusioned with the policies of the current government, Afrikaner farmers therefore looked to Apartheid as a system whereby the state would intervene to ensure an equitable distribution of African labour between urban and rural areas, without farmers having to compete with the manufacturing sector for labour in an open market.

The AHI and SAAU alike, therefore, expressed no discomfort over deepening white dependence on African labour.

No, a person must be practical. It must be acknowledged that the non-white worker already constitutes an integral part of our economic structure, that

---

[130] The SAAU tended to represent the interests of the more prosperous farmers most vocally. This is evident, e.g., in the SAAU's strong condemnation of the labour-tenancy system, the inconveniences of which were more pronounced on the more capitalised, larger farms (see later).

he is now so enmeshed in the spheres of our economic life that, for the first fifty to one hundred years (if not longer), total segregation is pure wishful thinking. Any government which disregards this irrefutable fact will soon discover that it is no longer in a position to govern.[131]

The 'practical' notion of Apartheid derived from the conviction that renewed economic integration was not fundamentally irreconcilable with white economic and political supremacy. The political problems currently generated by African proletarianisation could be solved by improved state control, rather than by fundamental restructuring of the country's labour markets.

Nor was it necessary to halt the process of African urbanisation, the AHI and SAAU argued, provided it was regulated according to white economic need. For, 'stable' urbanised labour was regarded as preferable to migrant workers who retained a permanent base in the reserves. As the AHI told the Tomlinson Commission, 'fundamentally, we are against migratory labour . . . Where you have an established industrial community such as you have on the Rand, such labour must be drawn from permanent residents and not from migratory labour.'[132] However, the AHI also opposed the sudden or drastic reduction of the flow of migrant labour into the cities to meet labour demands which were not met by the local African population. The need for migrant labour would diminish, not by the imposition of economically artificial restrictions, but by the continuing growth of the urbanised population, enlarged by permitting Africans taking up employment in the cities to settle there on a permanent basis.

Contrary to the conventional wisdom,[133] the SAAU also accepted the presence of a growing urbanised African proletariat as a necessary condition of the country's economic prosperity.[134] The larger the settled urban population, the SAAU reasoned, the fewer the jobs available for Africans deserting the white farms in search of more lucrative employment. The SAAU therefore saw no need to prohibit workers and their families from the reserves from settling in

---

[131] *Volkshandel*, June 1948, cited in O'Meara, *Volkskapitalisme*, p. 175

[132] UNISA, Tomlinson Commission Hearings (TCH), vol. 87, 13 Feb. 1953, pp. 8007, 8006.

[133] Most scholars share M. Legassick's view that 'both farming and gold-mining retained an interest in limiting or preventing permanent African urbanisation' ('Legislation, Ideology and Economy in post-1948 South Africa', 14).

[134] UNISA TCH, vol. 10, 19 May 1952, p. 533.

the towns, provided employment and suitable accommodation were available.[135]

Another reason for the SAAU's preparedness to accept the growth of the urbanised African population was farmers' vested interest in the limited development of the reserves. The total segregationists stressed that, in order for the reserves to absorb the desired exodus of Africans from the towns, vigorous agricultural development programmes were necessary. And to this end the reserves would ultimately have to be enlarged in size. The SAAU vehemently opposed both prospects. Farmers were reluctant to foster competition from thriving African farms in the reserves. Moreover, some of the reserves bordered on areas which held valuable water sources. Intent on preserving white control of this vital resource, the SAAU preferred the prospect of an expanding urban African proletariat to the enlargement and development of the reserves necessitated by programmes of urban population removals.[136]

The AHI's and SAAU's mutual acceptance of continuing African urbanisation together with deepening economic integration led them to advocate fundamentally similar influx control policies, although with differing emphases reflecting their respective immediate priorities. Both saw an influx control policy as a means of regulating Africans' access to the cities according to the size of the urban labour demand. As long as employment was available, African work-seekers should be entitled to enter the cities, accompanied by their families if they wished to settle there. In this respect, their 'practical' influx control policy bore striking resemblances to the Fagan Commission's stance on African urbanisation and industrial employment. Unlike the Fagan Commission, however, Afrikaner capitalists thought that African families should be permitted to settle in urban areas only if the male bread-winners found work there. Deploring the presence of widespread agricultural labour shortages, both the AHI and SAAU called for the removal of 'work-shy' unemployed Africans from the towns to white farms.

The SAAU also proposed separate, more stringent, influx control regulations for farm-born Africans, as opposed to Africans from the reserves. This call was largely a response to the perceived inadequacies of the labour-tenancy system. Farmers complained that the

[135] UNISA TCH, vol. 10, 19 May 1952, pp. 537–8.
[136] Ibid. 551.

time which adult male labour tenants and their young sons spent in urban employment represented a 'wastage' of farm labour, and inhibited the improvement of agricultural productivity.[137] To solve this problem, the state should phase out the labour-tenancy system and replace it with policies compelling farm-workers into full-time agricultural employment. The farming community was divided over the pace at which such changes should be instituted. Under-capitalised farmers were typically in less of a hurry, having fewer resources to utilise the land occupied by labour tenants. Also, engaging a full-time work-force meant paying cash wages all the year round, a financial burden which many smaller farmers felt they could not carry.[138] But the overwhelming consensus, reflected in the SAAU's 1944 memorandum, was that new forms of state control over farm labour were immediately required.[139] Administratively, they should be based on a rigid differentiation between agricultural and industrial labour,[140] to be created by erecting insurmountable influx control barriers to farm-workers' migration townwards. It was solely Africans from the reserves, rather than those from the farms, to whom the SAAU conceded the right to settle in those towns where their labour was in demand.

Clearly the ideological slogan 'Apartheid' straddled two incompatible blueprints for the preservation of white supremacy. What then was the relative influence of each version of Apartheid within the alliance on the eve of the 1948 election? O'Meara insists that, by the late 1940s, the 'practical' conception of Apartheid was ideologically hegemonic within Afrikanerdom, a reflection of the political dominance of the Economic Movement within the nationalist alliance. In his view, it was merely a small cluster of politically and ideologically marginal ivory-tower intellectuals who endorsed the total segregation blueprint.[141] But, asserting rather than proving the ideological hegemony of Afrikaner capital,[142] O'Meara's argument underestimated the powers wielded by the organisations and individuals espousing total segregation. Leading journalists defended this

[137] Morris, 'The Development of Capitalism', pp. 334–5.
[138] See ibid. 335.
[139] Ibid. 335.
[140] UNISA TCH, vol. 10, May 1952, p. 560.
[141] O'Meara, *Volkskapitalisme*, p. 175.
[142] See D. B. Posel, 'The Meaning of Apartheid before 1948: Conflicts of Interests and Powers within the Afrikaner Nationalist Alliance', *JSAS* 14/1 (1987), 134.

position in the columns of the Afrikaans Press. Afrikaner academics, far from being confined to secluded ivory towers, exerted considerable influence over debates within the inner circles of the Broederbond.[143] Indeed, as mentioned previously, SABRA's 'scientific' exploration of the total segregation position had been authorised and sponsored by the Broederbond. And, as O'Meara himself argues, the Bond played a crucial role in orchestrating the Afrikaner nationalist alliance and mobilising support for the NP's policies.[144] The IV, too, was well placed to shape Afrikaner opinion, having been set up (like other affiliates of the FAK) to foster a sense of Afrikaner identity by publicising the Afrikaner nationalist cause. The IV had considerable authority in some quarters; for example, the Pretoria City Council's evidence to the Fagan Commission was a near *verbatim* copy of that presented by the IV, both being a vigorous defence of total segregation.

The absence of a single, ideologically hegemonic, concept of Apartheid on the eve of the 1948 election was demonstrated *prima facie* by the substance of the Sauer Report (1947), endorsed by the NP as party doctrine.

### *The Sauer Report*

The unresolved conflict between the competing conceptions of Apartheid was reproduced in the Sauer Report in two ways: in its declaration of the long-term objectives of Apartheid and, more conspicuously, in its proposals concerning the means by which these would be achieved.

The Report began by advocating 'total Apartheid between whites and Natives' as the 'eventual ideal and goal'.[145] Hence the assertion, at odds with the 'practical' conception of Apartheid, that 'the ideal which must be focused on is the gradual extraction of Natives from industries in white areas, although it is recognised that this can only be achieved in the course of many years'.[146] Again in line with the total segregationist rather than the 'practical' position, the Report also called for the ultimate removal of urbanised African communities from 'white' areas, on the grounds that 'the urbanisation of

---

[143] For more detail, see Posel, 'The Meaning of Apartheid', 134–5.
[144] O'Meara, *Volkskapitalisme*, p. 244.
[145] 'Sauer Report', p. 3.
[146] Ibid. 11.

Natives conflicts with the policy of Apartheid'.[147] Yet the Sauer Report also acknowledged the importance of 'practical' considerations, stressing that the implementation of Apartheid would, 'as far as it was practically possible, be pursued gradually, always taking into account the national needs and interests and with the necessary care to avoid the disruption of the country's agriculture, industries, and general interests'.[148]

A similarly ambiguous combination of purist and 'practical' recommendations informed the Report's proposals for the immediate steps necessary to embark on the Apartheid road. On the one hand, the Report took a leaf out of SABRA's book in calling for 'a plan for the gradual reduction of the number of detribalised Natives in the urban areas by making other arrangements for them'.[149] The Report also recommended the imposition of labour quotas within the urban areas, to restrict the rate of growth of the urban African work-force according to fixed ratios of African to white workers.[150] But other short-term measures prescribed by the Report bore the mark of more 'practical' thinking. The call for labour quotas was vague, even hesitant. Quotas were to be imposed 'wherever practical and desirable',[151] rather than as a general rule. Also, despite having decried the deepening integration of Africans into the country's economy, the Report nevertheless insisted that 'everything possible must be done to deter the exodus of natives from the [white] farms'.[152] The Report also recommended the institution of a labour bureaux system, premised on an acceptance that continued economic growth necessitated the deepening economic integration of Africans. The labour bureaux system's principal objective was to harness sufficient numbers of African workers to meet the growing demands of white urban and rural employers alike.[153] This process would in turn foster an expansion (rather than a contraction) in the size of urban African communities. In short, although proffered as part of the 'transition' to total segregation, the labour bureaux system would in fact take the country increasingly further from this goal.

The Report's acceptance of the continuing growth of the urban African population fell short of the Afrikaner capitalist position, however. The AHI and SAAU had recommended that, in order to 'stabilise' the urban work-force, Africans entering employment

---

[147] Ibid. 11.    [148] Ibid. 3.    [149] Ibid. 10.
[150] Ibid. 11.    [151] Ibid.    [152] Ibid. 9.    [153] Ibid. 12.

should be permitted to settle permanently in the cities with their families. But the Sauer Report proposed a freeze on further urbanisation, insisting that African workers recruited from the rural areas should remain 'temporary sojourners', unaccompanied by their families.[154]

Contrary to O'Meara's view, therefore, the Sauer Report did not bear the imprints of a single hegemonic conception of Apartheid. It was rather an internally contradictory and ambiguous document—contradictory, because it wove together strands from mutually exclusive conceptions of Apartheid, and ambiguous, because it did not finally choose between them.

Chapter 1 pointed out that in much of the academic literature on Apartheid, the Sauer Report is seen as having crystallised and synthesised the interests of the Afrikaner nationalist alliance, in a single, largely uncontested, and consistent programme of Apartheid. The newly elected Nationalist government's policies are then explained as the immediate and simple translation of the Sauer Report's recommendations into political practice. This chapter has revealed, however, that the Sauer Report's recommendations manifested an unresolved conflict between disparate sets of policy proposals, rather than a single, consistent plan. The newly elected Nationalist government therefore lacked a compelling, unambiguous, and uncontested blueprint from which state policies could simply be read off, step by step. Instead, after 1948 the contest between the opposing factions within the Nationalist alliance was transposed into the state itself. An alternative explanation of the making of Apartheid during the 1950s is therefore required, one which carries the theme of intra-Afrikaner conflict over into an examination of the constraints, interests, and priorities which shaped NP policy, and its solution to the influx control problem in particular, during the course of the decade.

---

[154] 'Sauer Report', p. 10.

# 3

# *Apartheid and Influx Control Strategy in the 1950s*

THE NP took office in 1948 with attention focused squarely on the phenomenon of African urbanisation and its attendant dilemmas and dangers. The first Minister of Native Affairs, E. G. Jansen, declared that 'the position in the urban areas has become intolerable';[1] 'the biggest problem in connection with Native administration today is the situation in the urban areas'.[2] A 'Native influx of alarming proportions', he warned, had produced an 'urgent and serious' housing problem, coupled with the 'social danger' of 'detribalisation' which left 'nothing to replace . . . the tribal form of control'.[3] The urban areas had become political tinder boxes. In Verwoerd's words,

Europeans and non-Europeans in recent years have been working up to a crisis . . . Under the previous government, we saw more and more trouble blowing up, clashes in the towns, crimes, the creation of all sorts of hamlets on the borders of the towns full of poverty and misery, clashes on the trains, assaults on women. Wherever you go, and in every field, you find an increasing tension between Europeans and Non-Europeans.[4]

The impact of the problem was not confined to the urban areas. With white farmers suffering the burden of critical labour shortages which the previous government had failed to tackle effectively, the newly elected Nationalist leaders stressed the need to keep a keen eye on the interests of white farmers. As NP Senator Verwoerd told the Senate in 1948, one of the NP's principal objectives was 'the imposition of state control in matters of labour in such a way that the necessary farm labour will be sufficiently assured'.[5]

The political inflammability of the townships and farm labour

---

[1] *HAD* (1948), vol. 62, col. 1663.
[2] *HAD* (1950), vol. 71, col. 4702.
[3] NAD, 'Native Policy of the Union of South Africa' (Native Affairs Fact Paper no 9; 1951).
[4] Union of SA, *Senate Debates* (1948), col. 227.
[5] Ibid., col. 239.

shortages were immediate and pressing problems, demanding swift action by the state. Yet these problems were also symptoms of a more profound dilemma to which the NP had as yet failed to provide a consistent, unambiguous solution. The 'problem' of influx control exemplified exactly the issue which divided competing conceptions of Apartheid, namely, whether or not deepening white dependence on African labour in the towns was fundamentally injurious to the cause of white political supremacy. The Sauer Report had prevaricated on the issue, producing an internally inconsistent strategy for tackling the problems in the towns. This chapter begins by examining and accounting for the conception of Apartheid which emerged within the design of state policy during the 1950s, and then explains the influx control strategy which issued from it.

## Debates about Apartheid during the 1950s

The prospect of reconciling economic integration and political segregation remained a source of division and controversy within Nationalist ranks throughout the 1950s. The DRC, which enjoyed a large Afrikaner membership, exercised considerable moral authority within the *volk*, in upholding Apartheid as a properly Christian doctrine. The moral foundation of Apartheid, it was argued (at least during the early 1950s), lay in its promise of total segregation. Thus, in 1950, the Church's annual congress 'adopted a policy of eventual total separation of white and black', including 'a complete reorganisation of the existing economic structure so that all industries would in time be manned wholly by whites'.[6] But the then Prime Minister, D. F. Malan, spoke for many other Nationalist MPs in his swift rebuttal of the Church's position.

Total segregation is not the policy of our party and it is nowhere to be found in our official declarations of policy . . . I said it clearly on platforms, that total territorial separation was impracticable under present circumstances in South Africa, where our whole economic structure is to a large extent based on Native labour. It is not practicable and it does not pay any party to endeavour to achieve the impossible.[7]

[6] SAIRR, 'The Economic Development of the Reserves' (Fact Paper no. 3; 1959), p. 4.
[7] *HAD* (1950), vol. 71, col. 4142.

Still, Malan's version of NP policy was contested by several Nationalist MPs, who called for immediate moves towards the goal of 'economic apartheid'.[8] The second Minister of Labour, Senator J. de Klerk, recommended the 'purification' of industries, so that 'black spots in the white areas could be cleared'.[9] T. E. Donges, the first Minister of the Interior, held a similar view,[10] along with prominent Nationalist MPs, such as N. Diedrichs and M. C. de Wet Nel.[11]

Calls for the extrication of African labour from the 'white' economy were echoed in the Afrikaans Press. In 1955, for example, a leading article in *Die Burger* rebuked the 'bad' industrialists and farmers who demanded more African labour, together with the 'bad' housewives who could not do without African servants.[12] In the same year *Die Vaderland* appealed for a vigorous white immigration drive, to enable white employers to wean themselves from African labour.[13] In short, as A. Hepple, leader of the South African Labour Party, declared, 'we have heard the National Party speak with many voices on the question of their Native policy'.[14]

It was the voices of the NAD's policy-makers which soon came to dominate discussions about Apartheid. The Minister of Native Affairs had a strategic advantage in the design of Apartheid policies, because his portfolio covered the key problem area for Apartheid, the so-called 'Native question'. Its urgency and prominence in the early 1950s gave Jansen the opportunity to start refashioning his Department into a more powerful and self-sufficient policy-making organ, a process which was to continue throughout the decade. In 1951 two assistant Ministers of Native Affairs were appointed. (No comparable positions existed in any other government department.) This move was an assertive bid to expand the Minister's executive authority within the Cabinet: the Minister and two assistant Ministers (both members of the Native Affairs Commission), together with a third member of the Commission, 'constituted a

---

[8] e.g. *HAD* (1951), vol. 76, col. 7796; (1955), vol. 88, col. 3442.
[9] *HAD* (1955), vol. 88, col. 4033.
[10] Ibid., col. 3770.
[11] See, e.g., *HAD* (1948), vol. 62, cols. 2988–94 (Diedrichs); *HAD* (1950), vol. 71, cols. 4775–6 (de Wet Nel).
[12] Cited in *HAD* (1955), vol. 87, col. 1723.
[13] Ibid., vol. 87, col. 1209.
[14] *HAD* (1950), vol. 71, col. 4743.

sub-Cabinet for dealing exclusively with Native matters'.[15] In addition, the size of the NAD's bureaucracy grew steadily. In his first two years in office, Jansen saw to the creation of 308 new posts for whites along with 230 new posts for Africans.[16] By 1960 the number of whites employed by the NAD exceeded 3,000, as compared with approximately 1,750 in 1948.[17]

The scope of the NAD's activities also expanded. Jansen took the first step by appropriating some of the control exercised by the National Housing Commission over the provision of African housing. During 1950 the NAD and National Housing Commission established a 'Joint Committee . . . to co-ordinate all work undertaken by the two bodies in connection with Native housing, to ensure a uniform policy'.[18] The NAD's advance accelerated rapidly when Verwoerd took over as Minister of Native Affairs late in 1950. As Hepple put it, 'Verwoerd set about his new job like a giant unchained.'[19] By 1952 the NAD had established a sub-department of Labour, which effectively usurped the functions of the Department of Labour in respect of African workers. By 1953 the NAD also had its own sub-department of Housing, to deal with matters of African housing.[20] Policy matters concerning the reserves were colonised, too, leaving the Minister of Economic Affairs with little more than an advisory role.[21] Verwoerd also ensured that the NAD became self-sufficient in matters of policy research and planning, by creating an internal research division, staffed by SABRA members, to 'provide him with the necessary information for framing his policies'.[22] In short, the NAD was set to become, increasingly, a 'state within a state'.[23]

[15] *The Star*, 15 Aug. 1951.

[16] NAD, 'Progress Report for the Department of Native Affairs during 1949' (Fact Paper no. 10; 1951), p. 1.

[17] J. Lazar, 'Conformity and Conflict: Afrikaner Nationalist Politics, 1948–1961' (D. Phil. thesis, Univ. of Oxford, 1987), p. 124.

[18] Union of SA, *Report of the Department of Native Affairs for the Year 1950/1*, UG 30/1953, p. 26.

[19] Hepple, *Verwoerd*, p. 107.

[20] Union of SA, *Report of the Department of Native Affairs for the Year 1953/4*, UG 53/1956, p. 16.

[21] UW Ballinger Papers, B1.1.88, 'Tension Increases over Senate Bill', 20 May 1955, p. 4.

[22] *HAD* (1951), vol. 76, col. 7767.

[23] This is not to say that Verwoerd, or the NAD, was an autonomous author of state policy; the issue of the interests, pressures, and constraints which determined Verwoerd's and the NAD's decisions has yet to be addressed.

The transformation of the NAD from a once small and relatively minor department into the vanguard of Apartheid policy-making owed much to Verwoerd's personality and style of leadership. An autocratic and tireless Minister, Verwoerd kept a tight rein over the activities of the NAD.[24] Already much respected in the Senate, he rapidly acquired a formidable influence within the House of Assembly and Cabinet. His success derived partly from his skill and diligence as a politician. According to Hepple, 'by the time Verwoerd made his first speech in Parliament as Minister of Native Affairs, he was better informed than any of his predecessors'.[25] Verwoerd's private secretary also recalled the Minister's zeal for hard work and long hours.[26] But Verwoerd's power was also facilitated by the salience of 'the Native question' on the legislative agenda. The spate of bills concerning 'Native affairs' introduced in the early 1950s provided him with recurring opportunities to dominate parliamentary proceedings with lengthy, didactic speeches. In the Cabinet, too, Verwoerd's stature expanded along with the prominence of 'Native' issues, so that by 1955 fellow Nationalists referred to him publicly as 'the Big Boss'. As Senator M. Ballinger recalled, the Minister of Economic Affairs told Parliament in 1955 that issues of Apartheid 'were discussed by the whole Cabinet, and when they had finished discussing them, "the Big Boss decides"'.[27] Ballinger continued,

this was a new light on how policies are made in the Cabinet, and Parliament rose for a moment out of its lethargy to ask who was the Big Boss, the Prime Minister or Dr. Verwoerd. At that moment, Dr. Verwoerd entered the chamber to be greeted from the Nationalist benches with cries of 'Here comes the Big Boss'.[28]

From the early 1950s, then, Verwoerd, and to a lesser extent Jansen before him, wrested for the NAD the authority to define the concept of Apartheid on which its policies would be based.

---

[24] See F. Barnard, *Thirteen Years with Dr H. F. Verwoerd* (Johannesburg, 1967), p. 15.

[25] Hepple, *Verwoerd*, p. 109.

[26] Barnard, *Thirteen Years*, p. 15.

[27] UW Ballinger Papers, B1.1.88, 'Tension Increases over Senate Bill', 20 May 1955, p. 4.

[28] Ibid.

## The NAD's Conception of Apartheid

Jansen's and Verwoerd's positions on the nature of Apartheid were profoundly affected by the presence of conflict on the issue within Afrikaner ranks. Placed on the defensive by the UP's jibes about confusion and disarray within the NP, Jansen and Verwoerd were anxious to deny the existence of any real division on the issue. To create the impression of unity and consistency between the two versions of Apartheid, total segregation and 'practical' Apartheid were presented as if two separate phases of the same blueprint. It was a shrewd ideological device: the prospect of total segregation was upheld as the long-term ideal, whereas 'practical' policies were said to be necessary for the short term.[29]

In contrast to Malan and his fellow-thinkers, Verwoerd typically appropriated the language of the SABRA purists to describe the long-term goals of Apartheid. 'Economic integration . . . in its ultimate effect', declared Verwoerd, 'must also mean social and political integration'.[30] 'There are . . . only two courses of policy for the country. The one course undoubtedly leads to equality . . . And the other course leads in the direction of total segregation.'[31] South Africa was 'doomed', warned Verwoerd, if its policies allowed the African 'to improve his skill, draw better wages and provide a better market' within 'white' South Africa;[32] 'ultimately the Natives would have to be confined to their own reserves with their own industries to support them'.[33]

In the long term, therefore, Apartheid required

purposeful and deliberate economic segregation, not only by means of colour bars in regard to Bantu labour in white areas, but also by mechanisation of all labour activity to such an extent that the need for Bantu labour be reduced to a minimum; and furthermore, by planning new industrial development so that new industries be situated as close as possible to Bantu territories, in order to provide maximum labour for Bantu workers, while at the same time enabling them to be resident in their own territories with their families, in houses of their own.[34]

[29] e.g. *HAD* (1950), vol. 71, cols. 4475–6.
[30] *HAD* (1951), vol. 76, col. 7796.
[31] A. N. Pelzer (ed.), *Verwoerd Speaks* (Johannesburg, 1966), p. 13.
[32] *HAD* (1955), vol. 87, cols. 1322–3.
[33] *HAD* (1951), vol. 76, col. 7764.
[34] Verwoerd, cited in Barnard, *Thirteen Years*, p. 40.

When describing the short-term priorities of Apartheid, however, Verwoerd reverted to the language of 'practical' politics: the government can go no further than what was practicable in the light of our development,' he stated. 'The implementation of Apartheid must take into account economic realities.'[35] This short-term commitment to 'practical' policies involved the acceptance of at least three basic 'realities' which were said to be irrevocable 'for the forseeable future'.[36] First, in Verwoerd's words, 'we accept . . . that the economic organisation of [the] land and [the] interior will have the same character as it has now';[37] 'we're accepting the fact that the industry which starts here comes in here to stay'.[38] Secondly, these industries would continue to draw increasingly on African labour, since 'the presence of Natives in the European areas . . . as labourers is essential, at any rate for the present'.[39] No labour quotas restricting the ratio of African to white workers would be imposed. Instead, it would remain up to industrialists to decide how large a supply of African labour they required. Thirdly, it was accepted that the process of African urbanisation had created large 'detribalised' communities with little or no ties with the reserves. Verwoerd declared that it would be 'impractical' to deny this fact, by attempting to remove these communities from the 'white' areas to the reserves. In his words, 'a little less than one-third [of the African population] lives and works in the cities, of whom a section have become detribalised and urbanised. The Apartheid policy takes this reality into account.'[40] Ideologically, then, the NAD's discourse of 'practical' Apartheid differentiated between two categories of Africans: those who were 'detribalised' and thus *de facto* permanent city-dwellers, and those who retained 'tribal' identities and links. This distinction served to legitimate the fact that, despite the NP's declared long-term goal of relocating Africans in the reserves, in the short term millions would be permitted to remain in the 'white' cities. For, it

---

[35] Association of Chambers of Commerce (ASSOCOM), Non-European Affairs Files (NEAF), 'Interview with Minister of Native Affairs, on 11 May 1951', p. 3.

[36] BCC BMR 14/1/25, 'Conference between Native Affairs Department and Managers of Non-European Affairs . . . January 1953' (hereafter '1953 Conference'), p. 8.

[37] Ibid. 8.

[38] ASSOCOM NEAF, Verbatim untitled transcript of meeting between Assocom, FCI, and Verwoerd, 11 May 1951 (hereafter 'Verbatim Transcript'), p. 9.

[39] *HAD* (1950), vol. 71, col. 4710.

[40] Verwoerd, cited in Pelzer (ed.), *Verwoerd Speaks*, p. 26.

was claimed, 'practical' politics necessitated the pursuit of separate sorts of strategies in respect of each group.

While echoing SABRA's warnings about the long-term political dangers of economic integration, Verwoerd's proposals for the short term upheld Afrikaner capitalists' confidence in the state's powers to subvert these threats without having to intervene in the process of economic integration itself. The problems in the urban areas were labelled ideologically as merely problems of *control*, the solutions to which were simply a matter of 'creating . . . order out of the present chaos'[41] by the pursuit of 'better control, better influx control, better control over the people there [in the towns], better order, better combating of frustration'.[42]

In fact, Verwoerd's ideological depiction of Apartheid as a two-stage process was internally contradictory.[43] The 'practical' policies of the first stage would take the country along a different route from that leading towards the purported ideal of total segregation. The economic integration of Africans would be deepened by the continuing expansion of industries increasingly dependent on African labour in the principal industrial regions of the country. The size of the urban African proletariat would also grow. Thus, the policies deemed impractical at the onset of the first stage of Apartheid because they failed to take account of economic realities would become all the more impractical as the first stage progressed.

This contradiction was effectively suppressed, however, since the language of 'practical' politics also discounted the immediate relevance of long-term objectives. In Verwoerd's words,

total territorial segregation . . . is the ideal and in the process of achieving that—and it will take a long time—each generation should formulate its own attainable political policy and state what it wants to do.[44]

While on the one hand the policy of Apartheid has to be implemented, at the same time it has to be done step for step [*sic*] in such a way that the country can bear the implementation of that policy . . . At no stage could

---

[41] *HAD* (1950), vol. 71, col. 4711.

[42] BCC BMR 14/1/25, '1953 Conference', p. 8.

[43] Note that this contradiction was not a duplication of the Sauer Report's prevarication between competing blueprints for Apartheid. The Sauer Report reproduced elements of each in both its short- and long-term blueprints.

[44] *HAD* (1955), vol. 87, col. 199.

one give a so-called 'blueprint' (as we are often asked to do in regard to Apartheid) of what the next or final stage would be.[45]

Whereas the Sauer Report had vacillated between 'practical' and purist strategies, Verwoerd's approach to the short term was more consistently 'practical' (although, as will be shown later, the substance of Verwoerd's 'practical' conception of Apartheid did not wholly coincide with that of Afrikaner capital). Despite echoing the purists' long-term objectives, Verwoerd shelved questions about how to attain them as 'matters for future generations and their policies'. Why, then, if the ideal of total segregation was politically so remote during the early 1950s, was it ideologically so prominent? On the other hand, why was Verwoerd so scrupulous in distancing his Department's actual policies from those expounded by the purists?

The ideological combination of both purist and 'practical' approaches, as if two stages in a single process, served an immediate strategic purpose in deflecting Opposition charges of disunity within Afrikaner ranks. But this is not the sole explanation of the NAD's version of Apartheid. However distant and elusive the ideal of total segregation, it served an important ideological purpose in legitimating the state's immediate, more 'practical' plans. Arguably, the principal function of state ideology is to depict the exercise of power in terms which legitimise it as morally right. Ideologically, total segregation was characterised as a moral defence of white political supremacy, since Africans and whites would enjoy 'equal rights' in separate territories. By describing its 'practical' policies as the first step along the road towards the ideal of total segregation, the state provided whites with a way of redescribing the existing realities of white domination as the means towards a moral end. This rhetoric also conveyed the impression of direction and foresight to policies which were often fundamentally reactive, with little systematic thought given to their long-term implications.

The discourse depicting total segregation as Apartheid's ideal was also an indication of the influence of SABRA within the NAD. W. M. Eiselen, a founder member of SABRA, was appointed Secretary of Native Affairs in 1951, over the heads of more

---

[45] Ibid., vol. 88, col. 3760.

experienced, long-serving NAD officers. Also, Verwoerd's departmental research division was dominated by SABRA members. The
Native Affairs Commission, a long-standing body created to monitor
and advise on the implementation of departmental policy, was
rapidly purged of its allegedly 'liberal' influences,[46] and M. C. de
Wet Nel, a SABRA executive member, was appointed its deputy
chairman (with Verwoerd as chairman). Such appointments probably signified efforts to co-opt SABRA into the state apparatus, so as
to pre-empt division and opposition. But the need for this sort of
strategy was itself an indication of the seriousness with which
SABRA's views (which in turn expressed the basic standpoints of the
Broederbond) were appraised. The process of co-option was largely
successful, in so far as Verwoerd's authority in the NAD was seldom
questioned. But the ideologically influential positions offered to
SABRA intellectuals in order to secure their political support enabled them to leave their mark on the state's discourse on Apartheid.

The commitment to 'practical' politics 'for the forseeable future'
reflected a different set of powers, priorities, and constraints.
Although Afrikaner capitalist interests were not hegemonic within
either the NP or that NAD, they did exercise considerable power
over the design of NAD policy. The interests of white farmers, as
represented by the SAAU, had a regular and privileged hearing in
the Department. As a NAD memorandum explained,

there is in existence a liaison committee (usually referred to as 'Die Skakelkommittee') between the Minister of Native Affairs and his Department on
the one hand, and the SAAU and the various provincial agricultural unions
on the other. All Native labour matters affecting agriculture, such as
questions of the supply of labour, wages and conditions of employment and
policy generally, are discussed by this Committee, which is presided over
either by the Minister or the Secretary for Native Affairs, and which meets
as and when necessary.[47]

This Liaison Committee had been launched in 1944, in a collabor-
ative bid by the NAD and the SAAU to tackle the problem of
farm labour shortages. By the late 1940s repeated meetings of the

---

[46] *HAD* (1950), vol. 71, col. 4757.
[47] UW A989Mfe/Portfolio 7, Industrial Legislation Commission of Inquiry,
Miscellaneous Memoranda: NAD Memorandum on 'Native Labour Bureaux', 17
Aug. 1949, p. 7.

committee had established the basis for a 'very intimate relationship'[48] between the NAD and the SAAU, which was entrenched and extended once the NP came to power. By 1953 the SAAU spoke enthusiastically of the 'sincere co-operation'[49] it received from the NAD. No comparable arrangement existed between the NAD and any other business organisation.

One indication of the SAAU's power to block the pursuit of SABRA's brand of Apartheid was the NAD's ambivalence towards developing the reserves. Central to SABRA's blueprint for Apartheid was an immediate and vigorous programme for improving agriculture in the reserves, and extending the size of reserve lands if necessary. So committed was SABRA to this goal that it spearheaded the appointment, and proceedings, of the Tomlinson Commission, briefed to examine the prospects for developing the reserves.[50] SABRA's influence and direction also made its mark on internal NAD research on this subject. And the SABRA-dominated Native Affairs Commission (which advised the Minister on policy matters affecting the reserves) framed its recommendations within SABRA's vision of 'a long-term policy . . . to build a future for the Native in his own areas'.[51] Yet Jansen's and Verwoerd's positions on developing the reserves were deeply affected by white farmers' opposition, both to the prospect of competition from peasant farmers in the reserves and the possible extension of reserve lands. For example, when in 1948 the Native Affairs Commission recommended the purchase of more farms in the Pietersburg and Louis Trichardt areas of the Northern Transvaal to assist African agricultural production in adjoining reserves, Jansen yielded meekly to protests from white farmers.[52] The small sums of money allocated to the reserves during the early 1950s indicated that the development of the reserves was also relatively low on Verwoerd's list of priorities.[53]

[48] Quoted in H. Bradford, 'Getting Away with Slavery: Capitalist Farmers, Foreigners and Forced Labour in the Transvaal, *c*.1920–1950' (paper presented to History Workshop Conference, Univ. of Witwatersrand, 1990), p. 10.

[49] SAAU, *Report of the General Council for the Year 1953/4 for Submission to Annual Congress* (Pretoria, 1954), p. 3.

[50] Interview with N. J. Olivier, 5 July 1985.

[51] Union of SA, *Report of the Native Affairs Commission for the period 1 January 1948 to 31 December 1952*, UG 36/1954, p. 21.

[52] *HAD* (1950), vol. 71, col. 4711.

[53] Ibid., col. 4720.

The NAD's 'practical' attitude to Apartheid 'for the forseeable future' is also partly explained by the interests of Afrikaner commerce and industry. Due largely to the efforts and investments of the Economic Movement, the 1940s had seen the spectacular expansion of Afrikaner business. Between 1939 and 1949 the number of Afrikaner-owned manufacturing concerns increased from 1,293 to 3,385, with turnover expanding from £6,000,000 to £43,600,000. Commercial establishments numbered 9,585 by 1949, as compared with 2,428 in 1939, and their turnover jumped from £28,000,000 to £203,700,000.[54] However, as O'Meara points out, 'many of these [new businesses] were small and under-capitalized'.[55] Were the state to have taken a purist approach to Apartheid, insisting that employers make proportionately more use of white (and therefore more costly) labour and invest more in mechanisation, a spate of fledgling Afrikaner businesses would have collapsed. Ironically, SABRA's proposals would have inflicted a far heavier burden on Afrikaner capital than on its English-speaking counterpart. Most of the larger capital-intensive industries capable of surviving any such onslaught from the state were owned by English-speakers. The 1950 'Ekonomiese Volkskongres',[56] however, reiterated the NP's commitment to enhancing the prosperity and competitiveness of Afrikaans business.

There was more to the NAD's 'practical' priorities, however, than simply the power of Afrikaner capitalist lobbies. Another critical factor was the NAD's still limited powers and resources *vis-a-vis* urban local authorities. In at least one important respect, the economic organisation of the country was not in the hands of the NAD, nor any other central government department. Decisions as to how much urban land would be set aside for industrial development rested with the elected city councils, which, together with the municipalities employed to serve them, constituted the local arm of the state.[57] As the NAD was well aware, the local authorities had a vested interest in the expansion of local industries, which boosted the employment prospects and general economic prosperity of the

[54] S. Trapido, 'Political Institutions and Afrikaner Social Structures', *American Political Science Review*, 57/1 (1963), 80.

[55] O'Meara, *Volkskapitalisme*, p. 184.

[56] Literally the 'economic congress of the nation', this was convened to 'set the course for the future' of Afrikaans business (ibid. 248).

[57] I have used the term 'local authorities' to refer to elected city or town councils and municipalities jointly, when appropriate.

area. Although vexed by the local authorities' monopoly on such key decisions, the NAD had not yet developed the political and administrative muscle to usurp these powers. Indeed, such a confrontation would have done enormous damage to the newly installed Nationalist leadership in the NAD, heavily dependent on the co-operation of local authorities.[58]

'Practical' pressures from capital and local authorities weighed heavily on the NAD. But its pragmatic orientation was not entirely a submission to powerful lobbies. Like any state institution, the Department had its own vested interest in policies which nurtured economic growth. The accumulation process is the source of the taxation and finance which are the lifeblood of state practices. Because the purists' proposals for diminishing white dependence on African labour threatened the vitality of the capitalist economy, they conflicted with the state's own interests. (So, even in the 1960s when the NAD's policy-makers took seriously a more purist position on economic integration, the state's 'institutional self-interest' mitigated the adoption of a wholeheartedly purist approach.)[59]

Finally, the NAD's notion of Apartheid is also partly explained by the fact that the foundations of the key Apartheid policies of the decade were laid during the Nationalists' first term of office, from 1948 to 1953. During these years the logic of electoral politics prevented anything but a cautious, short-term approach to Apartheid. The Nationalists had won the 1948 election by a narrow margin of seats, not votes.[60] Uncertain of re-election, policy-makers were working with a timetable of up to five years in the first instance. It was, therefore, expedient and important to make visible inroads into immediate problems rather than to embark on a tortuous route towards long-term goals.

For all these reasons, then, the NAD ideologically postponed the pursuit of 'separate development' for 'future generations and their

---

[58] The NAD's reliance on local authorities is discussed later in the chapter. See also Ch. 4.

[59] See Ch. 9, where it is shown that by the early 1960s the NAD was calling for curbs on the scale of 'economic integration'.

[60] Strictly speaking it was the Herenigde Nasionale Party (HNP) which won the election with 70 seats (the Afrikaner Party won 9 seats, the UP 65 and the Labour Party 6). The HNP got only 39.4 per cent of the vote. The HNP and Afrikaner Party then merged in 1949 to form the National Party (NP), so for the sake of convenience this discussion refers simply to the NP. (K. Heard, *General Elections in South Africa, 1943–1970* (Oxford, 1974).)

policies', which meant that the purists' blueprint for total segregation was overruled as a basis for policy-making. Instead, NAD policies accorded far more closely with the 'practical' version of Apartheid expounded by Afrikaner capitalists, yet without simply mimicking the AHI's or the SAAU's policy proposals. The NAD opted for a blend of 'practical' priorities, tempered by the characteristically purist anxiety about the political dangers of ongoing African urbanisation.

This synthetic conception of Apartheid was embedded in the NAD's strategy for resolving the influx control problem. But this plan was rooted in more than simply the contest between 'practical' and purist policy blueprints. As well as drawing on the Stallardist legacy of past policies, the NAD was also profoundly influenced by the recommendations of municipal administrators, particularly those on the Witwatersrand represented by the Association of Administrators of Non-European Affairs. The authority of municipal administrators in matters of urban policy derived from their expertise and experience; they were 'virtually the sole custodians of the practical knowledge of dealing with the bewildering complexity of urban African administration'.[61] From the 1920s 'urban Native administration' had become an increasingly specialised occupation, governed by a formidable plethora of laws and regulations. Particularly during the early 1950s, the NAD's policy-makers could make little headway through this morass on their own. Jansen had been a lawyer before taking up his appointment as Minister; Verwoerd had been editor of the Afrikaans newspaper *Die Transvaler* and a Senator before succeeding Jansen; and Eiselen took up his position as Secretary for Native Affairs after a career as a university professor and then a government inspector of education. Moreover, the activities of the NAD's more experienced and informed officers, the Native Affairs Commissioners, were largely confined to the rural areas of the country. Without advice and suggestions from leading municipal organisations such as the Association of Administrators of Non-European Affairs, therefore, the Ministry of Native Affairs could not have generated a suitably informed and comprehensive influx control policy.

---

[61] J. F. Holleman, 'The Tightrope Dancers: Report on Seventh IANA Conference' (1958), p. 1.

Policy recommendations were particularly prolific from municipal officials in the late 1940s and early 1950s. The NAD's failure to have provided a clear or decisive lead to local authorities during the 1940s had forced them to take the initiative in dealing with their local problems of African proletarianisation. Urban administration became a laboratory for local authorities to introduce and test their own strategies, which in turn provided the new Nationalist regime in the NAD with fertile suggestions for its national influx control strategy (as discussed in the next section).

The NAD's influx control strategy, then, was a compound of several distinct priorities and interests, rather than a simple transcription from any of the prevailing blueprints for Apartheid. This admixture of determinants is underlined by the following discussion of the dual imperatives and principal features of the NAD's influx control strategy.

### The NAD's Principles of Influx Control

The NAD looked to its influx control policy as the means to marry twin imperatives in the urban areas. Firstly, in accordance with its notion of 'practical' politics, the NAD undertook to ensure an adequate supply of African labour to white employers in both the urban and the rural areas. From an economic point of view, the NAD saw its influx control policy as the vehicle of a 'rational' distribution of African labour between the cities and the white farms. The urban areas should accommodate only as much African labour as was necessary to meet the urban labour demand. In this way, the drain on would-be agricultural labour supplies would be diminished.

Verwoerd's pragmatism extended to the recognition that the match of labour supply and demand in the cities could never be wholly precise. He told municipal administrators, 'you can't draw a line delimiting labour needs exactly; you will have to make provision for a small measure of surplus to take account of the constant turnover'.[62] But the surplus would not extend beyond a 'certain

---

[62] BCC BMR 14/1/25, '1953 Conference', p. 8.

small margin of available labour'[63] in order to protect the interests of white commercial agriculture.

The second imperative of the influx control strategy was to restrict the numbers of Africans in the urban areas as far as possible. In the state's view, the larger the urban African proletariat, the greater the concomitant threats to the country's political stability and industrial peace. These fears about the political dangers engendered by African urbanisation were stated by the government commission investigating disturbances in Krugersdorp and other townships on the Rand during 1949–50. According to the commission's report, these 'riots' had

resulted largely from a growing antagonism to authority ... [which] assumes alarming proportions on account of the fact that Natives and especially urbanised Natives, who are largely the product of a society subject to deteriorating social bonds, constitute a fertile field for propaganda, the authors of which aim to gain power and status out of chaos.[64]

The cities were seen as breeding grounds of 'communistic'[65] onslaughts on white economic and political supremacy. As Malan told parliament in 1948,

communism has been allowed to play its part in the country and its chief field for propaganda is provided by the non-Europeans. They are incited against the Europeans, and the position is aggravated more and more by the unrestricted influx which has been occurring ... from the Native areas to the European areas. Everything indicates that the position is becoming graver.[66]

The NAD, therefore, saw its influx control policy as having to fulfil dual roles: in addition to providing an instrument for controlling the allocation of African labour, the policy would also secure 'better control' over the cities by limiting the growth of the urban African population. To meet both objectives simultaneously, the NAD devised a policy with six principal features, discussed in turn.

---

[63] *HAD* (1952), vol. 77, col. 1315.

[64] Union of SA, *Report of the Commission Appointed to Inquire into Acts of Violence Committed by Natives at Krugersdorp, Newlands, Randfontein and Newclare*, UG 47/1950, para. 229, p. 12.

[65] The term 'communism' was used by the state loosely to encompass all militant African resistance.

[66] Cited in Department of Foreign Affairs, *Dr Malan Explains Apartheid* (1948).

*1. The Introduction of Labour Bureaux to Control the Movement of
African Labour into Urban Areas*

The NAD's influx control policy rested on the same Stallardist
foundations as those on which the 1937 Native Laws Amendment
Act had been grounded: 'those (Africans) living in the cities are only
entitled to be there if they are prepared to work and there is work
available for them'.[67] By the late 1940s urban local authorities were
at pains to point out that this Stallardist principle could not be
effectively operationalised unless Africans' residence in urban areas
was strictly co-ordinated with control over the allocation of employment there.[68] The transfer of the registration of service contracts to local authorities went some of the way towards this goal;
but the next step, strongly urged by the Association of Administrators of Non-European Affairs, was the establishment of a centralised, national system of labour bureaux, to control the placement
of African workers with urban and rural employers.[69]

This proposal was not entirely new; as a departmental memorandum pointed out in 1949, 'the Department of Native Affairs had
aimed at the establishment of Native labour bureaux practically
since the time of Union'.[70] Necessary provision for this was first
made by the Native Labour Regulation Act of 1911, but private
labour recruiting networks were too lucrative and powerful for the
NAD to have competed successfully.[71] It was only in 1946 that the
NAD first established a sprinkling of urban labour bureaux, some
for the purpose of administering the Unemployment Insurance Act
and others to take over the registration of service contracts from the
NAD.[72] A few local authorities had also established labour bureaux

[67] Verwoerd, quoted in Federated Chamber of Industries (FCI) NEAF, 'Government Policy with regard to Natives in Urban Areas', 12 Mar. 1956, p. 5.
[68] BCC BMR 14/1/30, 'Minutes of Special Meeting of Administrators of Non-
European Affairs . . . 12 December 1946: Memorandum to Fagan Commission',
p. 15.
[69] Ibid. 12–15.
[70] UW A989Mfe/Portfolio 7, Industrial Legislation Commission of Inquiry,
Miscellaneous Memoranda: NAD Memorandum on 'Native Labour Bureaux',
17 Aug. 1949, p. 1.
[71] State-controlled, but clandestine, labour bureaux in rural areas of the Transvaal
had been supplying white farmers with foreign labour since the mid-1920s, effectively
competing with private recruiters. See Bradford, 'Getting Away with Slavery',
pp. 4–7.
[72] UW A989Mfe/Portfolio 7, 'Native Labour Bureaux', p. 5.

on their own initiative. But the scope of the system was still small and fragmented. Both the Fagan Commission and the Sauer Report had stressed the need to extend and formalise the labour bureaux system on a national basis; but both failed to specify how such a system should be set up and run. It was the Association of Administrators of Non-European Affairs which had dwelt more thoroughly and intensively on the issue, and whose recommendations to the Fagan Commission (which were then extended by a committee of the NAD) therefore played a key role in fashioning the NAD's plans. Following the Association, and in consultation with the United Municipal Executive, the NAD proposed to establish a nation-wide network of 'local' labour bureaux in the cities and 'regional' bureaux in rural areas, co-ordinated by a 'central' labour bureau under the control of the NAD's Director of Labour.[73] Each local labour bureau would gain comprehensive control over African employment in its area, because all employers and African work-seekers there would be compelled to register with the bureau and abide by its decisions.[74]

## 2. *Recognition of 'Residential Rights' for the 'Urbanised'*

The basic tenet of the NAD's influx control policy, that access to urban areas would be governed by their labour demands, fell squarely within long-standing Stallardist traditions. But, in the name of 'practical' politics, the NAD's influx control programme also made an important, if anomalous, departure from the Stallardist policies of the past. Differentiating between 'detribalised' and 'tribalised' Africans in the cities, the NAD conceded the 'detribalised' group a degree of residential security at odds with a thoroughgoing Stallardism. Accepting that 'detribalised' Africans had little or no real ties with 'tribal' communities in the reserves, the NAD ruled out mass urban removals as an option for 'the forseeable future', being both impractical and certain to provoke an outcry from industrialists and farmers.[75] According to Verwoerd, 'it is quite clear that the situation now to be handled is that of stabilising the

---

[73] BCC BMR 14/1/30, SNA to Town Clerks, 'Draft Regulations for the Establishment, Management and Control of Native Labour Bureaux', 10 Sept. 1951.
[74] Ibid. 12–15.
[75] Pelzer (ed.), *Verwoerd Speaks*, p. 3.

present population and providing for their needs, before attacking further problems of population distribution'.[76]

The basis of the NAD's influx control strategy was, therefore, the construction of a rigid administrative barrier between 'detribalised' communities comprising permanent city-dwellers, and those allegedly living temporarily in the cities, retaining a permanent home in the rural areas. In the name of 'practical' politics, the architects of influx control policy acknowledged that 'detribalised' Africans had earned the 'residential right' to remain in urban areas on a *de facto* permanent basis, 'for the forseeable future'. 'Detribalisation', Verwoerd conceded, entitled these people to certain 'guarantees, security, and stability'.[77] Most notably, their presence there was not conditional on their remaining in employment, a significant departure from the thoroughgoing Stallardism of the 1937 Native Laws Amendment Act.

These so-called 'residential rights' should not be mistaken for political rights, however. The NAD's policy-makers underlined the fact that, 'while it is admitted that Natives should remain in urban areas . . . it is explicitly stated that they should have no political or equal or social or other rights with Europeans'.[78]

### 3. A Freeze on Further Urbanisation

The concept of residential rights was a pragmatic concession to irreversible 'realities', rather than a liberal or humanitarian impulse on the part of the Nationalists. So, while the NAD's policy-makers grudgingly accepted the existence of a relatively privileged 'detribalised' urban population, they were determined that the urbanisation process should not advance any further. Afrikaner capitalists favoured continuing African urbanisation, as a means of 'stabilising' the work-force. But the NAD heeded the purists' concern for a brake on further urbanisation in the interests of political control. As Jansen put it,

the object is to prevent the further accumulation of Native families in the urban areas . . . The number of detribalised Natives in the urban areas

---

[76] NAD, 'Progress Report for . . . 1950', p. 19.
[77] *HAD* (1952), vol. 77, col. 1311.
[78] NAD, 'Native Policy', p. 5.

should be frozen . . . to prevent further detribalisation of families which can lead to an increase in the numbers in the urban areas.[79]

In order to effect this urbanisation freeze, residential rights would be denied to all Africans born outside already urbanised communities. In this way, the boundary dividing urban 'insiders' from 'outsiders' would be wholly impenetrable: no Africans born in a rural area would be permitted to settle in an urban area. Their presence in the urban area would always be contingent on their remaining in employment.

## 4. *Extending the Influx Control System to African Women*

The NAD's determination to halt the urbanisation process placed a particular premium on controlling the movements, marriage patterns, and economic activities of African women—all of which the NAD set out to achieve by extending the influx control system to encompass African women.

During the 1940s several municipal administrators on the Witwatersrand had vainly petitioned the NAD to intensify legal controls over the movement of African women. Requests along these lines from the Association of Administrators of Non-European Affairs had been impotent, largely because the NAD was reluctant to tamper with what were considered politically explosive measures.[80] But the municipal advocates of stricter controls over the movements of African women found a more sympathetic audience in Jansen, Eiselen, and Verwoerd.[81] Rhetoric vilifying 'undesirable women' in the cities became part of the NAD's position on 'the urban problem'. Elastic and expansive, the category of 'undesirable women' could be stretched to encompass all single women uncontrolled by men. Such women, particularly those who brewed beer and ran

[79] *HAD* (1950), vol. 71, col. 4711.

[80] BCC BMR 14/1/30, 'Minutes of Native Affairs Advisory Committee . . . 26 June 1942'; and 'Minutes of Monthly Meeting of Association of Administrators of Non-European Affairs . . . 15 February 1945'.

[81] See, e.g., BCC BMR 14/1/25, '1953 Conference', pp. 43, 47–8. Note that the proceedings of this conference also show that municipal administrators were by now more divided on the issue of influx control for women, several having become wary of provoking disturbances in their areas by intensifying controls over women's movements—a reaction, in large measure, to the anti-pass protests of the early 1950s (see Ch. 4).

shebeens illegally, were held responsible for bringing moral decay, juvenile delinquency, and high levels of urban crime to the townships. Indeed, virtually the entire urban malaise could be blamed on the erosion of traditional patriarchal relationships. As Jansen put it, 'it is constantly being said that the Natives in the cities deteriorate. The undesirable conditions are largely caused by the presence of women, who in many cases leave their homes contrary to the wishes of their fathers or guardians and contrary to tribal custom.'[82] The NAD's strategy of improved urban control thus included a commitment to 'building up . . . [urban] family life' by 'having the patriarchal system introduced again'.[83]

The NAD also regarded the large numbers of urban women occupied in the informal sector as economically 'redundant', since they were not 'ministering to white needs'. In addition to rehabilitating 'traditional' family relations, the NAD was, therefore, keen to channel economically active African women into 'respectable' work—that is, formal employment by whites.

While the cautious regime in the NAD during the 1940s had been wary of inciting unrest, the new Nationalist government thus regarded the benefits of extending the influx control system to African women as too tempting to bypass. Not only would the migration of women to urban areas be restricted in accordance with white labour demands; the influx control laws could also be used as an instrument for restoring and buttressing African men's control over women. For, apart from those who were already fully urbanised, women would not be permitted to settle in urban areas unless they either 'ministered to white needs' or were formally married to a man permitted to be in the area.

## 5. Opening the Cities to Single Work-seekers

Given their 'practical' premises, the architects of influx control policy did not intend to barricade the cities altogether. Africans from rural areas whose labour was required by white employers within urban areas would be permitted to live there for the duration of their employment contracts. But, in line with the plan to freeze

[82] Quoted in C. Kros, *Urban African Women's Organisations, 1953–1956* (Johannesburg, 1980), p. 23.
[83] *HAD* (1952), vol. 80, col. 7882.

the process of 'detribalisation', these workers would remain temporary residents, barred from joining the ranks of the 'urbanised'. Instead, they would be 'periodically returned to their homes to renew their tribal connections'.[84]

In order to relieve the urban authorities of some of the burden of influx control, the NAD proposed to institute controls over the townwards migration of Africans at its source. An African leaving his or her district of origin to take up employment in a town would first have to secure permission from the labour bureau in this district. In the case of Africans living on white farms, the written permission of the farmer would also be required.

A different set of restrictions was intended to govern the access of foreign Africans (that is, citizens of other African countries) to the urban areas. Previous governments had treated Africans from the Protectorates in the same administrative category as Union-born Africans, allowing 'tens of thousands'[85] into the towns. But, according to Jansen, Africans from the Protectorates, like all other foreign Africans, were 'superfluous' inhabitants of the urban areas. Their presence, he argued, exacerbated an already desperate housing shortage; also, foreigners were known to have participated in urban riots, and foreign women were culprits in the 'illicit liquor trade'.[86] Moreover, if all foreign Africans were debarred from the cities, Jansen reasoned, the likelihood of their accepting work on white farms would increase. Indeed, one of the principal motives for a particularly strict influx control policy towards foreigners was to provide a means of 'diverting . . . foreign labour to the farms'.[87]

### 6. *The Urban Labour Preference Policy*

The NAD's administrative entrenchment of a permanent urbanised population in the 'white' cities sat uncomfortably with the Nationalists' ideological and political principle that the presence of Africans in the towns was justified by white economic needs alone. The conferral of residential rights created a category of city-dwellers entitled to remain there whether or not they were unemployed and

---

[84] *HAD* (1948), vol. 62, col. 1660.

[85] NAD, 'Native Policy', p. 8.

[86] Ibid. 8.

[87] W. M. Eiselen, quoted in Institute of Administrators of Non-European Affairs (IANA), 'Proceedings of 1953 Annual Conference', p. 23.

therefore 'surplus' to white needs. The NAD was anxious to curtail the size of this group as far as possible, for several reasons. In addition to exposing a profound ideological anomaly, the build-up of urban labour 'surpluses' was a symptom of exactly one of the problems which the NAD's influx control policy was intended to solve—the alleged maldistribution of African labour between urban and rural areas. In terms of the NAD's simplistic economic reasoning, 'idleness' amongst city-dwellers signified a waste of would-be farm labour.[88] As Nationalist MP Mr Papenfus put it, 'if we want to put a stop to the stream of labour from the platteland to the cities, we shall first of all have to make use of all those idlers in the cities'.[89] Ensuring that labour 'surpluses' did not build up within the urbanised community was, therefore, an integral part of the NAD's plan for a 'rational' distribution of African labour.

The NAD had not undertaken any systematic nation-wide investigation into the extent of unemployment amongst Africans in urban areas. However, by extrapolating from the findings of various local authorities, the Department's policy-makers concluded that this problem had taken on grave proportions.[90] During the early 1950s the Pretoria City Council, for example, reported that 4,800 men out of a total of 13,000 known to reside in the town were 'idle'.[91] Figures showing the proportion of the unemployed who were 'detribalised' were unavailable; but the NAD deduced the prevalence of 'idleness' amongst this group from their so-called 'job choosiness' in refusing the notoriously unpopular and arduous jobs paying the lowest wages. As the NAD put it, 'urbanisation of the Native produces the avoidance of certain jobs'.[92]

Tackling unemployment amongst so-called 'temporary' city-dwellers who were not protected by residential rights presented little problem to the NAD. Any idle Africans in this category could be forcibly removed from an urban area, since their presence there was contingent on their remaining in employment. However, a different

---

[88] Ibid.

[89] *HAD* (1952), vol. 77, col. 749.

[90] Note that the NAD did not differentiate between unemployment and underemployment. To square the NAD's findings with those of the Fagan Commission, it must be assumed that the NAD's counts of 'idle' Africans in the townships accommodated a high measure of underemployment.

[91] BCC BMR 14/1/25, '1953 Conference', p. 45.

[92] Ibid. 45.

strategy was required to eliminate unemployment within the urbanised community (as defined by the NAD), since their residential rights were not conditional on continuous employment. The solution proposed by the NAD's policy-makers drew on an urban labour preference principle, already in use by the Johannesburg municipal Non-European Affairs Department (NEAD) and firmly endorsed by the Association of Administrators of Non-European Affairs as 'a cardinal principle of policy'.[93] In terms of this principle, Eiselen claimed, the NAD could ensure that 'optimal' economic use was made of the resident urbanised population. To date, he argued, white employers in the urban areas had not exhausted the full labour supply available on their doorsteps, meeting their labour needs by importing workers from the rural areas instead. In order to eliminate this 'appalling' and unnecessary 'wastage'[94] of African labour in the cities, Eiselen declared, 'it is essential that measures be instituted to utilise all available labour resources in the urban areas'.[95] Unemployment amongst urbanised Africans would be eradicated, not by exporting the problem to the reserves, but by channelling the 'idle' holders of residential rights into employment ahead of African workers newly arrived from the reserves.

The NAD's influx control strategy thus hinged on an urban labour preference policy (ULPP) which specified that 'until all permanent urban labour resources had been utilised, further influx was undesirable';[96] 'in regard to the movement of Union Natives . . . the policy was to prevent additional natives entering a district where existing Natives were sufficient to supply labour needs'.[97] This ULPP marked the limit of employers' autonomy in stipulating their own labour needs. The NAD's pragmatism extended as far as permitting employers in urban areas to dictate the *numbers* of African workers they required. But the ULPP denied them the right to specify a demand for migrant labour in preference to urbanised workers. As long as the urbanised labour pool had not been fully drained

---

[93] BCC BMR 14/1/30, Association of Administrators of Non-European Affairs, 'Report of Sub-Committee . . . to Consider Establishment of a Regional Organisation on the Reef to Administer Registration of Native Service Contracts, Influx Control and Unemployment Insurance Act', 30 July 1947, p. 3.

[94] Union of SA, *Report of the NAD for the Year 1951/2*, UG 37/1955, p. 20.

[95] BCC BMR 14/1/25, '1953 Conference', p. 45.

[96] Ibid. 46.

[97] ASSOCOM NEAF, Sec. to Pres. Federated Hotel Associations of Southern Africa, 4 Aug. 1954.

(irrespective of the particular qualifications, training, or preferences of the workers in it), employers would be denied access to additional migrant workers recruited from beyond the urban boundary.

The ULPP conflicted starkly with the realities of African employment in the towns. While the journals of organised commerce and industry sang the praises of a 'stable' urbanised work-force, individual industrialists often preferred the services of migrant workers, particularly for unskilled work. 'Rural labour' was purportedly less 'job choosy', more 'docile' and disciplined, and prepared to work for lower wages than urbanised workers (see Chapter 6). From the NAD's point of view, however, such preferences were irrational. Farmers were deprived of would-be farm-workers while surpluses of urban labour accumulated in the towns.[98] In order to restore 'rationality' to the urban labour market, the NAD thought it necessary to restructure it forcibly, overruling employers' preferences. The implementation of the ULPP would, therefore, depend on the creation of a national system of labour bureaux, to establish systematic and comprehensive control over the allocation of labour to employers in the urban areas. Denied the right to recruit labour independently, urban employers would be compelled to accept the labour allocated to them by labour bureaux officials, who could then ensure that local work-seekers had first claim on all available jobs.[99]

The ULPP was also intended to fulfil another less direct role in ensuring a 'rational' distribution of African labour. Addressing the FCI in 1951, Eiselen underlined other symptoms of the prevailing 'irrationality' of urban African employment. Labour turnover was extremely high, and labour productivity correspondingly low, he claimed. As a result, the number of Africans drawn into the urban labour market was excessive. Were the labour market to operate according to a 'different conception of Native labour'[100] which stressed the benefits of a more stable and productive work-force, Eiselen argued, the growth of the African work-force could be considerably pared. He recognised that the onus in effecting these changes devolved largely on employers themselves. But he saw the

---

[98] Eiselen, quoted in IANA, Proceedings of 1953 Annual Conference', p. 18.
[99] *HAD* (1952), vol. 77, cols. 550–1.
[100] W. M. Eiselen, 'Plan to Rationalise South Africa's Native Labour' (NAD Fact Paper no. 13; 1950), p. 5.

ULPP as the state's means of expediting the shift towards greater stability and productivity. For, denied unlimited access to migrant labour, employers would become less nonchalant in hiring and firing their workers, and would have to make better use of 'stable' labour available on their doorsteps. As the Minister of Labour explained,

the trouble with the employers is that they know they have an unlimited supply of Native labour, with the result that they are not concerned with the aptitude of the individual worker. They are not concerned about the training of that worker . . . the result is that there is usually a 60–70 per cent turnover. The result is also that the productivity of the worker is extremely low and his efficiency is of a very low standard.[101]

It is a very good thing . . . to see to it that there is no unrestricted supply in any particular area, because, as a result of that, productivity will be increased and efficiency will be improved.[103]

The ULPP was intended to apply to adult women and youths (aged 15–18), as well as to adult males. By encouraging employers to take on local women in certain jobs previously filled by male and female migrant workers—such as domestic service—the NAD hoped to limit the number of migrant workers necessary to meet white needs. As J. van Heerden of the NAD told a conference of departmental and municipal officials in 1953, if more use was made of 'Native women's labour, . . . the labour position in the country will improve considerably'.[103]

The same sort of argument was advanced in respect of African youths who were neither attending school nor already in white employ. Rampant youth unemployment was a source of considerable concern within the state. In 1951 an inter-departmental committee reported 80 per cent unemployment amongst youths aged 15–20 in Pretoria. In Johannesburg, 20,000 youths were found to be unemployed.[104] These figures alarmed NAD officials, who suspected all 'idle' youths of being political 'agitators' or criminals. Their suspicions were fanned by the *Report of the Commission . . . to Inquire into Acts of Violence Committed by Natives at Krugersdrop, Newlands, Randfontein and Newclare* (1950), which reported 'mass intimidation' in the townships by 'a large number of educated and

---

[101] *HAD* (1952), vol. 77, cols. 1148–9.
[102] Ibid., col. 1151.
[103] BCC BMR 14/1/25, '1953 Conference', p. 45.
[104] Ibid. 45.

other youths without any visible means of support'.[105] For the NAD, then, channelling youths into the employ of whites represented a form of political and social control—'saving the Native youths in the city from the drift into tsotsidom'[106]—in addition to a strategy for the 'better utilisation' of resident urban labour power.[107]

As part of its ULPP, the NAD, therefore, intended to 'take all necessary steps to place young Natives born in the cities, into employment'.[108] Industrialists would have to make use of 'local youths . . . before further labourers are allowed to come in'.[109] Since employers generally disdained the services of the young, Eiselen announced that the NAD had persuaded the Department of Labour to permit the payment of lower wages to youths doing the same jobs as adults in Pretoria, the Witwatersrand, Port Elizabeth, Durban, East London, Bloemfontein, Witbank, and Vereeniging.[110] He declared, too, that the NAD was 'working towards the ideal of youths of the locations becoming domestic servants and this eventually assisting in removing surplus natives from the urban area'.[111]

The features of the ULPP described above were designed to apply to urban areas nation-wide. But the ULPP was also intended to a serve an additional, regionally specific, function in the Western Cape. At a meeting in 1951 with representatives of ASSOCOM and the FCI, Verwoerd alluded to his Department's intentions to apply additional restrictions on the employment of African labour in the Western Cape.[112] But it was not until 1954 that the substance of these restrictions was announced. As Eiselen explained, the NAD's influx control policy in the Western Cape would operate from the ideological premiss that 'the Western Cape was the natural home of the Coloured people, and they have the right to be protected against the competition of Natives in the labour market'.[113]

---

[105] Union of SA, *Report of the Commission . . . into Acts of Violence . . . at Krugersdorp, Newlands, Randfontein and Newclare*, UG 47/1950, p. 3.

[106] *HAD* (1952), vol. 77, col. 751.

[107] See, e.g., *HAD* (1952), vol. 77, col. 634.

[108] IANA, 'Proceedings of 1953 Annual Conference', p. 24.

[109] *Senate Debates* (1951), vol. 3, col. 4148.

[110] IANA, 'Proceedings of 1953 Annual Conference', p. 24.

[111] Killie Campbell Library (KCL), KCF 46, Durban Municipal Records (DMR), 'Minutes of Meeting of Durban City Council Delegation with Eiselen, 10 Sept. 1954', p. 7.

[112] ASSOCOM NEAF, 'Verbatim transcript', p. 18.

[113] Eiselen quoted in F. Snitcher, 'The Eiselen Scheme', *Africa South*, 1/3 (1957), 40.

In the eyes of the NAD, the growth of the urban African population in the Western Cape was especially threatening. It was in the
Western Cape that the country's so-called 'Coloured' population was
largely concentrated. The prospect of growing numbers of Africans
and Coloureds living and working together excited fears of a united
black working class, with formidable economic bargaining powers.[114]
There were other dangers too. As Donges, Minister of the Interior,
explained,

the potential danger of the Coloured vote has persisted . . . in South
Africa . . . it is not just primarily the natural increase of the Coloured
population which presents the greatest menace . . . the danger lies mainly
in the fact that we have this tremendous Native reservoir which by inter-
marriage may potentially be responsible for the number of Coloured people
in the country increasing.[115]

Adapting the ULPP to the specific conditions and problems of the
Western Cape provided the state with what it deemed an economically 'practical' means of subverting these threats: the number of
Africans entering the region would be more rigidly restricted than
elsewhere in the country, but without thereby depriving white
employers of a sufficient supply of labour.[116] The local urban labour
supply would in this case comprise the resident Coloureds. In line
with the ULPP, African migrant labour would not be permitted into
the urban areas of the Western Cape until the resident Coloured
labour supply had been fully utilised. In the Western Cape, then,
the ULPP took the form of a 'Coloured Labour Preference Policy'
(CLPP).[117] It was in these terms that the prospect of the CLPP was
first raised by Verwoerd in parliament in 1952.[118]

[114] This issue is discussed in more detail in I. Goldin, 'Coloured Preference Poli-
tics and the Making of Coloured Political Identity in the Western Cape Region of
South Africa, with Particular Reference to the Period 1948–1984' (D.Phil. thesis,
Univ. of Oxford, 1984).

[115] Quoted in D. W. Kruger, *South African Parties and Policies* (London, 1960),
322.

[116] This objective, however, does not fully explain the introduction of the
Coloured Labour Preference Policy (CLPP). For more detail on other determinants,
see Goldin, 'Coloured Preference Politics'.

[117] This argument is made in greater detail in D. B. Posel, 'Coloured Labour
Preference Policy in the Western Cape in the 1950s in the Context of National
Policy on African Urbanisation' (paper presented to the conference on 'Western
Cape: Roots and Realities', Univ. of Cape Town, 1986).

[118] *HAD* (1952), vol. 77, col. 1126.

The ULPP was clearly central to the NAD's proposed solution to the problem of influx control in the early 1950s. By limiting the number of migrant workers permitted to enter the urban areas, and forcing employers to resort to more productive and less 'wasteful' employment practices, the ULPP married the NAD's commitment to 'practical' labour policies with its determination to curb the growth of the urban African population as far as possible. In so doing, the ULPP also testified to the limits of the NAD's economic pragmatism. Yet, most scholars have paid little attention to the ULPP, which has prevented a full understanding of the state's strategy of influx control in the 1950s. Martin Legassick, for example, saw the distinguishing feature of Apartheid as the state's extension of the migrant labour system operative on the mines and farms to secondary industries in the towns, so as to guarantee them an adequate supply of cheap African labour.[119] Legassick's thesis is partly correct, in so far as the NAD planned to limit new entrants to the towns to migrant workers, rather than to permanent residents. However, the NAD also planned to impose new restrictions on the operation of the migrant labour system itself, by refusing industrialists unconditional and unlimited access to migrant labour. Legassick failed to take account of these restrictions and the effect they would have had on African wages. Had the NAD's intention been simply to supply industrialists with cheap labour, permitting them unrestricted access to migrant labour would have been a more appropriate influx control policy. Legassick ignored the ULPP, because his argument stresses the fundamentally economic determinants of the state's proposed solution to the influx control problem. However, the particular form of the migrant labour system proposed by the NAD for secondary industry reflects the combination of economic and political interests shaping the design of this influx control policy.

It is also inaccurate to claim, as many scholars have done,[120] that the state's influx control policy conformed directly to the policy preferences of Afrikaner capitalists. The NAD went along with the AHI and SAAU in accepting the growing demand for African labour amongst whites, and heeded their calls for the state to ensure that

---

[119] Legassick, 'South Africa: Capital Accumulation and Violence', p. 276.

[120] See, e.g., O'Meara, *Volkskapitalisme*; Hindson, *Pass Controls and the Urban African Proletariat*.

the supply of African labour to urban and rural areas was sufficient to meet this demand. However, whereas Afrikaner capital favoured the economically regulated growth of the urbanised African population, the NAD proposed an immediate and total freeze on the urbanisation process. Moreover, in so doing, the NAD dismissed the AHI's and SAAU's calls for the gradual phasing out of the migrant labour system. The AHI and SAAU had called on the state to permit the 'stabilisation' of the urban work-force by permitting rural Africans taking up urban jobs to settle there permanently with their families (see Chapter 2). But the NAD, while reiterating the benefits of a 'stabilised' African work-force, had very different ideas about how to achieve this end. As the NAD saw it, by denying employers unlimited access to migrant labour, the ULPP would force them to reduce their labour turnover and make better use of the labour already in their employ. Labour 'stabilisation', in the NAD's eyes, would be won by changing employers' attitudes to African labour, rather than by 'stabilising' the workers' place of residence and life-style. Calls for labour 'stabilisation', therefore, did not deter the NAD in its proposals to entrench the migrant labour system as the sole basis for rural Africans' access to urban employment in the future.

# 4

# *Struggles over Influx Control Legislation*

THE legislative foundations of influx control policy during the first phase of Apartheid were laid during the Nationalist government's first term of office, between 1948 and 1953. Uncertain of re-election in 1953, the NP was intent on making a swift and conspicuous impact on the pressing economic and political problems unleashed by African migration to the cities. Jansen, the first Minister of Native Affairs, therefore wasted little time in tabling the legislation necessary to implement the proposed programme of influx control. By the end of 1952, with the promulgation of the Native Laws Amendment Act, the principal pillar which would support the state's influx control policy for the decade to come had been built.

This chapter examines the substance and passage of this legislation, to assess the effects of parliamentary and extra-parliamentary opposition to the NAD's original influx control strategy. The passage of the Native Laws Amendment Bill through parliament has not attracted much attention in the academic literature. It is worth examining, however, because it shows that early Nationalist legislation was fundamentally shaped by pressures of the historical moment, to be expected particularly from a government yet to entrench itself in power and buffeted by immediate problems and priorities. This discussion also reveals the key interests and powers which shaped the official influx control policy of the decade, notably, those of capitalist agriculture, industry, and commerce, and, to a lesser extent, mining; various African political organisations; parliamentary opposition to the NP; and local authorities. It is argued that the Native Laws Amendment Act differed in important respects from the form in which it was originally drafted. In the face of powerful opposition, Verwoerd (as Minister of Native Affairs) made concessions which departed from the NAD's original influx control strategy, and introduced significant loopholes and contradictions into the official influx control policy enshrined in the 1952 Native Laws Amendment Act. However, the NAD's success in taking

only four years to place much of its proposed influx control programme on the statute books reflected the breadth of white support
for what was seen to be an orderly and thoroughgoing solution to
the problem of influx control. The UP tried to discredit the NP by
presenting its policy proposals as ideologically uncompromising and
economically damaging, compared with the allegedly more moderate
and reasoned proposals of the Fagan Commission. But Verwoerd
succeeded in reassuring organised capital and the white electorate
at large that the Department's influx control Bill was suitably
'practical' and would be implemented in a similarly pragmatic spirit.

It was shown in the preceding chapter that the NAD's influx
control strategy was two-pronged: it was designed, on the one hand,
to effect a 'rational' distribution of African labour between urban
and rural areas; and, on the other hand, as a means of controlling
the growth and composition of the urban African population. In
1949 the NAD tabled two bills, the Native Laws Amendment Bill
and the Urban Areas Amendment Bill, to amend the existing
legislation on African labour and urban population control respectively. These Bills are examined in turn.

### The 1949 Native Laws Amendment Bill

The Native Laws Amendment Bill proposed amendments to the
1911 Native Labour Regulation Act to facilitate the introduction of
a nation-wide system of labour bureaux for the 'canalisation'[1] of
African labour. All African employment in agriculture and urban
areas would be controlled by labour bureaux, which would allocate
African workers to white employers. To ensure that African labour
was 'rationally' distributed between urban and rural areas, the
bureaux would have to place all available urban labour in employment in the cities before authorising the importation of migrant
labour from rural areas.

The interests of capitalist agriculture loom large in an explanation
of how and why this Bill took shape. Jansen first mooted the idea

---

[1] See, e.g., *HAD* (1950), vol. 71, col. 4707; (1952), vol. 77, col. 552. S. Kahn,
MP, pointed out that Nationalist MPs had become 'captivated' with the phrase, as a
'honeyed' way of describing a system of 'forced labour' (*HAD* (1952), vol. 77, col.
739).

of a labour-bureaux system in parliament as his government's solution to farmers' labour problems.[2] The Native Laws Amendment Bill was then drafted in close consultation with the Liaison Committee of the SAAU.[3] But it is simplistic to reduce the Bill simply to an expression of white agricultural interests.[4] The Native Laws Amendment Bill was devised to pursue the NAD's objectives in both rural and urban areas. In addition to tackling the farm labour shortage, the Bill was the legal vehicle for the ULPP, which was integral to the NAD's strategy for controlling African urbanisation. The ULPP would limit the numbers of rural workers drawn into the urban African proletariat, to restrict its growth as far as was 'practically' possible. The NAD regarded these curbs on population growth in the cities as a vital instrument for containing the threat of urban African resistance. As Nationalist MP F. Mentz put it during a subsequent parliamentary debate, the labour bureaux system was designed to

avoid the massing together which one finds in many cities . . . We say that we can no longer allow the uncontrolled flow of Natives from one part of the country to the other because, if we allow it, we are creating problems in the face of which we shall be powerless in the near future.[5]

In order to maximise the social and political control afforded by the ULPP, Verwoerd insisted that the labour bureaux system should encompass all Africans, male and female, over the age of 15. In the eyes of white officialdom, all unemployed youths were unruly 'tsotsis', caught up in lives of political 'agitation' as well as violent crime.[6] In an effort to combat 'tsotsism', the Native Laws Amendment Bill therefore defined all Africans above the age of 15, male and female, as 'work-seekers', which meant that they were automatically subject to the conditions of the labour bureaux system.

The labour bureaux system proposed by the Bill was also designed to guarantee an adequate supply of African labour to white employers in the urban areas. Indeed, this system had an in-built

---

[2] *HAD* (1948), vol. 62, col. 1664.

[3] UW A989Mfe/Portfolio 7, Industrial Legislation Commission of Inquiry, Miscellaneous Memoranda: NAD Memorandum on 'Native Labour Bureaux', 17 Aug. 1948, p. 7.

[4] O'Meara, e.g., argues that 'Apartheid sought primarily to secure a stable labour supply for agriculture' (*Volkskapitalisme*, p. 177).

[5] *HAD* (1952), vol. 77, cols. 1094–5.

[6] e.g. *Senate Debates* (1951), vol. 111, cols. 4147–8.

urban bias: it was only once the urban demand for African labour
had been satisfied that labour bureaux would step in to redirect
work-seekers based in the reserves away from the cities to the white
farms. Labour bureaux were not empowered to satisfy rural demands for labour first, before allowing Africans to seek work in the
cities.

That agricultural interests were not monolithic in shaping the
Native Laws Amendment Bill is also illustrated by the Bill's stance
on the issue of the compulsory or voluntary registration of work-
seekers with labour bureaux. The issue was extremely contentious.
The UP, following the recommendations of the Fagan Commission,
had approved the idea of a nation-wide labour bureaux system, but
insisted that the registration of work-seekers with labour bureaux be
voluntary. The white farming lobby, however, had a strong interest
in a system of compulsory registration. The farm labour problem
had arisen primarily because large numbers of Africans chose city
jobs over employment on white farms paying considerably lower
wages. White farmers looked to the state to supply them with
African labour without their having to offer competitive wages. In
order to do so, the labour bureaux system would clearly have to
withdraw Africans' freedom to choose urban over rural employment.

Agriculturalists' preferences aside, the NAD also had other
reasons to make the labour bureaux system compulsory. Its strategy
for channelling African labour to white farms depended upon the
labour bureaux having the power to place urbanised work-seekers
into jobs ahead of rural migrants. Unless all work-seekers were
compelled to register with labour bureaux, the bureaux' officials
would lack the information and control necessary to institute this
strategy.

Yet, the 1949 Native Laws Amendment Bill failed to declare a
consistent position on the registration issue, making provision for
the 'voluntary or compulsory registration of Natives with labour
bureaux'.[7] Clearly the Nationalist government's political muscle was
not yet strong enough to back the agricultural lobby against the stiff
opposition from the UP. The Native Laws Amendment Bill's
prevarication on the issue was nevertheless sufficient to have
provoked the Opposition's outrage. But the controversy was cut
short by Jansen's withdrawal of the Bill late in 1949.

[7] *HAD* (1949), vol. 69, col. 7375.

## The 1949 Urban Areas Amendment Bill

Anticipating a lengthy debate over the Native Laws Amendment Bill, Jansen vainly hoped that the Urban Areas Amendment Bill, a far shorter Bill introduced later in 1949, would enjoy a smooth enough passage to be passed within a single session of parliament.[8] The most contentious clause in this Bill proposed amendments to section 10(1) of the 1945 Natives (Urban Areas) Act. The 1945 version of section 10(1) had read as follows:

10.(1) The Governor-General shall, if requested to do so by a resolution adopted by a duly constituted meeting of any urban local authority, by proclamation in the Gazette, declare that from and after a date to be specified therein no native shall enter the urban area under the jurisdiction of that urban local authority for the purpose of seeking or taking up employment or residing therein, otherwise than in accordance with conditions to be prescribed by the Governor-General in that proclamation; and the Governor-General may at any time after consultation with the urban local authority concerned, of his own motion issue any such proclamation in respect of any urban area.

The 1945 legislation, then, did not compel urban local authorities to institute influx control regulations. However, for those urban local authorities who chose to do so, section 10(1) allowed for a blanket ban on the entry of all Africans—male and female—into the urban areas in question.

In terms of the 1949 Urban Areas Amendment Bill, section 10(1) was amended to prescribe the compulsory application of influx control to all urban areas nation-wide. The bill having divided the country up into 'proclaimed' (primarily urban) and 'non-proclaimed' areas, the amended section 10(1) then laid down that:

10(1) No Native shall . . . remain for more than seventy-two hours in an urban or in a proclaimed area . . . unless he was born and permanently resides in such area or permission so to remain has been granted to him by an officer designated for the purpose by that urban local authority.[9]

This would apply to African men and women alike.

As well as making new inroads into the autonomy of local

---

[8] Ibid., col. 7308.
[9] *Senate Debates* (1951), vol. 111, col. 4186.

authorities in matters of influx control, section 10(1) of the Urban Areas Amendment Bill was also unprecedented in differentiating the resident urban African population into two groups: those entitled to remain there on the grounds of having been born and permanently resident there, and those who, having been born else-where, could only remain there for as long as the local authority permitted them to do so. Moreover, the boundary between the two groups was rigid: in line with the proposed freeze on further urbanisation, no one born outside the area would gain the right to remain there unconditionally, no matter how long he or she had been employed there.

This amendment to section 10(1) was highly controversial. But parliamentary debate on it was pre-empted by the withdrawal of the Urban Areas Amendment Bill, along with the Native Laws Amendment Bill. Acknowledging Opposition accusations that the two Bills were fundamentally interlinked and ought to be considered conjointly, Jansen announced his intention to reintroduce both Bills in an amalgamated form to a future session of parliament. The NAD's drive to institute its influx control programme was thus suspended for a year, during 1950.

The year 1950 proved to be a stormy one, politically. In Verwoerd's words, 'the feelings of restlessness and discontent which have been evident among the Native people for some years past, persisted . . . [and] led to rioting and dislocation of essential services'.[10]

On 29 January a police raid in search of illegal liquor in New-clare, Johannesburg, provoked clashes between the police and an African crowd of over two hundred, during which twenty-seven Africans were shot. These disturbances, together with others which had occurred in Krugersdorp and Randfontein late in 1949, were sufficiently disconcerting to the NAD to have prompted the ap-pointment of a commission of inquiry into the causes of all three sets of riots. But one of the main focuses of organised African resistance during 1950 was the Suppression of Communism Act, which gave the state draconian powers to apprehend anyone promoting 'any political, industrial, social, or economic change . . . by the promo-tion of disturbance or disorder . . .'.[11] A May Day stay-away in

---

[10] NAD, 'Progress Report for the Department of Native Affairs during 1950' (NAD Fact Paper no. 11, 1951), p. 1.
[11] Lodge, *Black Politics*, p. 33.

protest against this law and low African wages was called by the ANC, in accordance with the tactic adopted by its 1949 Programme of Action of 'civil disobedience, non-cooperation, boycotts, and politically directed strikes'.[12] Supported by the CPSA and the South African Indian Congress, the protest 'evoked a significant response'[13] amongst African communities, particularly on the Reef.

Probably the most explosive political issue was the state's declared intention to subject African women to all the notorious rigours of the pass system. As Senator M. Ballinger was told in a letter from a Johannesburg resident,

the papers yesterday had headlines on 'passes for native women'; what a stir it has caused. In all my years of dealing with natives never have I seen such a spontaneous resentment to any measure. One native put it to me, Let them do it, then go to Orlando to apply it, Newclare riots will be nothing to what will happen.[14]

Mass demonstrations erupted in many cities. A wide range of organisations, such as the ANC, SAIRR, CPSA, and the National Council of Women, sent angry deputations to the NAD. Even the politically moderate and timid Location Advisory Boards' Congress (LABC) was drawn into the fray. The advisory board system had been instituted by the state in 1923, in the belief that the advisory boards would provide local authorities with a means of co-opting the support of urban community leaders. It was hoped that advisory board members, aware of and responsive to local grievances, would play an important role in maintaining order in the townships by pre-empting militant 'agitation'. In terms of the 1923 Urban Areas Act, advisory boards members were either elected or nominated to represent the interests of individuals in their community to the local authority, and were permitted merely to advise local and central government on policies affecting the townships. The LABC was then instituted in 1928, to provide a national forum to 'further the interests of Location Advisory Boards'[15] and gain the ear of 'central government, provincial administrators, municipal councils and

---

[12] S. Trapido, 'African Opposition in South Africa, 1949–1961', in *Collected Papers on Opposition in the New African State* (London, 1967–8), 99.
[13] Lodge, *Black Politics*, p. 33.
[14] UW Ballinger Papers, A410 B2.5.25 File 3, W. R. Grant to M. Ballinger, 24 Mar. 1950.
[15] G. Xorile Papers, Location Advisory Boards' Congress (LABC), 'Memorandum on the Bill to Amend the Natives (Urban Areas) Consolidation Act' (undated), p. 1.

other public bodies'[16] implicated in the country's urban 'Native policy'. By 1950, although many individual advisory board members were outspoken critics of government policy, the LABC was a meek and moderate body with little influence or credibility within the wider African community. However, the LABC was one of the few African organisations which maintained regular, if obsequious, contact with the NAD, by means of which the Minister of Native Affairs kept abreast of conservative African opinion. So, when the LABC sent a deputation to the Minister politely protesting against the prospect of African women being subjected to the influx control regulations,[17] the NAD was confronted with the fact that such opposition spanned the entire spectrum of African political opinion. Recognising the potential for a bitter confrontation on the issue, Jansen backed down, and, on 7 April 1950, issued a statement that African women would not have to carry passes.[18] With this, the wave of protest subsided temporarily.

This interim victory for African resistance was not to last. Jansen then resigned, replaced temporarily by C. R. Swart, until Verwoerd took over as Minister of Native Affairs in October 1950. When the influx control legislation was finally revived, in May 1951, Jansen's reprieve for African women had been forgotten. The NAD had reverted to its original plan to encompass African men, women, and youths alike within the scope of a national system of influx control.

## The 1951 Native Laws Amendment Bill

The twin influx control bills withdrawn late in 1949 were reintroduced into parliament in 1951, in the form of a single omnibus Native Laws Amendment Bill. Verwoerd took the highly unconventional step of introducing this Bill into the Senate, rather than the House of Assembly, first. Non-Nationalist MPs were outraged, protesting that,

once a Bill has been passed in that revising Chamber [the Senate], it makes it very difficult for this House, when the matter is reintroduced here, to give

---

[16] G. Xorile Papers, p. 1.
[17] UNISA A. W. G. Champion Papers 15.4 LABC, 'Deputation to the Minister of Native Affairs', 17 Apr. 1950.
[18] *HAD* (1952), vol. 77, col. 737.

the fullest consideration which we would otherwise give it. It becomes very difficult to send such a measure to a Select Committee; and what is more, it means that the parties in this House are very often inclined to consider themselves committed to a decision of the Other House, instead of coming to their own decisions which can then be reviewed by the Other House.[19]

Hastening the Bill's passage through the House of Assembly was exactly what Verwoerd was after. The drafting of the omnibus Bill was only completed in early May 1951. (Thus most Senators had not seen a copy before the first reading of the Bill in the Senate on 15 May.) With the next general election pending some time before May 1953, there would have been little chance of the Bill being passed before then if it had followed the conventional path. Verwoerd already knew from the debates in the House of Assembly over the previous two years that the new Bill would provoke considerable controversy in the Lower House. The likely appointment of a Select Committee would have prolonged this debate still further. Also, the Opposition would have exerted strong pressure to have the Bill discussed with representatives of African organisations. The process of debate in the Senate, on the other hand, was likely to be far shorter, since the Senate was merely a review body, in which Select Committees were highly unusual. Senators were less likely to debate the principles of the Bill, concentrating more on technicalities, as befitted their expertise. Also, the authority and stature of Senate would probably ensure that, once the Bill was passed by the Senate, debate in the House of Assembly would be brief and inhibited.

This tactic obviously depended on securing the Senate's approval. Verwoerd soon discovered that this was not automatic. The majority of Senators had no serious objections to the clauses of the Native Laws Amendment Bill which dealt with labour 'canalisation', and supported them without amendment. Nor did they object to the Bill's failure to specify whether the registration of work-seekers would be voluntary or compulsory. It was the Bill's amendments to section 10(1) of the Natives (Urban Areas) Act which met with a more critical response. Objecting to the clause as unduly harsh, UP Senators moved an amendment which would extend the right to live permanently in urban areas more widely to include the many thousands of Africans who, although born in rural areas, had lived in urban areas sufficiently long to have become urbanised. Periods

---

[19] Ibid., col. 428.

of three or five years were suggested as appropriate yardsticks of urbanisation.[20]

This call was all the more forceful for the support it received in other prominent quarters. One of these was the Association of Administrators of Non-European Affairs, which had long since maintained regular and influential contact with the NAD. In its submission to the Fagan Commission, the Association had declared that Africans permitted to live in an urban area should be limited to 'persons born in an urban area or persons who can clearly establish their intention of making the urban area their permanent home'.[21] The previous chapter identified the NAD's lack of expertise and experience in township administration, which gave municipal administrators considerable leverage in the formulation of the NAD's urban policies. This influence was enhanced by the fact that these policies could not have been implemented without municipal co-operation. The extent of the NAD's authority over the local authorities in matters of 'urban Native administration' had been ambiguous ever since the Act of Union ruled on the matter in 1909. One section of the Act gave local authorities control over municipal affairs, while another section gave the central government control over African affairs.[22] At SABRA's suggestion,[23] Verwoerd took steps to increase the degree of departmental control, such as requiring the managers of municipal NEADs to hold a licence from the Minister of Native Affairs which could be revoked if departmental policy was flouted. But the NAD had neither the strength nor the resources for a major confrontation with the local authorities, who remained the principal agents of departmental policy in the urban areas. As far as influx control was concerned, this meant that municipal administrators would have to apply and enforce the terms of the proposed section 10(1). Also, municipal officers would staff the labour bureaux situated in the towns (local labour bureaux) and thus control the issue of work-seekers' permits.

The LABC, too, urged Verwoerd to confer urban residential

---

[20] *Senate Debates* (1951), vol. 111, cols. 4189, 4191.

[21] BCC BMR 14/1/30, 'Minutes of Special Meeting of Association of Reef Managers of Non-European Affairs . . . on 12 December 1945', p. 3.

[22] E. Hellman, 'Urban Areas', in E. Hellman (ed.), *Handbook on Race Relations* (Cape Town, 1949), p. 232.

[23] SABRA, *Die Naturellevraagstuk: Referate Gelewer op die Eerste Jaarvergadering van SABRA* (Stellenbosch, 1950), p. 108.

rights more generously, to include those who had settled permanently in the cities.[24] A deputation from the LABC which met Verwoerd in April 1951 complained that 'the exemption from the operation of this Act [the Native Laws Amendment Act] which referred only to those who were born and resident in the urban area would make thousands of urban Africans homeless'.[25] Securing the (limited) support of the LABC by making some concession to their demands offered Verwoerd a means of retaliating to the repeated criticism from the Opposition parties in parliament that the Native Laws Amendment Bill had been drafted without consulting the African community.

Finally, the largely English-speaking organisations representing commercial and industrial interests—the FCI and ASSOCOM—generally favoured a more open policy on African urbanisation as a means of promoting the 'stabilisation' of the urban African workforce, although they did not react specifically to the terms of the proposed section 10(1). The urbanisation process ought to be fostered rather than hindered, argued the FCI and ASSOCOM, since 'migrant Natives are not as productive as permanent workers'.[26] They urged, too, that 'detribalised' Africans who, although born in rural areas, had settled permanently in urban areas and abandoned their 'tribal' ties should be accepted by the state as permanent and fully urbanised city-dwellers. The FCI, for example, prepared a memorandum on 'The Native in Industry' in January 1951, which recommended that 'recognition should be given to the fact that, in order to gain the maximum productivity of the Native, a stable Native force is required and that facilities should be created to give that stability to the detribalised urban Native'.[27]

Facing strong pressure to ease the conditions for residential rights, and anxious to get the support of the Senate with minimum controversy and delay, Verwoerd informed the Senate that he would modify section 10(1), but with a considerably less generous yardstick of 'urbanisation' than had been suggested by UP Senators. A further sub-clause, section 10(1)(b), was added, which allowed that Africans who had been employed in the same proclaimed area by

---

[24] *Senate Debates* (1951), vol. 111, col. 4194.
[25] UNISA Champion Papers 18.3.1 LABC, 'Report on Deputation to Minister of Native Affairs', 28 Sept. 1951.
[26] FCI NEAF, 'The Native in Industry' (1951), p. 1.
[27] Ibid. 4.

one employer for a minimum of ten years, or by several employers
for not less than fifteen years, could join the ranks of the 'urbanised',
permitted to live in that area without further permission. As Verwoerd observed when defending this amendment in the House of
Assembly,

of whom can one say, fundamentally: 'We are not going to interfere with
you. We regard you as Natives of the city'? Surely they are those who were
born there and reside there permanently, and who have their families with
them. They are, secondly, those who are such good workers that they have
stayed for a long time with one employer, and they are, thirdly, those who
have been a long time in the city, although with different employers. *All
these people are urbanised.*[28]

The Senate accepted Verwoerd's amendment, but then challenged the Native Laws Amendment Bill's provisions dealing with
African women. Senators were unperturbed that the Bill reneged on
Jansen's earlier promise, and subjected women to the full gamut of
influx control restrictions. But objections were raised to the fact that
the Bill denied rural-born wives the automatic right to join their
husbands living in urban areas. The Native Laws Amendment Bill
had not addressed the issue directly, thereby leaving intact the
existing provision that a woman could join her husband provided he
had been employed in the urban area for at least two years. An
amendment was moved in the Senate to scrap the two-year restriction. But it failed to receive a majority vote. It was only towards the
end of the Bill's passage through the House of Assembly that section
10(1) was amended to confer residential rights on the wives and
dependent children under the age of 18 of men living and working
permanently in the cities. Again an important concession was made
partly as a trade-off against getting the Bill through parliament
before the pending election.

The final version of section 10(1) thus conferred residential rights
on three categories of Africans, as follows:

10(1) No Native shall remain for more than seventy-two hours in an urban
area or in a proclaimed area . . . unless
  (a) he was born and permanently resides in such area; or
  (b) he has worked continuously in such area for one employer for a
      period of not less than ten years or has lawfully resided in such area

---

[28] *HAD* (1952), vol. 77, col. 1310 (author's italics).

for a period of not less than fifteen years, and has thereafter continued to reside in such area and is not employed outside such area and has not during either period or thereafter been sentenced to a fine exceeding fifty pounds or to imprisonment for a period exceeding six months; or

(c)  such native is the wife, unmarried daughter or son under the age at which he would become liable for the payment of general tax under the Native Taxation and Development Act, 1925, of any native mentioned in paragraph (a) or (b) of this sub-section, and ordinarily resides with that native;

Section 10(1)(d) then went on to specify that Africans who were not eligible for residential rights in terms of the three sub-clauses above could not stay in an urban area longer than seventy-two hours unless they had registered as work-seekers with the local labour bureau or had permission from the local authority to remain there.

The Native Laws Amendment Bill was finally passed by the House of Assembly in 1952, along with the misnamed Abolition of Passes and Documents Act, which required all Union-born Africans, male and female, to carry a reference book authorising them to live and work in a specified proclaimed or non-proclaimed area. (Foreign Africans living in South Africa had to carry identity documents.) Later the same year the NAD also issued the 'Labour Bureaux Regulations', a series of administrative instructions governing the creation of labour bureaux, the institution of the ULPP, and associated procedures. This armoury of influx control legislation was complemented, too, by the 1950 Group Areas Act, which restricted Africans living in allegedly 'white' areas to segregated residential areas, and the 1951 Prevention of Illegal Squatting Act, which prohibited Africans from squatting on land beyond municipal jurisdiction.

In what ways did the influx control policy established by this legislation accord with, or deviate from, the NAD's original intentions? The remainder of this chapter considers the relationship between the 1952 influx control legislation, and each of the twin prongs of the NAD's influx control strategy—the labour 'canalisation' programme and the plan to curb African urbanisation—in turn. In each case, it is shown that the political powers of various capitalist interests, African resistance, and white parliamentary opposition to the NP played major roles in determining the extent to which the NAD's objectives gained the status of law.

## Implications for the Labour 'Canalisation' Plan

With the promulgation of the 1952 Native Laws Amendment Act, the NAD's policy-makers succeeded in swiftly placing their strategy for labour 'canalisation' on to the statute book largely as planned. The Act authorised the creation of a pyramidal system of 'local', 'district', and 'regional' labour bureaux. At the base of the pyramid, local labour bureaux would be instituted in all proclaimed areas. Staffed by municipal officers, the local labour bureaux would control the placement of registered African work-seekers in vacancies registered with the bureaux by white employers. The crucial issue, of whether the registration of African work-seekers would be voluntary or compulsory, was ultimately settled the way the NAD had originally intended: all work-seekers were required to register, so that the local labour bureaux would have the information and control necessary to ensure that migrant workers were not taken on until surpluses of local labour had been used up. When additional migrant labour was needed, authorisation was required from the nearest district labour bureau, headed by a Native Affairs Commissioner, before the local labour bureau could issue the necessary work-seekers' permits. The Native Affairs Commissioners were in turn answerable to the chief Commissioner running the regional labour bureaux. Officers of the NAD, rather than local authorities, would exercise overriding power over the allocation of African labour to the cities. The Native Laws Amendment Act, then, created the legal avenues necessary for the central state to exercise an unprecedented degree of control over the distribution of African labour between urban and rural areas.

The 1952 Native Laws Amendment Act also gave the NAD unprecedented powers to prohibit any further employment of foreign Africans in the urban areas. Local authorities were denied any say in the matter. Requests by urban industrialists for foreign labour would be dealt with directly by the NAD.

The fact that the NAD's labour 'canalisation' plan became law without modification depended to a large extent on the NAD having received tacit or active support from much of the agricultural, mining, industrial, and commercial sectors. The strong backing from agricultural capital for the Native Laws Amendment Bill is unsurprising, given the prominent role played by the SAAU in the formulation of the Bill. Indeed, the Native Laws Amendment Bill demonstrated the NP's staunch commitment to addressing the needs of capitalist agriculture. However, the successful passage of the Bill's labour control plan did not depend on backing from agricultural capital alone. The political power and prominence of mining capital was sufficient to have ensured that its views and interests were always taken seriously by the government of the day. Had the mining industry voiced strong opposition to the proposed labour-bureaux system, the passage of the Native Laws Amendment Bill might well have been considerably less swift and smooth.

In fact, the mining industry had good reasons to support the NAD's labour strategy. As Verwoerd told parliament in 1952, mining industrialists were anxious to improve their supply of African labour: 'Not only does the mining industry need all the labour it can get today, but it needs 40% more. The industry only has 60% of the labour it needs.'[29] The labour bureaux system proposed by the Native Laws Amendment Bill did not address such problems directly: the system was designed such that urban labour 'surpluses' were first and foremost a solution to agricultural labour shortages. Indeed, the mining industry was specifically excluded from the scope of the labour bureaux system, a reflection of the dominance of the mining industry's own labour-recruiting organisations in the supply of African labour to the mines. Nevertheless, the interests of mining capital were indirectly well served:

the legislation gave employers in the mining sector a decided advantage over their competitors for labour in manufacturing industry. No obstacles were placed in the way of men in the reserves wishing to go to the mines; to get permission to go to work in a factory was far more difficult.[30]

The potential gains to the mining industry were especially pronounced in respect of foreign workers. Throughout its history the mining industry had depended heavily on African labour drawn from beyond the country's borders. By 1946 Mozambique, Botswana, Lesotho, and countries further north supplied 56.9 per cent of the African work-force on the mines.[31] However, increasing numbers of foreign workers had been heading for the cities, to take

[29] *HAD* (1952), vol. 77, col. 769.
[30] F. Wilson, *Labour in the South African Gold Mines, 1911–1969* (Cambridge, 1972), p. 81.
[31] Ibid. 70 (using figures from the Transvaal Chamber of Mines).

up better-paid jobs in manufacturing and commerce. According to the Tomlinson Commission, by 1951 there were approximately 215,000 foreign workers in secondary and tertiary industries, fast approaching the figure of 225,000 in mining.[32] The mining industry, therefore, had a strong vested interest in the singularly strict restrictions proposed by the Native Laws Amendment Bill on the employment of foreign Africans in the secondary industry and commerce.

Clearly, mining capital had no reason to oppose the NAD's plans; but Verwoerd took steps nevertheless to ensure support from the Transvaal Chamber of Mines (TCM). At some stage before 1953[33] Verwoerd sounded out the Chamber on the prospect of establishing rural African villages outside the reserves, as an additional source of mine labour. It was the new influx control legislation, he explained, which would make this strategy possible. As subsequent discussions between Verwoerd and the TCM revealed in 1953,

the Minister had in mind the classes of Natives who held no land in the reserves, or were without housing or useful employment in the urban areas. In respect of the latter, his general idea was that the operation of his new Urban Native Control Regulations would have the effect of forcing the Natives into the new rural villages which he proposed to establish. The villages would consist of freehold plots, but would not be large enough to allow the families to live by agriculture alone, and they would be obliged, therefore, to spend the greater part of their time working on farms or in factories or in the mines. The Minister's object, in approaching the Chamber, was to put forward his view that the Mining Industry, by assisting in his scheme, might be able to improve its supply of Native labour.[34]

The agricultural and mining sectors, then, were generally well satisfied with the NAD's labour 'canalisation' programme. Its advantages were less clear-cut, however, for organised commerce and industry. The ULPP threatened to eradicate the large urban labour surpluses which depressed wage levels, and limit employers' freedom to recruit migrant labour when it suited them. The fact that

---

[32] Union of SA, *Tomlinson Commission*, p. 39.

[33] Anglo-American Corporation, Industrial Relations Archive, 'Notes on 36th Meeting of Native Administration Committee (Orange Free State)... 26 August 1953', p. 8. It is clear from these minutes that the idea of rural villages was first mooted to the TCM before 1953, although no exact date is given.

[34] Ibid. 8.

neither the FCI nor ASSOCOM nor the AHI opposed the Native Laws Amendment Bill therefore warrants explanation.

The FCI took a stronger stand in favour of the principle of influx control than ASSOCOM. According to the FCI's 1951 memorandum on 'The Native in Industry', 'the movement of the Natives from rural to urban centres (should) . . . be regulated and controlled'.[35] The FCI recognised, too, that 'the institution of an organised network of labour bureaux'[36] was the appropriate vehicle of influx control. ASSOCOM, on the other hand, expressed its view on influx control in the words of Report no. 13 of the Social and Economic Planning Council:

the townward movement which has characterised all racial groups, but which is now becoming particularly marked among the Natives, is . . . a natural response to economic pressure. From an economic point of view it is generally to be welcomed, since it usually implies a movement of labour to much more productive employment and hence an increase in the national income. The movement must, of course, give rise to severe social stresses. But . . . it would be wrong to try to eliminate these stresses by the futile attempt to stem the townward drift. Rather should the adjustment to the urban environment be assisted by positive measures such as the provision of adequate housing facilities and social services.[37]

In ASSOCOM's view, therefore, 'in general, it is submitted, this migration of Natives to the cities should be allowed to continue'.[38] A labour bureaux system should simply provide 'guidance' to Africans in search of employment in the cities; it should not forcibly control their movements.[39]

The FCI and ASSOCOM were unanimous in their condemnation of economically 'artificial steps to prohibit the migration of Natives to the European areas of the country'.[40] For, as the Fagan Commission had explained, 'in estimating labour requirements one has to remember that, where there is great industrial activity, it is also necessary that there should always be a substantial reserve of labour—people who are ready to step in when others fall out or

[35] FCI NEAF, 'The Native in Industry', p. 5.
[36] Ibid. 5.
[37] ASSOCOM NEAF, 'Memorandum for Submission to Planning Commission on Socio-Economic Development of Native Areas within . . . South Africa' (1952), p. 7.
[38] *Commercial Opinion*, Apr. 1952, p. 455.
[39] Ibid.
[40] Ibid. 457.

when there is increased activity in some industry; and there are many industries that are constantly contracting and expanding for seasonal and other reasons'.[41]

NAD policy-makers were committed to maintaining an adequate supply of African labour to the cities. But, in their eyes, this did not require a large urban labour reservoir. Indeed, in defending the Native Laws Amendment Bill in parliament, Verwoerd declared war on the 'large'[42] surpluses of African labour in the urban areas, associated with the high labour turnover in industry and commerce. In response to the criticism that the Bill 'was too strict and that it was impossible not to have a labour reservoir where there was an industry',[43] Verwoerd replied,

> it is not the duty of the state to supply a labour surplus. The duty of the state is to try to ensure that every person can find a proper sphere of employment . . . In the ordinary course of circumstances there will be a certain small margin of available labour, but it must not be expected that plussage can be large.[44]

ASSOCOM and the FCI were, therefore, initially anxious that the NAD's labour 'canalisation' plans levelled a serious threat to the profitability of urban industry and commerce. In January 1951 the FCI called for a national conference, to provide a forum for commerce and industry to discuss 'the social and economic aspects of the Native issue' with the Ministers of Economic and Native Affairs.[45] Rejecting the idea of a national conference, Verwoerd agreed to a closed meeting with representatives of ASSOCOM and the FCI on 11 May 1951. Here, Verwoerd succeeded in allaying ASSOCOM's and the FCI's fears about the economic dangers of the NAD's labour strategy, by stressing that 'the implementation of Apartheid had to take into account economic realities'. 'The overriding consideration', he declared, 'was that the Government could go no further than what was practicable in the light of [the country's] development.'[46]

[41] Union of SA, *Fagan Commission*, p. 18.

[42] *HAD* (1952), vol. 77, col. 1315.

[43] Ibid., col. 1314.

[44] Ibid., cols. 1314–15.

[45] FCI NEAF, Director of Executive Council to Constituent Members, re 'The Native in Industry', 8 Jan. 1951.

[46] ASSOCOM NEAF, 'Precis of Discussion with Minister of Native Affairs . . . 11 May 1951', 29 May 1951, pp. 2–3.

Reassured by Verwoerd's pragmatic response to their queries, the FCI and ASSOCOM then took tactical decisions not to challenge the NAD on policy matters, and to direct their energies instead towards ensuring that departmental policy was sufficiently flexibly applied. As the FCI Parliamentary Secretary explained in a letter to the ASSOCOM President about the 1951 meeting,

if [Verwoerd's] . . . words are to be interpreted in a manner which industry regards as 'practicable', we probably will have nothing further to say. In other words, I do not think that the Chamber will interest itself overmuch in the theoretical implications of the so-called broad policy, but rather that we will concentrate our efforts on seeing that the policy will be pursued in a 'practical' manner.[47]

The FCI's response to the Native Laws Amendment Bill followed this strategy exactly. As the secretary of the FCI's parliamentary committee explained, the FCI agreed to support the Bill on the strength of the NAD's undertaking to implement it in a loose, 'practical' way: 'It was only when the Department indicated its intention to maintain a floating Native reserve from which various industries would draw according to their requirements that the parliamentary committee . . . agreed to let the Bill pass without any objection.'[48]

The decision by organised commerce and industry to opt largely for a 'politics of concession' also derived from the political culture of the day, which decried the open politicisation of business, particularly when predominantly English-speaking and substantially pro-UP.[49] The NAD did not establish regular and formal links with the FCI and ASSOCOM, of the sort enjoyed by the SAAU Liaison Committee. A strong ideological taboo within the NP, against the 'political' interference by urban business people (but not farmers!), entrenched this distance between the NAD and the predominantly English-speaking FCI and ASSOCOM. 'Hoggenheimer' (an ideo-

---

[47] FCI NEAF, FCI Parl. Sec. to ASSOCOM Pres., re 'Native Policy', 30 May 1951.

[48] FCI NEAF, 'Extract from Minutes of Second Parliamentary Committee . . . 16 Feb. 1954', item. 12.

[49] For more detail on this point, see D. B. Posel, 'Interests, Conflict and Power: The Relationship between the State and Business in South Africa during the 1950s' (paper presented to conference of Association for Sociology in Southern Africa, 1985), pp. 21–4.

logical caricature of 'big' English-speaking capital) symbolised to Afrikaner nationalists the danger of an unhealthy subordination of the political process to the profit motive.

It is difficult to establish the role played by the Afrikaans chamber of commerce, the AHI. This testifies to the organisation's policy of keeping a low profile on political issues; its communication with the NAD was hidden behind closed doors. In the absence of further evidence, therefore, the fact that the NAD's labour 'canalisation' plans were successfully promulgated on the statute books can be interpreted as a sign of either approval or impotence on the part of the AHI in the matter. But it is more likely the former, since Verwoerd's reassurances to ASSOCOM and the FCI would have been applicable to the business community at large.

Another important source of support for the NAD's programme for controlling the allocation of African labour came from municipal administrators. As the Secretary for Native Affairs pointed out in a circular to local authorities, the 'Regulations for the Establishment, Management and Control of Native Labour Bureaux', drafted in conjunction with the Native Laws Amendment Bill, were 'drawn up in consultation with representatives of the Municipal Executive of South Africa'[50] and managers of the NEADs of some of the principal municipalities.[51] Particularly influential was the Association of Administrators of Non-European Affairs, which had come out firmly in favour of a national labour bureaux system, compulsory for all urban and rural employers and workers, to improve the distribution of African labour across the country.[52] Indeed, as the previous chapter explained, the Association's recommendations regarding labour bureaux had had a profound influence on the NAD's original policy proposals in this regard.

All in all, therefore, the rapid and smooth promulgation of the NAD's labour 'canalisation' plan reflected the existence of a hegemonic consensus within the white electorate at large about the need for an improved system of influx control based on the demand for labour in the cities. Indeed, in essence, the NAD's plan was

---

[50] The United Municipal Executive comprised representatives of the country's four provincial Municipal Executives.

[51] BCC BMR 14/1/30, SNA to Town Clerks, re 'Draft Regulations for . . . Labour Bureaux', 10 Sept. 1951, p. 1.

[52] BCC BMR 14/1/30, 'Minutes of Special Meeting of Administrators of Non-European Affairs . . . on 12 December 1946'.

profoundly similar to the recommendations concerning the distribution of African labour which had been made by the Fagan Commission and endorsed widely within the English-speaking population. For example, this Commission, too, had stressed the need for a nation-wide system of influx control, overseen by central government rather than local authorities. It had also called for the establishment of a national network of labour bureaux, as one of the principal vehicles of influx control.[53] The main differences between Fagan's proposals and the NAD's had centred, first, on whether the registration of work-seekers with labour bureaux should be compulsory or voluntary, and, secondly, on the size of the labour reservoir permitted to build up in the cities. However, the divisiveness of these issues was diminished by the fact that the NAD prevaricated over the first until the final stages of debate over the Native Laws Amendment Bill, and reassured the business community of its pragmatic approach in respect of the second.

Lastly, the swift and smooth promulgation of the NAD's labour bureaux proposals was also facilitated by the absence of popular African resistance focused specifically on this issue. Protests against the NAD's influx control legislation were directed principally against the general principle of influx control and its application to African women.

### Implications for the Proposed Urbanisation Freeze

The 1952 Native Laws Amendment Act, together with the Abolition of Passes and Documents Act, substantially extended the state's capacity to control the growth and composition of the urban African population. Section 10(1) narrowed the candidates for permanent urban residence to three groups, which excluded the many thousands of Africans who had long since settled clandestinely in urban areas. A large proportion of these people were women, struggling to survive by taking on part-time or casual work if full-time jobs were unavailable. Despite fierce protest, the Native Laws Amendment Act applied to African women and men alike. All illegal city-dwellers were threatened with the prospect of being 'endorsed out' of the proclaimed area to a life of even starker poverty in the

---

[53] Union of SA, *Fagan Commission*, p. 49.

reserves. Section 10(1) ensured, too, that only a fraction of legal township residents acquired the security of 10(1)(a), (b), or (c) status. Africans who had lived and worked in an urban area legally, but for less than ten years, faced expulsion once unemployed. The same prospect threatened those who had been legal city-dwellers for up to ten years but who had changed jobs during that time. Since the African labour turnover in industry at the time was extremely high,[54] the majority of legal workers would have had to wait a full fifteen years before earning the right to settle in urban areas on a permanent basis, accompanied by their families. The concessions contained in section 10(1)(b) and (c), both exacted by effective opposition to the original version of section 10(1), were certainly not generous. Still, they cannot be dismissed as wholly inconsequential. The final version of section 10(1) introduced two important loopholes into the official influx control policy of the 1950s, loopholes which seriously impeded the state's capacity to control African urbanisation in the ways it had originally intended.

First, the final version of section 10(1) compromised the NAD's plan to freeze further African urbanisation. Although this clause placed considerable obstacles in the way of further African urbanisation, it also left open two narrow, but significant, avenues whereby Africans born in rural areas could *legally* gain acceptance as 'urbanised' city-dwellers. In terms of section 10(1)(b), ten years' continuous service with one employer or fifteen years with several employers entitled a migrant worker to remain permanently in the proclaimed area without further permission, even if unemployed. And in terms of section 10(1)(c), an African woman living in a rural area who married a man with 'urbanised' section 10(1)(a) or (b) status could join him in the urban area. Their children would likewise gain the residential rights of permanent city-dwellers. Contrary to intention, then, section 10(1) licensed 'the phenomenon of continuous growth of the urban Bantu population . . . irrespective of whether or not the labour requirements of a particular urban area justifies such a large urban Bantu population'.[55]

---

[54] Studies of factories in East London and Cape Town in 1956 and 1957 showed average labour turnovers of 119 per cent p.a and 138 per cent p.a respectively (D. Hobart Houghton, 'Men of Two Worlds: Some Aspects of Migratory Labour in South Africa', *South African Journal of Economics*, 28/3 (1960), 184).

[55] M. C. Botha, 'Opening Address', in IANA, 'Proceedings of 1962 Annual Conference', p. 89.

Secondly, the final version of section 10 contradicted the logic of the ULPP, the pivot of the NAD's labour 'canalisation' programme. Intent on eliminating labour surpluses in the cities, the NAD looked to its ULPP to ensure that white employers made 'optimal economic use' of the urban African population before being permitted to recruit migrant workers from rural areas. Ironically, this ULPP was seen as working hand in hand with the allocation of residential rights to urbanised Africans. These rights would identify the Africans who, if unemployed, would be 'channelled' into employment ahead of rural work-seekers. The final version of section 10, which allocated these rights, thus lay at the heart of those Labour Bureaux Regulations which instituted the ULPP:

> unless a Native was born and is permanently resident in a urban area, or is otherwise legally entitled to remain in the area, the Native will not be allowed to register for or take employment in the area if there are unemployed work-seekers in the area who are legally entitled to be there.[56]

Yet, section 10(1)(a), (b), and (c) was simultaneously the principal obstacle in the way of the ULPP. Implicit in the ULPP was the thoroughly Stallardist assumption that Africans had no right to live in the cities except when ministering to white needs. The entire urban African population was thus regarded as a labour reservoir, at the disposal of white employers. Section 10(1)(a), (b), and (c), however, delineated three groups of Africans *whose presence in urban areas, whether employed or not,* was to be accepted, and indeed protected, by the state. In Verwoerd's words, the clause conferred 'guarantees, security, and stability'[57]—specifically, protection from removal if unemployed—to those acknowledged as 'urbanised'. Eiselen reiterated the point when addressing the Institute of Administrators of Non-European Affairs (IANA) in 1953: the category of 'surplus' Africans liable for removal from the cities, he pointed out, did not include those 'protected by section 10(1)(a) and (b)'.[58] Section 10(1)(a), (b), and (c), therefore, denied the labour bureaux the means to compel 'idle' members of the urbanised population into taking work. Yet the elimination of 'idleness' amongst urbanised

---

[56] FCI NEAF, Sec. to Members of Non-European Affairs Committee, re 'Industrial Native Labour in Urban Areas', 22 Dec. 1955, para. A(4).

[57] *HAD* (1952), vol. 77, col. 1311.

[58] IANA, 'Proceedings of 1953 Annual Conference', p. 22.

men, women, and youth was precisely what the ULPP was designed to achieve.

This contradiction in the legislation was in fact latent in the NAD's intended strategy from the start. The concept of residential rights for the urbanised undermined the basic premiss of the ULPP, that the urbanised population (men, women, and youth) could be located in employment at the behest of the state. However, the final version of section 10(1) promulgated in 1952, which enlarged the number of candidates for residential rights beyond the NAD's original intentions, magnified and thus underlined the contradiction.

The reasons why section 10(1) emerged in a form clearly at odds with the NAD's intentions has received little attention in the literature.[59] To explain the discrepancies between the original and final versions of section 10(1), this chapter has drawn attention to various power struggles which the NAD was not yet strong enough to win. Central among these was the NAD's response to vehement African opposition to the original influx control Bills, from moderate and more militant organisations alike. With the ANC and CPSA committed to anti-pass campaigns, Verwoerd refrained from exacerbating the opposition by alienating even moderate bodies such as the LABC. The power struggles within white electoral politics also had an important bearing on the final version of section 10. In the face of a widespread white consensus on the need for a more flexible policy on African urbanisation, Verwoerd could not afford to be wholly intransigent. As N. J. Olivier commented during a 1985 interview, before 1953 'Verwoerd wouldn't do things to estrange the voters, because it was still a toss-up between the UP and NP, and there was always the possibility of switching governments'.[60] The concessions made were the barest minimum needed to win support for the Native Laws Amendment Bill amongst the

---

[59] D. Hindson's thesis, 'The Pass System and the Formation of an Urban African Proletariat', contains a brief but unconvincing discussion of the introduction of section 10(1). Hindson argues that, in introducing and promulgating section 10(1), the state set out to provide a legal instrument for reproducing 'differentiated forms of labour power in the cities' (pp. 166–7) in line with employers' interests. This argument takes no account of the intended role of the ULPP as a means of overruling employers' preferences for migrant labour to do unskilled work (which accounted for a substantial proportion of the African work-force in the 1950s).

[60] Interview with N. J. Olivier, 7 July 1985.

majority of UP Senators, whose position would in turn influence UP thinking in the House of Assembly.

The impact of these contests and concessions shows, then, that the influx control policy of the 1950s, one of the pillars of the early Apartheid system, was not simply transcribed from an Afrikaner nationalist grand plan on to the statute books. Non-Afrikaner nationalist groupings, such as the larger municipal NEADs, played a direct role in fashioning the legislation. So, too, did the electoral pressures of the historical moment. Also, although fervent African opposition failed to bar the passage of the Native Laws Amendment Bill, it was partly responsible for the two concessions over the terms of section 10(1) of the Native (Urban Areas) Act, which flew in the face of the NP's intended influx control strategy.

# 5

# *The Practical Effects of Influx Control*

BY 1952 the state was legally entitled to exercise vast powers over African movement, residence, and employment. Africans required official permission both to travel and not to travel, to work and not to work. Permits were necessary for every journey from a non-proclaimed to a proclaimed area, and between proclaimed areas. The right to stay in one place also required official authorisation. Permits were required to look for jobs, to take jobs, and then to change jobs. Confident of its powers to exact compliance forcibly, the NAD had taken little account of the individual needs, preferences, and interests of Africans themselves. They were relegated to the status of blank counters on the drawing-board of NAD policy, to be moved around wholly at the behest of the state.

Putting this system of influx control into operation clearly required enormous bureaucratic resources. A range of permits had to be issued, renewed, or cancelled. (Verwoerd admitted in 1952 that the services of 950 clerks were required merely to issue the various influx control authorities with the necessary forms.)[1] The labour 'canalisation' programme depended upon the institution of a nation-wide network of labour bureaux, each requiring clerical and managerial staff. In addition, the enforcement of the influx control regulations necessitated an extensive police force. The amended section 10(1) of the Natives (Urban Areas) Act did not restrict Africans entering the urban areas; all Africans were allowed seventy-two hours in a proclaimed area without permission. The NAD's capacity to detect the many thousands of Africans who outstayed the seventy-two hours without permission depended entirely on ubiquitous policing.[2]

---

[1] H. J. Simons, 'Passes and Police', *Africa South*, 1/1 (1956), 53.
[2] Africans without section 10(1) permits were assumed to be guilty of contravening the 72-hour clause unless they could prove otherwise.

When Jansen took over as Minister of Native Affairs in 1948, the apparatuses of 'Native administration' were far too small to have undertaken the ambitious system of influx control envisaged by the architects of Apartheid. Native Affairs Commissioners administered all aspects of NAD policy in the rural areas, while urban Native administration was undertaken largely by the generally small, municipal NEADs.[3] This allowed for considerable regional variations at the administrative level. The municipal NEADs had had a particularly free hand. Unlike the Native Affairs Commissioners, who were departmental employees, municipal officers were employed by, and answerable to, elected town or city councils. This had allowed the party political orientation of these councils to exercise a major influence over municipal administration. After 1948, however, the NAD's policy-makers were intent on establishing a uniformly rigorous system of influx control country-wide, a goal which required the rapid expansion of the NAD's own administrative bureaucracy, as well as measures to bring municipalities firmly in line with NP thinking and NAD policy.

The NAD undertook both tasks zealously. During Jansen's first year of office, 308 new posts for whites were created, along with 230 new African posts, giving a total of 3,937.[4] The previously combined post of Chief Native Affairs Commissioner for the Witwatersrand and national Director of Labour was subdivided, and a new Sub-Department of Labour was instituted soon after 1952. Under its auspices a network of local and district labour bureaux was set up. By 1960 nearly 300 local (urban) labour bureaux and 280 district (rural) labour bureaux had been created.[5]

The NAD made a concerted effort to fill as many administrative posts as possible with NP supporters. Jansen made this intention plain in the House of Assembly in 1950, declaring that 'the officials of the [Native Affairs] department have of latter years been directed along a certain course, a liberal course . . . It is high time for new blood to come into the department.'[6]

---

[3] Until the late 1940s the NAD controlled the registration of service contracts. But in the late 1940s and early 1950s this power was transferred to the NEADs (see Ch. 2).

[4] NAD, 'Progress Report for . . . 1950', p. 2.

[5] Union of SA, *Report of the Bantu Affairs Commission for the Period 1 January 1957 to 31 December 1960*, UG 36/1961, p. 7.

[6] *HAD* (1950), vol. 71, col. 4757.

Particularly during the second half of the decade,[7] the Broederbond played a leading role in recruiting suitable candidates for posts at the top echelons of the NAD. According to N. J. Olivier, then himself a Broederbond member, the Broederbond extended its sphere of influence in the civil service either by placing its own members into prominent positions there, or by recruiting high-ranking civil servants into the organisation.[8] In this way, several municipal Managers of Non-European Affairs[9] and many of the more senior labour bureaux officials, for example, were or became Broederbond members.[10]

This process of expanding the bureaucracy by inserting NP supporters was hampered early on in the decade by a dearth of suitably qualified Afrikaner applicants for the jobs being opened up. Jansen declared that in 1950, relative to the number of bureaucrats needed to 'cope with expanding services', the NAD's 'staffing position . . . was strained'.[11] At the beginning of 1950 132 further posts were created, but '126 former posts were abolished, owing mostly to inability to find candidates to fill them within the stipulated six months'.[12] The problem was unsurprising considering the level of Afrikaner educational achievement in the first half of the decade. By 1955 only 16 per cent of Afrikaner pupils in standard 6 in the Transvaal went on to complete their secondary education. By 1960 this figure had risen to 29 per cent.[13] Nevertheless, by 1960 only 11 per cent of the total Afrikaner population had finished twelve years of education.[14] The shortage of Afrikaans-speaking matriculants probably did not affect staffing levels in the lower echelons of the bureaucracy. But candidates for the higher, more responsible positions required a matriculation certificate (i.e. twelve years of schooling), so that the expansion of the NAD bureaucracy during the course of the decade was partly bound up with the advance of Afrikaner secondary education.

---

[7] During the early 1950s the Broederbond was principally involved in the expansion of Afrikaner cultural activities (see Lazar, 'Conformity and Conflict').

[8] Interview with N. J. Olivier, 7 May 1985.

[9] Interview with W. J. P. Carr, 17 Apr. 1984.

[10] Interview with N. J. Olivier, 7 May 1985.

[11] NAD, 'Progress Report . . . for 1950', p. 2.

[12] Ibid. 2.

[13] The number of Afrikaner matriculants in the Transvaal was higher than in the other provinces.

[14] These calculations were made by John Lazar, using 1960 census figures.

The growth of the Native administration bureaucracy was accompanied by the increasing centralisation of control in the NAD, particularly in the latter half of the decade. Verwoerd instituted a departmental licence for all managers of municipal NEADs, which could be revoked if departmental policy was flouted. In at least one case—in Johannesburg in 1958—the NAD went further, and appointed a watchdog committee to check that the Johannesburg City Council's UP majority was not subverting the rigorous enforcement of influx control.[15] Municipal autonomy on specific policy matters was also eroded as the decade wore on, as Chapters 6 and 8 will show.

Putting the influx control regulations into practice depended not only on the expansion of the NAD's administrative resources, but also on the enlargement of the urban police force. Accordingly, the decade saw successive increases in the size and powers of the police presence in the 'white' areas of the cities and in the African townships (the latter including a municipal force as well as the South African police (SAP)). The size of the SAP rose from 14,743 in 1946 to 23,016 in 1955, which, 'allowing for the increase in population during that period, [entailed that] the number of police per 1,000 rose by almost exactly 25 per cent'.[16] From 1951 efforts were also made to place more African policemen in the townships. Between 1951 and 1953 the number of blacks (including Africans) employed by the SAP increased from nearly 8,000 to just under 11,000.[17] The powers and numbers of municipal police (employed by local authorities, rather than the SAP) expanded too. Legislation promulgated in 1955 (Act No. 56 of 1955) enabled more aggressive municipal policing, by giving municipal African constables powers of arrest without a warrant, within township boundaries.

How effectively did the NAD marshall these expanding administrative and policing resources, to apply and enforce the influx control laws? This chapter addresses the question in two parts. The first discusses the effects of influx control on the lives of Africans in the townships and beyond. The second part assesses the efficacy of the influx control system from the NAD's point of view, by comparing the degree of control achieved with the system's principal objectives.

[15] Interview with W. J. P. Carr, 23 Nov. 1984.
[16] C. F. Lucas, 'The Cost to Law and Order', *Africa South*, 2/4 (1958), 30.
[17] Horrell, *Non-European Policies*, p. 43.

## The Burdens of Influx Control

The expansion of the state's bureaucratic and policing powers during the 1950s weighed heavily on the lives of Africans. The application of the influx control regulations grew more rigorous and ruthless as the decade advanced. One index of this intensification was the rising number of convictions under the influx control laws in the courts, jumping from 164,324 in 1952 to 384,497 in 1962.[18] These figures entailed an average of 274,410 convictions per year, which, added up over the eleven years between 1952 and 1962, gives a total of 3,018,511 convictions. (In 1960, the population census recorded an urban African population of 3,443,950).[19] Many individuals would have received more than one conviction. The conviction statistics also include convictions incurred by those who were legally entitled to be in an urban area, but who had committed petty offences, such as failing to produce their reference book on demand. But, even so, by 1962 an enormous proportion of the urban African population had been caught by the courts in the net of the influx control laws.

While thousands of pass-law offenders were sent to prison, many more were 'endorsed out' of the urban areas altogether. By 1957 the Johannesburg NEAD, for example, had set up 'special mobile patrols . . . who are on constant duty in the African townships . . . to secure the apprehension and removal from this area of unauthorised Natives'.[20] Most other municipalities seem not to have gone to quite such lengths. Still, according to the NAD, between 1956 and 1963 at least 464,726 Africans were 'endorsed out' of twenty-three major towns[21] (although the larger proportion of these removals occurred between 1960 and 1963).[22] In the Western Cape the victims of this fate were mostly African women. According to unofficial estimates

---

[18] Hindson, 'The Pass System and the Formation of an Urban African Proletariat', p. 196.

[19] NAD, 'Verslag van die Interdepartmentele Kommittee insake Ledige en Nie-Werkende Bantoes in Stedelike Gebiede' (hereafter 'Botha Report') (1962), p. 44.

[20] W. J. P. Carr's Personal Papers, 'Commission of Inquiry into the Dube Riots 14–15 September 1957: Statement by W. J. P. Carr, Manager NEAD', 21 Jan. 1958.

[21] SAIRR, *Annual Survey of Race Relations in South Africa, 1964* (Johannesburg, 1964), p. 189.

[22] E.g. most of the 108,558 removals from Durban were accounted for by the 'clearance' of Cato Manor in the early 1960s.

by the SAIRR, 4,000 women were 'endorsed out' of the Cape Peninsula between January 1955 and July 1957 alone.[23] The NAD was also particularly aggressive in its attitude towards foreign Africans contravening the influx control regulations. According to the Minister of Labour, between 1948 and October 1959 no less than 800,000 foreigners had been deported,[24] an average of 71,000 per year during the eleven-year period.

Included in the number of Africans 'endorsed out' of the urban areas were pass-law offenders who had been dispatched to jobs on white farms by the district labour bureaux. In her important exposé in 1958 of the employment practices of white farmers in the Bethal district, Ruth First drew attention to the fact that

Africans arrested for petty contraventions[25] of pass laws . . . were being pressed to take farm work and promised that the charges against them would be dropped if they signed contracts with farmers . . . In the townships it was common knowledge that the labour bureaux of the Native Commissioners' courts and local pass offices were dragnets for farm labour, and in Alexandra Township every year, as the reaping season approached, the police raids for pass offenders became noticeably more frequent. Men trapped in the net of pass laws and fearful of being permanently endorsed out of the urban areas because they were unemployed . . . signed themselves away to farmers for six months in the hope that they would be allowed to re-enter the urban area after that period. Others signed because they thought they would be given labour in factories and then found themselves on lorries bound for the Eastern Transvaal. Still others put their fingers to documents and contracts they did not understand.[26]

First introduced in 1947 by the Native Commissioner's Court in Fordsburg, Transvaal,[27] this so-called 'scheme for the employment of petty offenders' became official national policy in 1954. A circular from the Secretary for Native Affairs to the authorities concerned outlined the substance and purpose of the scheme, revealing it to be essentially a system of forced labour.

---

[23] Cited in P. Ntantala, 'Widows of the Reserves', *Africa South*, 2/3 (1958), 13.

[24] A. Hepple, 'Unemployment by Race', *Africa South*, 4/2 (1960), 53. In order to make sense of these figures, in combination with the number of 'endorsements out' of 23 major towns between 1956 and 1963, it must be assumed that the latter refer to Union-born Africans only.

[25] The term 'petty contraventions' must be understood in the state's sense of the term which embraced all influx control offences.

[26] R. First, 'Bethal Case-Book', *Africa South*, 2/3 (1958), 20–1.

[27] A. Cook, *Akin to Slavery: Prison Labour in South Africa* (London, 1982), p. 14.

It is common knowledge that large numbers of Natives are daily being arrested and prosecuted for contraventions of a purely technical nature. These arrests cost the state large sums of money and serve no useful purpose. The Department of Justice, the South African Police and this Department [NAD] had therefore evolved a scheme, the object of which is to induce unemployed Natives now roaming about the streets in the various urban areas to accept employment outside such urban areas.

. . . The scheme has now been in operation in the larger centres for some time, and has been extended to urban areas throughout the Union.

Natives arrested by the police are merely detained and then removed under escort to the district labour bureau and handed over to the Employment Officer there.

Natives, who on account of their declining to accept employment are not released, are returned to the South African Police for prosecution.[28]

This 'operation involved thousands of people: over 3,000 men a year were sent to farms by the Fordsburg court alone'.[29] During 1949 38,000 petty offenders from the Witwatersrand had a similar fate.[30] Comprehensive national statistics for the number of pass-law offenders routed to farms in this way throughout the 1950s are not available. The NAD declared a figure of 92,843 Africans who had been placed by district labour bureaux into jobs on white farms in 1955.[31] But this includes Africans who were not participants in the petty-offenders scheme. Still, comparing this figure of 92,843 with the average of 274,410 pass-law convictions per year, it is clear that the number of pass-law offenders placed by the labour bureaux was considerably less than the number convicted in the courts. This trend was probably a reflection of the fact that many offenders who had seen through the petty-offenders scheme chose a prison sentence rather than a farm-labour contract.

The objective trends conveyed by all the statistics were reflected subjectively by African literature, journalism, and political manifestos of the day.[32] All testified to the ways in which the influx

[28] BCC BMR 14/1/69, Chief Native Affairs Commissioner (NAC), Witwatersrand, to Town Clerks (Reef), re 'Scheme for the Employment of Petty Offenders in Non-Prescribed areas', 26 Sept. 1955.

[29] Cook, *Akin to Slavery*, p. 14.

[30] F. Wilson, 'Farming 1866–1966', in M. Wilson and L. Thompson (eds.), *Oxford History of South Africa*, ii (Oxford, 1971), p. 149.

[31] M. Roberts, *African Farm Labour: Some Conclusions and Reflections* (Johannesburg, 1959), p. 124.

[32] See, e.g., B. Modisane, *Blame Me on History* ( Johannesburg, 1963; repr. 1986); H. Bloom, *Transvaal Episode* (Cape Town, 1956; repr. 1982); M. Dikobe, *The Marabi*

control system encroached on Africans' lives, as an instrument of the domination and discrimination intrinsic to their experience of Apartheid as a whole. These intrusions were multifarious and ubiquitous. The practice of influx control gave the structural subordination of African labour under Apartheid an immediacy in the daily experience of every African worker, legal or illegal. The Labour Bureaux Regulations made plain that the state regarded Africans as mere units of labour power at the disposal of white employers, with little right to choose if, where, and when they wanted to work. And the racism and violence which have pervaded the Apartheid system structured all the notorious routines of the influx control system: Africans having to wait in interminable queues for various permits, being bullied by impatient and abrasive officials, being manhandled and assaulted by police.

The harassment of Africans at the hands of the influx control authorities and the police was widely documented. For example, Dr A. B. Xuma, former leader of the ANC, told a government commission of inquiry in 1950 that 'flying squads, pick-up vans, troop-carriers, and mounted police are all abroad irritating and exasperating Africans by indiscriminately demanding passes, cause or no cause, often addressing and handling them in an insulting and humiliating manner'.[33]

As the implementation of influx control intensified during the decade, police methods grew more offensive still. Journalist D. Nokwe, for example, wrote of 'the humiliation of having to stop every few hours to produce these [pass] documents, the torture and cruelty of having to line up for hours in full view of the public, manacled, whilst the police waylay more victims'.[34] And reports of police brutality became commonplace.[35]

The influx control laws were wielded particularly ruthlessly against Africans suspected of political agitation. A circular from the Secretary for Native Affairs to Native Commissioners just after the 1952 Defiance Campaign specifically authorised this strategy.

*Dance* (London, 1973); also N. Mandela, *The Struggle is my Life* (London, 1978).
[33] UW Xuma Papers AD843/500301, A. B. Xuma, 'Evidence before Commission of Inquiry into Riots on [*sic*] Newlands, Krugersdorp, and Randfontein, 1 March 1950', p. 2.
[34] D. Nokwe, 'The South African Police: Laws and Powers', *Africa South*, 2/2 (1958), 18.
[35] See, e.g., H. Bloom, 'The South African Police', *Africa South*, 2/1 (1957), 10–12; Modisane, *Blame Me on History*, pp. 58–9.

As a result of recent disturbances in different towns [the circular read], the question was raised whether instigators of such disturbances should not be removed from urban areas . . . Natives whose presence in the area is for some or other reason regarded as undesirable should under no circumstances be permitted in terms of section 10 to reside there.[36]

The state also used the influx control regulations as a weapon of reprisal against whole communities in times of political malcontent. Early morning pass raids by the police were stepped up in the wake of protests or riots in the townships, and 'hundreds of Africans would be rounded up on infringements of the Pass regulations and other minor technicalities'.[37]

For Africans, the indignities of influx control cut across class or status differences. Governments before 1948 had issued so-called 'letters of exemption' from the influx control laws, to African men who were educated, affluent, or in positions of authority in their communities. But the Nationalists abandoned this practice. After 1952 influx control targeted all Africans on the grounds of their race, with no regard to their class. Indeed, the formulation of section 10(1) implicitly treated all Africans as guilty under the influx control laws until proven otherwise: the onus of proof that an African was legally entitled to remain in an urban area beyond the permissible seventy-two hours lay on the African. The police could therefore demand to see the reference book of any African at any time; and any one who failed to produce it, for whatever reason, was summarily arrested.

While the experience of influx control was not class-bound, it did vary, however, between men and women. Thanks to administrative concessions from the NAD after the passing of the 1952 Native Laws Amendment Act (discussed in Chapter 8), African women did not have to register as work-seekers until the following decade. Also, until the late 1950s the majority of African women were not compelled to apply for reference books. This allowed them a degree of freedom of movement denied to African men. Also, it was African men rather than women who were the principal targets of police pass raids and spot checks.

In addition to the burdens of influx control borne by the African population at large, the system incurred further economic and social

---

[36] BCC BMR 14/1/10, 'Extract from Minutes of Finance and General Purposes Meeting', 9 Mar. 1953.

[37] Modisane, *Blame Me on History*, p. 147.

costs for those who contravened the laws. First, the enforcement of the influx control laws exacerbated the widespread poverty within the townships and beyond. According to the SAIRR, in 1954 the minimum monthly subsistence budget for an African family of five was £23 10s. 4d. By 1956 this figure had risen to at least £26; but the average family income in the urban areas that year was £15 19s. 6d., leaving a monthly deficit of almost £10.[38] Pass-law offenders permitted to remain in the urban area (which was typical if theirs was a minor offence, such as not producing a reference book on demand) had the option of paying an admission of guilt fine, which was usually set at £2 or £3. For most families struggling to feed themselves, this sum was prohibitively high. The alternative was a prison sentence, as a result of which those in work probably lost their jobs. The self-employed, too, could ill-afford the loss of income while imprisoned. The routine of imprisonment for pass-law offences also scarred urban family life, removing fathers (and mothers, once these laws were imposed on women) from their children and burdening mothers and wives all the more heavily with sole financial and emotional responsibility for child care. The NAD frequently bemoaned the breakdown of parental discipline and family cohesion in the townships, and yet administered a pass system which imposed severe stresses on the urban African family.

Those who fell victim to the petty-offenders scheme, or who were 'endorsed out' of the proclaimed areas altogether, faced even bleaker prospects. However deprived life was for most in the townships during the 1950s, it was still far worse on the white farms or in the reserves. Between 1950 and 1952 the average farm wage went up by 12.5 per cent.[39] Still, by 1954, the average income of full-time male African farm-workers was £4 per month,[40] which was considerably lower than the average monthly wage of about £13 earned by industrial workers in the cities.[41] Even the Natal Agricultural Union conceded the serious financial predicament of African farm families. The Natal Agricultural Union's newsletter of August 1959 pointed out that the Department of Health estimated that £20 was the barest minimum necessary to clothe, feed, and house an African family of

[38] *Rand Daily Mail*, 23 July 1958.
[39] Horrell, *Non-European Policies*, p. 18.
[40] Cook, *Akin to Slavery*, p. 15.
[41] S. T. van der Horst, 'The Economic Implications of Political Democracy', *Optima* (1960), 27.

five; yet a survey of farm labour in the Eastern Cape had exposed an average monthly income of £9, in cash and kind (including accommodation), for a family of six.[42] The plight of farm-workers employed through the NAD's petty-offenders scheme was even more miserable: the NAD authorised wages of a meagre £3 10s. per month, for the duration of a ninety-day contract.[43]

Life for those 'endorsed out' to the reserves was similarly deprived. For the majority, the 1950s brought little, if any, alleviation of their economic difficulties. The Tomlinson Commission found that, by 1951, only a small and relatively prosperous sector of the peasantry in the reserves escaped the ravages of extreme poverty. An estimated 46.3 per cent of the income earned in the reserves was concentrated in the hands of 12.7 per cent of the population.[44] According to the Commission, 'the average family of slightly more than six persons, who has a stake in the land, earns £42 a year, £40 net' (i.e. after payment of tax).[45] The income of the growing number of landless families was lower still. Recognising the need to arrest the long-standing decline in living standards for the majority of reserve inhabitants, the report of the Tomlinson Commission in 1956 had recommended an ambitious and expensive programme of agricultural, industrial, and mining development in the reserves—at a cost of £104,000,000 for the first ten years of the scheme. But by the end of 1958 the government had allocated a mere £3,500,000 for reserve development,[46] having dismissed most of the Commission's recommendations. Thus, by the late 1950s only limited improvements in certain agricultural sectors and regions had been achieved. According to a 1959 report by the SAIRR on the progress of development in the reserves, 'useful development work is taking place in the reserves, but at a rate which one might term well-nigh infinitesimal in comparison with that advocated by the Tomlinson Commission'.[47]

After 1956 the NAD increased its investment in irrigation schemes, and undertook 'energetic programmes . . . for sugar production

---

[42] *NAUNLU* (official organ of the Natal Agricultural Union), Aug. 1959, p. 3.
[43] B. Turok, 'The African on the Farm', *Africa South*, 4/1 (1959), 29.
[44] Union of SA, *Tomlinson Commission*, p. 98.
[45] Ibid.
[46] SAIRR, 'The Economic Development of the Reserves: The Extent to which the Tomlinson Commission's Recommendations are being Implemented' (Fact Paper no. 3; 1959), p. 11.
[47] Ibid. 25.

(in the Umlazi, Imfune, Umnini and Umvoti reserves in Natal), fibre growing and afforestation (in Northern Zululand)'.[48] Also, soil-conservation work had 'been considerably speeded up since the Tomlinson Commission reported, and . . . Africans in the Reserves are taking a greater interest in these schemes'.[49] But, as the SAIRR pointed out, serious barriers on agricultural productivity remained intact. The government refused to change the existing system of one-man-one-plot (restricting a farmer to one small unit of land), or to arrange long- or short-term credit facilities for African farmers. The conservation work was 'still patchy, much depending on the interest and attitude of local officials'.[50] Furthermore, the dearth of any significant industrial or mining development in the reserves intensified the population pressure on the land. The Tomlinson Commission had recommended that, in order to relieve the prevailing congestion on the land, £30,000,000 should be allocated over ten years for the creation of 50,000 jobs in industry and commerce in the reserves. But by 1959 a mere '12 Africans [had] become employed in a small factory within the reserves and a few more in a sawmill, 967 further Africans [had] set up as general dealers and 5 more [had] engaged in other independent commercial activities'.[51] Agriculture remained the only realistic prospect of securing an income within the reserves; and typically its returns were still extremely limited. In most cases, then, Africans 'endorsed out' of urban areas to the reserves were dispatched to what P. Ntantala dubbed 'one monotonous song of droning flies, sick babies, dying stock, hunger, starvation, and death'.[52]

It was not only the Africans evicted from urban areas who suffered a drop in income and living standards. Nearly all African families in the reserves remained heavily dependent on the income of family members who became migrant workers. A 1954 survey by the NAD in the Willowvale area, for example, estimated that, of the £43 average annual income of a peasant family, £21 were earnings from migrant labour.[53] Economic pressures necessitated that virtually every able-bodied African male in the reserves became a migrant

---

[48] Ibid. 14.
[49] Ibid.
[50] Ibid.
[51] Ibid. 19.
[52] Ntantala, 'Widows of the Reserves', 13.
[53] G. Mbeki, *The Peasants' Revolt* (Harmondsworth, 1964), p. 70.

worker at some stage of his life.[54] This applied to increasing numbers of women too. Many more migrants left to seek work in the towns than had permission from the authorities. The NAD's growing powers to evict these illegal workers from the urban areas dealt a severe economic blow to their families in the reserves, by depriving them of nearly half their income.

In this way, then, the very enforcement of influx control intensified the economic pressures which prompted African work-seekers to leave the reserves for the towns in the first place. Yet, in the absence of serious efforts to improve economic conditions in the reserves, the NAD's strategy for coping with the growing illegal exodus from the reserves was to tighten the practice of influx control, and, with that, to exacerbate the original problem still further.

Violent and degrading, the system of influx control was clearly also economically debilitating and socially invasive. But did the operation of the system satisfy the NAD? The remainder of this chapter assesses the extent to which the implementation of influx control policy advanced the objectives underpinning the design of the policy.

### Comparing the Goals and Effects of Influx Control

The NAD's purpose in enforcing the gamut of influx control regulations was twofold, as we have seen. First, the influx control system was intended as a vehicle of labour 'canalisation', to effect an 'even distribution of Native labour'.[55] Secondly, the influx control system was also designed as an instrument of state control over the growth and composition of the urban African population, to keep the numbers of Africans migrating to the cities down to the economically indispensable minimum and prevent their settling there permanently. To what extent, then, did the imposition of influx control foster these twin objectives? The following discussion assesses in turn the extent to which each of these objectives was realised.

---

[54] Union of SA, *Tomlinson Commission*, p. 53.
[55] BCC BMR 14/1/30, SNA to Town Clerks, re 'Powers and Duties Regarding . . . Native Labour Bureaux', 17 Nov. 1952.

*Influx Control and Labour 'Canalisation'*

The principal aim of the NAD's labour redistribution strategy was to redistribute urban labour 'surpluses' to rural areas experiencing labour shortages, thus eliminating African unemployment in the urban areas and easing labour shortages on the white farms. The efficacy of the programme should, therefore, be evaluated on both the urban and rural ends.

There was no official statistical record of African unemployment during the 1950s. This makes an assessment of the extent to which the NAD succeeded in eliminating unemployment in the urban areas unavoidably impressionistic. Nevertheless, there were several pointers, emanating both from within and beyond the NAD, that urban African unemployment went up, not down, during the course of the 1950s. According to an ASSOCOM report on 'Incomes and Economic Growth in South Africa', there were at least 160,000 unemployed African males in the urban areas in 1958.[56] The years 1958–60 saw an economic recession, which pushed unemployment levels higher still. In his study of unemployment, A. Hepple claimed that, by July 1960, official unemployment figures had escalated 'to the highest level recorded for over twenty years'.[57] While these statistics did not include Africans, Hepple argued that unemployment rates amongst Africans would have risen similarly, because 'Africans occupy the jobs where labour turnover is highest and where permanency is rare'.[58]

The state's awareness of rising levels of African unemployment in the cities was evidenced by the appointment in 1962 of an inter-departmental committee, chaired by M. C. Botha (then Deputy Minister of Bantu Affairs) to investigate the extent of 'idleness and unemployment' amongst Africans in the urban areas. Dismissing the labour bureaux' records of the number of registered work-seekers in the cities without jobs as an inaccurate indication of urban African

[56] ASSOCOM NEAF, 'Incomes and Economic Growth in South Africa', 3 Oct. 1962. On the basis of the statistics provided in Table 4, Ch. 6, of the numbers of African men in the urban work-force by 1959/60, even 160,000 unemployed (an underestimate since unemployment levels increased between 1958 and 1960) entailed an unemployment rate of at least 23 per cent. It must be stressed, however, that such calculations are an extremely imprecise and unreliable estimate, given the problems associated with the compilation of Table 4 (as explained in note to Table 4).

[57] Hepple, 'Unemployment By Race', p. 48.

[58] Ibid.

unemployment, this committee produced its own calculation of the extent of the problem.[59] The report of the Botha committee claimed that, by 1960, 452,000 Union-born African males over the age of 15 were unemployed within the country at large. This figure was upped to 500,000 to include Union-born African women.[60] The Botha Report then argued that 200,000 of the unemployed male Africans over the age of 15 were located in the urban areas.[61] However, the Report found it impossible to estimate the extent of urban unemployment amongst African women.[62]

Amongst township youths, unemployment remained particularly high throughout the course of the decade. The alarming level of urban unemployment amongst African youth in the early 1950s, particularly in Reef towns,[63] was one of the problems which the NAD's labour 'canalisation' strategy had been designed to solve and exploit. From the NAD's point of view, had better use been made of the labour power of urban youths who had left school, the need for additional migrant labour in urban areas would have dropped. But the NAD achieved little success on this front. Research on 'juvenile delinquency' presented to the 1957 annual conference of the IANA by one of its members concluded that 'it can . . . definitely be stated that by far the greater majority of youths in the locations under the age of 20 years who do not attend school, are still unemployed'.[64]

The persistence of high levels of urban unemployment was closely linked to the failure of the ULPP. The NAD was unable to restructure the urban labour market in line with its policy dictates, so that urban labour 'surpluses' (in the NAD's sense of the term) continued to grow through times of economic recession and growth. The ULPP was designed as part of the state's solution to the problem of urban unemployment: as long as the resident labour supply in a given urban area was not fully utilised, the importation of further

---

[59] These figures were derived by subtracting the number of economically active Union-born Africans (2,180,000) from 'the Bantu labour potential' (2,632,000). The latter represented 94 per cent of the total African male population over the age of 15, the assumption having been made that 6 per cent of this population was not suitable for work.

[60] NAD, 'Botha Report', pp. 7–8.

[61] Ibid. 117.

[62] Ibid. 47.

[63] P. Bonner, 'Family, Crime and Political Consciousness on the East Rand, 1939–55', *JSAS* 14/3 (1988), 11.

[64] IANA, 'Proceedings of 1957 Annual Conference', p. 128.

migrant labour into the area would be prohibited. The urban unemployed would be placed in all available employment ahead of
migrants. In theory, therefore, the rate of importation of migrant
labour into the area ought to have followed the ebbs and flows of its
particular business cycle, declining in times of limited expansion and
rising again with the rate of growth of the work-force. The practice,
however, was markedly different. The ULPP failed to place the
urban unemployed at the head of the job queue. So, irrespective of
the particular economic pulse of the urban area in question,[65] the
numbers of migrant workers permitted into it continued to climb.
During the mid-1950s, at a time when industrial output was beginning to decline,[66] municipal administrators admitted the persistent
'under-utilisation' of the urbanised labour reservoir; yet the FCI
noted that the 'percentage of migratory workers . . . is increasing
annually'.[67] The Johannesburg NEAD registered these dual trends
by reporting an increase in the number of work-seekers holding
section 10(1)(d) permits 'despite the fact that there is an ever-
growing surplus of 10(1)(a), (b), (c) labour'.[68] By the end of the
decade, the trend was unchanged. The Botha Report of 1962 recognised that the NAD was still confronted by the very syndrome which
the ULPP had been designed to correct: 'the anomaly exists, that
work-seekers from outside the urban areas are admitted in, despite
the fact that there is already a surplus in the towns'.[69]

Persistent urban African unemployment was thus made worse for
the NAD by the fact that it coexisted with the expansion of the
migrant work-force. This was a symptom of exactly the 'maldistribution' of the African labour supply which the NAD's labour 'canalisation' policy had set out to correct.

Influx control failed to rectify what the NAD saw as the

[65] This is not to say that the business cycle had no effect on the growth of the
migrant work-force; the point is rather that resistance to the ULPP was not overruled
during periods of contraction.

[66] After a growth of 7.2 per cent in 1954, the increase in industrial output dropped
to 4.4 per cent in 1955. By 1957 it had fallen to 2.3 per cent (D. Innes, *Anglo American
and the Rise of Modern South Africa* (Johannesburg, 1984), p. 173). Note, however,
that during this period the expansion of labour-intensive industries was proportionately greater than those which were more highly mechanised.

[67] FCI NEAF, 'Native Labour Problems of the Urban Areas Act', 1956, p. 3.

[68] West Rand Administration Board Archives (hereafter WRAB), Johannesburg
Municipal Records (hereafter JMR), A78/1, 'Minutes of 832nd Ordinary Meeting of
Non-European Affairs and Housing Committees', 30 Aug. 1955, p. 743.

[69] NAD, 'Botha Report', p. 4.

'maldistribution' of African labour in another respect too. Surpluses of urbanised labour often coexisted with shortages of labour in certain job categories, within the same town. These labour shortages were twofold. First, organised commerce and industry complained of shortages of skilled labour, caused by the state's policy of restricting Africans' access to skilled jobs.[70] In practice, many employers had the go-ahead from the state to promote African workers covertly into skilled positions by reclassifying the jobs as semi-skilled.[71] But, according to the FCI, the ideological and political barriers deterring employers from opening skilled jobs more fully to Africans remained overwhelming. The FCI told the Viljoen Commission in 1958, that

the Chamber considers that one of the most serious impediments to the expansion of industry which exists today is the confusion and uncertainty which surrounds the present and future utilisation of non-Europeans in factory employment . . . Over all industries there hangs the threat that Section 77 of the Industrial Conciliation Act[72] may be applied in order to impose a predetermined labour structure on them along racial lines, regardless of the consequences to the employees and the economic operation of the industries concerned.[73]

So, despite a large reservoir of unemployed Africans in the townships, secondary industry was beset by a mounting shortage of skilled labour.

This anomaly manifested one of the internal tensions within the design of the Apartheid system as a whole. On the one hand, the NAD's labour redistribution policy was formulated with an eye to boosting the productivity of African labour and reducing labour turnover, in line with what Eiselen had called 'a different conception of Native labour' (see Chapter 3). By restricting employers' access to migrant labour, the NAD hoped to force them to pay more attention to training and 'stabilising' their African work-forces.[74] A more

---

[70] ASSOCOM NEAF, 'Notes on Official Statements of Policy', 8 May 1951, p. 3.

[71] ASSOCOM NEAF, 'Notes on . . . Interview with Minister of Labour on 22 November 1950 . . . ' (n.d.), p. 2.

[72] The Industrial Conciliation Act, no. 28 of 1956, made provision for the restriction of certain types of work for persons of particular racial groups.

[73] FCI NEAF, untitled extract from FCI's evidence to Viljoen Commission, 1958, pp. 16–17.

[74] See, e.g., Eiselen, 'Plan to Rationalise South Africa's Native Labour', pp. 5, 10.

skilled and productive urban African work-force was highly desirable to the NAD, since it would have reduced the labour turnover and hence the number of African workers needed in the cities. Yet, as the FCI's evidence to the Viljoen Commission (cited above) showed, other facets of the state's labour policies gave employers a conflicting message. Uncertainty amongst employers about the state's attitude to Africans' advance into skilled positions was one of several disincentives against following the NAD's call for a 'different conception of labour'. The state's discriminatory employment policy worked against exactly the labour 'stabilisation' which the NAD hoped the ULPP would encourage.

The second sort of labour shortage occurred at the opposite end of the job spectrum, amongst the worst paid and most arduous unskilled jobs which were notoriously unpopular among migrant and urbanised work-seekers alike. Labour shortages in these jobs (such as domestic service, and heavy manual labour in the engineering and metal industries, stone quarries, and brickfields) were a recurrent feature of urban African employment throughout the decade, and the focus of mounting complaints from white householders, as well as from organised commerce and industry. A shortage of domestic servants reported by the Johannesburg NEAD in 1950 was a common and pervasive trend in many towns.[75] By 1955 the NAD had acknowledged the existence of 'acute' labour shortages in the heavy metal and engineering industries,[76] and had allowed certain relaxations of the ULPP in an effort to ameliorate the problem (see Chapter 6). However, complaints from the FCI suggest that these shortages continued to worsen. In a letter to Eiselen in 1956, the FCI admitted the absence of any major overall labour shortage in secondary industry, but also drew attention to growing shortages in certain heavy metal job categories, as well as more widespread seasonal labour shortages.[77] Many factories which retrenched their African workers during slack periods, being seasonal in nature, had difficulty in recovering their full complement of labour during peak periods.

[75] IANA, 'Proceedings of 1953 Annual Conference', p. 91; IANA, 'Proceedings of 1957 Annual Conference', p. 197.
[76] BCC BMR 14/1/25, SNA to Chief NAC, Johannesburg, re 'Employment of Ex-Mine Natives as Domestic Servants', 16 July 1955.
[77] FCI NEAF, Non-European Affairs Sec. to SNA, re 'Native Labour', 28 Aug. 1956.

The extent of such shortages of unskilled labour varied between regions. Whereas the Northern Transvaal Chamber of Industries issued no such complaint, the problem was a cause of concern in the Western Cape, for example. But it was on the Witwatersrand in particular that unskilled labour shortages were most widely reported. By 1957 the problem on the Witwatersrand loomed large enough to have prompted a meeting between the NAD, the Transvaal Chamber of Industries, and the Johannesburg NEAD, followed by a series of four meetings within a month between the Transvaal Chamber of Industries and the Johannesburg NEAD.

The rural effects of the labour bureaux system were mixed, partly a function of the changing, and varying, labour needs of white commercial agriculture during the 1950s. These in turn reflected conspicuous processes of restructuring and reorganisation within the agricultural sector. After 1950 the number of white farm units began to decline, falling from 116,848 in 1950 to 105,859 in 1960.[78] At the same time, the total area devoted to commercial agriculture rose, from 101,480,108 morgen in 1950 to 107,165,190 morgen in 1960.[79] The dominant tendency, therefore, was one of land concentration and farm-unit consolidation. But a parallel, albeit a lesser, tendency was simultaneously gathering pace. At the other end of the spectrum, smaller farm units were being further fragmented and subdivided. In 1950 72,014 farm units, representing 61.6 per cent of the total number of holdings, comprised 500 morgen or less. By 1960 the number in this category had dropped to 58.7 per cent of the total number of holdings, but the average size of each holding had dropped from 165.23 morgen in 1950 to 149.63 morgen in 1960.[80] Such farming operations were often unprofitable. The 1959/60 'Commission of Inquiry into European Occupancy of Rural Areas' was disturbed at the increasing number of uneconomic farms using inefficient and outdated farming methods, as much as 70 per cent of farms in some areas.[81]

On the larger, more productive, commercial farms, important steps in the rationalisation of production were being taken. One of these was advancing mechanisation, indicated in part by the

[78] Marcus, *Restructuring in Commercial Agriculture*, p. 4.
[79] Lazar, 'Conformity and Conflict', p. 101.
[80] Ibid. 102–3.
[81] Ibid.

dramatic growth in the number of tractors used.[82] The overall figure of 48,423 tractors in use in 1950 shot up to 122,218 by 1961.[83] The number of wheat and maize combines also increased, from 5,304 in 1950 to 10,223 in 1960.[84] But mechanisation was uneven, varying in different areas and according to the type of farming. Generally, mechanisation proceeded more rapidly in pastoral than in arable farming.[85] Significant variations occurred within each type of farming, too. For example, by the end of the 1950s wheat-farming was highly mechanised; but the same could not be said for maize. M. de Klerk's study of farming in the Western Transvaal showed that, by 1968, only '25–30% of the area planted with maize was being harvested by combine'.[86]

The effects of these developments on farmers' labour needs were similarly varied, depending on the type of farming, region, and degree of mechanisation. But a few overall trends could be discerned. The first was an increase in the absolute size of the agricultural work-force (see Table 2) accompanying the extension of the scale of production, particularly arable cultivation. (The volume of agricultural output increased by more than 50 per cent between 1948 and 1960.)[87] The second was a rise in the ratio of seasonal/casual farm labourers to full-time workers,[88] although this trend was itself more pronounced in arable production.[89] In other words, although the demand for farm labour grew all-round, the proportionately greatest increase was in the need for seasonal or casual labour.

---

[82] As Marcus points out, mechanisation is not simply equivalent to 'tractorisation'. Mechanisation should be understood as the application of mechanical power in general—a broad definition which 'not only encompasses tractive power, including tractors, but which is also able to include machine-based technology such as milking machines, sprinkler irrigation, micro- and macro-jet spray technology, etc.' (Marcus, *Restructuring in Commercial Agriculture*, p. 13).

[83] Lazar, 'Conformity and Conflict', p. 100.

[84] Ibid. 101.

[85] D. Budlender, 'Mechanisation and Labour on White Farms: A Statistical Analysis' (Carnegie Conference Paper no. 26, Univ. of Cape Town, 1984), p. 18.

[86] M. de Klerk, 'Seasons that will never Return: The Impact of Farm Mechanization on Employment, Incomes, and Population Distribution in the Western Transvaal', *JSAS* 11/1 (1984), 88.

[87] Lazar, 'Conformity and Conflict', p. 100.

[88] C. Simkins, 'African Population, Employment, and Incomes on Farms outside the Reserves, 1923–1969' (Carnegie Conference Paper no. 25; Univ. of Cape Town (1984)), p. 8.

[89] Marcus, *Restructuring in Commercial Agriculture*, p. 63.

Thirdly, the advance of mechanisation generated a growing demand for more semi-skilled farm-workers who were permanently settled, full-time workers, rather than labour tenants working for a portion of the year. This led the SAAU, reflecting the interests of the larger, more highly capitalised farming operations, to call for the abolition of labour tenancy, so as increasingly to stabilise the agricultural work-force and improve its productivity.[90]

The still sizeable number of farmers running small, less profitable concerns had different labour problems and priorities, however. The Natal Agricultural Union, for example, reported that many farmers in Natal stood by the labour-tenancy system, expressing little if any need for more full-time workers. For under-capitalised farms, labour tenancy still offered the most reliable means of attracting labour at low wages, which outweighed its disadvantages—such as the under-utilisation of labour and the sacrifice of part of the farm land for use by the labour tenants. Indeed, most of these farmers could not have afforded to exploit the extra land.[91]

The labour bureaux system responded to these varying needs in

TABLE 2. *Labour bureaux' agricultural placements and growth in African agricultural work-force, 1952–1957*

|      | Labour-bureaux placements (male)[a] | Regular & domestic agricultural work-force (male) |
|------|------|------|
| 1952 | 28,545 | 592,488 |
| 1953–4 | 72,670 | 605,991 |
| 1955 | 92,843 | 623,705 |
| 1956 | 75,613 | 631,290 |
| 1957 | 87,996 | 623,837 |

[a] Labour-bureaux placements were presumably most, if not all, male, since women were not subject to the Labour Bureaux Regulations.

*Sources*: C. Simkins, 'African Population, Employment and Incomes on Farms outside the Reserves, 1923–1969', (Carnegie Conference Paper no. 25, Univ. of Cape Town, 1984), p. 8; M. Roberts, *African Farm Labour: Some Conclusions and Reflections* (Johannesburg, 1959), p. 124.

[90] See, e.g., SAAU, *Report of the General Council for the Year 1959 for Submission to the Annual Congress* (Pretoria, 1960), p. 52.
[91] *NAUNLU*, 18 Mar. 1960.

different ways: first, by redirecting workers from urban areas to farms, and, secondly, by restricting the exodus of farm-workers to urban areas. As the following discussion shows, the 'canalisation' programme was principally a conduit for seasonal or casual labour. The labour bureaux aided the 'stabilisation' of farm labour only to the extent that the efflux from farms was reduced. Yet, in both cases, the record of the labour bureaux was mixed. Farmers' labour shortages were often significantly eased, and, as Table 2 shows, the overall performance of the labour bureaux in allocating labour to farmers improved as the decade passed. But the achievements of the bureaux nevertheless fell far short of the NAD's objectives.

A significant number of those 'placed' on farms were foreign work-seekers, thanks to direct intervention on farmers' behalf by the central co-ordinating labour bureau in the NAD. For example, in 1953,

once messages were received that huge numbers of foreign natives were entering the country through Mafeking in the Cape, the matter was immediately investigated [by the central Bureau] and by March, approval had already been secured to use that supply for agriculture . . . A few weeks ago the head of the [central] Bureau himself paid a visit to chiefs in the northern areas in an attempt to relieve the continuing demand [for labour] in the Transvaal Highveld.[92]

Although the statistics should be treated warily, the trend for the proportion of foreign Africans employed on white farms to increase seems unmistakable. According to the Froneman Committee (1962), which reported on the foreign African population of the country, by 1961 approximately 270,000 and 120,000 foreign African men and women respectively were employed in agriculture,[93] as compared with the Tomlinson Commission's estimate of a total of 210,000 in 1951.[94]

The majority of those sent to the farms were routed from the urban areas of the country. According to government figures, of the 28,545 Africans placed in agricultural employment by the district labour bureaux during 1952/3, 21,823 were redirected from urban

[92] CAD NTS 2230 463/280, Eiselen to Minister of Native Affairs, re 'Plaasarbeid: OFS', 8 July 1953.

[93] K. Owen, *Foreign Africans: Summary of the Report of the Froneman Committee of 1962* (Johannesburg, 1964), p. 45.

[94] Union of SA, *Tomlinson Commission*, p. 41.

areas.[95] Comparable figures are not available for subsequent years. But, judging from the NAD's report for the period 1954–7, the proportion of labour bureaux placements made by deflecting work-seekers from urban areas must have been large: according to the report, 'the greatest contribution of the bureaux in supplying agriculture labour was drawn from the urban areas and not from the Bantu areas'.[96]

Most of the bureaux' placements were casual or seasonal labour, the type of labour for which farmers' demand was growing at the fastest rate. Exact statistical breakdowns of the number of seasonal and casual workers placed on farms are unavailable. But there are several indications that the labour bureaux were well attuned to farmers' casual and seasonal labour needs. Included in the bureaux' placement figures were an unspecified number of petty offenders press-ganged into agricultural employment for ninety days, as an alternative to prison sentences for pass-law offences. As Ruth First pointed out (in the passage quoted earlier), the petty-offenders scheme was particularly aggressively applied during the harvesting season. The central labour bureau in the NAD also frequently rose to the occasion. For example, one of the tasks of the central bureau was to rally all available sources of labour as the mealie harvest drew near. As Eiselen explained, for approximately six months before the harvest the central bureau acted in concert with the police to 'canalise all surplus urban labour to agriculture'.[97]

The movement of allegedly 'surplus' urban labour to farms suffering labour shortages was in line with the NAD's labour redistribution strategy. But this picture of the bureaux' successful performance needs to be qualified in several important respects. The bureaux did not succeed in redirecting anything like the full 'surplus' of Africans seeking urban employment into farm labour. A far greater number of African work-seekers were refused entry into the urban areas than accepted farm work. For example, in 1953/4 over 71,000 Africans were refused work-seekers' permits in the Witwatersrand alone,[98] but 72,670 were placed in agricultural employment by the labour

[95] Roberts, *African Farm Labour*, p. 124.

[96] Union of SA, *Report of Department of Native Affairs for the Years 1954–7*, UG 14/1959, p. 40.

[97] CAD NTS 2230 463/280, Eiselen to Minister of Native Affairs, re 'Plaasarbeid: OFS', 8 July 1953.

[98] Roberts, *African Farm Labour*, p. 124.

bureaux nation-wide.[99] In Johannesburg, in the month of December 1958, 710 Africans were refused Section 10(1)(d) permits, but of these only 232 signed farm contracts.[100] Also, the placement figures inflated the bureaux' performance in supplying farmers with labour, because the figures concealed high desertion and labour-turnover rates.[101] The number of workers dispatched to the farms was far greater than the number who stayed to work there. Finally, the bureaux' contributions to farmers' labour needs were consistently dwarfed by the Department of Prisons' '9*d*.-a-day scheme' to supply farmers with convict labour. Prisoners were purportedly 'volunteer labourers', but several reports confirmed a high degree of coercion and abuse. As a result, in 1952 the '9*d*.-a-day scheme' forced some 40,500 on to the farms, 30 per cent more than the number channelled through the labour bureaux.[102] By 1957/8 the number of prison labourers on farms had shot up to 200,000,[103] more than double the number of labour bureaux placements for the year.

The labour bureaux' principal contribution to the 'stabilisation' of farm labour (in line with the labour needs of the more capital-intensive farms) was through the imposition of so-called 'efflux controls'—that is, the restriction of the movement of farm labour at source. Farm-workers were to be issued with reference books, which would have to be signed by their employers before the Native Affairs Commissioner at a district bureau would consider giving them permission to enter a proclaimed area, even if temporarily. The scheme was only partially successful, however. By the end of the 1950s it had certainly become more difficult for farm-workers to desert and head for the towns. Overall, therefore, the introduction of labour bureaux was associated with a slow-down in the rate of African emigration from the white farms. This was reflected in the increasing growth rate of the African farm population. According to official census figures, between 1951 and 1960 the annual percentage growth rate of the African population on white farms was 1.74 per cent, as compared with 0.96 per cent between 1946 and 1951 and 1.13 per

[99] Ibid.
[100] Turok, 'The African on the Farm', 29.
[101] Ibid. 30.
[102] Marcus, *Restructuring in Commercial Agriculture*, p. 118.
[103] Ibid. 127.

cent between 1936 and 1946.[104] But the bureaux' powers of efflux control were severely limited, both by rural resistance to the issuing of reference books and by widespread illegal migration. In several areas of Natal, for example, male farm-workers flatly refused to hand over their identity documents to farmers in order to receive reference books, in many cases deserting the farm in protest.[105] The agricultural journal *The Farmer* reported in 1958 that enforcing the signing of

*dompasses* [reference books] has caused a labour upset in the Middlerust area . . . Some farmers are badly hit by the exodus . . . of labourers leaving the district . . . and a labour crisis is threatening. One farmer, after completing milking, transports his labourers to a neighbour to milk there, for the latter has no labourers.[106]

Nor did the district bureaux have the resources to prevent large numbers of Africans deserting farm work and heading for the towns illegally. Defiance of the influx control laws by farm-workers carried the added danger of reprisals by the farmer to their families left behind on the farm. But, with the legal avenues to the city drastically narrowed, bypassing the labour bureaux system was usually the only means of securing a job in town.

## *Influx Control and African Urbanisation*

Before addressing this issue, certain doubts about the reliability of official South African population statistics should be noted. The population censuses generally miscalculated the size of the urban African population. Clandestine township residents, of whom there were several hundreds of thousands, had obvious reasons to elude the census-takers. Moreover, when censuses were undertaken in the wake of political upheavals, legal and illegal city-dwellers alike were ill-disposed towards the census-takers, regarded as agents of the state monitoring their movements. The 1960 census in particular

---

[104] Simkins, 'African Population, Employment and Incomes', p. 2. Note, however, that the growth rate of the farm population is not a precise indicator of the decline in urban migration. Other factors, such as a declining mortality rate, may also have contributed to the increasing population growth, although this is impossible to establish definitively because rural African infant mortality figures are not available.

[105] *NAUNLU*, 24 Jan. 1958.

[106] *The Farmer*, 11 July 1958.

is suspect for this reason, having been conducted soon after the Sharpeville shootings, in a time of widespread political turmoil in the townships. Estimations of the inaccuracies in census figures caused by such factors vary, ranging from 5.2 per cent for the urban areas generally[107] to as much as 50 per cent for particular cities.[108] Still, in the absence of any comprehensive alternative to the official censuses, demographers have little option but to attempt to correct for some measure of error. Wherever possible in the following discussion, both official and corrected statistics are cited. While the latter are more accurate, it was the former which guided politicians and administrators in their appraisal of the effects of influx control and subsequent revisions of it in the 1960s (as discussed in Chapter 9).

According to official figures cited by the Botha Report, the size of the resident urban[109] African population (foreign and Union-born) increased from 2,328,534 in 1951 to 3,443,950 in 1960, an increase of 47.9 per cent.[110] By 1960 the urban African population comprised 31.8 per cent of the total African population, as compared with 23.7 per cent and 27.2 per cent in 1946 and 1951 respectively.[111] Charles Simkins's figures, corrected for census-miscalculation, show an increase in the (foreign and Union-born) urban African population from 2,559,200 in 1950 to 3,825,500 by 1960, which represents a population growth of 49.5 per cent.[112] Simkins's statistics for Union-born urban Africans alone show a higher proportionate growth of 54.37 per cent over the decade (an increase from 2,204,300 to 3,402,700).[113]

---

[107] J. Sadie, cited in G. Maasdorp and A. S. B. Humphreys, *From Shantytown to Township* (Cape Town, 1975), p. 6.

[108] Ibid. 9.

[109] The 1951 Population Census extended the definition of 'urban area' used in the 1946 Census (see Ch. 2 n. 1) to include 'sub-urban areas' and 'quasi-townships'. 'Sub-urban areas', characteristic of 'large towns', were 'those residential areas situated outside but adjoining the municipal boundaries'. 'Quasi-townships' were detached and distant from large towns, and were 'urban in character', such as 'mission stations, railways, mining and industrial towns'. (Union of SA, *Classification and Status of Urban and Rural Areas*, p. 4.)

[110] NAD, 'Botha Report', p. 9.

[111] Welsh, 'The Growth of Towns', p. 173; calculated using census reports.

[112] I have derived this figure from Simkins, *Four Essays*, pp. 70–2, 53–4.

[113] Ibid. 71.

It was NAD policy to place drastic curbs on the numbers of foreign Africans in the cities. Only those foreign workers already in employment were entitled to live in the urban areas; the urban areas would be closed to all further employment of foreign Africans. The statistical records of the growth in the foreign African population in the cities are particularly suspect. The Froneman Committee, which specifically investigated the number and distribution of foreign Africans living and working in cities, doubted the reliability of any of its figures.[114] Indeed, successive calculations in the Committee's report were wholly inconsistent. On the one hand, it estimated the foreign African population in the urban areas in 1960 at 416,080.[115] Yet, on the other hand, the Committee reproduced labour bureaux statistics showing a resident foreign population of the cities comprising about 50,000 male workers and 25,000 to 50,000 women and dependents.[116] According to Simkins, between 1950 and 1960 the number of foreign Africans in the urban areas increased by 22.2 per cent from 354,100 to 432,800.[117] However, this increase was concentrated in the towns, the foreign population in the metropolitan areas having fallen slightly.[118] While the number of foreign Africans living in the metropolitan areas dropped by 4.5 per cent from 276,000 in 1950 to 262,800 in 1960,[119] the number living in the towns shot up by 117.7 per cent from 78,100 to 170,000.[120] (These figures do not include the foreigners living illegally in the cities, of whom, according to the Froneman Committee, there were many.)[121]

The NAD was privately disconcerted by the continuing expansion of the urban African population.[122] In terms of its 'practical' approach to Apartheid, the NAD had accepted that the urban

[114] Owen, *Foreign Africans: Summary of . . . Froneman Committee*, p. 3.

[115] Ibid. 3.

[116] Ibid. 45.

[117] Calculated from Simkins, *Four Essays*, pp. 70–4.

[118] Simkins uses the official classification of 'metropolitan area' as compared with 'town'. A 'metropolitan area' referred to a 'unit of urban concentration' which 'may comprise more than one legally constituted local authority area in addition to "suburban" areas' (see n. 109). A 'town', on the other hand, comprised a local authority area which lacked 'sub-urban' areas. (Union of SA, *Classification and Status of Urban and Rural Areas*, p. 5.)

[119] Simkins, *Four Essays*, pp. 70–2.

[120] Ibid. 70, 73–4.

[121] Owen, *Foreign Africans: Summary of . . . Froneman Committee*, p. 19.

[122] This response is clear, e.g., throughout the Botha Report. For further discussion, see Ch. 9.

African population would continue to expand, but in accordance with the growth of the African work-force in the cities. Yet during the 1950s the numbers of Africans resident in the cities swelled in the face of rising unemployment.

Publicly, however, the NAD's leaders stressed what they saw as the positive feature of the population statistics, namely, the fact that between 1951 and 1960 the annual growth rate of the urban African population was less than that during the period 1946–51. Census figures showed a decline in the annual rate of growth of the urban African population after 1951, from 5.1 per cent p.a. between 1946 and 1951, to 4.2 per cent p.a. between 1951 and 1960 (although the latter figure was nevertheless slightly higher than the comparable figure of 4.1 per cent for the period 1936–46).[123] The Nationalist government hailed this change in the 1950–60 period as a victory for its influx control policy.[124] Such claims were only partly true. Economic factors also played an important role. The increase in the annual population growth rate during 1946–51 had reflected the effects of the extraordinary post-war industrial expansion. A. J. Norval points out that the greatest percentage increase in South Africa's manufacturing work-force took place in 1948/9, which also saw a considerable increase in the number of manufacturing establishments.[125] Urban industrial expansion then slowed down considerably between 1955 and 1959,[126] and with it the demand for African labour.

The degree to which influx control succeeded in stemming urban population growth must also be understood in relation to the Nationalists' anti-squatting drive. Jansen, recognising shanty towns as focal points of uncontrolled urbanisation, had wasted little time in introducing the 1951 Prevention of Illegal Squatting Act. This law authorised the removal of 'anyone who has entered any African location or village, or anyone who remains on land despite warning to depart'.[127] So-called 'site and service schemes' were then devised to accommodate the remaining legal squatters. Squatters who were legally entitled to live in a proclaimed area were to be resettled on serviced sites, on which they could erect shacks until such time as

[123] SAIRR, *Annual Survey of Race Relations in South Africa, 1964*, p. 188.
[124] e.g. *HAD* (1964), vol. 11, cols. 6086, 6090.
[125] Norval, *A Quarter of a Century of Industrial Progress*, p. 2.
[126] Ibid. 22.
[127] M. Horrell, *Legislation and Race Relations* (Natal, 1971), p. 35.

permanent houses were built. The clearance of uncontrolled shanty settlements thus afforded the NAD the opportunity to identify and remove illegal squatters. Yet the decision to initiate these site and service schemes rested with local authorities, whose attitudes varied. Some, such as Benoni, responded vigorously to the scheme. In Benoni, the entire Apex Squatters' Camp, accommodating some 23,000 Africans, was rapidly flattened, and those legally resident in the area then resettled on serviced sites.[128] Other local authorities, such as Durban and Cape Town, were tardier in combating squatting,[129] leaving squatter settlements intact for much of the decade.

The influx control system was far less effective in keeping African women out of the urban areas, than African men. According to the official census data, the percentage increase in the number of African females resident in the urban areas between 1951 and 1960 (59.59 per cent) exceeded the corresponding percentage increase for men (40.48 per cent).[130] Simkins does not give figures for the number of foreign African women resident in the urban areas in 1950. His data show that the number of Union-born urban African women grew from 894,000 in 1950[131] to 1,500,000[132] in 1960, an increase of 67.8 per cent. During the same period the number of Union-born African men resident in the urban areas grew by 45.21 per cent from 1,310,300 to 1,902,700.[133] As the decade wore on, African women thus constituted an increasing proportion of the expanding resident urban African population.

Another index of this trend was the diminishing masculinity ratio (the ratio of men to women) within the urban African population. A look at masculinity ratios for various urban areas also gives some indication of the extent to which Africans in urban areas were living under family conditions as *de facto* permanent residents. Under normal circumstances the urbanised population of any city would comprise roughly equal numbers of men and women. A high masculinity ratio in a city at any given time thus reflects an influx of

---

[128] D. Humphriss and D. Thomas, *Benoni, Son of my Sorrow* (Cape Town, 1968), pp. 122–3.

[129] *Rand Daily Mail*, 16 Nov. 1960.

[130] NAD, 'Botha Report', p. 44.

[131] Simkins, *Four Essays*, p. 53.

[132] Ibid. 54 (I have used the population figures he compiles which include Umlazi in Durban; Umlazi became part of Kwazulu during 1960).

[133] Ibid. 53–4.

single, childless men who were not born there. A diminishing masculinity ratio over time, on the other hand, could reflect one of two trends: either the tendency for an increasing proportion of Africans migrating to the city to settle and raise families there; or a proportionately greater increase in the number of temporary female migrants, relative to the number of temporary male migrants. The patterns of migration amongst African women have not been fully researched. An unknown proportion of women migrating to the towns from reserves or farms remained temporary migrants. However, according to the Tomlinson Commission, it was widely accepted that the majority of African women came to the urban areas with the intention of settling there.[134] On the assumption, then, that the number of rural African women who came to the towns to settle was greater than those who remained temporary migrants, falling masculinity ratios in the urban areas during the 1950s give some indication of the increasing scale of urbanisation there.

According to the uncorrected census figures, the ratio of (foreign and Union-born) urban African men to women, considered nationwide, fell from 166 : 100 in 1950 to 143 : 110 by 1960.[135] Simkins's figures for Union-born urban Africans show a drop in masculinity ratio from 146 : 100 in 1950 to 126 : 100 by 1960.[136] These trends suggest, then, that, contrary to plan, the NAD's influx control system failed to decelerate, let alone freeze, the process of African urbanisation.

Some striking regional differences are worth noting, however. Population trends in the Western Cape, and Cape Town in particular, seem to have conformed most closely to the NAD's plans. According to the Botha Report, the resident urban African population in the Western Cape grew by 33.5 per cent, as compared with the national average of 47.9 per cent.[137] In Cape Town itself, census figures show a growth of only 25.5 per cent.[138] The census figures take no account of illegal residents, of whom there seemed to have been large numbers in the Western Cape.[139] Still, the NAD's drive

---

[134] Union of SA, *Tomlinson Commission*, p. 28.

[135] NAD, 'Botha Report', p. 44.

[136] Simkins, *Four Essays*, pp. 53–4.

[137] NAD, 'Botha Report', p. 44.

[138] Republic of SA, *Statistical Year Book 1964* (Pretoria, 1964), A–15.

[139] This is claimed, e.g., by the Cape Chamber of Industries (FCI NEAF, 'Some Notes on Native Labour Availability and Influx Control', 24 Nov. 1955, p. 6).

to contain the numbers of Africans entering and settling in the Western Cape was unusually effective. Moreover, the Western Cape was probably the only region (and certainly the only metropolitan region) in which the masculinity ratio did not drop (but again with the *caveat* that these figures exclude a count of illegal residents, which might well have included a far greater proportion of women than men). According to the Botha Report, between 1951 and 1960 the masculinity ratio in the Western Cape remained constant at 200 men to 100 women.[140] This was the highest masculinity ratio in a metropolitan area in 1960.[141]

In Port Elizabeth, on the other hand, a wholly different trend emerged. Between 1950 and 1960 the population growth was 75.77 per cent,[143] and the masculinity ratio dropped from 111 : 100 to 100 : 100.[144] In this case, a higher than national average population growth was accounted for by an increasing proportion of women, indicating an accelerating trend towards permanent urban migration.

Urban areas in the rest of the country fitted somewhere between the two extremes occupied by the Western Cape and Port Elizabeth. For example, according to the Botha Report, the masculinity ratio in the Durban–Pinetown metropolitan area fell from 250 : 100 in 1950 to 167 : 100 by 1960.[144] In the (urban) Southern Transvaal region, a drop from 200 : 100 to 143 : 100 was recorded.[145] Figures for Johannesburg in particular show a drop from a ratio of 148 men to 100 women in 1951[146] to 106 men to 100 women by 1960.[147]

Masculinity ratios, and the extent of permanent urban migration, also differed markedly between metropolitan areas and smaller towns. Table 3, drawn from Simkins's data, shows that throughout the decade the resident Union-born African population of the smaller towns was proportionately more urbanised than that in metropolitan

---

[140] NAD, 'Botha Report', p. 14.

[141] The masculinity ratio in the Cape Town township of Langa grew particularly high following the construction of large hostels for migrant workers. According to M. Wilson and A. Mafeje, whereas in 1949/50 the masculinity ratio in Langa was 457 : 100, by 1959 it had reached 1055 : 100 (M. Wilson and A. Mafeje, *Langa: A Study of Social Groups in an African Township* (Cape Town, 1963), p. 4).

[142] Union of SA, *Statistical Year Book, 1964*, A–15.

[143] NAD, 'Botha Report', p. 14.

[144] Ibid.

[145] Ibid.

[146] Simkins, *Four Essays*, p. 9.

[147] Calculated from WRAB JMR A 10/3, 'Population Trends', 9 May 1963.

TABLE 3. *Percentage population increases and masculinity ratios in resident Union-born African population of metropolitan urban areas and towns, 1950–1960*

| Union-born Africans | Metropolitan areas | | Towns | |
|---|---|---|---|---|
| | 1950 | 1960 | 1950 | 1960 |
| Population increase | | 61.9% | | 39.8% |
| Masculinity ratio | 166 : 100 | 139 : 100 | 116 : 100 | 104 : 100 |

*Source*: C. Simkins, *Four Essays on the Past, Present and Possible Future of the Distribution of the Black Population of South Africa* (Cape Town, 1983), ch. 2.

areas (indicated by the consistently lower masculinity ratios for the towns). The fact that by 1960 the masculinity ratio in the towns had dropped to 104 : 100 indicates the presence of a proportionately smaller male migrant population than in the metropolitan areas, where the masculinity ratio stood at 139 : 100. However, even in the metropolitan areas, the falling masculinity ratio between 1950 and 1960 indicates that there, too, the rate of permanent migration was on the increase.

The discussion so far has relied on census figures, corrected and uncorrected. But, arguably, even the corrected statistics miscalculated the extent of African urbanisation during the decade, having taken insufficient cognisance of clandestine settlement in the towns. In the absence of more precise information, municipal adminstrators accepted as a rule of thumb that at least 20–25 per cent of African residents under their jurisdiction were illegal.[148] The illegal population included single migrant workers evading the labour bureaux system (as discussed in Chapter 6) but not necessarily intending to settle in the urban area on a permanent basis. However, many male and female 'illegals' were *de facto* permanent urban residents, whose presence was another sign of the NAD's failure to have placed a brake on African urbanisation.

To conclude, the practice of influx control during the 1950s, which intensified as the decade wore on, incurred heavy economic, social, and psychological costs for the victims of the influx control laws. Compounding the existing burdens of poverty, the influx control system also broke up families, and reinforced racist practices

[148] Interviews with J. Rees, 26 July 1984, and S. B. Bourquin, 16 Apr. 1985.

which cast Africans in socially servile roles. Even legal city-dwellers were treated as offenders until they could prove themselves innocent. Yet, from the NAD's point of view, by 1960 the influx control system had yielded an unsatisfying mixture of failures and successes in respect of both its twin prongs. On the labour 'canalisation' front, the NAD's partial success in directing large numbers of Africans to the farms must be juxtaposed with serious shortcomings on the urban end. Urban African unemployment levels rose, reflecting in part the failure of the ULPP. Urban labour 'surpluses', particularly amongst the youth, worsened at the same time as the migrant workforce expanded. Yet these surpluses also coexisted with growing labour shortages in certain job categories.

By 1960 the NAD had achieved an uneven degree of control over the growth and composition of urban African population. Overall, the urban African population growth rate fell, but the proportion of Africans settling in the urban areas went up, not down as intended. The expansion of the urbanised population was reflected in the fact that increasing numbers of African women continued to settle in the urban areas, and to a proportionately greater extent than men. Some regions, however, approximated more closely to the NAD's objectives than others. The Western Cape was particularly striking in this regard (although the extent of illegal residence detracts somewhat from this conclusion). The NAD's success in barricading the cities to foreign Africans was also regionally variable, being far greater in the metropolitan areas than in the smaller towns. Indeed, it seems that large numbers of the foreigners denied access to jobs in the metropolitan areas were simply deflected to the towns.

The NAD's reaction to this mixed record of influx control during the 1950s is examined in Chapter 9. Before that, Chapters 6, 7, and 8 account for practical shortcomings of influx control, by examining how the influx control policy was applied and the power struggles which ensued. Two sorts of factors impeded the smooth and effective functioning of the influx control system according to plan. First, its administrators found their hands tied in various ways by the substance of the influx control policy itself. In particular, the contradiction between the terms of the amended section 10(1) and the ULPP (identified in Chapter 4) became a major hindrance in the administrative process. Secondly, while the influx control legislation entitled the NAD to lay claim to systematic and comprehensive powers, the exercise of these powers was not uncontested. The

NAD's capacity to implement its influx control programme effectively depended upon securing the consent or acquiescence of at least three key sets of actors: white urban employers of African labour; Africans living and seeking work in the cities; and the municipal administrators of NAD policy. Chapters 6 and 7 (which discuss the implementation of labour 'canalisation' measures) and Chapter 8 (which examines the implementation of anti-urbanisation measures) show that each group brought varying sorts of powers and pressures to bear upon the implementation of influx control policy, which thus became a process of continuing negotiation and struggle for the NAD.

# 6

# *Influx Control and Urban Labour Markets*

THE NAD's labour 'canalisation' programme was couched in the language of the 'rationality' of the market. Its objectives were to 'match' labour supply and demand; to improve economic 'efficiency' by eliminating the 'wasteful' use of labour; and to 'rationalise' the distribution of labour by removing labour bottlenecks and easing labour shortages. In fact, however, what the NAD labelled as economically 'irrational' behaviour and the source of a 'maldistribution' of African labour was partly the *result* of market forces having come to dominate the African labour market. The allegedly 'wasteful' use of urban labour reflected the fact that the supply price of urban labour was generally higher than that of migrant labour. Also, it was the low wages paid for unpleasant and demanding industrial work which were largely responsible for the 'inefficiently' high labour turnover in urban industries. Still, even the lowest urban wages were higher than those paid to African workers on the mines and farms. And it was these wage differentials which were the principal cause of the alleged 'maldistribution' of labour between urban and rural areas.

The mechanisms of the labour market were not wholly economic, however. A variety of social and cultural factors, of which the state's policymakers took no account whatsoever, also structured employment patterns. Workers' age, gender, ethnicity, exposure to migrant networks, degree of familiarity with the job market, prior experience and training, as well as employers' ideological prejudices and preferences, were thoroughly enmeshed with the economic pressures of labour supply and demand.

Still, in theory, neither economic forces nor sociological tendencies ought to have obstructed the labour redistribution strategy, since it was premised on the capacity of the labour bureaux system to *restructure* the African labour market in line with the dictates of NAD policy. Economic 'rationality' in the NAD's sense of the term was to be legally and administratively orchestrated.

The previous chapter has shown that the labour bureaux's success on this front was limited. The supply of African labour to white farms was enlarged, but without rationalising the utilisation of labour in the cities. Indeed, urban unemployment and urban labour shortages in certain categories worsened simultaneously. Also, the turnover of African labour remained high, perpetuating the allegedly 'wasteful' patterns of employment. Why did the NAD's urban labour 'canalisation' programme fail so dismally? This chapter examines the urban economic realities of the day, and the impact of the migrant labour system and influx control legislation upon them. The next chapter then assesses how and why the labour bureaux system failed to 'rationalise' the urban labour market in line with the prescriptions of NAD policy.

The ULPP was at the centre-stage of the NAD's labour redistribution strategy. The architects of the ULPP intended the policy to correct the conspicuous and common tendency amongst employers to avoid urban African workers, in favour of migrant workers, for unskilled work. For it was this tendency which caused the urban African work-force to expand in the midst of persistent urban unemployment. Setting out 'to employ every possible Bantu legally domiciled in town',[1] the NAD intended the ULPP to ensure 'the placement of the city Bantu in jobs which are now in practice reserved for migrant labourers'.[2] Also, by thus restricting the supply of migrant labour to the cities, the NAD hoped to engineer a shift towards a more productive, 'stable', and efficient urban work-force.

Yet, despite the salience of the ULPP, the NAD offered remarkably little in the way of an economic explanation or defence of how the policy would work. The ULPP was glibly referred to as an economically 'rational' policy, on the grounds that it facilitated the matching of labour supply and demand. But this process was crudely conceived in quantitative terms, treating labour supply and demand as if homogenous and inert quanta. Thus if, in any given town, the collective demand was for $x$ number of African workers and the size of the local economically active African population was $x + n$, then there was purportedly no good economic reason to bring more labour into the area, until the growth in the size of the local demand

---

[1] W. M. Eiselen, 'The Demand for and the Supply of Bantu Labour', *Bantu*, 5 (1958), 9.

[2] Ibid. 13–4.

exceeded *n*. The ULPP took no account of the differentiation between skilled, semi-skilled, and unskilled work, and its effects on employers' demands. Urban job-seekers would be channelled into *all* jobs, skilled or unskilled, ahead of migrants. The segmentation of the labour supply by gender and age, and its effects on the demand for labour, were similarly presumed irrelevant, but for the single concession that African women and youths would be unsuitable for heavy industrial work. In all other jobs categories, however, men, women, and non-school-going youths over the age of 15 were treated as if interchangeable units of labour power.

Not surprisingly, then, the NAD's model of a homogenous labour market bore little resemblance to the prevailing reality of a segmented urban labour market, structured by several variables: the degree of skill required for a job, workers' age, gender, ethnicity, level of education and training, familiarity with the job market, length of time spent in the city, access to migrant support networks, as well as the ideological stereotypes which informed employers' choices and priorities. In order to distinguish some of the distinct urban employment patterns which prevailed during the decade, the following discussion looks at the cases of adult men, women, and youths separately. It is shown in each case that the economic, ideological, and cultural barriers to the implementation of the ULPP were unwittingly compounded by the terms of the NAD's influx control legislation itself. Chapter 4 exposed the contradiction between the ULPP and the terms of section 10(1), by showing that section 10(1) gave urbanised Africans (in the legal sense of the term) the security and protection to resist the ULPP. This chapter explores this contradiction more fully, and shows how it was played out in the labour market. On the one hand, section 10 was an essential vehicle of the ULPP, in differentiating between migrants and urbanised Africans. Yet, on the other hand, section 10 was simultaneously one of the major obstacles to the ULPP, in entrenching the very employment patterns which the ULPP was designed to change.

### The Urban Employment of African Men

This section examines the prevailing patterns of urban labour demand, and the effect of the migrant labour system and influx control laws on the incorporation of adult male workers into the

T ABLE 4. *Composition of urban African work-force, 1949/50–1959/60*

|  | 1949/50 | | 1959/60 | |
|---|---|---|---|---|
|  | Total | Male | Total | Male |
| Manufacturing | 241,857[a] | 236,869[a,b] | 348,529[a] | 320,652[c] |
| Construction | 50,529 | 50,518 | 75,084 | 74,899 |
| Electricity | 14,707 | 14,707 | 17,164 | 17,159 |
| Commerce[d] (1952–60) | 110,995 | 107,583 | 138,240 | n.a.[e] |
| South African Railways & Harbours (1949–59) | 80,528 | 80,493 | 101,303 | 101,263 |
| Post Office (1949–59) | 4,681 | | 7,930 | |
| Public Services (1951–60) | | | | |
|   Central Govt. | 100,000[f] | | 105,508 | 90,185 |
|   Provincial Admin. | | | 56,737 | 45,736 |
|   Local Auth. | 80,000[f] | | 95,929 | 94,059 |
| Private Services | | | | |
|   Laundries | 6,242 | 5,771 | 9,053 | 8,109 |
|   Accom. Services (1946/7–1958/9) | 24,559 | 20,403 | 28,888 | 23,441 |
| Others (1958/9) | | | 13,102 | 11,508 |
| Domestic Service (1951–60) | 300,000 | 114,861 | n.a.[e] | n.a.[e] |

*Notes:* This table is compiled from different sources (see below) which are not always wholly comparable. But, since no single source supplies all the information required, they have all been used. The table should therefore be treated as a rough guide to trends, rather than as a fully reliable record of the absolute numbers in employment.

The table omits African professionals, since they are largely excluded from the scope of the subsequent discussion of labour market trends.

[a] Includes motor industry.

[b] These figures are cited by the 1964 Statistical Year Book, but do not tally with the fact that by 1946, according to the 1946 Population Census, 10,198 African women were already in industry.

[c] Excludes motor industry.

[d] Excludes working proprietors.

[e] Not available.

[f] Rough estimates supplied by NAD, 'Memorandum' (see below).

*Sources:* Union of SA, *Population Census 1946*, vol. 5, UG 41/1954; *1951*, vol. 1, UG 42/195; Republic of SA, *Statistical Year Book 1964* (Pretoria, 1964); NAD, 'Memorandum on Availability of Native Labour' (1951); H. J. Simons, *African Women: Their Legal Status* (London, 1968), p. 274; S. Greenberg, *Race and State in Capitalist Development* (Johannesburg, 1960), p. 426.

urban work-force. The resultant dual tendencies in the labour market are then summarised.

## The Demand for Skilled, Semi-skilled, and Unskilled Labour

Table 4 shows the growth in African employment generally, and male employment in particular, in those sectors which were concentrated in the urban areas.

The urban demand for skilled and semi-skilled African labour was largely concentrated in manufacturing. Having received an immense boost during the Second World War, manufacturing expanded impressively until the late 1950s. Between 1948/9 and 1957/8, the number of private manufacturing establishments rose from 13,879 to 16,838, and the value of their gross output grew from £610,000,000 to £1,503,000,000. Also, the trend towards capital intensification, which had been boosted by a massive injection of capital into manufacturing after the war, continued into the 1950s—as is indicated by the fact that between 1948/9 and 1957/8 total capital investment in the private manufacturing sector grew by 270 per cent, as compared with an increase of 42 per cent in the total number of employees in private manufacturing.[3] These developments reinforced the trend, established in the early 1940s, for African workers to move up the job ladder. The shortage of white artisans continued to draw Africans into more skilled work, although their numbers were limited by pressure from white trade unions and ideological barriers amongst employers.[4] The more significant trend was the incorporation of an increasing proportion of Africans into semi-skilled operative positions, created as new machinery was installed and erstwhile skilled tasks were deskilled.[5]

Quantifying these advances by Africans into skilled and semi-skilled work is hampered by the fact that the prevailing definition of skill was partly ideological. In order to allow employers the benefits

---

[3] Norval, *A Quarter of a Century of Industrial Progress in South Africa*, pp. 2–3.

[4] *Commercial Opinion*, Nov. 1958, p. 7.

[5] Semi-skilled openings for Africans in industry were most numerous in the metal and engineering industries, which were also the classes of industry employing the largest number of Africans overall. Semi-skilled openings were fewest in the stone, clay, earthenware, and glass industries. The semi-skilled work-force was also concentrated regionally in the Southern Transvaal, which accounted for 53% of the total manufacturing work-force in 1949/50. (M. Horrell, *South Africa's Non-White Workers* (Johannesburg, 1956), pp. 71–2.)

of skilled African labour without antagonising the white trade unions, the state permitted the reclassification of skilled jobs performed by Africans as 'semi-skilled'.[6] The problem of measuring Africans' skills is further complicated by the fact that occupational censuses grouped semi-skilled operatives and unskilled workers into the same category. Nevertheless, according to J. L. Sadie, between 1936 and 1960 the percentage of skilled and semi-skilled workers in the African manufacturing work-force rose from 9.5 per cent to 16 per cent.[7]

While continuing capital intensification was an important feature of manufacturing development during the 1950s, it is also important to recognise the constraints on that process. Although the proportion of African manufacturing workers in skilled and semi-skilled positions continued to rise during the decade, the overwhelming majority of Africans employed in manufacturing—84 per cent in 1960—remained unskilled workers.

The proportion of Africans in skilled and semi-skilled positions in commerce was even smaller than in manufacturing. According to the Tomlinson Commission, only 11 per cent of Africans working in wholesale and retail trade were not unskilled in 1951.[8] And jobs in the service sector, which accounted for the highest number of African workers in the cities (see Table 4), were almost all unskilled, apart from a relatively small, but growing, number of African clerks.

Overall, therefore, while the urban demand for African labour to fill skilled and semi-skilled positions grew during the 1950s, it was altogether dwarfed by the demand for unskilled labour. A study in 1957 of African employment in the Cape Peninsula, for example, showed that 90 per cent of the representative sample of African workers in the region was employed in unskilled jobs.[9] And a survey in Durban's Lamontville and Chesterville townships, also in 1957, showed that 70 per cent of the sample of workers was unskilled.[10]

[6] ASSOCOM NEAF, 'Notes on . . . Interview with Minister of Labour on 22 November 1950', p. 2.

[7] Cited in S. J. Kleu, 'Industrial Policy', in J. Lombard (ed.), *Economic Policy in South Africa: Selected Essays* (Cape Town, n.d.), p. 120.

[8] Union of SA, *Tomlinson Commission*, p. 37.

[9] S. T. van der Horst, 'A Note on Labour Turnover and the Structure of the Labour Force in the Cape Peninsula', *SAJE*, 25/4 (1957), 275.

[10] O. Horwood, 'Some Aspects of Urban African Employment in the Durban Area' (SAIRR Natal Region paper, 1958), p. 6.

*Effects of Migrancy and the Influx Control Laws*

From an economic point of view, jobs open to Africans in the towns were ranked on a scale of popularity according to their wages and working conditions.[11] At the top of the scale were skilled, clerical, and semi-skilled jobs offering the highest rates of pay. In Johannesburg and Germiston, for example, experienced machinists in the clothing industry were paid £6 14s. 2d. per week,[12] which was considerably higher than the average unskilled industrial wage of about £3 per week. Job options then descended through a range of semi-skilled and unskilled work with worsening wage levels and working conditions, which varied between regions. In 1957 in Cape Town, for example, 'oil companies, factories, garages, builders and bakeries were the most important groups paying wages above the average' of £3 per week.[13] In 1959 in Durban, among the highest-paid unskilled industrial workers were those in the leather, match, rubber, furniture, and clothing industries, where wages varied between £2 16s. 10d. and £4 per week (including cost-of-living allowance). The lowest-paid unskilled industrial jobs were those in the sugar, tobacco, fruit-drying, heavy chemicals, wood-working, and catering industries, where wages ranged from as little as £1 15s. 0d. to £2 2s. 0d. per week.[14] Unskilled jobs in the service sector tended to compare with the lower end of the wage spectrum in manufacturing. By 1959 approximately 97.7 per cent of Africans in municipal services nation-wide (almost all unskilled labourers) earned between £5 and £10 per month.[15] Job-seekers also ranked unskilled work according to the degree of manual labour and number of working hours involved. Jobs requiring arduous manual labour—such as in the heavy metal and engineering industries, stone quarries, brickfields, and coal transportation—were notoriously unpopular. So, too, were domestic service and the catering and dairy industries, which imposed long or irregular working hours.

Both the migrant labour system and the influx control legislation promulgated in 1952 had marked effects on the economic priorities

[11] See, e.g., Wilson and Mafeje, *Langa*, pp. 23–5; B. A. Pauw, *The Second Generation: A Study of the Family amongst Urbanised Bantu* (Cape Town, 1963), p. 32.
[12] A. Hepple, 'The Fiery Cross of Job Reservation', *Africa South*, 2/3 (1958), 44.
[13] Van der Horst, 'A Note on Native Labour Turnover', 283.
[14] KCL Bourquin Papers, KCM 55268, SAIRR Natal, 'The Cato Manor Framework' (1959), p. 2.
[15] Welsh, 'A Tax on Poverty', 57.

and bargaining powers of Africans seeking work in the urban areas. Demographically, the migrant labour system created three categories of Africans working in the urban areas: first, urbanised workers who were already permanently settled there; secondly, those who had recently migrated to the towns with the intention of settling there; and, thirdly, temporary or oscillating migrants, who had spent varying lengths of time in urban areas but who maintained a permanent home elsewhere (usually in a rural area or outside the country). The influx control legislation, however, treated the second and third groups as a single category. All Africans who had migrated permanently to a particular urban area less than ten or fifteen years ago (depending on whether they had had one employer or several) were defined legally in the same way as oscillating migrants: as 'temporary sojourners' in the urban area, whose permission to remain there was wholly contingent on their being employed.[16] These discrepancies between the demographic and legal senses of the terms 'migrant' and 'urbanised' complicate an assessment of the effects of migrancy and influx control on urban employment patterns.[17] The emergent picture is therefore clearest at the opposite poles of the spectrum where the two definitions coincide: on the one end, in the case of the new migrant with little experience of city life or work and whose links with his rural home and culture remained strong; and, on the other, in the case of the urbanised man, acknowledged and protected as such by the law (in terms of section 10(1)(a) or (b)). The trends are messier and less predictable in the case of men occupying the middle grey area: first, those who were urbanised in a demographic sense (having settled for several years in the cities), but classified legally as 'migrant' because they had not fulfilled the narrow specifications of section 10(1)(a) or (b) (that is, ten or fifteen years' continuous registered service with one or more employers in the same proclaimed area); and, secondly, the long-serving oscillating migrant, who had spent many years in the city as an experienced worker but who retained strong rural attachments and regularly returned to his rural home.

---

[16] Migrants in the legal sense were, therefore, all those whose residence in the urban area was governed by the terms of section 10(1)(d) if they were Union-born, or section 12 if they were foreigners (see Ch. 4).

[17] The following discussion specifies as far as possible whether these terms are being used in their demographic or legal senses, unless this is made plain by the context of their usage.

Reports from administrators, organised commerce and industry, and scholars of the day all indicate that African men permanently settled in the townships were more discriminating in their choice of work than their migrant counterparts, particularly those recently arrived, or directly recruited, from the reserves. As the FCI noted in 1955, 'Native workers, especially the permanent urbanised Native, are becoming more selective as to their employment occupations.'[18] Increasingly, urbanised job-seekers refused to take work at the bottom end of the job spectrum. According to a municipal official in Pretoria, for example, Africans resident in the city's townships 'refuse work paying £3 to £5 per month, and lie around idle for months on end waiting for work paying higher wages, usually £6 to £8 per month'.[19] B. Pauw's East London study revealed similarly that 'occupations of the "rough and heavy" type . . . seem to attract hardly any town males'.[20] And the FCI reported the same trend in industrial employment country-wide, that 'in the majority of cases, manual or menial work will only be accepted by Natives of the migratory type'.[21] As a result, municipal administrators reported a concentration of urbanised workers in the best-paid categories of work: 'generally speaking, 10(1)(a), (b) & (c) Natives enter classes of employment where wages are higher than those paid to 10(1)(d) Natives'.[22]

The preparedness amongst migrants to accept 'lowly paid and menial work' reflected, in the first instance, the vulnerabilities engendered by the migrant labour system and exacerbated by the influx control legislation. The capacity to wait for preferred work, rather than take a job in haste, irrespective of the wage, surely depended on the likelihood of preferred jobs becoming available within a reasonable period of time. It would have been irrational to

---

[18] FCI NEAF, 'Memorandum on Results of Survey on Availability of Native Labour', 21 June 1956, para. 19.

[19] UNISA Ziervogel Papers, C. W. Prinsloo, 'Stedelike Naturelle-Administrasie met Besondere Verwysing na Arbeidsdistribusie' (n.d., c.1952), p. 19.

[20] Pauw, *The Second Generation*, p. 32. See also Wilson and Mafeje, *Langa*, pp. 20–1.

[21] FCI NEAF, 'Summary of Memorandum on Results of Survey of Availability of Native Labour', para. 7.

[22] WRAB JMR A78/1, 'Minutes of 832nd Ordinary Meeting of Non-European Affairs and Housing Committee, 30 August 1955'. See also a similar claim by the Benoni NEAD, cited in P. Bonner and R. Lambert, 'Batons and Bare Heads: The Amato Textile Strike', in Marks and Trapido (eds.), *The Politics of Race, Class, and Nationalism in Twentieth Century South Africa*, p. 344.

wait for better-paid work if there was little chance of any coming up. How long work-seekers were prepared to wait depended on their financial circumstances, and how much more they stood to earn once they secured the sorts of jobs they were after. Generally, well-established township-dwellers were more likely to hold out for the more popular jobs because they had a competitive edge over new migrants in several respects—such as, a better knowledge of the job market and a greater network of friends and relatives in the townships who could introduce them to employers, inform them about appropriate vacancies, and assist financially while they were temporarily unemployed. Still, it must be said that this was by no means invariably the case. P. Delius has shown that, during the 1950s, migrant associations among the Pedi on the Rand cushioned the arrival of a new male migrant to the city in exactly these ways, directing him to employment in particular factories or enterprises along with other Pedi men, and perhaps tiding him over materially until he secured a job.[23] Generally, however, 'job choosiness' depended on the sort of experience and information more likely in the case of urbanised than newly arrived migrant workers.

The second precondition of urban workers' relative 'choosiness' in the job market was the existence of a thriving informal sector in the townships. Without this safety net providing an alternative source of income, the pressure to find formal employment would have been far greater. Once again, the migrant labour system and influx control laws tended to prejudice particularly the new migrants' access to the world of petty entrepreneurship. On the whole, the recently arrived migrant, living in a hostel or still searching for a place to stay, found it difficult to insert himself rapidly into the informal networks of township trading. And, lacking spare cash, he could ill afford the time and initial costs to set himself up. Still, participation in the informal urban economy was not restricted solely to the urbanised. The Pedi migrant associations, for example, gave some of their members an entrée to various trading networks amongst migrant communities on the Rand.[24] But, for new migrants lacking such support, the pressures to secure a wage were usually immediate and compelling. The deepening poverty of the majority of African peasants and the landless in the reserves during the 1950s (see

---

[23] Delius, 'Sebatakgomo', 593, 604.
[24] Ibid. 594, 604.

Chapter 5) accelerated the process of labour migration amongst job-seekers who could ill afford to turn down poorly paid work. The influx control laws compounded the urgency, allowing urbanised Africans protected by section 10(1)(a) or (b) more room for manœuvre and bargaining power in the labour market than migrants. Section 10(1)(a) and (b) conferred the right to remain in an urban area whether employed or not. Those who held these qualifications were thus legally entitled to take as much time as they wanted to find suitable employment. Migrants, on the other hand, were far more insecure and constrained. A section 10(1)(d) work-seeker's permit gave Union-born migrants fourteen days in which to find a job, failing which they would be 'endorsed out'. All 10(1)(d) permit-holders were thus under considerable pressure to find employment as soon as possible, in order to secure or retain a legitimate place in the cities. Foreign migrants were even more vulnerable. Although section 12 of the Urban Areas Act prohibited any further employment of foreign Africans in the cities, in practice foreigners were sometimes given permission to enter the cities provided they took the notoriously unpopular jobs (see later). As the imposition of influx control intensified during the course of the 1950s, particularly in respect of foreigners, the insecurity and vulnerability of migrants (in the legal sense) worsened accordingly.

All in all, then, migrants, and more particularly those doubly disadvantaged by their urban inexperience and the influx control laws, were generally less likely than urbanised job-seekers to refuse what the FCI termed 'obnoxious work'.[25] As the Johannesburg NEAD reported, migrant job-seekers were 'prepared to accept lower wages and menial work . . . in order to obtain a foothold in Johannesburg',[26] a remark equally applicable to other urban areas. But, since this trend was a function of several variables, the avenues of choice open to individual migrants would have varied, depending on the extent of their poverty, inexperience in the job market, length of stay in the city, and access to urban support networks.

Migrants' job choices were not shaped solely by their disadvantaged position in the labour market, however; they also reflected the ways in which migrant workers organised collective bulwarks against

---

[25] FCI NEAF, 'Memorandum on Native Labour Availability and Influx Control', 24 Nov. 1955.
[26] WRAB JMR A78/1, 'Minutes of 832nd Ordinary Meeting'.

the insecurities and stresses of migrancy. From at least the 1930s
many male migrants found jobs in town with guidance from migrant
associations, typically ethnically particularist and regionally based.[27]
By the 1950s the principal role of such migrant associations seems to
have been their bid to control the corrosive effects of proletarianisation on migrants' rural ties, by forging bonds of solidarity, mutual
dependence, and discipline with like-minded men. 'Through such
networks', W. Beinart found, 'workers could retain contact with
home and establish defensive structures at work.'[28] Research on
migrancy by Beinart and Delius suggests that migrant associations
were complexly determined, changing over time, and varying according to members' ethnic identity, home region, level of education, and degree of traditionalism.[29] This brief discussion of patterns
of migrancy cannot do justice to their many facets; it merely draws
attention to some of the apparently common ways in which migrant
associations linked home and workplace. The first was to provide a
channel into the urban labour market. By colonising particular types
of jobs or places of employment, migrants' associations offered their
members the opportunity to work alongside others from the same
region, clan, or district—a welcome security for migrants new to the
city and unfamiliar with its job market. The second was to build a
cultural bridge between workers' rural and urban milieux. Talking
about matters back home, reproducing traditional structures of
authority in the workplace, sharing leisure activities, and distinguishing themselves from urbanised people by their style of dress
were some of the ways in which members of migrant associations
crafted individual and group identities which held urban cultural
influences at bay. As Beinart points out, this was not a simple duplication of rural preoccupations in an urban context; the cultural
medium of migrants' associations should be seen as a refraction of

---

[27] Beinart suggests that Christian migrants were exceptions to this trend; more
readily assimilated into the urban cultural milieu, they did not form migrants'
associations (W. Beinart, 'Worker Consciousness, Ethnic Particularism and Nationalism: The Experiences of a South African Migrant, 1930–1960', in Marks and Trapido
(eds.), *The Politics of Race, Class and Nationalism in Twentieth Century South Africa*,
pp. 299–300.

[28] Ibid. 289.

[29] Beinart, ibid., and 'The Origins of the Indlavini: Male Associations and Migrant
Labour in the Transvaal' (unpublished mimeo, 1987); Delius, 'Sebatakgomo'.
(Beinart's work is partly a response to the anthropological literature on migrant
associations, notably the work of Philip and Iona Mayer.)

rural norms and values through the lens of particular experiences of proletarianisation.[30]

Further research is needed to assess the scale and impact of migrant associations nation-wide.[31] But Beinart's and Delius's work suggests that, at least amongst workers from Transkei and Sekhukhuneland, membership of migrant associations was widespread and led ethnically or regionally defined groups of migrants to cluster in particular types and places of work. For example, in many cities it was Bhaca migrants who dominated municipal sanitation services. Increasing numbers of Pedi migrants converged on ISCOR in Pretoria from the late 1930s.[32] In some cases, the clustering was district- or village-based: 'Harry's Hat Factory in Doornfontein, for example, became a mecca for men from Manganeng.'[33]

Employers perceived and recorded workers' priorities and preferences in an ideological catalogue of the costs and benefits of 'urban or detribalised' as opposed to 'tribal' labour.[34] The 'location man' was stamped as 'job choosy', 'lazy', and 'cheeky',[35] especially when 'semi-educated'. In the words of a senior compound manager for Union Steel Corporation,

the detribalised . . . group has today become a problem. He [*sic*] is the young, semi-educated, arrogant, demanding and won't-work type. He is difficult to handle because he is very prone to disobedience and has, invariably, no inclination to work unless forced to do so . . . The result is you have a worker performing a task which he is forced to do and does so inefficiently.[36]

'Tribal' migrants, on the other hand, were held to be 'more obedient, harder working, and . . . more easy to satisfy and control'.[37] Employers looked upon a worker's 'tribal' identity as a safeguard against 'communistic' leanings, and the source of discipline

---

[30] Beinart, 'The Origins of the Indlavini', p. 35.

[31] e.g., to my knowledge, the prevalence and form of migrant organisation amongst Zulu workers has not been studied.

[32] Delius, 'Sebatakgomo', 594.

[33] Ibid. 593.

[34] Employers typically recognised only one category of migrant, the 'tribal' worker who retained strong ties with his rural home. This encompassed both the newly arrived city-dweller and the oscillating migrant who had not been 'detribalised'.

[35] Interview with W. J. P. Carr, 23 Nov. 1984.

[36] R. C. McLean, *How to Use Industrial Native Labour Efficiently* (Johannesburg, 1958), p. 3.

[37] Ibid. 2.

and docility.[38] Many employers, therefore, established their own rural recruiting networks, built around chiefs whose co-operation was likely to have enhanced the discipline and loyalty of the workers recruited.

This stereotype of the 'tribal' worker was reinforced by employers' experience of the so-called 'raw Native', inexperienced, untrained, and vulnerable, as far less likely than the city-dweller to refuse 'obnoxious' employment on the grounds of low wages or poor working conditions. Foreign migrants, according to the FCI, were the least 'job choosy' and 'work shy' of all: 'experience has proven that foreign Natives are more than willing to accept . . . obnoxious employment'.[39] 'Rural labour' was also considered 'better suited to heavy industrial work',[40] offering strength uncorrupted by the 'decadence' of city life.

As is the case with all ideological constructions, the employers' view of 'rural labour' as more docile and disciplined than 'detribalised' workers, was grounded to some extent in reality. The urgency of securing a cash wage, inexperience in the job market, and vulnerability imposed by influx control were all contributing factors. So, too, was the self-disciplining role of migrant associations within the work-force. Many male migrant associations were hierarchically structured, with clear lines of authority.[41] These hierarchies were transposed into the workplace, as a source of internal control among workers who belonged to the migrant association.[42]

Employers also described the characteristics of 'tribal labour' in terms of ethnic stereotypes. According to W. Carr, Johannesburg's Manager of Non-European Affairs, it was common cause amongst employers in the city that Zulus were 'strong and motivated', Xhosas more 'troublesome', while Sothos were 'lazy smart alecs'.[43] The content of such stereotypes was fluid, however, enabling employers in various cities to explain and accept the ethnic and regional clustering in migrant employment in terms of an 'ideal' match

---

[38] F. J. Language, 'Native Housing in Urban Areas', *Journal of Racial Affairs*, 1/2 (1950), 29.

[39] FCI NEAF, 'Memorandum on Native Labour Availability and Influx Control', 24 Nov. 1955.

[40] McLean, *How to Use industrial Native Labour*, p. 2.

[41] See, e.g., Beinart, 'Worker Consciousness, Ethnic Particularism and Nationalism', p. 299.

[42] Thanks to Philip Bonner for this information.

[43] Interview with W. J. P. Carr, 23 Nov. 1984.

between particular ethnic groups and types of work. For example, according to research by a Pretoria municipal official, 'ISCOR (Pretoria) have found that the Zulu make outstanding watchmen and police, the Tsonga are good cleaners and sanitation workers, the Pedi are intelligent machine workers, the Transvaal Ndebele work well with picks and shovels, etc.'.[44]

It was widely conceded, however, that employing 'tribal' migrant labour also had its disadvantages. 'Instability' was often, although not invariably, alleged to be one of them. Large numbers of migrants left the cities for the reserves annually for about three months during the ploughing season, and their return to the same job could not be guaranteed.[45] As a study of labour turnover in the Dunlop Rubber Factory in Durban showed, in the case of migrants 'the moral and economic necessity or obligation to return to the Native areas still influences their working behaviour'.[46] Also, employers generally regarded a migrant's 'quality of labour'[47] for more skilled work as poorer than that of a 'detribalised' worker, in so far as the latter was typically more literate, numerate, and fluent in English or Afrikaans.

### Dual Tendencies in the Urban Labour Market

No doubt individual employers attached different importance to the relative pros and cons of taking on 'tribal' as opposed to 'detribalised' workers, and individual migrants succeeded to varying degrees in transcending the handicaps imposed on them by migrancy and the influx control system. But, overall, two basic tendencies structured the adult male labour market in the urban areas.

First, the demand for, and the supply of, skilled and semi-skilled labour was concentrated amongst those job-seekers with a firm foothold in the urban area. The men who were best placed for such work were generally those who were urbanised in the demographic and legal senses of the term. This tendency derived in the first instance from job-seekers' choices and options, as discussed previously.

---

[44] UNISA Acc. 147, Ziervogel Papers, C. W. Prinsloo, 'Stedelike Naturelle Administrasie, met Besondere Verwysing na Arbeidsdistribusie', p. 18.
[45] FCI NEAF, 'Memorandum of Results of Survey on Availability of Native Labour', 21 June 1956, p. 3.
[46] S. B. Ngcobo, 'The Response of Africans to Industrial Employment', *Race Relations Journal*, 21/1 (1954), 13. The study was conducted in 1946, using a sample of 1,100 workers.
[47] Ibid. 4.

Least constrained were those work-seekers who were long-standing permanent city-dwellers protected by the terms of section 10(1)(a) or (b). Men who were urbanised in the demographic sense but classified legally as migrants (because they still held section 10(1)(d) permits) were often as familiar with the job market and as experienced on the job as men born and bred in the city, which gave them the edge over the so-called 'raw' migrant. But they were disadvantaged, nevertheless, by the terms of section 10(1)(d). Many oscillating migrants, too, had had several years' experience in city life and employment; but, in addition to the pressures of 10(1)(d), their bargaining power was often weakened by an annual return home for the ploughing season.

Workers' choices and interests shaped, and were reinforced by, employers' preferences. Thus the tendency for the more urbanised workers to monopolise the more skilled jobs also derived from the widespread (although not monolithic) preference amongst employers for 'stable' workers to do skilled and semi-skilled work. As the FCI explained,

the increasing productivity and specialisation of Native labour in semi-skilled and operative categories . . . is dependent on stability of labour and maintenance of training and occupational advancement. Unlike the mining and agricultural industries where bulk manual labour is used and where each working unit can be substituted for by another working unit, secondary industry has to follow a more individual employee basis, where each working unit is trained for a particular purpose and cannot be removed from that purpose without the sometimes lengthy training of a replacement.[48]

Practical experience has proven that the productivity of the migrant worker cannot reach the same peak as that of a permanent worker.[49]

For employers, the efficiency of the training process also depended on the 'quality of labour'. Here, urbanised workers enjoyed the advantage of a better basic education and initial command of English or Afrikaans than migrants. But the longer a migrant's experience of urban life and work, the less the 'quality' of his labour would have been hampered by educational disadvantages.

Articulating the views of the larger industrial concerns in which semi-skilled African labour played an increasingly important part, the FCI therefore declared in 1957 that, in general, 'the need for

[48] FCI NEAF, 'Native Labour Mobility', 18 Mar. 1957, p. 1.
[49] FCI NEAF, 'The Native in Industry', 8 Jan. 1951, p. 4.

specialisation, and increasing and improved training, is resulting in the establishment of a labour pattern whereby . . . the semi-skilled operative positions are usually occupied by permanent urbanised workers'.[50]

It must be stressed, however, that this was a tendency rather than the rule. In some cases, employers ranked the advantages of employing 'raw' migrant labour above those of urbanised labour, irrespective of the level of skill or training involved. Union Steel Corporation's compound manager, for example, reported a generalised prejudice against 'the detribalised group': 'Industries in my area have discovered that this group has become unsound and uneconomical labour to employ because they [*sic*] leave when they wish, and for the slightest provocation or reprimand.'[51] Partly for this reason, firms such as Union Steel promoted migrants already in their employ, training them for semi-skilled work once they had proven their ability and loyalty.

Also, employers' experiences did not always confirm the widespread belief that migrant workers were less 'stable' than their 'detribalised' counterparts. As the Tomlinson Commission reported, the evidence on this issue was 'contradictory in nature': 'some data reveal the settled labourer as a more steady worker, while others suggest that the migrant worker is superior in this regard'.[52] A study by Hobart Houghton also found that 'some men whose wives and families lived in the reserves were found to have ten years' service or more with the same firm. They returned home only for their annual leave or occasional week-ends. Conversely some of the unstable workers were town-born.'[53]

Several studies during the decade indicated that the 'stability' of labour was also a function of age and marital status: labour turnover amongst urbanised male workers was generally higher among young, single men than older, married men.[54]

Lastly, in areas where the proportion of workers permanently settled in urban townships remained relatively small, such as

---

[50] FCI NEAF, 'Native Labour Mobility', p. 1.

[51] McLean, *How to Use Industrial Native Labour*, p. 3.

[52] Union of SA, *Tomlinson Commission*, p. 95.

[53] D. Hobart Houghton, 'Labour in African Development', in E. A. G. Robinson (ed.), *Economic Development for Africa South of the Sahara* (London, 1964), p. 327.

[54] e.g. ibid. 327; Ngcobo, 'The Response of Africans to Industrial Employment'; Glass, *The Black Industrial Worker: A Social Psychological Study*.

Durban, employers often had little option but to employ oscillating migrants, irrespective of the sort of work involved.

The second overall trend in the labour market was the relegation of the less popular categories of unskilled work to migrant workers, particularly the inexperienced and those perceived as still 'tribalised'. This tendency derived partly from the handicaps and vulnerabilities inflicted on migrants by the migrant labour system and influx control legislation (as discussed earlier). These in turn generated an overwhelming demand among employers for 'tribal' migrants to do unskilled work because for employers, different priorities dominated the recruitment of labour for unskilled, as opposed to skilled and semi-skilled, jobs.

Economists of the day, along with organised commerce and industry, echoed Eiselen's lament that 'our present economic life bears the stamp of very expensive cheap labour' in the form of a 'low standard of efficiency and . . . huge turnover of African labour'.[55] Employers were repeatedly exhorted to improve the productivity of African labour by means of

better selection and placement of workers . . . better supervision, better opportunities for advancement and promotion of workers, systems of wage payment which provide incentives to increase output, more attention to physical working conditions and welfare facilities, and to industrial safety and health.[56]

But these calls generally fell on deaf ears.[57] As IANA put it in 1957, 'employers jib at modernising their old-fashioned organisations . . . Planned training of employees and cultivating a sympathetic attitude is absent in most cases.'[58]

Employers' intransigence over unskilled wage levels was all the more assertive for the tacit backing they received from the Wage Board.[59] Whereas Eiselen called on employers to 'raise wages . . . as efficiency improves',[60] the Wage Board responded to pressure from

---

[55] Eiselen, 'Plan to Rationalise South Africa's Native Labour', p. 10.

[56] N. N. Franklin, *Economics in South Africa* (Cape Town, 1954), p. 171.

[57] *Commercial Opinion*, Mar. 1957, p. 13. See also Franklin, *Economics in South Africa*, p. 173.

[58] IANA, 'Proceedings of 1957 Annual Conference', p. 131.

[59] The Wage Board was a state body which set and monitored minimum wage levels.

[60] Eiselen, 'Plan to Rationalise South Africa's Native Labour', p. 7. Also see the discussion of his 'different conception of Native labour' in Ch. 3.

white farmers to stem urban wage increases which would lure even larger numbers of rural Africans into the towns.[61] Thus, 'for the first ten years of the Nationalist government . . . the Wage Board went into comparative hibernation compared to its previous activity',[62] doing nothing to stop real wage levels from falling.[63] (Clearly the issue of urban African wages was a source of tension and division within the state itself, as well as within the business community.)

The calls for unskilled wage increases became more urgent and vociferous after 1957, when a three-month bus boycott in Alexandra Township alarmed organised industry and commerce about the political dangers of poverty wages. The Johannesburg Chamber of Commerce hastily established a Wage and Productivity Association, to persuade employers of the need to increase unskilled wages. The Wage Board then agreed to reassess minimum wage levels in several unskilled occupations, but by 1959 few changes had been instituted.[64] Many employers, too, were still largely unmoved. Had they faced a strongly unionised unskilled work-force exerting unrelenting pressure for increased wages, it might have paid them to raise wages and 'modernise' their operations. But 'tribal' migrants supplied a sufficiently cheap and docile unskilled work-force for employers to sustain profitability without taking steps to increase labour productivity and 'stabilise' their work-force. Therefore, as F. J. Language, Brakpan's municipal Manager of Non-European Affairs, pointed out,

many employers of unskilled labour prefer to engage the 'raw' Native who does not belong to any trade union, who is unaware of industrial legislation, and wage regulations, and who is quite content, temporarily at least, to submit to the stipulations and demands of the employer in all respects concerning an ordinary contract of service. There is a tendency among private employers of native labour to prefer the immigrant labourer to the town native, the deciding factor being the fact that the wage of the former is much lower than that demanded by the town native.[65]

As 'raw' migrant workers gained experience and became more familiar with the urban labour market, so many of them moved on to

[61] H. R. Griffiths and R. A. Jones, *South African Labour Economics* (Johannesburg, 1980), p. 99.

[62] Ibid.

[63] W. F. J. Steenkamp, 'Bantu Wages in South Africa', *SAJE*, 30/2 (1962), 98.

[64] A. Hepple, *Poverty Wages* (Johannesburg, 1959), p. 5.

[65] Language, 'Native Housing in Urban Areas', p. 29.

other jobs.[66] The bottom end of the job spectrum was thus characterised by a high labour turnover, which continually reproduced the demand for more 'raw' rural labour.

Able to exploit both the vulnerabilities and cultural networks of 'tribal' migrants, most employers paid little heed to the three-day stayaway called by the South African Congress of Trade Unions (SACTU) in 1958, to pressure employers into increasing the minimum wage to £1 a day. Indeed, according to A. Hepple, real wage levels continued to drop as the decade drew to a close, forced down by the rise in African unemployment which accompanied the recession of 1959–60.[67] Persistently poor wages and working conditions perpetuated the preference for 'tribal' migrants, which in turn allowed unskilled wages to stay low.

In short, then, the combined effect of the migrant labour system and the influx control legislation of the day was to structure the urban labour market in the following ways. 'Tribal' migrant labour tended to be the preferred source of unskilled labour, while 'detribalised' workers generally stood a better chance of securing the better paid, more skilled jobs. Since the demand for unskilled labour far outweighed the demand for skilled and semi-skilled labour, the labour market was dominated overall by the 'strong prejudice . . . against the employment of Native labour already domiciled and housed within the confines of a particular town'.[68] As municipal administrators reported, overall 'employers prefer this . . . migratory class of worker to the urban Native'.[69]

### Urban Employment of African Women

The NAD's purpose, in extending the ULPP to African women, was to ensure the 'better utilisation' of the labour power of the women already living in the townships. The NAD accepted that women workers were ill-suited to heavy manual work, but reasoned that absorbing increasing numbers of urban women into the lighter grades of work would help to diminish the overall need for male and

[66] IANA, 'Proceedings of 1953 Annual Conference', p. 88.
[67] Hepple, *Poverty Wages*, p. 9.
[68] IANA, 'Proceedings of 1953 Annual Conference', p. 88.
[69] WRAB JMR A78/1, 'Minutes of 832nd Ordinary Meeting'. See also IANA, 'Proceedings of Annual Conference', 1953 p. 38; 1956, p. 15; 1961, p. 19.

female migrant labour, and thereby contain the expansion of the resident urban population. Once again, however, the NAD's policy model bore little resemblance to the realities of the urban labour market.

African women's job options differed in several respects from men's. Paradoxically, African women, urban and migrant alike, had fewer options but greater freedom of choice than African men. As a result, the differentiation between migrant and urbanised women in the labour market was less marked than in the case of men. Nevertheless it was still the case that migrant women tended to concentrate in the worst paid, least popular jobs, which urbanised women resisted. But the more formidable obstacle to the ULPP in the case of women lay in the expansion of women's informal economic activities in the townships, a worsening 'wastage' of the female urban labour pool in the NAD's eyes. A significant proportion of women, both urbanised and migrant, were either marginalised in the labour market or resisted wage labour because participation in the township economy was more lucrative. And, ironically, the influx control regulations gave them all the more space in which to do so. The following discussion looks, first, at African women's occupational options in the cities, and, secondly, at how these were affected by the migrant labour system on the one hand, and the influx control legislation on the other.

### Occupational Options in the Cities

'Perhaps the most outstanding characteristic of the urban African community is its poverty.'[70] So wrote L. Longmore in her study of women's lives in Johannesburg's townships in the 1950s. Married or not, almost all urban African women had to take a major, if not the sole, responsibility for supporting themselves and their children. E. Kuzwayo, then a social worker in Johannesburg, alleged that, even in stable relationships, 'the majority of fathers do not give a reasonable proportion of their earnings for the use of their families'.[71] But even those fathers who handed over their entire wage could

---

[70] L. Longmore, *The Dispossessed: A Study of the Sex-Life of Bantu Women in Urban Areas in and around Johannesburg* (London, 1959), p. 108.

[71] E. Kuzwayo, 'The Role of the African Woman in Towns', (SAIRR paper RR 207/1960), 22 Nov. 1960, p. 1.

not meet their families' basic needs. According to the SAIRR's estimates, the minimum subsistence costs of an urban African family of five in 1956 was £26 per month.[72] Yet the vast majority of male workers were then earning less than £16 monthly. Small amounts earned by adolescent children or other family members might have lessened the deficit; but, in the majority of families, the mother was an important bread-winner.[73]

A large proportion of women were in the unfortunate position of having to provide for their families largely single-handed. This was partly a reflection of the late marrying age amongst urban Africans; as had been the case in the previous decade, many men and women postponed marriage until their thirties.[74] Most women had therefore had at least one child, and usually more, before marrying.[75] But, increasingly, women were not marrying at all. The trend, already evident in the 1940s, for men and women to enter into transient 'vat en sit' relationships ('informal unions') was all the more pervasive during the 1950s. As Longmore discovered, 'it may well be that the new urban African generation is dispensing with marriage in its old forms';[76]

it is not unusual for urban 'husbands' to change frequently, leaving the home in the charge of the women and her growing brood of children. These loose unions, irregularly formed, have given rise to the temporary family, which affords no security to the children born into them.[77]

Reliable and complete national statistics are unavailable. But several studies show that the proportion of female-headed urban households was on the increase (although with significant variations between regions[78]). For example, B. Pauw's survey of East London townships reveals that 40 per cent of the households sampled were run by women.[79] M. Wilson and A. Mafeje discovered that this was

---

[72] *Rand Daily Mail*, 23 July 1958.

[73] See, e.g., Kuzwayo, 'The Role of the African Woman in Towns'; G. Maasdorp and A. S. B. Humphreys, *From Shantytown to Township* (Cape Town, 1975), p. 48; Walker, *Women and Resistance*, p. 146.

[74] H. J. Simons, *African Women: Their Legal Status* (London, 1968), p. 70.

[75] Longmore, *The Dispossessed*, p. 50.

[76] Ibid. 52.

[77] Ibid. 58.

[78] e.g., a study in Klerksdorp in 1957 found that only 12 per cent of the sample of households surveyed were not headed by married men (see Steyn and Rip, 'The Changing Urban Bantu Family', 507).

[79] Pauw, *The Second Generation*, p. 146.

a 'common' tendency in Langa township (Cape Town),[80] as did M. Marwick in his survey of five hundred Nguni households in a Reef township.[81]

Economic pressures on urban women, then, were greater, in many cases, than they were on the men. Yet the range of job options open to African women in the urban areas, at least in the formal labour market, was far narrower than that encountered by African men. Statistical data on the female work-force are patchy, but reveal clearly that the demand for female African labour was largely restricted to the service sector, and domestic service in particular. (Durban was something of an exception, in that domestic service was still dominated by African men in the 1950s.) On one estimate, between 1951 and 1960 the number of female African workers in services increased by 18.4 per cent from 274,060 in 1951 to 324,585 in 1960. Of the latter, 87 per cent were domestic workers.[82] The demand for African women workers in manufacturing was far smaller, although it did increase strikingly during the course of the decade, from 11,126 in 1951 to 22,285 in 1960—a rise of 100.2 per cent.[83] Most female industrial workers were concentrated in 'those areas of manufacturing which corresponded broadly to traditional female occupations'—in clothing, textiles, and food.[84] The limited number of industrial openings for African women also narrowed their access to skilled or semi-skilled work. Particularly in the garment industry, some women did become operatives.[85] But, overall, a far larger proportion of female workers than male workers in the cities did unskilled work.

African women's wages were generally lower than men's, partly because women were more heavily concentrated in unskilled jobs, but also because women were typically paid less than men for the same work. Thus, according to the Botha Report, for example, in

[80] Wilson and Mafeje, *Langa*, p. 79.

[81] C. Simkins, 'Household Composition and Structure in South Africa', in S. Burman and P. Reynolds (eds.), *Growing Up in a Divided Society: The Contexts of Childhood in South Africa* (Johannesburg, 1986), p. 26.

[82] Simons, *African Women: Their Legal Status*, Tables 12 and 13.

[83] Ibid., Table 13. Note that these figures are not altogether consistent with those cited in Table 3 earlier in this chapter.

[84] Walker, *Women and Resistance*, p. 116.

[85] I. Berger, 'Solidarity Fragmented: Garment Workers of the Transvaal, 1930–1960', in Marks and Trapido (eds.), *The Politics of Race, Class and Nationalism in Twentieth Century South Africa*, p. 139.

1962 86 per cent of female industrial workers earned less than £2 10*s*. 0*d*., as compared with 9 per cent of male industrial workers.[86] The Tomlinson Commission found that in 1952 most African women in commerce earned a little over half the wages of African men in this sector. Whereas the average wage for African males in commerce was £108 p.a., African women were paid between £52 and £58 on average, and in some cases as little as £24 p.a.[87] Nevertheless, African women generally stood to gain more from an industrial or commercial job than from domestic service.[88] Wages for domestic work, which were not subject to Wage Board rulings, varied from employer to employer, but were generally notoriously bad. A survey of wages earned by women in Johannesburg in 1942, for example, shows that, in some cases, African women in commerce earned more per week than domestic workers pocketed per month.[89] And there is no reason to suppose that the discrepancy changed significantly during the 1950s.

The types and numbers of jobs open to African men were, therefore, far more diverse than those available to women; and men's wages, which were extremely low in relation to the cost of living, were considerably higher than those to which African women could aspire. Under these conditions, the township economy was a vital source of income for African women, more so than for the men. In terms of the ULPP, the growth of the informal sector represented a 'waste' of urban labour power. But large numbers of women had found that they could earn more from part-time domestic work and/or various petty-entrepreneurial activities than from full-time wage labour. And many of those in formal employment had to supplement meagre wages with extra income from such informal sector work.

In their survey of the urban informal sector of Johannesburg, K. Beavon and C. Rogerson locate the period from 1945 to the mid-1960s as the third of four phases in women's participation in the urban informal sector. It was a phase distinguished by three key features: 'the demise of the formerly common income source of

---

[86] NAD, 'Botha Report', p. 48.
[87] Union of SA, *Tomlinson Commission*, p. 37.
[88] Pauw, *The Second Generation*, p. 33.
[89] UW SAIRR Papers, AD 843 B17.1, 'Analysis of Helping Hand Club Hostel Residents, July 1942'.

washing'; 'the growth in women's participation in new spheres of informal economic activity', notably coffee-cart trading; and the further consolidation of already important economic activities, such as beer-brewing.[90] Washing, initially dominated by African men, had become an important source of income for urban African women during the 1920s and 1930s; but by the 1950s competition from the laundry business had forced women to find more lucrative alternatives. Coffee-cart trading was one of the more popular enterprises, at least in Johannesburg. Again, women established their hold as men relinquished theirs. By 1953 58 per cent of coffee-carts in Johannesburg were operated by women.[91] But the operations of most coffee-cart traders were precarious. Lacking the required hawkers' licence, many were frequently prosecuted and fined by municipal authorities.[92]

The most widespread, and often the most profitable, petty-entrepreneurial activity for women was the brewing and sale of sorghum beer and/or the sale of so-called 'European' liquor. Both activities were illegal, and punishable by heavy fines or imprisonment. The 1937 Native Laws Amendment Act had given municipalities a monopoly on the production and sale of sorghum beer, as a major source of revenue for township administration. Only the small handful of township residents issued with brewing permits, renewable every year as of 1950, were entitled to compete with the municipal beer-halls. But defiance of these restrictions was ubiquitous. Longmore estimated that in Eastern Native Township in Johannesburg, for example, more than 60 per cent of the residents engaged in the illicit liquor trade.[93] Numbers were higher still in larger townships which were more difficult to police (such as Orlando in Soweto) and in freehold areas beyond municipal control (such as Sophiatown or Alexandra and Cato Manor). State officials stereotyped the woman brewer as 'loose' and 'undesirable'; but many 'respectable' married women were heavily involved in the trade.

One of the reasons for the prevalence of the brewing trade was its

[90] K. Beavon and C. Rogerson, 'The Changing Role of Women in the Urban Informal Sector of Johannesburg', in D. Drakakis-Smith (ed.), *Urbanisation in the Developing World* (London, 1986), p. 211.

[91] Ibid. 219.

[92] C. Rogerson, 'The Council vs. the Common People: The Case of Street Trading in Johannesburg', *Geoforum*, 17/2 (1986), 206.

[93] Longmore, *The Dispossessed*, p. 212.

lucrativeness relative to the meagre wages offered by formal employ-ment for women. The selling price of sorghum beer represented a substantial mark-up on the cost of the ingredients. In Eastern Native Township, for example, 'an expenditure of 6 shillings on yeast, malt, sugar and oatmeal brings in over 24 shillings'.[94] But the profit-ability of the liquor business varied widely, dependent on a range of factors—such as the (illegal) availability of so-called 'European liquor' in the shebeen, the proximity of the shebeen to 'white' suburbs, and the degree of police surveillance in the area in which the shebeen was located. The most successful brewers ran shebeens in the larger townships or freehold areas, offering liquor on credit to regular customers. In such cases, the woman's takings seem often to have been considerably higher than anything an African woman could earn in formal employment (although comprehensive statistics are unavailable). In 1951 in Sophiatown, for example, some brewers took in £10 per week.[95] And several 'shebeen queens' there must have earned still more, enough to build large and extravagant houses.[96] But such substantial profits were probably not the norm. In Eastern Native Township, for example, Longmore did not find

a single well-to-do shebeen queen . . . such as the prosperous ones to be found in Sophiatown and other areas where people who specialise in this type of business compete favourably with business men who own stores. The brewers at Eastern Native Township are amongst the poorest inhab-itants, except those who undertake brewing as a sideline, and are at the same time earning more money by working for Europeans in town.[97]

Still, even the less successful brewers were able to protect themselves financially to some extent, by forming rotating credit associations.[98] Each member would make a monthly contribution, and could then periodically withdraw a lump sum from the pool, an insurance against illness, arrest, or deportation.

Prostitution was another well-established economic activity amongst township women, which could also yield substantially more than formal employment. During the 1940s it was already clear to

---

[94] Ibid. 220.
[95] Lodge, *Black Politics*, p. 97. Similar earnings are reported by Bonner, '"Desirable or Undesirable Sotho Women?"', p. 35.
[96] Longmore, *The Dispossessed*, p. 212.
[97] Ibid.
[98] Bonner, '"Desirable or Undesirable Sotho Women?"', p. 35.

the Joint Council of Europeans and Africans that prostitution was common amongst 'young girls because the average monthly wage earned in legitimate employment was too low to satisfy the girls' requirements'.[99] In Sophiatown, by the late 1950s, some prostitutes were earning as much as £20 a day,[100] enough to persuade several husbands or lovers to encourage the practice, offering to stand guard against exposure by the police.[101] But, in other areas, takings were more modest (although still impressive in comparison even to industrial employment)—for example, £5 a day on weekends for prostitutes working in the vicinity of the Denver hostel, in Johannesburg.[102]

### Effects of Migrancy and the Influx Control Laws

As in the case of African men, the migrant labour system had a significant effect on the employment patterns of African women. Dual trends emerged. First, although the evidence is sparse, it seems that urban women tended to dominate the industrial and commercial jobs, which occupied the top end of the wage spectrum.[103] Women living in the townships could draw on the same sorts of contacts, information, and familiarity with the job market which gave urban men the edge over inexperienced migrants in the competition for popular jobs. (There is some evidence, however, that 'home-girl' networks amongst migrant women did fulfil a similar function to male migrant associations, informing and guiding women in their choice of work).[104]

Secondly, migrant women, particularly those who had recently arrived in the urban area, tended to cluster at the bottom end of the job spectrum, being less discriminating in their choice of employment than women already well-established in the area. The dearth of alternative forms of employment meant that domestic service accounted for the majority of female workers, urban and migrant alike. But the proportion of 'tribal' women in domestic service was

[99] CAD NTS 2223 430/280, 'Memorandum of the Joint Council of Europeans and Africans', 1942.
[100] Longmore, *The Dispossessed*, p. 143.
[101] Ibid.
[102] Ibid. 142.
[103] See, e.g., Pauw, *The Second Generation*, p. 33.
[104] Thanks to Belinda Bozzoli for this information.

nevertheless generally higher than that of urbanised women. As Pauw discovered in East London townships, for example, 'domestic employment is less common among town women than it is for the East London Bantu female population as a whole'.[105] Several factors accounted for this trend. Domestic service was notoriously unpopular with urban women, because of the abysmal wages paid, long working hours, and the fact that most white householders insisted that their domestic workers live on the premises. For migrant women separated from their families, having to live outside the townships was less of a drawback. Also, women new to the city were often prepared to enter domestic service as a first step, planning to move on once they were more familiar with their urban surroundings.

In the case of African men, the influx control legislation entrenched and heightened the ways in which the migrant labour system disadvantaged migrant work-seekers in the urban labour market. The terms of section 10(1)(d) and section 12 (in the case of foreigners) rendered inexperienced migrant men all the more vulnerable to unscrupulous employers and 'obnoxious' work. In the case of African women, however, the influx control system had the opposite effect, levelling the options of migrant and urbanised women in some respects, at least until the end of the 1950s. On paper, the 1952 Native Laws Amendment Act subjected African women to the same influx control restrictions as African men. But, in practice, women did not bear the full brunt of these laws until the 1960s. Confronting a storm of protest over the 1952 Act, Verwoerd made two administrative concessions in 1952: women would not yet have to carry reference books; nor would they be subject to the Labour Bureaux Regulations (see Chapter 8). During the 1950s, therefore, women did not have to register with labour bureaux in order to seek work legally, or report there if unemployed. Nor were they compelled to find work within fourteen days. As a result, section 10(1)(d) and section 12 women were spared one of the more powerful pressures forcing their male counterparts to find employment as quickly as possible, settling for 'obnoxious' work in the absence of ready alternatives.

It was also considerably easier for section 10(1)(d) and section 12 women to enter the informal sector without falling foul of the influx control authorities than it was for men. Only men protected by

---

[105] Pauw, *The Second Generation*, p. 33.

section 10(1)(a) or (b) were permitted to avoid formal employment; men on section 10(1)(d) or section 12 permits were liable for 'endorsement out' once they ceased to minister to white needs. In the case of women, however, although section 10(1)(d) and section 12 permit-holders were legally required to work, the fact that they were exempt from the Labour Bureaux Regulations meant that the labour bureaux lacked the authority to police their economic activities.[106]

Ironically, then, the economic incentives for women to enter the informal sector were administratively reinforced. Large numbers of women, migrant and urbanised, therefore continued to resist wage labour, swelling the ranks of the alleged urban labour 'surplus' which the ULPP was intended to eradicate. The NAD had set out to force an increasing proportion of women on to the urban labour market, but unwittingly promoted a conflicting tendency. As one would expect, its effects were most visible at the bottom end of the job spectrum—particularly domestic service—which became increasingly unpopular during the course of the decade (although it remained the single largest employer of African women). In Johannesburg in 1953, for example, the Manager of the municipal NEAD reported that 'the experience of my Department's Employment Bureau indicates quite clearly that the number of Natives who are prepared to take up domestic service is growing steadily smaller over the years'.[107]

## Employment Patterns amongst Township Youth

The ULPP had been premised on the assumption that township youths (aged 15–20) could move into domestic service and the lighter unskilled jobs, releasing adult men for more arduous employment (see Chapter 3). However, youths were marginalised in the labour market by a generalised prejudice amongst employers against the unreliability of youth and the 'cheekiness' of Africans who had

---

[106] This did not mean, however, that women were entirely free from police harassment. Many were arrested and prosecuted on other counts, such as trading without a hawkers' licence or dealing in illicit liquor.

[107] IANA, 'Proceedings of 1953 Annual Conference', p. 91.

strayed from 'tribal' ways. The youths, in turn, often disdained regular employment, particularly if low-paying and involving manual labour, which prevented them from putting their years of schooling to profitable use. More could be earned, and in more adventurous ways, through petty crime organised by youth gangs. As P. Bonner wrote in his study of African townships on the East Rand,

to a greater extent than with urban labour in general, employers found urban youth undisciplined, unreliable, unpunctual, prone to absenteeism and dishonest. Partly this was prejudice, partly it had some basis in fact, but always the prejudice itself helped to cultivate those characteristics of urban youth that employers so deplored. The longer urban youth stayed out of work, the more likely they were to be immersed in the youth gang culture of the townships and to end up, in the language of the Inter-Departmental Committee on Native Juvenile Unemployment, as 'unfit for regular and disciplined work'.[108]

In an attempt to enlarge the numbers of youths employed in the lighter grades of unskilled work, the NAD persuaded the Department of Labour to authorise lower minimum wages for youths than for adults doing the same work. But most employers were unmoved, preferring the services of adult workers to those of youths, no matter how cheap their labour. All the NAD's wage deal did was reinforce the youths' case against formal unskilled employment.

Paradoxically, moreover, this 'job choosiness' (to use the NAD's language) was protected to some extent by the influx control legislation itself. Township youths with residential rights, in terms of section 10(1)(a) or (c), were not legally obliged to find work in order to remain in the cities.[109]

The upshot was what Eiselen called 'an alarming increase of unemployed juveniles who have grown up in the city'.[110] In the words of the Witwatersrand Regional Commissioner, youths 'for whom suitable employment in industry, mining and commerce was not available, were reluctant to accept work as domestic servants, farm

---

[108] Bonner, 'Family, Crime and Political Consciousness on the East Rand, 1939–1955', p. 12.

[109] Section 29 of the Urban Areas Act allowed that section 10(1)(a), (b) and (c) qualifiers could be prosecuted and removed from the area if declared 'idle and undesirable' by the courts. However, municipal administrators complained that this procedure was cumbersome and often ineffectual.

[110] Eiselen, 'The Demand for and the Supply of Bantu Labour', 10.

labourers or in heavy industry, and tended to roam around the streets'.[111]

To conclude, skill differentials, age, gender, ethnicity, and the existence of migrant networks, together with the differentiation between settled workers with section 10(1)(a), (b), and (c) rights and 'migrant' workers with section 10(1)(d) or section 12 permits, all played important roles in segmenting the urban labour market. From an economic and sociological point of view, then, the NAD's model of a homogenous undifferentiated labour market made little sense. Moreover, the economic illogic in the ULPP was symptomatic of an internal contradiction within NAD policy as a whole. Section 10 was, on the one hand, the instrument of the ULPP. It was section 10 which differentiated between urbanised and migrant job-seekers, in order to enable the labour bureaux to place city-dwellers in work ahead of migrants. Yet, on the other hand, the terms of section 10 heightened and entrenched the economic forces militating against the ULPP. Section 10(1)(a), (b), and (c) unwittingly sponsored the 'choosiness' of urbanised job-seekers in the face of 'obnoxious' employment. And the vulnerability and insecurity of a section 10(1)(d) or section 12 migrant played into the hands of employers intent on keeping African wages low at all costs.

Nevertheless, in theory, the labour bureaux system ought to have surmounted all the economic and social obstacles to the ULPP by sheer administrative fiat. The labour bureaux were intended to exercise comprehensive and systematic control over the allocation of African labour to white employers, so that the preferences of job-seekers and employers alike would be flatly overruled by the terms of the ULPP. The failure of the ULPP was, therefore, also a reflection of inadequacies in the operation of the labour bureaux system. The following chapter, which discusses how the labour bureaux system functioned in practice, examines the conflicts between the labour bureaux, employers, and workers over the ULPP, and shows why the labour bureaux submitted to the forces which the ULPP should in theory have overridden.

---

[111] BCC BMR 14/1/30, Regional Employment Commissioner (REC) to Chief NAC, Johannesburg, re 'Inspection of Local Labour Bureau, Brakpan', 18 Jan. 1956, p. 5.

# 7

# *The Workings of the Labour Bureaux*

'PROPER labour planning' in the cities and on the farms, declared the NAD, 'was the ultimate objective of the labour bureaux.'[1] And in the simplistic world of NAD economics, the way to achieve this goal on the urban end was simply to ensure that the number of African job-seekers in any city matched the number of vacancies, allowing for 'a certain limited plussage'.[2] Then each city would be allocated neither too large, nor too small, a supply of African labour. Yet, the inauguration of the labour bureaux system brought worsening labour surpluses and shortages in its wake. Paradoxically, the labour bureaux were both too weak in some respects, and too strong in others, to have undertaken the NAD's labour 'canalisation' programme effectively. This chapter shows that, on the one hand, the labour bureaux exercised *too little* control over the urban labour market to have imposed the ULPP effectively. Surpluses of urban labour were not dislodged, despite the fact that further migrant labour continued to stream into the cities. And, on the other hand, the labour bureaux imposed *too much* control to prevent the simultaneous build-up of labour shortages in various categories. For the ULPP was not wholly inoperative, and, when enforced, its·effect was to exacerbate labour shortages at the bottom end of the job spectrum. Furthermore, the immobility of labour between urban areas was built into the very design of the labour bureaux system. This thrust another spoke into the wheel of the labour redistribution drive, by jamming labour surpluses and shortages on opposite sides of municipal boundaries.

## The Limits of the Labour Bureaux's Control

The labour bureaux's powers to implement the ULPP were thwarted in two ways. First, the majority of employers and job-seekers simply

[1] P. S. van Rensburg, 'Die Instelling van Arbeidsburo's, *Bantu*, 9 (1954), 12.
[2] *HAD* (1952), vol. 77, col. 1315.

bypassed the system altogether; and, secondly, those employers who did participate in it were generally (although not invariably) powerful enough to override the ULPP. These trends are examined in turn.

### *Resistance against the Labour Bureaux System*

It was easier for African women than men to bypass the labour bureaux system. Indeed, the labour bureaux's powers to control female employment were wholly thwarted from the start. Verwoerd's concession in 1952, that the Labour Bureaux Regulations would not apply to women, introduced a sizeable loophole into the ULPP: the labour bureaux had no legal means to force urban or migrant African women into taking any employment, 'obnoxious' or not. The NAD could do little to close the loophole, other than by urging municipalities to entice African women voluntarily into the labour bureaux system. A departmental circular was duly issued in 1952, in which 'all labour bureaux are . . . earnestly requested to endeavour by guidance to impress upon female work-seekers and employers of female workers alike the desirability of their making use of the labour bureaux'.[3] But few municipalities complied, and, when they did, African women generally did not.

The subjection of all men and youths to the Labour Bureaux Regulations only partially strengthened the labour bureaux's hands. A survey by the FCI in 1956 revealed that only 38 per cent of its sample of firms in the Northern Transvaal, for example, used the labour bureaux to fill their vacancies for African workers. Moreover, the survey found that, overall, workers capable of filling semi-skilled or other sought-after positions tended to bypass the labour bureaux system.[4] This entailed, in turn, that employers offering such jobs generally preferred to meet their labour needs without the assistance of labour bureaux.[5]

As far as the more skilled and experienced job-seekers were

---

[3] BCC BMR 14/1/30 NAD 'Guide . . . to Management of Local Labour Bureaux', 3 Nov. 1952, p. 3.

[4] FCI NEAF, 'Memorandum of Results of the Survey on the Availability of Native Labour', 21 June 1956, para. 14. Note, however, that the memorandum also reported generalised complaints about the 'quality of labour', whether supplied by labour bureaux or not.

[5] Ibid., para. 6.

concerned, the labour bureaux system offered them nothing. Poised at the head of the queue for the more popular jobs, they had no reason to surrender their independence to the labour bureaux, which denied job-seekers the right to select their preferred type of work. This bureaucratic levelling of the labour supply also explained why employers in search of labour for skilled or semi-skilled work had compelling reasons to bypass the labour bureaux. Working with the simplistic model of a homogenous labour market described in the previous chapter, the architects of the labour bureaux system had treated all workers as equally suitable for all jobs. They had, therefore, failed to make provision either for the selective placement of different types of workers, or for aptitude tests and other assessments of individual abilities or training. Thus, as the NAD itself admitted in later years,[6] the labour bureaux system was essentially geared towards 'bulk-hiring', which was only appropriate for 'activities requiring mere manual labour'.[7]

Evasion of the labour bureaux system was not confined to the top end of the labour market, however. It was also rampant amongst unskilled job-seekers and their employers. The fact that the more inexperienced migrant workers in particular, were relegated to the less popular jobs was partly a reflection of how heavily dependent they were on finding work relatively quickly, even if poorly paid. The labour bureaux, however, had the power to prevent migrants from coming to the urban areas to take any work at all. Many thousands of Africans propelled to the cities by desperate poverty in the reserves or beyond the country's borders, therefore, chose to seek work illegally, without authorisation from the labour bureaux.

Employers were in turn able to capitalise on this choice. As a municipal official put it, illegal migrants 'had their backs to the wall to an even greater extent'[8] than legal migrants. Dependent on employers' preparedness to flout the regulations, and ever vulnerable to the threat of exposure to the authorities, illegal workers had little bargaining power to challenge 'obnoxious' working conditions and abysmal wages. As the Master Builders' Association pointed out, 'these unregistered Bantu . . . show a loyal [*sic*] and willingness

---

[6] NAD, 'Botha Report', p. 54.

[7] FCI NEAF, 'Memorandum in Regard to Non-European Unrest', 2 June 1958, p. 18.

[8] Interview on 6 Nov. 1984 with a past Manager of the Johannesburg NEAD who did not want to be named.

to work not always evidenced by those possessing passes which permit them to easily leave [*sic*] one job and find another'.[9] Therefore, much to the chagrin of the NAD, 'exploitation by unscrupulous employers, who rely on the fact that the workers' presence in the area is irregular, is an everyday occurrence'.[10]

Bypassing the labour bureaux system was also necessary if workers and employers were to make use of migrant associations as informal labour-recruiting networks. As explained in the previous chapter, migrants who found work through the auspices of a migrant association enjoyed a relatively protected and structured entry into the labour market. For the employer, this arrangement offered several advantages. Not only were workers 'on their best behaviour [because] . . . they came in illegally';[11] employers could also rely to some extent on existing structures of authority within the migrant association as a source of discipline and loyalty within the work-force (see Chapter 6). The labour bureaux system, however, was poised to subvert this arrangement. The bureaux claimed a monopoly on labour recruitment and placement which would override employers' preferences. And the ULPP threatened to undermine migrant associations, either by barring migrants' access to the urban labour market altogether or by atomising their employment, allocating workers individually to whatever job happened to arise at the time.

The cumbersome and time-consuming red tape endemic to any dealings with the labour bureaux created further incentives to employers to engage workers illegally. A request to a labour bureau for labour was a lengthy procedure, as a wad of labour requisition forms was processed by a labyrinthine and inefficient bureaucracy. Adding insult to injury, employers were then required to pay a services levy for every worker sent to them by the bureaux.[12] Finally, the penalties for non-compliance were too mild to have provided much of a deterrent to employers. As the Botha Report

[9] WRAB JMR A78/2/2 Master Builders' Association, 'Draft Memorandum', 17 Apr. 1967.

[10] WRAB JMR A78/2/8, 'Memorandum on . . . Establishing Labour Supply Company for Building and Allied Industries in Johannesburg', 20 Aug. 1968. The remark was made in 1968, but was equally applicable to the 1950s.

[11] Interview with J. Knoetze, 15 July 1985.

[12] In 1952 the NAD introduced a compulsory 'native services levy', payable by employers for every registered African worker, to be used to fund the provision of basic services in the townships.

complained, the courts looked benignly on employers' contravention of the Labour Bureaux Regulations.[13] Convictions were relatively infrequent, and, even then, the fines imposed were low, ranging from £5 to £10.[14]

Having given employers and job-seekers across the board strong incentives to defy the Labour Bureaux Regulations, the labour bureaux system had created a problem of illegal employment on a scale far too large to control. Lacking the personnel to inspect all business premises to check for violations of the Regulations, the labour bureaux could do little to exact greater compliance from employers. On the contrary, punitive raids against employers were seldom conducted. Nor did the state make any effort to stiffen the penalties. Instead, efforts to contain the scale of illegal employment were focused on the townships, rather than in the factories. Labour bureaux relied on the SAP and municipal police to expose illegal workers during dawn pass raids on township homes and spot checks on the streets.

The state's inertia in the face of illegal practices by employers was a good indication of the power of business interests at the administrative level. As the Riekert Commission recognised decades later,[15] policing employers more ruthlessly would have been a far more efficient way of preventing illegal employment than raiding the townships and arresting pass-law offenders. These arrests were so commonplace that they were little or no deterrent. And, however many 'illegals' the police caught, there were thousands more who succeeded in evading the law.

### Resistance within the Labour Bureaux System

The labour bureaux were patronised largely by those employers who failed to secure cheap unskilled labour on the open market.[16] Ironically, the operation of the labour bureaux was, therefore, almost wholly confined to that sector of the labour market where employers' preference for 'tribal' labour was strongest. A conflict between the demands of employers and the prescriptions of the

---

[13] NAD, 'Botha Report', p. 36.

[14] Ibid. 81.

[15] Republic of SA, *Report of Commission . . . into Legislation Affecting Utilisation of Manpower*, RP 32/1979, p. 259.

[16] This excludes, of course, employers who obeyed the law for its own sake.

ULPP thus came to dominate the daily operation of the labour bureaux.[17] It was a conflict which exposed a latent tension between the twin objectives of the NAD's influx control strategy. The architects of this strategy were committed to curtailing the growth of the urban African population, on the one hand, and ensuring an adequate supply of African labour to the cities, on the other. The ULPP was proffered as the means of reconciling the two. However, as the previous discussion showed, the realities of the urban labour market were such that intransigent attempts to impose the ULPP would have thwarted one of the principal functions of the labour bureaux, namely, to supply urban employers with the numbers of workers they required.

The overwhelming demand amongst urban employers was for unskilled labour, which in most cases was expressed as a strong preference for 'tribal' labour. Employers' opposition to the ULPP, therefore, confronted the NAD with the necessity to rank one priority of the influx control policy over the other. Different rankings provoked conflicts between competing factions within the state. But the fact that the ULPP remained largely inoperative gives some indication of the overriding primacy of the economic imperative.

In some cases, the labour bureaux's surrender to the realities of the labour market was authorised from the top echelons of the NAD. The go-ahead came from Verwoerd, who stated bluntly that employers' demands took preference:

if there is a demand for labour in industries or in the sphere of domestic service, the person handling the permits . . . will grant concessions to the Natives to the extent that it is necessary to meet the demand for labour . . . No harm, no difficulties can arise. *The test is always the demand for labour.*[18]

The first of these concessions followed from an amendment to the Natives (Urban Areas) Act in 1954, waiving the ULPP when employers specifically requested the services of individual Africans known to them. In such cases, 'a permit to seek work can . . . be issued to a particular individual for a particular type of employment in spite of any surplus of labour which may exist elsewhere'.[19]

---

[17] Interview with W. J. P. Carr, 23 Nov. 1984.

[18] *HAD* (1955), vol. 87, col. 1802 (author's italics).

[19] FCI NEAF, SNA to FCI, re 'Natives (Urban Areas) Amendment Bill', 5 May 1954.

According to the Witwatersrand's Chief NAC, once this concession was introduced,

both employers and Bantu . . . soon found ways and means of abusing [it]. Bantu illegal entrants streamed in from the reserves, without regard to the labour bureaux system, made the acquaintance of employers and were then applied for, to be introduced as special cases . . . Under this abuse, the exception became the rule. The whole labour bureaux system became undermined.[20]

Then, in 1955, acknowledging that there was an 'acute [labour] shortage experienced by employers in heavy industry',[21] Eiselen authorised labour bureaux on the Witwatersrand to offer Africans caught living illegally in the townships the option of heavy manual jobs as a means of legalising their presence there. A similar concession was offered specifically to workers who had completed their contracts on the mines. Under normal circumstances, the influx control legislation barred them from entering the cities. However, the NAD agreed to lift this barrier for ex-mine-workers provided they took heavy manual work or jobs in municipal services, in areas where such labour was in short supply.[22] In 1956, following representations from IANA, the NAD's Director of Labour, van den Berg, agreed to extend the scope of these concessions countrywide.[23] In its bid to meet employers' demands, the NAD thus resorted to exactly the tactic already noted amongst employers, of exploiting the influx control system as a source of cheap labour for 'obnoxious' employment.

The NAD was internally divided, however, over the relative priority of fuelling the labour supply to cities, as opposed to enforcing the ULPP. In 1957 P. van Rensburg, exponent of a more rigid application of the ULPP, took over as the NAD's Director of Native Labour. Addressing an ASSOCOM congress that year, he insisted that labour shortages in unpopular categories of work 'would not be met by allowing Natives to drift into urban areas,

[20] WRAB JMR A78/7/1, Chief Bantu Affairs Commissioner, Witwatersrand, to Manager, Johannesburg NEAD, re 'Difficulties . . . with Reference Book System', 30 Aug. 1965.
[21] BCC BMR 14/1/30, SNA to Chief NAC, Johannesburg, re 'Employment of Ex-Mine Natives as Domestic Servants', 16 June 1955.
[22] BCC BMR 14/1/30 Minutes of Native Affairs Committee, item 32, 13 Feb. 1956.
[23] IANA, 'Proceedings of 1956 Annual Conference', p. 85.

since the Department could not allow large numbers of unemployed Natives to remain in urban areas'.[24] Van Rensburg ensured that his predecessor's undertaking to IANA was not instituted, and in March 1957 Eiselen's concession to labour bureaux on the Witwatersrand was withdrawn on the grounds that it undermined the ULPP. All Native Affairs Commissioners on the Witwatersrand were informed that 'the Department can no longer tolerate the practice whereby ex-mine Natives and other illegal entrants of your area are being absorbed in industry, which, in fact, means an evasion of the policy regarding the canalisation of Native labour'.[25]

Top-level concessions were, therefore, erratic and unreliable, reflecting conflicts amongst the NAD's leading decision-makers over the practical primacy of the ULPP. But the ULPP was regularly compromised by the daily decisions of lower-ranking NAD officers and municipal administrators. Employers' powers to command the labour of their choice depended in the first instance on the distribution of control between the local and district labour bureaux. The municipal officials who ran the local bureaux were generally, but not invariably, more sympathetic to employers' interests than the departmental bureaucrats running the district bureaux. The Labour Bureaux Regulations required that requests for migrant labour be submitted by the municipal labour bureau to the Native Affairs Commissioner in the nearest district labour bureau. But, in practice, the Commissioners often delegated their authority to admit or bar migrant labour into an urban area to the municipally run bureaux. According to W. Carr and J. Knoetze (both past municipal Managers of Non-European Affairs), this trend was especially marked in the case of local bureaux run by members of the NP, SABRA, or the Broederbond.[26]

Municipal officials, however, were not invariably sympathetic to employers' requests. The ULPP was sometimes enforced, the priority of stemming the migrant tide having been ranked more highly than economic considerations (see later). But, overall, municipal administrators responded sympathetically to employers. As the FCI found in its 1956 survey of 'Native Labour Availability' in secondary industry, 'local labour bureaux are not complying

[24] *Commercial Opinion*, Nov. 1957, p. 27.
[25] BCC BMR 14/1/77, Chief NAC, Witwatersrand, to NAC, Brakpan, re 'Native Labour Bureaux', 8 Mar. 1957.
[26] Interviews with W. J. P. Carr, 23 Nov. 1984, and J. Knoetze, 15 July 1985.

strictly with the Regulations but are responding in a far more lenient manner to the requirements of employers of Native labour'.[27]

There were several reasons for this trend. First, as employees of elected town or city councils, municipal officials' decisions were shaped to a large extent by the exigencies of local government. In particular, local authorities had vested interests in promoting the industrial and commercial expansion in their areas, not least because the rates paid by businesses made an important contribution to the local authorities' coffers. Local capitalists were also influential members of the white constituency which elected the local authority. Therefore, as the Municipal Association of the Transvaal put it, 'if local authorities are in a position to help industries by increasing their efficiency and competitiveness, it is their duty to help'.[28]

In some respects, the expansion of local industry presented the municipalities with a double-edged sword. A growing African work-force entailed a growing demand for township housing, the costs of which were borne by the local authority. The expense of supplying extra accommodation was, therefore, a countervailing factor, which led some municipalities more than others to tighten their grip on employers. But most local authorities had no ambitions of housing all workers. Despite the accelerated construction of African housing during the 1950s, the housing shortage remained too formidable for local authorities with limited housing budgets to have eliminated altogether. In Durban, for example, the NEAD estimated an accommodation shortage of at least 15,000 houses and 20,000 hostel beds in 1960. Yet in that year only 3,528 houses were built.[29] Johannesburg, too, had what the City Council called a 'chaotic Native housing shortage'. At the end of 1958 about 17,000 families still required housing.[30] Under these conditions, most municipalities simply stopped measuring the demand for housing; and the work-force carried on expanding.

Another reason for municipal laxness with the ULPP was the fact that municipalities understood the preference for 'tribal' labour

[27] FCI NEAF, 'Native Labour Availability: Summary of Memorandum', 21 June 1956.
[28] WRAB JMR A14/2 IANA, 'First Addendum to Agenda of 62nd Ordinary Meeting of Institute Council', 28 Aug. 1962.
[29] KCL DMR KCF 46, Bourquin to SAIRR, 5 Dec. 1960.
[30] ASSOCOM NEAF TCI Labour Division, 'Memorandum', 4 Apr. 1955.

well, being party to it themselves.[31] As large employers of unskilled African labour, paying wages at the lower end of the spectrum, municipalities had labour needs which were directly at odds with the ULPP too. In Johannesburg, for example, as the NAD's Director of Labour had explained in 1948, 'for its sanitary service, the municipality must recruit 100 natives from outside Johannesburg per week. The municipality pays £2 per week and they cannot get the natives in Johannesburg. In certain factories they pay 12/6 per day.'[32]

Ironically, the bureaux's administrative procedure also created incentives for their officials to waive the ULPP. The performance of a labour bureau was measured by the NAD in terms of the number of service contracts registered. Bureaux officials who took a hard line on the ULPP ran the risk of alienating employers from the labour bureaux altogether, and thereby depleting the registration statistics. Also, labour bureaux officials were widely suspected of taking bribes from employers, one of the more lucrative ways of improving the statistical records.

Durban was a good example of the trend for employers' demands for migrant labour to be upheld when local labour bureaux were controlled *de facto* at municipal level. Despite the fact that the local authority was dominated by the UP, it had a relatively free hand. The labour bureaux were run according to so-called 'City Council Policy', which dismissed the ULPP.[33] Since Durban's urbanised African population was relatively small, its employers relied heavily on migrant labour. A ULPP, therefore, had no place in the City Council's scheme of things, which permitted employers to draw freely on 'tribal' labour from seven designated rural areas.[34] It was not until 1959/60, in the wake of the political upheaval triggered by the 1959 Cato Manor riots (see Chapter 9), that the NAD ordered the Durban NEAD to follow departmental policy more scrupulously.

In the main, then, when employers' demands for 'tribal' labour were dealt with by municipal administrators, they were generally (although not uniformly) upheld. However, the typical experience

[31] Interview with W. J. P. Carr, 23 Nov. 1984.
[32] CAD NTS 2229 463/280, 'Notas van Vergadering tussen die Department van Naturellesake en die Skakelkommittee', 1 Nov. 1948.
[33] Durban City Council, *Mayor's Minute*, 1959/60, p. 116.
[34] Horwood, 'Some Aspects of Urban African Employment in the Durban Area', p. 6.

of employers in Johannesburg illustrates that, even when an unsympathetic Native Affairs Commissioner dominated the operation of the labour bureau, the interests of local business usually prevailed over the ULPP. The UP majority in the Johannesburg City Council fanned suspicions within the NAD that 'liberal' influences corrupted the reliability of the NEAD, so much so that, in 1958, Verwoerd appointed a watchdog committee of departmental officials to check that NAD policy was strictly enacted. With Verwoerd's eye keenly trained upon it, the Johannesburg municipal labour bureau dutifully referred all requests for migrant labour to the Native Affairs Commissioner. According to W. Carr, then Manager of the Johannesburg NEAD, an acrimonious battle usually ensued, with the NEAD taking the employer's side against the Native Affairs Commissioner. But even then, according to Carr, the Commissioner 'nearly always . . . would have to give way'.[35]

In Cape Town, too, the Commissioner generally yielded under pressure, until 1959/60. The inauguration of the CLPP in 1955 had supposedly placed an absolute prohibition on further African employment in the area until all Coloureds looking for work had been employed. But, since most Coloureds refused the lowest-paid menial work, initial moves to enforce the CLPP were stalled by pressure from the Cape Chamber of Industries. The Chamber persuaded the Native Affairs Commissioner that the shortages of unskilled labour in Cape Town were already 'so critical'[36] that blocking industrialists' access to African migrant labour would incur serious economic harm.

Employers' preferences prevailed partly because of the power of local job-seekers to defy the ULPP. As Carr observed, the Native Affairs Commissioners had to give in because 'local labour was not prepared to take the jobs'.[37] Even if employers had relented to taking on local labour, section 10(1)(a), (b), and (c) deprived the labour bureaux of the powers to marshall urban job-seekers into jobs they did not want. So, had the Commissioners simply refused to give way on the ULPP issue, they would have created massive labour shortages in the cities without reducing the size of the existing

---

[35] Interview with W. J. P. Carr, 23 Nov. 1984.

[36] FCI NEAF, 'Native Labour Availability and Influx Control', 24 Nov. 1955, p. 6.

[37] Interview with W. J. P. Carr, 23 Nov. 1984.

urban labour surpluses. The labour bureaux system would thus have become a far more thoroughgoing failure than it was, and the NAD's undertaking to supply urban employers with the number of workers they required, entirely discredited.

To conclude, therefore, the realities of the labour market tended on the whole to structure the labour bureaux system, rather than vice versa as intended. There are important exceptions to this trend, which are dealt with in the next section. But, overall, as the FCI remarked, the ULPP was

rarely, if ever, applied . . . In practice, labour bureaux in urban areas have been unable to meet the demands for labour with the labour available from the local residents in those areas. Supplies of native labour have therefore had to be brought into the urban area from extra-urban areas.[38]

### The Excesses of Labour Bureaux Control

One of the purposes of the labour bureaux system was to 'allow an easy flow of labour from areas where there is no work to areas where there is work'.[39] Verwoerd, therefore, assured parliament in 1952 that 'there will be no restrictions controlling movement from a proclaimed area with a labour surplus to a proclaimed area with a labour shortage'.[40] He was mistaken, however. Labour mobility between proclaimed areas was seriously thwarted by the substance of the Labour Bureaux Regulations in conjunction with the terms of section 10(1).

Organised commerce and industry complained of a worsening problem of labour immobility, manifest in two forms. First, if labour was in short supply in one part of an industrial region and in abundance in another, the nature of the labour bureaux system tended to inhibit the transfer of labour between them. This led to the creation and entrenchment of artificial pockets of regional unemployment—artificial, because they coexisted with adjacent or nearby surpluses for comparable categories of work.[41] For example,

---

[38] FCI NEAF, 'Industrial Native Labour in South Africa', 22 Nov. 1955, p. 2.
[39] *HAD* (1952), vol. 77, col. 552.
[40] Ibid., cols. 551–2.
[41] See FCI NEAF, 'Native Labour Availability and Influx Control', 24 Nov. 1955, p. 4; TCI, 'Minutes of Meeting of Non-European Affairs Committee . . . 12/4/55', pp. 5–6.

by the mid-1950s industrialists in Nigel (on the East Rand) complained that they suffered labour shortages but were unable to utilise the labour surplus in nearby Germiston.[42] Likewise, Roodepoort (outside Johannesburg) was unable to draw labour surpluses from Johannesburg.[43]

Secondly, employers complained of difficulty in transferring their own employees between factories in different proclaimed areas—a problem on the increase on the Rand, for example, where 'the expansion of industry . . . resulted in a gradual movement away from Johannesburg . . . to properly planned and developed industrial zones'.[44] This problem was particularly vexing to firms wishing to transfer their more skilled and experienced African workers. Industrialists complained that a dearth of skilled and semi-skilled labour was inhibiting expansion and retarding productivity. The NAD's influx control policies aggravated this problem, by making it difficult, if not impossible, for firms transferring their operations to a different municipal area to retain the services of the more highly trained Africans in their employ. Instead, as the FCI complained, such transfers subjected firms to the inefficient and illogical process of having to take on African workers anew and repeat the training process from scratch.

This, in addition to the considerable administration and expenses involved, also introduces the ludicrous position that Natives with industrial experience and training and who should obviously be retained in the urban areas, are moved to occupations and areas for which they are totally unsuited, while industrial employers are forced to meet their labour shortages with new recruits from the reserve areas who have to be specially trained in all spheres of industrial activity.[45]

The root of the immobility problem in each case was the economically arbitrary and irrational delineation of a local labour bureau's area of jurisdiction. Designated part of the municipal administration, a local labour bureau operated within municipal boundaries, administratively sealing off its area from others within the same industrial region. The Witwatersrand, for example, while economically

[42] FCI NEAF TCI, 'Minutes of Meeting of Non-European Affairs Committee . . . 12/4/55', pp. 5–6.
[43] Ibid. 6.
[44] FCI NEAF, Sec., Non-European Affairs Committee, to All Members, re 'Native Labour Mobility', 18 Mar. 1957.
[45] Ibid. 4.

a single region, was fragmented into a series of discrete administrative zones, each controlled by a separate local labour bureau. The Labour Bureaux Regulations then made no specific provision for the direct transfer of work-seekers between local labour bureaux. In fact, the Regulations tacitly shunned such a procedure by specifying that work-seekers wishing to enter a proclaimed area required authorisation from a district labour bureau. A local labour bureau facing a shortage of labour in its area applied for additional labour from the Native Affairs Commissioner in the nearest district labour bureaux, and not from adjacent or nearby local labour bureaux which had not found work for all the work-seekers registered with them. As a result, the African population of the urban area grew, while labour surpluses remained intact, exactly the trend which the NAD had set out to eradicate.

These administrative barriers to the transfer of African labour between proclaimed areas were yet another symptom of the NAD's simplistic model of a homogenous labour market. By treating all labour as interchangeable, the architects of the NAD's labour 'canalisation' policy had seen no need to make special provisions for the transfer of semi-skilled or skilled workers.

Confronted with the immobility problem soon after the Labour Bureaux Regulations had been promulgated, the NAD reacted in much the same way as it did to employers' pressures on other fronts: by making concessions. In 1954 the NAD authorised that, when labour shortages and surpluses occurred in adjacent proclaimed areas, African men with section 10(1)(a), (b), or (c) qualifications in the one area could move directly to the other area, provided they took up employment there.[46] But the terms of section 10 introduced a catch which effectively nullified the concession. Section 10(1)(a), (b), and (c) qualifications were not transferable between proclaimed areas; in fact, they were forfeited once employment was taken in a different proclaimed area from that in which the qualifications were issued. A section 10(1)(a), (b), or (c) qualifier moving to a job in a different proclaimed area had to settle for section 10(1)(d) status in the new area, which denied his wife and family the right to move with him. A section 10(1)(d) permit also carried no protection against being 'endorsed out' to the reserves if he became unemployed.

---

[46] WRAB JMR A78, REC, Witwatersrand, to Manager, Johannesburg NEAD, re 'Bantu Labour Bureaux: Bantu Women . . . ', 22 June 1959.

Understandably, therefore, few, if any, men were prepared to make the sacrifice. 'The effect of section 10(1)(a) and (b)', as the IANA Council reported, was 'therefore to rule out movement of Bantu workers from the area of one local authority to another'.[47]

Labour immobility engendered by section 10(1) lay at the heart of rising levels of unemployment in Vereeniging, for example. During the 1950s most vacancies for Africans in Vereeniging were in heavy manual jobs concentrated in its steel and steel-based industries (mainly ISCOR). Local job-seekers often refused this work, or were turned down by employers preferring the purportedly superior strength and discipline of a 'tribal' migrant worker. However, were the 'detribalised' men and women of Vereeniging to have left the area to take preferred clerical, commercial, or industrial jobs in neighbouring towns, they would have sacrificed their section 10(1)(a), (b), or (c) status in Vereeniging. It was only by remaining unemployed in Vereeniging that their residential rights were secure, an ironic inversion of the ULPP, which had been designed to secure full employment within urbanised communities issued with these rights.

The administrative problems in transferring workers between proclaimed areas were not confined to section 10(1)(a), (b), and (c) qualifiers. Memoranda from organised commerce and industry suggest that various municipal labour bureaux officials would have been prepared to condone the transfer of employees with section 10(1)(d) status between proclaimed areas if they were accompanying their employers to new factories or businesses.[48] Yet, however amenable the municipal authorities might have been to this arrangement, the workers in question often had good reason not to participate in it. With desperate housing shortages in many areas, particularly those of rapid industrial expansion, workers were unlikely to find accommodation in the area to which they transferred. Those section 10(1)(d) workers who had secured accommodation in one proclaimed area were therefore reluctant to move. As the Transvaal Chamber of Industries put it, 'the Native prefers to stay where the house is and relinquish the job'.[49]

---

[47] WRAB JMR A14/2 IANA, 'First Addendum to Agenda of 62nd Ordinary Meeting of Institute Council', 28 Aug. 1962.
[48] FCI NEAF, 'Minutes of Non-European Affairs Committee', 12 Apr. 1955, p. 6.
[49] Ibid. 4.

From the mid-1950s organised commerce and industry placed mounting pressure on the NAD to tackle the problem of labour immobility. The FCI, for example, recognised that the problem derived from the economically arbitrary delineation of a proclaimed area to which section 10(1) qualifications, housing, and work-seekers' permits were restricted. A memorandum from the FCI in 1956, therefore, recommended that 'legislation affecting the employment of Natives in industry established in the Urban Areas of the Union, should be made to apply on a unitary basis comprised of an economic area or an industrial area in preference to the present municipal or Urban Areas of application'.[50] The FCI drew confidence in its representations from the fact that Verwoerd claimed to favour the principle of regional control over urban African housing and employment.[51] But the FCI's recommendations were stillborn, blocked by municipal administrators intent on retaining direct control over Africans housed and employed within their areas of jurisdiction. It was municipal administrators who had earlier thwarted a similar proposal by W. Carr, Manager of the Johannesburg NEAD. In a paper at the 1953 IANA Congress, Carr had called on fellow administrators and the NAD to consider the 'principle of accepting the Reef or similar areas of industrial and commercial concentration as one economic and labour unit'[52] throughout which section 10(1) qualifications would be valid. However, as Carr had anticipated, the proposal was stifled through 'lack of support from some of my colleagues'.[53] Their objections were focused on the issue of administrative control: who would administer the influx control system when applied over enlarged proclaimed areas? Suspicious that the Johannesburg NEAD would dominate any new regional authority created for this purpose, other municipalities in the region were reluctant to cede their direct authority over Africans' access to jobs and employment within the municipal area.

The point has been made several times that, during the 1950s, the NAD had neither the strength nor the resources wholly to restructure the parameters of administrative control over urban African

---

[50] FCI NEAF, 'Economic Areas as Units for Application of Legislation', 27 Mar. 1956, p. 1.
[51] Ibid.
[52] IANA, 'Proceedings of 1953 Annual Conference', p. 85.
[53] Ibid.

housing and employment. Therefore, despite Verwoerd's inclination to support Carr's proposals, the NAD yielded to the municipal consensus.

Leaving the existing structure of the labour bureaux system intact, the NAD had few palliatives for the business community. At its meeting with the FCI, ASSOCOM, and the Transvaal Chamber of Industries in 1955 over the issue of labour immobility, all the NAD could do was to undertake to advise municipal administrators that Africans should be permitted to live in one proclaimed area and work in another.[54] Most municipalities, however, were unreceptive to the suggestion. Some complained that there was no uniform official procedure by which to co-ordinate and keep track of such an arrangement. The Labour Bureaux Regulations did not preclude employment in one area and residence in another; but they did not specifically authorise it either. And most administrators made little effort to come to some arrangement between themselves. For they had more serious objections to the very principle of the NAD's scheme. The costs to the local authority of providing basic services to township residents were partially recouped from a services levy, payable by the employer for each African worker registered with the local labour bureau. If a local authority agreed to continue accommodating Africans who found employment in other areas, then it would have to bear the cost of supplying them with services without drawing in their services levies. Local authorities were also reluctant to bear the cost of housing Africans who were not 'ministering to white needs' within the municipal area. Therefore, as A. S. Marais, Manager of the Boksburg NEAD, told IANA 'local authorities will not accept responsibility for Bantu housing unless they are also able to control the Bantu influx into their particular areas'.[55]

Persistent labour shortages in unpopular categories of work represented another barrier to 'proper labour planning' unwittingly created by the substance of NAD policy itself. The shortage of unskilled labour for 'obnoxious' industrial work, acknowledged by the NAD to be 'acute' in 1954, did not let up as the decade wore on. In 1956 the FCI reported that, while the labour bureaux system had 'not resulted in any starvation of industrial labour in the urban

[54] FCI NEAF, 'Minutes of Non-European Affairs Committee', 12 Apr. 1955, p. 6.
[55] WRAB JMR A14/2/2 IANA Transvaal Division, 'Minutes of Meeting of 23 August 1961'.

areas',[56] industrialists on the Witwatersrand particularly reported worsening labour shortages in certain heavy manual categories.[57] By 1958, this trend seems not to have changed, despite the NAD's preparedness to waive the ULPP in certain instances and the generally pragmatic attitude to the ULPP on the part of many local labour bureaux officials. In an address to the Johannesburg Chamber of Commerce in March 1958, Eiselen admitted that 'in recent months there have been several reports of grave labour shortages in many spheres'.[58] This included municipal and domestic service.[59]

The root of these shortages was low wages and poor working conditions. Had industrialists, municipalities, or householders been prepared to increase wages for unskilled work, it would have been more attractive to job-seekers within and beyond the townships. However, the fact that the labour bureaux system usually *did* deliver a cheap and vulnerable supply of labour led employers to respond to the labour shortages by blaming the labour bureaux, rather than reassessing unskilled wage levels.

There was some truth in these accusations. Employers' demands for 'tribal' labour were sometimes blocked by intransigent administrators who stood by the ULPP willy-nilly.[60] And, as discussed earlier in this chapter, the realities of the urban labour market, together with the logic of Section 10 rights, ensured that the enforcement of the ULPP exacerbated local labour shortages, leaving local surpluses intact. Unless a supply of 'tribal' labour was forthcoming, 'obnoxious' vacancies tended not to be filled. However, the more resounding blow to employers' interests was inflicted by the NAD's efforts to curb the employment of foreign Africans in the cities.

By 1951, foreign Africans comprised a large proportion of the urban African workforce. On one estimate, approximately 215,000 foreigners were then employed in secondary and tertiary industries. Foreigners were also well-represented in the service sector, parti-

---

[56] FCI NEAF, 'Memorandum on Results of Survey on the Availability of Native Labour', 21 June 1956.

[57] FCI NEAF, Sec. of Non-European Affairs Committee to SNA, re 'Native Labour', 28 Aug. 1956.

[58] W. Eiselen, 'The Supply of, and the Demand for, Bantu Labour', *Bantu* 5 (1958), 14.

[59] BCC BMR 14/1/30, REC to NACs, Witwatersrand, re 'Arbeidstekort: Witwatersrand', 29 Nov. 1957. See also O. Horwood, 'Some Aspects of Urban African Employment in the Durban Area', 7.

[60] Interview with J. Knoetze, 15 July 1985.

cularly in hotels. Most were unskilled workers[61] to whom the stereo-typical attributes of the 'raw' migrant worker—obedience, strength, discipline—were particularly strongly attached. The Tomlinson Commission, for example, reported on a 'number of undertakings' in which 'the management preferred foreign Natives, because they were said to be more efficient workers'.[62] The FCI noted, too, that foreigners were more likely than Union-born workers to accept low wages and 'obnoxious work',[63] a pattern confirmed by the Federated Hotels' Association.[64]

It was NAD policy, however, to deflect foreign work-seekers from the urban areas, to the mines and white farms. In terms of Section 12 of the Natives (Urban Areas) Act (as amended in 1952), no further employment of foreign workers was permitted in the urban areas. In a bid to ensure strict and uniform adherence to this policy, Verwoerd circumvented the municipalities and centralized the issue of Section 12 permits in the office of the Secretary for Native Affairs. By 1955, Eiselen had instructed labour bureaux that 'no foreign Native shall be permitted to remain in the service of an employer [in urban areas] for longer than two years'.[65] Employer bodies reacted angrily. The Federated Hotels' Association, for example, sent a deputation to Verwoerd in 1954, to protest the 'difficulties created for the industry by . . . the repatriation of foreign Natives'.[66] Verwoerd's response was markedly different from his generally pragmatic attitude to the employment of Union-born migrants. According to the Federated Hotels' Association, 'the Minister stated that "in regard to foreign Natives, we are merciless". He realised that this might deprive the industry of good employees, but he believed Union Natives could, with training, be made to fill their place.'[67]

Business pressure was not wholly ineffectual, however. In 1956, in certain regions of the Witwatersrand, the two-year limit on a foreign worker's service contract was revoked, provided he or she remained

[61] Union of SA, *Tomlinson Commission*, 41.
[62] Ibid.
[63] FCI NEAF, 'Memorandum on Native Labour Availability and Influx Control', 24 Nov. 1955.
[64] ASSOCOM NEAF, Federated Hotels' Association of Southern Africa (FHA), 'Deputation to Minister of Native Affairs', 4 Aug. 1954.
[65] BCC BMR 14/1/30, 'Inspeksie van Naturelle Arbeidsburo', 9 Feb. 1956.
[66] ASSOCOM NEAF, FHA, 'Deputation . . .', 4 Aug. 1954.
[67] Ibid.

with the same employer.[68] Also, employers in smaller towns seem to have enjoyed a relatively flexible application of the regulations. As Chapter 5 showed, between 1950 and 1960, the foreign population of the metropolitan areas fell slightly by 4.5 per cent, but more than doubled in the towns. This suggests that Section 12 restrictions were more rigorously enforced in the metropolitan areas than in the smaller towns. Even in the metropolitan areas, however, employers resisted the NAD's restrictions by taking on foreign workers illegally. A comparison of population and employment statistics with labour bureaux' records suggests that such illegal employment must have taken place on a large scale. In 1950, approximately 215,000 of the 354,100 foreign Africans living in the urban areas were employed in secondary and tertiary industries. By 1960, according to Simkins, the foreign population of the urban areas had risen to 432,800.[69] Legally, foreign Africans were only entitled to live in urban areas if employed there, with the approval of the labour bureaux. Yet, in 1960, only 53,281 foreign workers (approximately 12 per cent of the foreign Africans living in the urban areas) were registered with labour bureaux.[70] The NAD's drive to enforce the ULPP against foreign workers did not entirely succeed, therefore. But the policy was rigid enough to have provoked continued complaints from industrialists. The FCI for example, protested to Eiselen that by blocking industrialists' access to foreign labour, the NAD was creating artificial shortages of labour in the most unpopular, poorly paid categories of work.[71]

To conclude then, this chapter has examined dual facets of the labour bureaux' failure to restructure the urban labour market in line with the NAD's idiosyncratic concept of economic 'rationality'. What the NAD deemed an 'irrational' labour market prevailed because of both the strengths and the weaknesses of the labour bureaux system. The labour bureaux were too weak to overrule resistance to the ULPP from employers and workers alike. The policy which was to have been the principal vehicle for 'ration-

---

[68] BCC BMR 14/1/30. 'Minutes of Native Administration Committee, Item 32', 13 Feb. 1956.

[69] See p. 142.

[70] K. Owen, *Foreign Africans: Summary of . . . Froneman Committeee*, 45.

[71] FCI NEAF, 'Native Labour Availability and Influx Control', 24 Nov. 1955, 4.

alising' the labour market was thus largely inoperative. Instead, the labour bureaux had to submit to the forces of a differentiated labour market, which tended to concentrate 'tribal' and 'detribalised' labour in different sorts of work. With a massive demand for 'tribal' labour for unskilled work, migrant workers continued to stream into the cities alongside surpluses of local labour.

The differentiations in the labour market also rendered the ULPP self-defeating when the labour bureaux *were* strong enough to impose it. Since local job-seekers refused to take 'obnoxious' work, the effect of the ULPP was to create (or aggravate existing) unskilled labour shortages, rather than to diminish urban labour surpluses. The labour bureaux system, therefore, failed to redirect surpluses of labour for more popular work, and to remedy shortages of labour for the unpopular jobs. Furthermore, the system was also unsuccessful in redirecting surplus job-seekers in one urban area to another area experiencing a shortage, even if the work available was agreeable to them.

In each case, the NAD's own amendment to section 10 of the Natives (Urban Areas) Act was one of the labour bureaux system's major stumbling blocks. First, section 10(1) subverted the ULPP on both the skilled/semi-skilled and the unskilled ends of the labour market. The labour bureaux had little recourse[72] against section 10(1)(a), (b), and (c) qualifiers who preferred 'idleness' to menial work. Section 10(1)(d), on the other hand, limited such selectiveness on the part of migrant workers. And the mere existence of the influx control legislation ensured that illegal migrants were the most vulnerable and insecure of all, and therefore a particularly attractive source of labour for unpopular work. Secondly, section 10(1) ensured that, even when employers did use the labour bureaux, the bureaux were forced to operate 'irrationally' (by their standards). The 'job choosiness' of section 10(1)(a), (b), and (c) job-seekers and the vulnerability and insecurity of 10(1)(d) workers ensured that, in order to supply employers with labour at all, the labour bureaux generally had to set the ULPP aside. Thirdly, the same factors ensured that, when the ULPP was enforced, its effect was to create

---

[72] Except by instituting court proceedings against Africans deemed to be 'idle and undesirable' (in terms of section 29 of the Natives (Urban Areas) Act)—a notoriously lengthy and often unsuccessful procedure (see Ch. 6 n. 111).

labour shortages, rather than eliminate surpluses. Fourthly, section 10(1) was also a considerable barrier against the mobility of African labour across municipal boundaries, since the residential rights of section 10(1)(a), (b), and (c) qualifiers were not transferable.

# 8

# *Influx Control and African Urbanisation*

AN instrument for the redistribution of African labour, influx control during the 1950s was also motivated by the NAD's determination to keep the resident urban African population as small as possible without scarring the urban economy. The Nationalist government found the prospect of an ever-enlarging urban proletariat politically alarming, looking upon the townships as hotbeds of 'communistic' dissent and agitation. Verwoerd and Jansen bemoaned the loss of 'tribal' discipline and identity amongst urbanised Africans, accompanied by the spreading appeal of the ANC and CPSA, and the growth of the African trade union movement. Such developments, they claimed, gave rise to 'all kinds of undesirable conditions'.[1]

The ULPP was to have played some role in the NAD's efforts to curtail the urban African presence by limiting the numbers of workers drawn into the cities from rural areas. But the NAD was also intent on prohibiting rural migrants from settling in the cities on a permanent basis with their families. While the continued, but controlled, growth of the migrant work-force was accepted as economically necessary, further African urbanisation was not. The NAD found the stream of women entering the towns from rural areas particularly disturbing, because it boosted the number of children born and bred in the cities. The NAD was perturbed, too, by the growing independence of what it called 'undesirable' women who had escaped the authority of parents or husbands.[2]

As Chapter 5 showed, the NAD's drive to curb further African urbanisation was largely unsuccessful. The absolute number, and relative proportion, of Africans settling in the cities went up, not down. One index of this process was the proportionately greater

---

[1] NAD, 'Native Policy of the Union of South Africa' (NAD Fact Paper no. 9; 1951), p. 1.
[2] BCC BMR 14/1/54, SNA to Town Clerks, re 'Control over Influx of Native Women into Urban Areas', 13 Oct. 1953. See also Ch. 3.

increase in the size of the female, than the male, urban African population. Despite having placed a greater premium on deterring women from moving to the cities, the NAD's influx control policy was far less effective in curbing the migration of women than of men.

The three sections of this chapter each examine one principal reason why the settled urban African communities in 'white' areas continued to expand during the 1950s, influx control barriers notwithstanding. The first section explores the impact within the state of mass protests against passes for women, in order to explain why, until late in the decade, African women enjoyed greater freedom of movement than African men. The second section assesses the practical effect of one of the legislative loopholes in the NAD's influx control programme. It examines the extent to which section 10(1)(a), (b), and (c) of the Urban Areas Act provided a protected avenue into the townships for originally migrant men and women and their families. The third part considers the effects of unorganised African resistance to the influx control laws. It was the determined evasion of the influx control system by many thousands of illegal city-dwellers that inflicted one of the most telling defeats on the NAD's efforts to curb urbanisation.

## Struggles against Influx Control for Women

From the start, the prospect of passes for women aroused what one municipal administrator called 'almost fanatical opposition'[3] from Africans across the board. The reasons for the protest varied between genders and social groupings. Familiar with the humiliation and harassment engendered by the pass system, many men did not want to see their spouses and daughters subjected to the same ordeals. It was commonly feared, too, that enforcing the pass laws would give the police a pretext for sexually abusing African women.[4] But 'the most frequently articulated male objection to women's passes was that they interfered with a man's authority over his own

---

[3] S. A. Rogers, 'The Administrative and Socio-Economic Problems Arising from the Presence or Absence of Bantu Women in Urban Areas', in IANA, 'Proceedings of 1957 Annual Conference', p. 160.

[4] e.g. George Xorile's Papers, 'Minutes of Twenty-Eighth Annual Session . . . of Location Advisory Boards' Congress . . . 9th to 12th January 1956', p. 7.

wife'.[5] A range of male-dominated organisations and institutions, therefore, championed the women's cause. The ANC, for example, vaunted the issue of passes for women as one requiring national mobilisation of men and women.[6] Even the moderate Location Advisory Boards' Congress took strong exception to the state's policy, as 'degrading and humiliating'.[7] But it was women who took the lead; their struggles were typically more vigorous and tenacious than the men's. According to the Federation of South African Women,[8] this often led to the withdrawal of active support for the women's struggles by men who disapproved of the women's militancy.[9]

The struggle against passes for women, then, was dominated by women; but the distinct groupings of women involved in it should be distinguished, since each was motivated by particular grievances and fears. Almost all the leadership of the anti-pass campaigns comprised trade unionists, teachers, or nurses, whose higher levels of education enabled them to take on organisational responsibilities such as compiling memoranda, delivering speeches, etc.[10] The mass support for the campaigns, however, was drawn principally from 'the women who had the most to lose economically from the advent of passes'.[11] As J. Wells observed,

it is precisely those women who lived as home-based workers, combining child-care responsibilities with economic activity, who responded with the strongest intensity . . . The flashpoint for resistance came at those times when state interference threatened to diminish or deny their ability to work in this way.[12]

The NAD's influx control laws levelled exactly this threat at home-based workers. One of the approved means for a woman to secure a pass (in terms of section 10(1)(d)) was to be formally employed by whites through the auspices of a labour bureau. In

---

[5] J. Wells, 'The History of Black Women's Struggle against Pass Laws in South Africa, 1900–1960' (Ph. D. thesis, Univ. of Columbia, 1982), p. 363.

[6] Walker, *Women and Resistance*, p. 190.

[7] George Xorile's Papers, 'Minutes of Twenty-Eighth Annual Session', p. 7.

[8] This was a non-racial national women's organisation, set up in 1954, which played a leading role in the fight against women's passes.

[9] Walker, *Women and Resistance*, p. 196.

[10] Wells, 'The History of Black Women's Struggle', p. 368.

[11] Ibid. 371.

[12] Ibid.

terms of the official rhetoric of influx control, women working at or from home were considered 'idle' and 'unproductive', and therefore liable for expulsion from the urban area, unless protected by section 10(1)(a), (b), or (c) residential rights.[13]

Single women, defending their social as well as their economic independence, were also vigorous participants in the anti-pass protests of the decade. Apart from formal employment by whites, the only remaining legal avenue into the urban areas for women was marriage to a man holding section 10(1) rights. Not only did the Nationalists' influx control laws threaten the livelihood of women engaged in informal economic activities; an attack was also launched on the pervasive urban patterns of late marriage and/or avoidance of marriage altogether in favour of informal unions (see Chapter 6).

The Nationalists first encountered the vehemence of women's anti-pass protests in 1950, in Durban, Langa, Kensington, and Elsies River in Cape Town, Uitenhage, East London, Phomolong, and Pietermaritzburg.[14] Alarmed by 'the whole uproar', Jansen had then promised women a reprieve. But Verwoerd had other ideas, and saw to it that the Native Laws Amendment Act, which contained the kernel of the NAD's influx control strategy, was applicable to women as well as men (see Chapter 4). The influx control arsenal created by this legislation comprised three main weapons: first, the 1952 amendments to section 10(1) of the Natives (Urban Areas) Act; secondly, the 1952 amendments to the Native Labour Act, authorising the creation of labour bureaux and associated procedures; and, thirdly, the 1952 Abolition of Passes and Documents Act, compelling all Africans over 16 to carry a reference book. Despite widespread popular outrage, Verwoerd was successful in ensuring that, legally, each of these three facets of influx control applied to African women, as well as to men. Verwoerd's only legal concession to women was to have extended section 10(1) to allow an automatic residential right for the wives of urbanised men (in terms of section 10(1)(c)).

In the early 1950s, then, the strength of popular feeling against passes for women had limited impact at the legislative level. But it

---

[13] Section 10(1)(a) or (b) status was determined by birth and/or lengthy continuous formal employment in the area, criteria which excluded large numbers of urban women.

[14] Walker, *Women and Resistance*, p. 129.

had a decisive effect at the administrative level. Once the legislation had been promulgated, Verwoerd then sought to defuse the popular outcry by promising an administratively lax approach. As localised anti-pass demonstrations raged during and after 1952,[15] Verwoerd tried to assure Africans that their protests were unnecessary: 'I repeat that notwithstanding the fact that these provisions are applicable to Native women, it is not our intention to proceed with its practical application at the moment because we do not think that the time is ripe for that.'[16]

Verwoerd's declaration was only two-thirds true, however. Women were exempted from the Labour Bureaux Regulations; that is, they did not need permission from the labour bureaux to seek or take work, nor did they have to report to the bureaux if unemployed. This was a substantial concession, since it severed the critical linkage in the NAD's influx control strategy between Africans' access to the urban areas and the availability of employment there. Also, Verwoerd conceded a temporary reprieve in the issuing of reference books to women. But African women were *not* exempted from the application of section 10(1) if they were domiciled in the Union, or section 12 if they were foreign.[17] In other words, they still required official permission in order to remain in an urban area longer than seventy-two hours. Clearly, therefore, Verwoerd was determined to wield at least one prong of the three-pronged influx control strategy against women. Indeed, his concessions on the Labour Bureaux Regulations and reference-book issue made the NAD all the more insistent that the application of section 10(1) and section 12 to women should proceed with 'extreme strictness', so as to 'limit [the] influx of Native women and get . . . rid of undesirable Native women'.[18]

The NAD could do little to police this instruction, however. For Verwoerd made another concession, this time in response to municipal pressure, which deprived the NAD of the power to enforce the desired 'strictness' in the application of section 10(1) and section 12 to women. The spate of anti-pass campaigns accompanying the

---

[15] See ibid. 130–1.

[16] *HAD* (1952), vol. 78, col. 2955.

[17] Before 1958 women from the Protectorates were treated administratively as if Union-born.

[18] BCC BMR 14/1/54, SNA to Town Clerks, re 'Control over Influx of Native Women into Urban Areas', 13 Oct. 1953.

passage of the Native Laws Amendment Bill had cautioned most local authorities to tread warily in their actions against African women, for fear of inflaming the townships under their jurisdiction.[19] They therefore prevailed upon Verwoerd, before the law was passed, to guarantee the local authorities the overriding power to decide if and how to apply the influx control regulations to African women.[20] As a result, until 1956[21] the extent to which women were incorporated into the influx control system varied markedly between regions. Whereas some municipal NEADs made determined efforts to impose section 10(1) on women, others were tardier.

The Cape Town NEAD was the first to act. By 31 October 1954 5,000 section 10(1)(d) permits had been issued, rising to 25,354 by 1957 (as compared to a mere 959 women with section 10(1)(a), (b), or (c) status).[22] Even so, women living in Cape Town illegally were seldom prosecuted.[23] Port Elizabeth, Outdshoorn, and Stellenbosch, in the Cape,[24] together with Vanderbylpark, Modderfontein, Krugersdorp, and Vereeniging in the Transvaal,[25] were among the NEADs similarly zealous in their application of the provisions of section 10(1) to women. Indeed, in Stellenbosch and Paarl, both political strongholds of SABRA which took a strong stand against African urbanisation, the number of African women resident within the municipal area dropped, following the removal of women living there illegally.[26] These municipalities were in the minority, however. By the end of 1956, 'most . . . large urban local authorities had not as yet implemented the provisions of Section 10 in so far as the women in their areas are concerned'.[27]

This pattern of municipal lethargy in imposing section 10 on

---

[19] In many instances, this represented a change of heart, as compared with the preference for stricter controls over women's movements which was expressed by many local authorities during the 1940s—see Chs. 2, 3.

[20] *HAD* (1952), vol. 78, col. 2960.

[21] After 1956 the application of section 10 to women became more widespread.

[22] IANA, 'Proceedings of 1957 Annual Conference', p. 161.

[23] Ibid. 163.

[24] Walker, *Women and Resistance*, p. 131.

[25] BCC BMR 14/1/30, REC to Chief NAC, re 'Inspection of Local Labour Bureaux: Brakpan', 18 Jan. 1956, p. 6.

[26] According to the 1954 SABRA newsletter, the Paarl municipality had recently removed 200 families, so that the number of women in the area dropped by 100. Similarly the Stellenbosch municipality had evicted 25 women.

[27] IANA, 'Proceedings of 1957 Annual Conference', p. 159.

women began to change in 1956, precipitated by the NAD's renewed determination to hinder women's access to the cities. Whereas the NAD had surrendered, at least partially, in the face of the anti-pass protests of the early 1950s, its approach during the latter half of the decade became increasingly aggressive and uncompromising. October 1955 saw the largest and most dramatic anti-pass demonstration to date, when approximately 2,000 women, mainly African, congregated outside the Union Buildings in Pretoria, armed with anti-pass petitions signed by thousands. But the NAD responded by turning the screw more tightly. In February 1956 the Regional Employment Commissioner of the Witwatersrand hinted at the NAD's switch to a more aggressive tack. Noting that the application of section 10(1)(d) to date had not deterred an 'influx of native women . . . of serious proportions', the Commissioner described

control over native women as a thorny question which requires serious attention and extremely careful steps . . . With an eye on the determination of a policy and procedure, the Department aims to have discussions with the Native Affairs Commissioners and the SAP in the near future.[28]

The clamp-down began with the NAD's withdrawal of its temporary reprieve exempting women from having to carry reference books. By September 1956 reference-book squads had issued about 23,000 reference books to women in thirty-seven small country towns, an average of 4,000 per month.[29] As Walker points out, 'these figures were a depressing indication that the government machine was moving forward, ponderously, but relentlessly'.[30] By mid-1958 reference books were being issued to women in Durban, Cape Town, Port Elizabeth, and on the East Rand, with little resistance encountered.[31] In October of that year it was the turn of domestic servants in Johannesburg, which provoked a week-long wave of demonstrations from African women in the city. Similar outcries met the reference-books squads as they moved on to other groups of African women.

Outbreaks of popular protest, which crossed the country after

---

[28] Reported in BCC BMR 14/1/30, 'Verslag van die Bestuurder, NEAD, Brakpan', 9 Feb. 1956, para. 8.
[29] Walker, *Women and Resistance*, p. 193.
[30] Ibid.
[31] Ibid. 215. One exception was the case of 250 women at Veeplaas in Port Elizabeth who refused to take reference books.

1956,[32] succeeded at best in delaying or obstructing the imposition of the reference-book system, but not preventing it. At the end of 1958 'the government announced that over 1.3 million reference books had thus far been issued to women',[33] although it was not until 1963 that the process was deemed complete.

The NAD's concerted drive to force reference books on women had important implications at the municipal level. In order for a reference book to be issued, a woman had to have secured the necessary permission from the local authority, in terms of section 10(1), to remain in the proclaimed area longer than seventy-two hours.[34] Therefore, as the Department's reference-book squads traversed the country, they provided the NAD with an opportunity to check up that Union-born women were being subjected to the terms of section 10(1). Municipal administrators were thus prodded into a more rigorous and systematic application of section 10(1) than had been the case before 1956.

Yet, even then, the NAD remained unable fully to control the migration of African women from rural to urban areas. Foreign women were subject to section 12, directly administered by the NAD. But the NAD lacked virtually any direct control over the application of section 10(1) to Union-born women. This continued to be the preserve of municipal administrators, whose interests and priorities often deviated from those of the NAD. Women from rural areas wishing to stay longer than seventy-two hours in an urban area could do so legally in one of two ways: either by securing a section 10(1)(d) permit, or by being admitted into the officially 'urbanised' community as the wife of an 'urbanised' man, provided she was 'ordinarily resident' with him (in terms of 10(1)(c)—see later). There were two ways of getting a section 10(1)(d) permit. First, Africans who wished to find employment in the area needed a work-seekers' permit (valid for fourteen days) from the local labour bureau there. And, secondly, the local authority had discretionary powers to issue section 10(1)(d) permits to Africans who were not

---

[32] Walker, *Women and Resistance*, p. 193. Demonstrations occurred in Winburg, Orange Free State, snowballing to Klerksdorp, Brakpan, Johannesburg, Durban, Port Elizabeth, Bethlehem, and others.

[33] Ibid. 222.

[34] Foreign African women in South Africa had to carry identity documents rather than reference books. It is not clear whether these documents were also issued to women by the reference-book squads.

work-seekers. Now, because women were exempted from the Labour Bureaux Regulations, they were not classed as 'work-seekers'. Therefore, women's access to section 10(1)(d) permits was entirely dependent on the discretion of municipal officials. The NAD could merely 'invite' the attention of municipal administrators to what 'the Department desires'.[35] This meant that, even after the NAD succeeded in prodding the local authorities into applying section 10(1) to women, the *ways* in which it was imposed varied widely, according to the different attitudes and priorities of the various municipal NEADs. For, as J. E. Mathewson, Manager of the Benoni NEAD, pointed out in 1956, 'leading local authorities still diverge considerably on the theory and practice of urban Native administration'.[36]

Some NEADs attempted to create their own administrative substitutes for the Labour Bureaux Regulations, until women's reprieve from these Regulations was lifted. Permits were issued only to women who were taking up employment. In Vereeniging, for example, the Town Council authorised the introduction of 'a registration system for (all) contracts of service entered into between European employers and Native females'.[37] The Vanderbylpark NEAD made similar moves in respect of women domestic servants, in a bid to curtail the number of servants sleeping on the premises in 'white' areas. All domestic servants were required to carry permits, which the NEAD issued preferentially to women seeking casual domestic work with more than one employer, rather than to those intending to work full-time and live in.[38]

Most municipalities, however, were wary of inflicting these sorts of restrictions on women,[39] and made little attempt, if any, to link women's rights to remain within prescribed areas systematically with the local demand for female labour. If women entering the area said they were looking for employment, this seems to have been sufficient to secure a section 10(1)(d) permit in most cases, despite the fact that the women were not obliged to register as work-seekers or report to the labour bureaux on entering or terminating

[35] BCC BMR 14/1/25, SNA to Town Clerks, 13 Oct. 1953.
[36] IANA, 'Proceedings of 1956 Annual Conference', p. 28.
[37] BCC BMR 14/1/30, REC to Chief NAC, re 'Inspection of Local Labour Bureaux', 18 Jan. 1956, p. 6.
[38] IANA, 'Proceedings of 1956 Annual Conference', p. 44.
[39] BCC BMR 14/1/25, '1953 Conference', p. 48.

employment. In East London, for example, where a restrictive application of section 10(1)(c) prevented a rural woman from joining her husband unless as a work-seeker in her own right, female work-seekers were issued with section 10(1)(d) permits 'fairly freely'.[40] And in Brakpan, 'it seemed that hardly any restrictions were being made on the entry of Native females in the prescribed area, provided they were either taking up employment with specified employers or merely visiting relatives and friends for short periods'.[41] But the Brakpan NEAD was 'cautious' in enforcing the employment requirement, so that very few women were prosecuted for living in Brakpan without the necessary permits.[42]

In most cases, then, the issue of section 10(1)(d) permits to women tended to be significantly more generous and less rigorous than it was to men. As the Johannesburg NEAD reported, 'on account of the lesser restrictions placed on female Bantu, a greater number are entering the urban areas as compared with the male Bantu, who are subject to the entire impact of influx control laws'.[43]

In Cape Town, the terms of the CLPP erected additional barriers against the settlement of rural women in the prescribed area. But, even there, until 1959/60, when the CLPP was more stringently applied, section 10(1)(d) permits were issued relatively freely to women by the Cape Town NEAD.[44] According to a SAIRR report on the application of influx control in the Cape Town area, 'women were more often [than men] allowed to remain in the area, even if they did not qualify for permanent residence, particularly if they were prepared to take "sleep-in" employment'.[45]

African women in different municipal regions encountered different degrees and types of difficulties in obtaining section 10(1)(d) permits. But the official population statistics and masculinity ratios cited earlier, which derive primarily from headcounts of legal city-dwellers, suggest that the sort of approach taken by the

[40] P. Mayer and I. Mayer, *Townsmen or Tribesmen* (Cape Town, 1961), pp. 57–8.
[41] BCC BMR 14/1/30, REC to Chief NAC, re 'Inspection of Local Labour Bureaux', 18 Jan. 1956, p. 6.
[42] Ibid.
[43] WRAB JMR A10/3, Johannesburg NEAD, 'Population Trends', 9 May 1963, p. 2.
[44] J. L. Mouat, 'The Application of the Pass Laws in the Cape Town City Council Area and Cape Divisional Council Area' (unpublished mimeo for SAIRR, 1961), p. 4.
[45] Ibid. 4. The fact that the masculinity ratios in Cape Town did not drop as the decade wore on must, therefore, reflect the large number of male migrants who secured employment there.

Johannesburg NEAD predominated. Indeed, this is the impression presented by the Botha Report, in its diagnosis of the application of influx controls during the 1950s.[46]

That municipal administrators tended to apply less stringent criteria when issuing section 10(1) permits to women than to men warrants explanation. After all, during the 1940s pressure for the intensification of state controls over women had come largely from municipal administrators. Moreover, by the 1950s local authorities had at least one good reason to reiterate this stance. As J. Knoetze, then Manager of the Vanderbylpark NEAD put it, 'the migration of the Bantu women to the urban area is usually of a permanent nature. Which means that in due course she will become a wife and mother and a house will have to be provided for her by the local authority.'[47]

Limited bureaucratic resources may have been one reason for the local authorities' relatively relaxed approach on the issue. During the decade, municipal NEADs had to take on considerably more work in administering the influx control policies for African men. Municipal officials had to staff the newly created local labour bureaux, issue reference books to African males in their areas, and, in so doing, process thousands of applications for section 10(1)(a) and (b) qualifications. These tasks probably left few personnel to tackle the application of section 10(1) to women.

A more important factor, however, was the shortage of domestic workers which persisted in most urban areas throughout the decade (see Chapter 5). As employees of the elected town or city councils, municipal administrators were generally responsive to local white householders' demands for African domestic workers. Domestic service, particularly if full-time, was more likely to attract migrant women than women settled in the townships with their families (see Chapter 6). But, even amongst migrant women, the turnover in domestic service was high, so that the demand for migrant women to take these jobs never subsided. Some administrators, therefore, permitted women from the rural areas to stay in town on condition that they take up domestic service. But in most cases this stipulation was not made, and women were given relatively free access to the cities, in the hope that at least some of them would meet the needs of white householders.

[46] NAD, 'Botha Report', p. 45.
[47] IANA, 'Proceedings of 1957 Annual Conference', p. 178.

Fear of igniting protest imposed another major constraint on the application of section 10(1) to women. Africans' protests to the NAD's plans to extend influx control to women in the early 1950s demonstrated plainly that the move was deeply provocative, so that by 1953 many local authorities were already reluctant to go this route.[48]

The application of section 10(1)(c) to women varied similarly between municipal areas. For, in practice, the NAD also left the application of section 10(1)(c) largely in the hands of municipal administrators. On paper, the conditions governing the issue of section 10(1)(c) rights were uniform, with no scope for municipal discretion. But, as the Johannesburg NEAD pointed out, the terms of the sub-clause were vague: how long did a wife have to be 'ordinarily resident' with her husband in order to qualify for section 10(1)(c) 'rights'?; was the seventy-two hours to which she was automatically entitled sufficient time?[49] Requests for clarification from the Johannesburg NEAD were not heeded by the NAD, so that administrators were left to supply their own interpretation of the ambiguous clause.

In interpreting the terms of section 10(1)(c),

some municipalities allowed the families of men who qualified for permanent residence to join their husbands and fathers. Others granted the concession only when accommodation was available for the family in the location. A third group prohibited women not normally resident in the area from remaining there permanently, even though their husbands qualified.[50]

In Johannesburg, for example, the City Council resolved that no women who entered the municipal area after 30 August 1955 could remain there permanently in terms of section 10(1)(c), irrespective of the legal status of their husbands.[51] However, it seems that the Johannesburg NEAD in turn partially relaxed this restriction by 'following a policy by which a Bantu man who qualifies to be in the area in terms of section 10(1)(a) or (b) . . . may bring a bride to Johannesburg from a prescribed area but not from a rural or

[48] BCC BMR 14/1/25, '1953 Conference', p. 48.

[49] N. Olivier posed the question at the 1957 IANA conference (IANA, 'Proceedings of 1957 Annual Conference', p. 175), and S. Rogers, Manager of Cape Town NEAD, replied that he, for one, had no answer (ibid. 198).

[50] Simons, *African Women: Their Legal Status*, p. 282.

[51] WRAB JMR A78/5, Acting Manager, Johannesburg NEAD, to All Superintendents, re 'Housing of Native Families: Influx Control', 6 Oct. 1958.

non-prescribed area'.[52] In Cape Town, on the other hand, a ban on any further acquisition of section 10(1)(c) status by African wives came into effect later, in 1961.[53]

The wording of section 10(1)(c) made no reference to whether or not the wives of section 10(1)(a) and (b) qualifiers lost their section 10(1)(c) status if they became widowed or divorced. Again, municipalities probably pursued discrepant policies. In Durban, for example, widows or divorcees lost section 10(1)(c) rights.[54]

In sum, then, Verwoerd's administrative compromises in the early 1950s left the NAD with little direct or decisive control over the numbers of African women joining the legal urban community. It was municipal influx control officers who wielded most of these powers,[55] and in most cases far less strictly than was necessary for the NAD's proposed urbanisation freeze to have taken effect.

It is not surprising, therefore, that, as the decade wore on, the NAD made several moves to challenge the local authorities' powers. The first step was made by the NAD's revision of its policy towards women from the Protectorates, as from 6 May 1958. Previously treated on a par with Union-born Africans, Protectorate women were now classed as foreigners, and were therefore subject to the direct authority of the Secretary for Native Affairs, in terms of section 12 of the Natives (Urban Areas) Act. This would allow Eiselen to ensure a uniformly uncompromising approach: all applications from such women for permission to enter and reside in a proclaimed area after 6 May 1958 were to be 'summarily refused as being against policy'.[56]

The decisive battleground, however, was over the discretionary powers in the issue of section 10(1)(d) permits, which the 1952 Native Laws Amendment Act had allocated to local authorities. This degree of autonomy was fiercely defended by most administrators. Without it, said the Manager of the Durban NEAD, S. Bourquin, municipal NEADS would be reduced to the role of

[52] WRAB JMR A78/7/1, Johannesburg NEAD, 'Certain Aspects Affecting Application and Administration of Pass Laws', 20 July 1965, p. 9.
[53] Mouat, 'The Application of the Pass Laws', p. 10.
[54] KCL Bourquin Papers, KCM 55268 File 4, SAIRR, Natal region, 'The Cato Manor Framework', 1959, p. 4.
[55] The exception was the issuing of section 12 permits, which was controlled directly by the NAD.
[56] BCC BMR 14/1/5, General Circular No. 24 of 1959 from SNA, re 'Bantu Women from High Commission Territories'.

merely rubber-stamping departmental decisions.[57] Of course, this was exactly what Verwoerd would have preferred. But, until the late 1950s he did not risk encroaching on the NEADs' terrain too much.[58] For, when Jansen and then Verwoerd took over as Minister of Native Affairs, urban 'Native administration' was almost exclusively the preserve of the NEADs, whose opinions and experience therefore carried considerable weight in the NAD (see Chapters 3 and 4). Also, the NAD needed the co-operation and the expertise of the NEADs in order to launch its influx control programme. After 1957 this diffidence and caution began to wane, as the NAD closed in on the discretionary municipal powers over section 10(1)(d). The first step was taken in 1957, when the Native Affairs Commissioners in Cape Town[59] and on the Witwatersrand[60] stipulated that section 10(1)(d) status could not be conferred unless 'approved accommodation' had been secured in advance of entry into the proclaimed area, a highly restrictive condition in view of the serious accommodation shortage in both areas. Then, in 1959, Eiselen made the decisive move, wholly withdrawing the discretionary issue of section 10(1)(d) permits. From then on, municipal influx control officers 'no longer had the right to allow females into the area in terms of Section 10(1)(d) of the Act'.[61] Also, as of 1 January 1959, the Labour Bureaux Regulations were applied to women. So, from 1959 women's access to section 10(1)(d) permits was solely by the way of the labour bureaux, and hence subject to the overriding authority of the Native Affairs Commissioners. The NAD had succeeded in usurping full control over women's movements to the urban areas, and in linking it in the desired manner to control over their employment there.

It took the NAD until 1959, then, to set up the full, triple-pronged system of influx control for African women and claim full powers over the administration of that system. Before that date the NAD had to yield to the local authorities, most of whom desisted

[57] Holleman, 'The Tightrope Dancers: Report on Seventh IANA Conference' p. 21.

[58] The furthest Verwoerd went was to license the officials of the NEADs, and threaten to revoke the licence if NAD policy was subverted. See Ch. 4.

[59] Mouat, 'The Application of the Pass Laws', p. 9.

[60] BCC BMR 14/1/30, Chief NAC, Witwatersrand, to NACs, re 'Kanaliseering van Arbeid', 11 July 1957.

[61] WRAB JMR A78/1/2, NEAD Manager to Town Clerk' re 'Influx Control: Native Women', 26 Feb. 1962.

from applying influx control provisions to women with anything like the 'extreme strictness' which the NAD had urged. As a result, for the duration of the decade, 'notwithstanding the control measures in section 10 . . . it appears that as a rule Bantu women entered and settled in the cities unhindered'.[62]

## The Application of Section 10(1)(a), (b), and (c)

Chapter 4 showed that the 1952 amendments to section 10 of the Natives (Urban Areas) Act unwittingly created legal avenues for Africans born in the rural areas to join the ranks of the officially urbanised—that is, to gain the residential right to live in a proclaimed area with their families, whether in the employ of whites or not. These official avenues into the settled urban community were far from generous: only those with ten or fifteen years' continuous service were eligible, and their wives or families had to wait until then before being accorded the same residential rights. But many departmental and municipal functionaries looked upon the loopholes created by section 10(1)(b) and (c) as one of the major obstacles to the state's anti-urbanisation drive,[63] and made various legal and administrative attempts to remove them. As the following discussion shows, their efforts were partially successful. The law was tightened up at various points, and additional administrative hurdles made section 10(1) residential rights harder to acquire than the law itself prescribed. But the legal gateways into the urbanised community remained open, allowing at least some long-serving migrant workers to earn the right to settle in urban areas, and some of the wives and dependent children of urbanised men to join them.

At an administrative level, conflicting interpretations of section 10(1)(a), (b), and (c) existed from the outset. Several municipal NEADs interpreted the law as stipulating that 'if somebody had not already had his 10 or 15 years service before 1952, they couldn't get 10(1)(b), because their aim was not to create an increasing pool of people who would qualify for 10(1)(b)'.[64] The Johannesburg NEAD, on the other hand, gave a significantly more generous

[62] NAD, 'Botha Report', p. 45.
[63] IANA, 'Proceedings of 1957 Annual Conference', p. 175.
[64] Interview with N. J. Olivier, 5 July 1985.

interpretation, allowing that 'all natives legally resident in the area prior to 1 January 1953 should be accepted as section 10(1)(a), (b), and (c) residents'.[65] 'Legal residence before 1953' in turn meant having had authorised employment. On the Johannesburg interpretation, then, simply the fact, rather than the duration, of employment, or the number of employers and of years' continuous residence, was the deciding factor. Other NEADs might well have followed Johannesburg's example, because it saved municipal officials the inconvenience of having to process and verify vast numbers of employment records, records of tenancy, etc., before classifying large resident communities in terms of their section 10(1) status.

Once the initial mass classification process was accomplished, however, the likelihood of a generous interpretation or application of section 10(1)(a), (b), and (c) dwindled sharply. Many local authorities then added their own extra requirements for these, and subsequent legal amendments to section 10(1) narrowed the field further.

One condition for section 10(1)(a) status was birth in the proclaimed area. Johannesburg was one town in which the number of section 10(1)(a) qualifiers was cut considerably by the NEAD's demands for a birth certificate to prove the place of birth, a document which relatively few Africans possessed. As G. Xorile, a member of the Johannesburg Native Advisory Board pointed out to the NEAD,

officials at the Influx Office want a copy of the child's birth certificate or baptismal certificate as proof that he was actually born in Johannesburg, and often this is very difficult to obtain as many children were not registered at birth. Many Africans belong to churches which are not recognised and which do not keep records of any kind.[66]

The Johannesburg Advisory Board also accused the NEAD of an arbitrary interpretation of section 10(1)(c).[67] Children born in Johannesburg but schooled outside the area were denied section

---

[65] WRAB JMR N15, Minutes of Non-European Affairs Committee, 'Housing of Bantu in Soweto', 16 Aug. 1966.
[66] George Xorile's Papers, 'Record of Informal Discussion between ... Non-European Affairs and Housing Committee and ... Native Advisory Board ... 28 March 1956'.
[67] Ibid.

10(1)(c) rights on their return. However, according to J. Rees, then a location superintendent in Johannesburg, this ruling was a departmental decision, applicable in all urban areas.[68]

The NAD also instructed NEADs to withhold residential rights from Africans 'whose presence in the area is for some or other reason regarded as undesirable'.[69] It is not clear how widely this strategy was followed, or how effective it was. For, as municipal administrators were well aware, claims for section 10(1)(a), (b), and (c) rights could be defended in court, where the NEAD would then have to justify its actions.[70] But, presumably, many unsuspecting people who did not fight their claims in court lost their residential rights in this way.

Various legal amendments also cut the number of people qualifying for section 10(1)(a), (b), or (c) status. After the courts upheld a claim for 10(1)(a) rights on behalf of an African man who had maintained a permanent home in the proclaimed area of his birth but had lived elsewhere, section 10(1)(a) was amended in 1955 to foreclose this possibility. After 1955 10(1)(a) rights were only issued to those who had lived continuously in the proclaimed area in which they were born.

The 1955 Natives (Urban Areas) Amendment Act also amended section 29, which gave the courts the power to expel Africans deemed 'idle and undesirable' from the proclaimed areas. Before 1955 the clause had not stipulated whether or not it applied to the holders of residential rights, and the courts often took the view that it did not. Section 29 was therefore amended so as specifically to include Africans with section 10(1)(a), (b), or (c) status.

Clearly, both the NAD and the municipal NEADs made various efforts to restrict the acquisition of section 10(1)(a), (b), and (c) rights. But they could not prohibit it altogether. Nor could they nullify the exemptions from influx control which these residential rights conferred. Administrators therefore complained that 'their powers of influx control are inadequate . . . because parliament has recognised a "permanent" urban community and given it security'.[71] SABRA too noted that 'various municipalities' had

---

[68] Interview with J. Rees, 1 Nov. 1984. Note that variations in the interpretation of section 10(1)(c) as it affected wives were discussed in the previous section.

[69] BCC BMR 14/1/10, Acting NAC to Manager of Brakpan NEAD, 16 Feb. 1953.

[70] See, e.g., IANA, 'Proceedings of 1956 Annual Conference', p. 38.

[71] Simons, 'Passes and Police', 59–60.

found that 'the Native . . . who enjoys exemption under Article 10 is actually beyond the control of the local authority'.[72] S. Bourquin, Manager of the Durban NEAD, complained that section 10(1)(c) prevented adequate controls over African children.[73] Rogers, Manager of the Cape Town NEAD, blamed section 10(1)(c) as partly responsible for his inability to curb 'tsostism'.[74] Roux, Manager of the Klerksdorp NEAD in 1956, complained that, 'if municipal officers ignored Africans' claims to rights on the basis of birth, they risked court proceedings'.[75]

Despite various legal and administrative attacks during the decade, the residential rights conferred by section 10(1)(a), (b), and (c) therefore generally did offer a degree of security and protection. Those who managed to secure these rights were able to gain a foothold in the cities as settled inhabitants, and raise their families there.

It was only in Cape Town, towards the end of the decade, that this trend was less uniform. In 1955 Eiselen declared the inauguration of the CLPP, which had, as one of its objectives, the 'ultimate elimination of the Natives' from the Western Cape, which was declared the 'natural home of the Coloured people'.[76] The CLPP was largely inoperative until late in the decade. But, once it was implemented, it was sometimes used to override the protection against removal implicit in the terms of section 10(1)(a), (b), and (c). According to a SAIRR report on influx control in the Western Cape from 1959,

those who 'qualify' to reside here permanently may be 'endorsed out' if they have been sentenced to a fine exceeding £50 or to imprisonment exceeding 6 months, or if they are deemed idle and undesirable, or if their presence is deemed detrimental to the maintenance of peace and order or if they have failed to observe the regulations issued by the local authority governing the terms and conditions of their residence.[77]

In sum, the issue of section 10(1)(a), (b), and (c) residential rights during the decade was less generous than the 1952 Native Laws Amendment Act originally prescribed. The legal loophole in the

---

[72] IANA, 'Proceedings of 1957 Annual Conference', p. 175.

[73] KCL Bourquin Papers, KCM 55167, Bourquin to Town Clerk, re 'Removal of Certain Bantu Women and Children from Urban Area of Durban', Jan. 1959.

[74] IANA, 'Proceedings of 1957 Annual Conference', p. 198.

[75] Ibid.

[76] Eiselen, cited in Snitcher, 'The Eiselen Scheme', 40.

[77] Mouat, 'The Application of Pass Laws', p. 12.

NAD's plan to curb African urbanisation was therefore partially narrowed by administrative means. Indeed, the number of people who gained the right to settle in an urban area by means of these rights must have been small in comparison to the size of the population increase. Nevertheless, this avenue was not closed off altogether, a fact which marked the limits of the NAD's powers to rectify administratively the legal anomalies which had been introduced into its influx control programme during the passage of the 1952 NLA Act.

### Informal Resistance to Influx Control

Perhaps the most crippling obstacle to the NAD's control over African urban migration was African resistance to the influx control system. This resistance took several forms, which had correspondingly different political effects. The most conspicuous and dramatic forms of resistance were organised anti-pass compaigns and spontaneous popular outbursts of protest against the pass laws, which dominated the black political landscape of the 1950s.[78] The scene had been set in 1950, with the spate of struggles against women's passes. Then the 1952 Defiance Campaign, which helped to launch the ANC as a mass movement, condemned the pass laws as one of the many 'which keep in perpetual subjection and misery vast sections of the population'.[79] In 1956, in one of the most spectacular anti-pass demonstrations of the decade, about twenty thousand women converged on the Union Buildings in Pretoria, one year after two thousand women had first gathered there to deliver thousands of anti-pass petitions. Women's protests continued to make their mark in the remaining years of the decade, 'generating an enormous response'[80] in 1957 and 1958. Finally, the ANC's and PAC's anti-pass campaigns of 1960 had an unexpectedly stormy impact after the massacre of protestors at Sharpeville (see Chapter 9).

Such struggles never succeeded in dislodging the influx control system. But, as mentioned previously, particularly early on in the

---

[78] The details of these struggles are eloquently covered in Lodge, *Black Politics*, and Walker, *Women and Resistance*. The following discussion is, therefore, but a brief summary of some of the key events.

[79] A. Luthuli, *Let my People Go* (London and Glasgow, 1962; repr. 1975), p. 105.

[80] Walker, *Women and Resistance*, p. 203.

decade, they played an important role in exacting the concessions which introduced serious loopholes in the NAD's influx control strategy, helping to subvert the ULPP, and thwarting the desired freeze on urbanisation. Also, the particularly determined protests against passes for women filled most municipal administrators with 'trepidation',[81] so that, until 1960, women were less hindered by the influx control laws than men. However, the state's defences against popular protests were strong, and some of the anti-pass campaigns lacked organisational cohesion and unified leadership.[82] Ironically, it was individual, unorganised acts of defiance of the pass laws, more than militant mass campaigns, which succeeded in wreaking havoc with the NAD's influx control strategy. C. van Onselen's remarks about resistance on the Southern Rhodesian mines are equally apt for an analysis of African resistance to influx control:

ideologies and organisations should be viewed essentially as the high-water marks of protest. At least as important, if not more so, were the less dramatic, silent and often unorganised responses, and it is the latter set of responses, which occurred on a day-to-day basis, that reveal most about the functioning of the system . . . It was the unarticulated disorganised protest and resistance which the . . . state found most difficult to detect or suppress.[83]

The municipal townships hosted thousands of illegal residents who devised various strategies for evading the authorities. They were aided and abetted by a substantial loophole in the law. Section 10(1) did not impose restrictions on Africans' entry into proclaimed areas; all Africans had the right to spend seventy-two hours in such areas without permission. Curiously, Verwoerd introduced this clause in the belief that it would enhance the NAD's control. Having to police every African entering the cities, he said, wasted time and effort on *bona fide* visitors, who had no intention of staying for very long. The so-called 'seventy-two-hour' clause was intended to concentrate the police's energies on those Africans who were attempting to find work and a home in the cities.[84] But how were the police to distinguish visitors from the rest? And how could they establish whether the Africans they confronted had been in the area for longer than seventy-two hours or not? The most obvious way for

---

[81] IANA, 'Proceedings of 1957 Annual Conference', p. 160.
[82] Walker, *Women and Resistance*, pp. 263, 211; Lodge, *Black Politics*, p. 78.
[83] C. van Onselen, *Chibaro* (London, 1976), p. 227.
[84] *HAD* (1952), vol. 77, col. 554.

an illegal resident to defy the system was simply to protest that he or she had only just arrived in the area. Wise to that tactic, the police sometimes ignored the seventy-two-hour clause, and simply arrested all those without permits. Nevertheless several administrators complained that the seventy-two-hour clause had in fact 'abolished . . . "influx control"'.[85]

Particularly in the larger cities, the 'illegals' found protection in numbers. The scale of illegal residence was simply too large for the police ever to contain, let alone curb. As J. Simons put it, the routine policing of the pass laws 'rather resembled the labour of a man who tries to empty a barrel of water with a sieve'.[86] Many of those who were 'endorsed out' either left the area only to slip in again undetected, or ignored the order altogether and remained in the area by eluding the authorities. But their lives were tense and insecure. As B. Modisane remarked, 'people were turned into cunning law-breakers, apprehensive and ready to flee from their homes to evade the processes of the law which required them to have permission in order to live in the peace and security of their homes'.[87]

Since the administration of the pass laws inflicted hardships on all Africans, legal or illegal, illegal township residents could usually count on support and assistance from their legal neighbours. Although section 10(1) divided Africans administratively into insiders and outsiders, there is little evidence to suggest that these divisions supplied the NAD with a means of buying off the insiders into exposing the presence of 'illegals' in their midst.

Many of the 'illegals' protected themselves to a degree by 'losing' their reference books (which bore the 'endorsement out' stamp) in order to secure a legitimate reprieve in the area while their application for a replacement was being processed. As all Africans in the cities knew, this bureaucratic procedure took months. First, a fingerprint was taken by a municipal official. This was then sent to the NAD central office in Pretoria to be matched against their existing records. After months, the Pretoria office would notify the NEAD that the applicant had been 'endorsed out' of the area. The applicant would then 'feign surprise and ignorance at this, and then "lose" the book again, and again if necessary'.[88]

---

[85] Simons, 'Passes and Police', 59–60.
[86] Ibid. 60.
[87] Modisane, *Blame Me on History*, p. 114.
[88] Interview with J. Rees, 1 Nov. 1984.

A safer but more expensive option was provided by the flour-
ishing illicit trade in forged reference books. The NAD acknowledged that in the first ten months of 1951 approximately 10,000
passes were forged in Johannesburg alone.[89] By 1965, according to
estimates from the Bantu Affairs Commissioner, this figure had at
least doubled.[90] Still, for many, forged passes remained prohibitively expensive. According to P. Ntantala, they sold for £15 to £20,[91]
more than the average monthly wage of male unskilled workers, and
nearly three times the monthly wage of African women employed in
commerce.

Fraudulent changes in house tenancy provided another cover for
illegal township dwellers. In Johannesburg, for example, the
registered tenants of township houses (legal residents) who left
the area frequently sold or gave their houses to illegal members
of the community, unbeknown to the township superintendent. The
new tenant then had a reasonable chance of remaining undetected
by paying the house rental in the name of the previous tenant.[92]
However, most of the townships' unofficial population lay low as
illegal sub-tenants, renting a room or part thereof, or even a chicken
run behind the house, from the registered tenant.[93]

'Illegals' also managed to secure a place in the highly controlled
and uncomfortable residential environment of the hostels for single
migrants.[94] Husbands were joined by wives who had entered the
area illegally; and workers without the required permits took
advantage of the already overcrowded conditions in the hostels,
joining the throngs sleeping in the passages or under beds.

Constantly in danger of arrest, illegal city-dwellers lived under
enormous stress. Also, their status prevented them from complaining to local authorities about the inadequate provision of services in
the townships and the desperate lack of decent accommodation. But
their defiance of the influx control laws was also a victory against the
state. Indeed, the cumulative effect was to deal a substantial blow to
the NAD's capacity to achieve its objectives. In 1955 the Cape

[89] *HAD* (1952), vol. 77, col. 1287.
[90] WRAB JMR 78/7/1, 'Certain Aspects affecting Application and Administration
of Pass Laws', 20 July 1965.
[91] Ntantala, 'Widows of the Reserves', 13.
[92] George Xorile's Papers, 'Minutes of Monthly Meeting of Joint Advisory Board
with Manager . . . 24 Jan. 1951', p. 4.
[93] Interview with J. Rees, 1 Nov. 1984.
[94] IANA, 'Proceedings of 1957 Annual Conference', p. 163.

Chamber of Industries, for example, claimed that 'a spate of illegal entrants was flowing into the Cape area from the reserves'.[95] And the Brakpan Manager of Non-European Affairs complained in 1957 that he felt 'disturbed by the considerably large number of Natives, particularly women, who are still present in the municipal area illegally . . .'.[96]

For the NAD, the solution lay in ever stricter applications of the existing laws, and the proliferation of still more rules and regulations. But in certain respects this approach was self-defeating. Multiplying the regulations simply stepped up the pressures on the already over-stretched policing and surveillance system. And a more ruthless enforcement of the regulations left increasing numbers of Africans no alternative but to defy the law. As S. Rogers, Manager of the Cape Town NEAD, pointed out, cutting down on the number of legal avenues into the towns simply turned many would-be temporary migrants into illegal permanent residents settled with their families;

> one has to take account that with the strict application of the Labour Bureaux regulations the native men in many cases are afraid to go back to their homes for fear that they may not be permitted to return to the Proclaimed Area . . . This frequently results in the wife coming to the Urban Area because her husband does not come home.[98]

Also, as Eiselen himself conceded, as the application of influx control grew stricter and the number of offenders multiplied, so the 'punitive system ceases to have any educative and remedial effect. The people implicated are no longer subject to any social stigma and therefore these sanctions lose their deterrent value'.[99] In Modisane's more caustic words, 'in our curious society going to jail carried very little social stigma, it was rather a social institution, something to be expected; it was Harry Bloom who wrote: more Africans go to prison than to school'.[99]

With the state's punitive weapons blunted by over-use, the very submission to the influx control system incorporated a healthy

---

[95] FCI NEAF, 'Some Notes on Native Labour Availability and Influx Control', 24 Nov. 1955, p. 6.

[96] BCC BMR 14/1/5, Manager, NEAD, to Location Superintendent, re 'Toes-tromingsbeheer', 20 May 1957.

[97] IANA, 'Proceedings of 1957 Annual Conference', p. 163.

[98] Ibid. 14.

[99] Modisane, *Blame Me on History*, p. 38.

contempt for that system. E. Kuzwayo's autobiography under-
lines the defiance registered in 'the shouting, singing, sometimes
stamping and laughter and very carefree behaviour by the so-called
[pass law] offenders', as they boarded the 'kwela-kwela' [police
vans].[100] As E. Genovese remarked *apropos* of Negro slaves in the
American south, even 'accommodation itself breathed a critical spirit
and disguised subversive actions, and often embraced its apparent
opposite—resistance'.[101]

In summary, then, despite the mounting stringency and aggres-
sion with which the influx control laws were enforced, thousands of
Africans found individual, unorganised ways of resisting these laws,
which cumulatively floored the NAD's efforts to combat illegal
urbanisation. The extent of these successes varied between regions,
Durban exemplifing the extreme case. The Grobelaar Committee of
Inquiry into rioting in Cato Manor in 1960 reported that 'the
Committee has no doubt whatever that there is, in actual practice,
no control over the influx of Bantu who have no right to be in
Durban'.[102] In Cape Town, however, by 1959/60, the NEAD had
tightened its application of the influx control laws considerably,
particularly in respect of African women.[103] Still, overall, the
NAD's drive to curtail the growth of the settled urban African
population was substantially slowed down by the scale of the
unarticulated, unorganised resistance to it.

Although the NAD's powers of influx control were far greater
during the 1950s than in previous decades, they were still insufficient to realise some of the key purposes of the NAD's influx
control strategy. For this was a strategy which made little effort to
co-opt support; its success depended entirely upon the NAD's
coercive powers to impose its rules and regulations on the local
authorities, employers, and Africans living and working in the
cities. But, during the course of the 1950s this proved too vast a
task. The following chapter, which deals with the shift into the
second phase of Apartheid, shows how the NAD set out to overcome
these shortcomings.

---

[100] E. Kuzwayo, *Call Me Woman* (London, 1985), p. 31.
[101] E. Genovese, *Roll Jordan Roll: The World the Slaves Made* (London, 1975),
p. 597.
[102] KCL Bourquin Papers, KCM 55224, 'Extract from Report of the Inter-
Departmental Committee of Inquiry in Connection with the Disturbances and
Rioting at Cato Manor, Durban, 24 January 1960', p. 5.
[103] Mouat, 'The Application of the Pass Laws', pp. 4, 10.

# 9

# The Shift into Apartheid's Second Phase, 1959–1961

THE prevailing tendency in the literature on Apartheid, as discussed in Chapter 1, is to see the Apartheid policies of the 1960s as simply the systematic extension of those of the preceding decade. The state's progress towards the policies which typified the late 1960s—such as homeland development, industrial decentralisation, population removals—is depicted as a continuous, cumulative process, each new step facilitated by the successful achievements accomplished with the previous one. This chapter illustrates, however, that between 1959 and 1961 Apartheid generally, and influx control policy in particular, shifted gear into a discrete second phase. This is not to deny certain unmistakable continuities between the 1950s and the 1960s; nor that the ambitious social engineering of the 1960s was enabled by some of the NP's key accomplishments during the 1950s. However, certain fundamental changes must be recognised alongside these continuities. Facilitated by important political realignments within Afrikerdom, the second phase of Apartheid inaugurated a series of new premises, objectives, and ideological tenets, in an attempt to remedy the perceived failures of existing urban policies. Before 1959 the NAD's annual reports acknowledged the initially tardy and tentative performance of new state apparatuses, such as the labour bureaux which needed time to strengthen their hold over the labour market. After 1959, however, the Department of Bantu Administration and Development (BAD)[1] began to see more in its failures of control than simply the teething problems of young and unpractised bureaucracies, diagnosing what it saw to be anomalies and loopholes at the very heart of the 'practical' influx control policies of the 1950s. As the Botha Report argued in 1962, 'the existing measures do not further the purposes

---

[1] In 1958 the then Native Affairs Department was renamed the Department of Bantu Administration and Development (at the same time as Bantu Education was reallocated to a new Department). This chapter refers to the Department as both the NAD and BAD, depending on the year in question.

for which they were introduced'.[2] This chapter begins by identifying the policy shift, and then looks at key features of the period 1959–61 to explain how and why the changes occurred. The final section briefly examines the extent to which the architects of the policy shift were able to realise their objectives, in both the legislative process and the administrative sphere.[3]

### Comparing Apartheid's First and Second Phases

During the 1960s many features of the Apartheid policies of the 1950s were retained and extended. The decade saw the continued enlargement of the state's already formidable armoury of repressive weapons. The commitment to the ULPP was reiterated. Also, restrictions on African migration to the cities, particularly in the case of foreigners, were further intensified. However, by 1960 the two key 'practical' premises which had shaped the influx control policies of the 1950s had been overturned. During the 1950s Apartheid had been designed, *inter alia*, to *accommodate* the growing urban demand for African labour. But during the following decade the BAD's policy-makers no longer accorded employers the right to stipulate the number of African workers they required, proposing instead that the state intervene in curtailing the process of economic integration itself. The BAD also now rejected its previous tenet, that 'detribalisation' was a reality which had to be accepted and incorporated into the design of Apartheid, by allowing detribalised Africans the residential right to live in white urban areas unconditionally. By 1960 the BAD had embarked on more drastic methods to reduce the urbanised African population, which included various assaults on the very principle of residential rights. These changes are discussed in turn.

### Changed Stance on Economic Integration

Throughout the 1960s the successive Ministers and Deputy Ministers of the BAD spearheaded moves to curb white dependence on

---

[2] NAD, 'Botha Report', p. 75.
[3] This discussion concentrates on those aspects of Apartheid relevant to an understanding of influx control policy.

African labour in the cities. Their arguments echoed some of the warnings which had been sounded by SABRA during the late 1940s, that economic integration was Apartheid's Achilles' heel. By having allowed industrial dependence on African labour to proceed unchecked, they declared, the state was now sitting on a political time bomb. As M. C. Botha, then Deputy Minister, told SABRA in 1963, 'it appears that in industry the ratio of Bantu to White workers has increased from 1:01 in 1928 to 2:2 now. If this process were to go ahead in an uncontrolled way, it would cause problems which would soon become . . . insoluble and fatal.'[4] M. de wet Nel (then Minister of BAD) expressed similar anxieties in telling N. Rhoodie, in 1964, that, 'if Apartheid should fail, it would probably be due to uncontrolled economic integration'.[5]

The BAD was divided over the appropriate corrective to 'uncontrolled economic integration'. Some leading BAD officials favoured the wholesale 'removal of Bantu labour from urban areas'.[6] But neither de Wet Nel nor Botha advocated such extreme measures. When the 1963 Transvaal congress of the NP appealed to the government to give 'final execution to its policy of Apartheid no matter what the sacrifices',[7] de Wet Nel was unsympathetic. His reply stressed the fact that, without some measure of dependence on African labour, 'our mines and industries would come to a complete standstill'.[8] However, he did deviate from the premisses of departmental policy during the 1950s, in underlining the need for the BAD to curtail the *scale* of economic integration in the cities. The BAD now recognised that an influx control policy limiting the supply of African labour to the cities in accordance with the prevailing demand, was too weak an instrument for containing the urban population growth. As B. Coetzee (then Deputy Minister of BAD) explained in 1966, 'how must we deal with the problem of the increase of Bantu labour on the Witwatersrand? . . . It is clear that influx control can never be more than an instrument to make

---

[4] WRAB JMR A14/5, M. C. Botha, 'Ons Stedelike Bantoebeleid teen die Agtergrond van ons Landsbeleid' (paper presented to 1963 SABRA congress), p. 1.
[5] Quoted in N. J. Rhoodie, *Apartheid and Racial Partnership in South Africa* (Academica, 1969), p. 98.
[6] WRAB JMR A14/5, vol. 1, Dr P. F. van Rensburg, 'Die Uitskakeling van Bantoe-Arbeid in Stadsgebiede' (address to 1963 SABRA Congress).
[7] *The Star*, 4 Sept. 1963.
[8] Ibid.

the flow of Bantu labour as orderly as possible. It can never be a solution.'[9]

Determined to institute 'positive measures' to deal with this problem, de Wet Nel threatened employers that the BAD 'would act firmly against people and organisations who did not co-operate with the government's plans to limit the number of Africans in white areas to the absolute minimum'.[10] The BAD thus embarked on a policy of imposing 'labour quotas of Bantu in each urban area'.[11]

The strategy of imposing labour quotas was closely interwoven with a programme of industrial decentralisation, formally instituted in 1960 with the creation of the Permanent Committee for the Settling of Border Industries. The BAD took the lead in articulating the aims and methods of this strategy. As Coetzee explained in 1966, the idea was to relocate labour-intensive industries from metropolitan to border areas. Industries situated on the border of the reserves could draw entirely on migrant African workers who lived in the reserves and journeyed to work each day—a way of sustaining industrial expansion without swelling the ranks of the urban African population. Industries remaining in metropolitan areas would have to reduce their complement of African labour by the 'utilisation of mechanisation, automation and computerisation'.[12] 'The emphasis', he continued, 'is on the elimination of the unskilled manual type of labour, the kind that is so prodigally used in South Africa because it is thought to be cheap'.[13]

The BAD also saw the agricultural and industrial development of the reserves as an important part of its strategy for reducing the growth of the African work-force within the white urban areas. The report of the Tomlinson Commission, recommending an extensive and expensive development programme for the reserves, was published in 1956. The government's White Paper on the report had rejected most of its specific recommendations, but adopted the language of 'development' used by the Commission to justify a far

[9] WRAB JMR A78/2, B. Coetzee, Address to National Development and Management Foundation's Symposium on 'Effective Bantu Employment', 21 June 1966, p. 7.

[10] *Rand Daily Mail*, 6 Oct. 1962.

[11] *Die Burger*, 29 Apr. 1961.

[12] WRAB JMR A78/2, B. Coetzee, 'Effective Bantu Employment', 21 June 1966, p. 21.

[13] Ibid. 25.

more limited 'five-year plan'.[14] By upgrading agriculture, and encouraging the establishment of new industrial and commercial projects, the BAD hoped to improve the economic carrying capacity of the reserves. For, as the strategies for reducing economic integration began to take hold, it would be necessary to create alternative avenues of employment for Africans within the reserves.[15]

### Changed Stance on African Urbanisation

The 1960s also saw a sustained onslaught on the concept of residential rights which had been fundamental to the influx control legislation of the 1950s. This change of tack must be understood in the context of another shift in the nature of Apartheid: the decision to transform the reserves into 'self-governing homelands'. As Verwoerd told parliament in 1961, this policy represented a departure from the government's original intentions; it 'is not what we wanted to see', he said.[16] During the 1950s the reserves were treated essentially as reservoirs of African labour at the disposal of whites. The commitment to separate development was largely the ideological means to legitimise the denial of the franchise to Africans living in the country. The reserves were defined as the permanent political home of all Africans, as a means of excluding them from the polity of white South Africa. But Africans had no political rights within the reserves.[17] By the 1960s, however, separate development was vaunted as a means of allocating Africans the right to self-government in their own homelands.

The notion of 'separate development' was thus redefined within a new ideological discourse of 'multi-nationalism' and 'ethnic self-determination'.[18] As Coetzee put it, 'our policy is . . . "multi-

---

[14] See, e.g., WRAB JMR A14/5, M. C. Botha, 'Ons Stedelike Bantoebeleid', p. 5.
[15] Ibid. 3.
[16] *HAD* (1961), vol. 107, col. 4191.
[17] The Bantu Authorities Act had been passed in 1951, which 'made provision for the establishment of tribal, regional and territorial authorities, and for gradual delegation to these authorities of certain executive and administrative powers, including levying of rates'. But there was 'no elective principle in the constitution of these authorities', and 'the system envisaged was for local government only'. (Horrell, *Legislation and Race Relations*, pp. 22–3.)
[18] This ideological stress on ethnicity accompanied the change in official nomenclature from 'native' to 'Bantu', signifying the replacement of the language of racial divisions with one which stressed ethnic identities and differences.

nationalism", and seeing that all nationalisms are exclusive, it is obvious that each group must have its own sphere where it can enjoy and exercise in full the privileges of a free society'.[19]

These ideological shifts formed part of the state's defences against increasingly severe international condemnation of Apartheid, which the Sharpeville shootings of 1960 (see later) had brought into sharp relief. Nationalist struggles for independence in colonial Africa during the late 1950s had focused international attention on the oppressive regime in South Africa, which put it under pressure to address the problem of African political rights. In an attempt to win some legitimacy in the eyes of its critics, the government's homeland solution mimicked the language of 'ethnic self-determination' used by African nationalists up north. But this strategy was seen expressly as a means of 'buying the white man his freedom and the right to retain domination in what is his country, settled for him by his forefathers'.[20]

The effects of an ideological discourse transcend its immediate instrumentality, however. The new language of ethnicity and 'multi-nationalism' also heralded the beginnings of a fundamental change in the BAD's attitude towards Africans in the white urban areas. The basis of the influx control policy of the 1950s had been the rigid ideological and administrative differentiation between rural and 'detribalised', 'urbanised' Africans. Recognising that 'detribalised' Africans had lost their 'tribal' identity and connections, the NAD conceded that their permanent home was in the so-called white areas. But by 1960 this 'practical' premiss was overturned, inaugurating a new commitment to levelling the status of all Africans inside and outside the 'urbanised' group. In marked contrast to the language of 'practical' politics, the BAD now discarded its earlier declaration that the 'fact' of 'detribalisation' entitled 'urbanised' Africans to certain 'guarantees, security, and stability'.[21] Indeed, the very notion of 'detribalisation' was scorned. Stressing the fundamental ethnic unity of Africans in the urban and rural areas, the BAD expressly rejected the idea that there were 'two kinds of Africans',[22] those who were urbanised and those who retained ties

[19] IANA, 'Proceedings of First Biennial Meeting of Officials', p. 7.
[20] *HAD* (1961), vol. 107, col. 4191.
[21] *HAD* (1952), vol. 77, col. 1311.
[22] W. M. Eiselen, 'Harmonious Multi-Community Development', *Optima* (1959), 18.

with the reserves. As Eiselen explained in 1959, 'our policy only recognises one Bantu community in its ethnic subdivisions'.[23] Or, as the then Deputy Minister (Coetzee) and Minister (Botha) of BAD put it in later years,

whatever the world may say, the Bantu city dweller is someone who still yearns for his homeland, and that yearning must be stimulated.[24]

The Bantu in the white urban areas cannot be dissected from their national relatives in the homelands, not even if they were born here in the white area. The Bantu in the white urban areas and those in the Bantu homelands are linked together into one nation by bonds of language—perhaps the most important ties—descent, kinship, tradition, tribal relations, customs, pride, material interests, and many other matters. The national consciousness of the Bantu is more deeply rooted than many people realise and are prepared to accept.[25]

This new language of ethnicity legitimised a sustained attack on section 10(1) rights. These residential rights were now declaimed as an indefensible 'deviation' from the principles of separate development.[26] Whereas the purpose of separate development was to allocate Africans their 'own sphere' in their ethnic homelands, argued the BAD, section 10(1) had

granted permanence . . . to Bantu . . . in European areas. Contrary to the basic aims . . . of 'separate development' . . . the Bantu has been allowed to make his home wherever he elects in the whole of South Africa, and this practice has necessarily created the impression that . . . the Bantu can . . . lay claim to the same rights as Europeans in the European areas.[27]

During the second phase of Apartheid, therefore, the BAD departed from its earlier limited acceptance of African urbanisation, which led to a sustained struggle to remove section 10(1) from the statute books. As the final section explains, this effort was unsuccessful. But the principle underpinning section 10(1) received a brutal blow from the BAD's urban removals policy. During the 1960s BAD policy encompassed several different types of removals

---

[23] Ibid. 18.
[24] IANA, 'Proceedings of First Biennial Meeting of Officials, 1966', pp. 8–9.
[25] *Senate Debates* (1967), col. 2830.
[26] IANA, 'Proceedings of 1959 Annual Conference', p. 27. See also Union of SA, *Memorandum Explaining the Background and Objects of the Promotion of Bantu Self-Government Bill, 1959*, NP 3–1959.
[27] Union of SA, *Memorandum*.

from rural and urban areas. Initially, the emphasis fell on relocating communities living in so-called 'black spots' in rural white areas to the homelands. By the mid-1960s urban removals were also becoming increasingly frequent. In some cases, entire townships were relocated on the other side of homeland boundaries; but in urban areas too distant from any of the homelands, the BAD concentrated on removing thousands of individuals classed as 'nonproductive'. As a BAD circular stated,

it is accepted Government policy that the Bantu are only temporarily resident in the European areas . . . for as long as they offer their labour there. As soon as they become, for some reason or another, no longer fit to work or superfluous in the labour market, they are expected to return to their country of origin or the territory of the national unit where they fit in ethnically if they were not born and bred in the homeland.[28]

Initiated as a national policy in 1961,[29] this policy grew more aggressive as the decade wore on. The categories of 'non-productive' people multiplied. By 1967 Africans living in the urban areas who were targeted for resettlement were

the aged, unfit, widows, women with dependent children and also families who do not qualify under the provisions of the Bantu (Urban Areas) Act, no. 25 of 1945 for family accommodation in the European urban areas . . . professional Bantu such as doctors, attorneys, agents, traders, industrialists, etc. Such persons are not regarded as essential for the European labour market . . . Normally they are well-to-do Bantu and by settling these people with buying power in the homelands, a great contribution can be made to the development of those territories.[30]

Clearly, the BAD had now rejected its prior 'practical' compromises of the Stallardist doctrine. All Africans, irrespective of their place of

[28] WRAB JMR A78/6/2, Sec. for BAD, 'Settling of Non-Productive Bantu Resident in European Areas, in the Homelands', 12 Dec. 1967.
[29] A 1961 conference of Chief Bantu Affairs Commissioners drew up the first procedures for the 'Removal of Surplus or Illegal Bantu in White Areas to Bantu Areas' (Department of Co-Operation and Development Library, 'Konferensie van Hoof Bantoesakekommissarisse te Pretoria, 16 tot 19 November, 1961'). Note that at least one 'black-spot' removal occurred before 1960, in 1957. But, arguably, the state's motives in this case derived from a long-standing concern about soil erosion in the area, more than from the inauguration of a national policy on 'black spots'. (See J. Starfield, '"A Documentary Drama": The Case of Malisela Letsoalo and the Banareng Tribe versus the Union Government' (Seminar Paper no. 229; African Studies Institute, Univ. of Witwatersrand, 1988).
[30] WRAB JMR A78/6/2, Sec. for BAD, 'Settling of Non-Productive Bantu'.

birth or length of employment, were entitled to remain in white areas only as long as they ministered to white needs.

The removals policy also heralded a new approach to urban unemployment. The influx control policy of the 1950s had sought to tackle unemployment in two ways. The first affected those without residential rights. Once unemployed, their presence in a proclaimed area was no longer legal and they could therefore be 'endorsed out'. However, unemployment amongst Africans who did have residential rights in the cities had to be tackled differently. These rights allowed their holders to remain in a proclaimed area despite being unemployed; therefore, the 'urbanised' unemployed could not simply be deported from the area. Instead, the NAD looked to the ULPP to ensure that surpluses of urbanised labour were used up. By the 1960s, however, although the BAD reiterated the ULPP, it had lost confidence in the policy's power to combat urban unemployment. The removals policy thus gave the BAD the power to remove all 'unproductive' Africans from the cities, whether they were urbanised or not.

## Accounting for the Changes

As the previous section showed, the new policies towards Africans in the urban areas were constructed within the ideological and legal framework of the homeland self-government policy, first introduced in 1959. The government's principal purpose in promulgating the 1959 Promotion of Bantu Self-Government Act was to address the problem of African political rights. However, the new homeland policy also created the possibility for new forms of control over the townships in white areas. By defining the urban townships as outposts of ethnic homelands, the BAD could attack the concept of residential rights for the urbanised. Also, the ideological commitment to developing the reserves legitimised the policies designed to diminish white urban dependence on African labour. Restricting the numbers of workers entering the cities was redescribed as part of the government's 'magnanimous' drive to boost the productivity of the reserves.

Still, the new homeland policy does not itself explain the BAD's drive to restructure its urban policies. It remains to consider when and why the possibilities for a new urban policy opened by the homeland policy were actively pursued by the BAD. They were, after all, the sort of moves which the architects of NAD policy in the early 1950s had dismissed as impractical and unnecessary. Unrestricted economic integration had been accepted as economically indispensable; and the NAD had yielded to the reality of a 'detribalised' urbanised population with no real ties with the reserves. Yet, by the late 1950s the BAD changed tack in the face of 'practical' obstacles which were now even larger than those identified early on in the decade. The size of the urban African work-force had grown, signifying the even deeper dependence of industrial profitability on African labour. Likewise, the size of the 'detribalised' population in the cities had expanded still further, their permanence now protected by legal residential rights.

As the following discussion shows, the major impetus within the BAD to restructure its urban policies derived from the escalation of urban African resistance in the late 1950s, which peaked in 1960 after the shooting of anti-pass protesters in Sharpeville, in the Vaal Triangle. As a result of these disturbances, the issues of African urbanisation and economic integration, which had dominated conflicts over the nature of Apartheid in the late 1940s and early 1950s, were again thrust to the forefront of debate within the Afrikaner nationalist alliance generally, and the BAD in particular. By 1960, however, the principal factors which had previously predisposed the NAD towards its 'practical' stance on these issues had changed. During the years 1948–53, when the legislative foundations of the first phase of Apartheid were laid, the NAD's 'practical' premises and objectives were shaped by several factors including, first, the power of Afrikaner capitalist interests, relative to those of primarily petty-bourgeois groupings such as SABRA, within the BAD; secondly, the NP's electoral uncertainty, which made for a cautious, short-term approach to policy-making; and thirdly, the power of local authorities within the NAD. But by 1960 departmental thinking was dominated by the views of the Broederbond and SABRA, backed now by the SAAU; the BAD's foray into new policies of social and economic engineering was fortified by the NP's strengthened grip on the reins of power; and the BAD had positioned itself for a frontal attack on the local authorities. Still, organised commerce and industry and several local authorities protested vigorously against the BAD's change of course. The 1960s thus saw a sustained struggle over the course of BAD policy. The following discussion examines in turn each of the factors shaping BAD policy.

*Escalation of Urban African Resistance in the Late 1950s*

The wave of urban African protest which rose in the late 1950s drew its momentum partly from the shop floor. Between 1955 and 1958 the number of industrial disputes and people on strike nearly doubled over the levels of the early 1950s.[31] However, by 1959 the main thrust of African protest came from within the townships, beginning with the squatter settlements of Cato Manor (outside Durban) early in 1959. Initially provoked by opposition to the state's plans to remove African squatters from the Cato Manor area, the disturbances raged for several months, inflamed by municipal raids on illegal beer stills. By August 1959 S. Bourquin, the Manager of the Durban NEAD, called a meeting with the Minister of the BAD to declare the local authority's impotence and defeat in the Cato Manor area. In Bourquin's words,

the authority of the Durban City Council—the civil governmental authority for the area—has been challenged and overthrown. That statement is not an exaggeration of the facts, for it is true to say that the City Council has been defeated at Cato Manor, and cannot restore its authority without the fullest co-operation and most active assistance of the Government.[32]

The tumult in Durban also made the headlines in the overseas Press. But this was a small sample of the more severe and damaging international censure soon to come. In December 1959, the Pan-Africanist Congress (PAC) and ANC both unveiled plans for national anti-pass campaigns. Their protests took an unexpectedly dramatic turn in March 1960, when the SAP opened fire on a crowd of PAC protesters in Sharpeville, Vereeniging. Sixty-nine people were killed and 180 injured. As the unrest spread to other areas of the country, a national state of emergency was declared, and a political storm broke. With the injustices of Apartheid now the subject of heated criticism abroad, South Africa withdrew from the Commonwealth. International confidence in the country's economic prospects dived, and during 1960 the country suffered a net outflow

---

[31] Griffiths and Jones, *South African Labour Economics*, p. 101.
[32] KCL Bourquin papers, KCM 55218 Durban NEAD, 'Notes for Meeting with Minister of BAD', 3 Aug. 1959.

of R180 million[33] and a 'balance of payments crisis more severe than any experienced since 1932'.[34]

As these political and economic crises dawned, the Afrikaner nationalist alliance was once again thrown into turmoil over the long-controversial issues of economic integration and the status of urban Africans. Debate and conflict over these questions, which had divided competing conceptions of Apartheid in the late 1940s, had persisted into the 1950s, albeit with less of the intensity than had characterised the pre-1948 controversies. But by the late 1950s conflict had escalated once more, with the DRC and SABRA wracked by internal divisions (see later). The Sharpeville crisis then fanned the flames, spreading the heat throughout Afrikaner ranks. Although this political blaze extended and perpetuated the controversies of the previous decade, the lines of division between competing factions which had characterised the debates of the late 1940s had now been redrawn, with decisive implications for the direction of BAD policy.

### Realignments within Afrikanerdom and the BAD

The Sharpeville shootings produced a resounding clamour, in South Africa and abroad, for 'liberal' reforms to the government's policies towards Africans in the urban areas. As the Liberal Party declared, the fact of a national state of emergency demonstrated to many that 'no urban stability could be built on the petty bureaucratic restrictions which the pass laws and influx control place on the lives of urban Africans'.[35] Some of these calls for reform emanated from within the state. In early April 1960 three senior Cabinet ministers— Donges, Sauer, and Schoeman—discreetly pressured Verwoerd to do away with the reference-book system.[36] Their request was sidelined by an assassination attempt on Verwoerd on 9 April. But while Verwoerd was recovering in hospital, Sauer (as acting Prime Minister) publicly called for 'a new deal for the African' by way of a far-reaching overhaul of the legislation affecting Africans in urban areas. 'The old book of South African history was closed at

---

[33] Innes, *Anglo American*, p. 173.

[34] D. Hobart Houghton, *The South African Economy* (Cape Town, 1964), p. 184.

[35] BCC BMR 14/1/92, Liberal Party Memorandum on 'The Bantu in European Areas Bill', 8 May 1961.

[36] B. Schoeman, *Van Malan tot Verwoerd* (Cape Town, 1973), p. 201.

Sharpeville a month ago,' declared Sauer; 'we must get rid of the pin-pricks which made the Native ripe for the propaganda of the PAC and ANC.'[37]

Sauer's pronouncements were echoed in several quarters of Afrikanerdom. The AHI, which had previously reserved its responses to government policies for private, behind-the-scenes negotiations, now made an overtly political intervention in the debate about urban Africans. Alarmed at the rapid decline in the country's appeal to foreign investors during the Sharpeville crisis, the AHI acted unusually assertively, taking the unprecedented step of aligning itself publicly with the primarily English-speaking FCI, ASSOCOM, the Steel and Engineering Industries' Federation of South Africa (SEIFSA), and Transvaal and Orange Free State Chambers of Mines. Recognising the Sharpeville disturbances as having been provoked by 'genuine grievances' on the part of urban Africans, these organisations published a joint memorandum in July 1960 of 'proposals to ease race tension'.[38] These proposals were based on

the realistic observation . . . that, owing to education, contact with a developed economy, etc., the Bantu can no longer be regarded as belonging to a single category . . . . In large cities, there is a settled urban Bantu population which it is desirable in certain respects to treat differently from those in the reserves.[39]

The memorandum thus called on the government to reform its policies towards Africans living and working in the cities, by drawing 'a clear distinction . . . between the settled urbanised Bantu who has resided for at least five years in an urban area, and has thus qualified for residence, and the migrant labourer'.[40] By permitting urbanised Africans greater freedom of movement and employment, it was argued, the government could stabilise the townships by securing the support of a 'loyal middle-class type Bantu'.[41] The AHI, then, accepted the view of English-speaking commerce and industry, that the antidote to urban African resistance was an extension of the existing differentiation between urbanised and

---

[37] P. Sauer, quoted in *The World*, 30 Apr. 1960.
[38] *Commercial Opinion*, July 1960, pp. 6–8.
[39] Ibid. 6.
[40] Ibid. 7.
[41] Ibid.

migrant residents of the cities. Once the state's grip over the movements and employment of urbanised Africans was loosened, their sense of grievance would diminish.

The call for a similarly co-optive strategy to ameliorate the plight of urban Africans was also heard from dissident factions within the DRC and SABRA. Although initially an outspoken protagonist of total segregation, by the mid-1950s the DRC had generally thrown its weight behind the state's version of Apartheid. A more liberal faction within the DRC, however, had begun voicing criticism of the migrant labour system and its disruptive effects on family life.[42] These murmurings grew louder in the wake of the Sharpeville crisis, issuing in insistent pleas to review the effects of Apartheid on urban Africans. 'Educated Christian Bantu individuals', it was argued, should be viewed in a 'different light' from Africans in the reserves.[43] A gathering of leading Afrikaner churchmen in December 1960, the Cottesloe Consultation, echoed this dissatisfaction with existing Apartheid policies, calling for a review of the migrant labour system, job reservation, and the appallingly low wages and poor living conditions of urban Africans.

A similar lobby was mounted by a minority faction within SABRA. Its dissatisfaction with state policy was rooted in a conflict with Verwoerd in the late 1950s over his response to the findings of the Tomlinson Commission. According to N. Olivier (a founder member of SABRA), the Tomlinson Commission, briefed to examine the prospects for the socio-economic development of the reserves, was appointed by Jansen at SABRA's behest.[44] Tomlinson, himself a prominent SABRA figure, was joined by other leading SABRA members in collecting and presenting the Commission's findings. It is not surprising, then, that the Commission's report reiterated the familiar SABRA call on the government to develop the reserves into economically viable entities (see Chapter 2). A figure of £104,000,000 over ten years was estimated for the task. Verwoerd, however, as Minister of the department responsible for the reserves, refused to allocate such a large sum of money.[45] His plans for developing the reserves were far more limited, aiming

---

[42] Lazar, 'Conformity and Conflict', p. 263.
[43] Ibid. 266.
[44] Interview with N. Olivier, 5 July 1985.
[45] *HAD* (1956), vol. 91, col. 5305.

merely to contain the African population which was surplus to the labour needs of white areas. By the late 1950s Verwoerd's powers over SABRA had expanded to the point where the dominant faction in the organisation had meekly succumbed to his view, softening its stance on total segregation. The majority within SABRA now called merely for stricter controls on African urbanisation and economic integration, within a framework of the limited development of the reserves. Only a minority group of what J. Lazar calls the 'visionaries' stood by the original SABRA prescription for thorough-going total segregation.[46] Conflict between the visionaries and the SABRA mainstream which backed Verwoerd came to a head at the 1960 SABRA conference (held a month after the Sharpeville shootings), which was dominated by debates over the position of urban Africans. The visionaries, recognising that Verwoerd's opposition to total segregation was unassailable, adopted an unexpectedly—and impermissibly—reformist stance. As long as the government was not seriously committed to total segregation, they argued, the only effective bulwark against continual turbulence in the townships was to ameliorate the position and living conditions of urbanised Africans. As Professor Joubert, a Transvaal executive member, told the conference, 'thousands and thousands of Bantu with their families are settled in our urban White areas. To regard them as visitors or migrant labourers would be, from a sociological point of view, unrealistic ... While they are there, life must be made economically bearable for them.'[47] Ironically, the AHI's calls for the acceptance of an economically integrated and permanently settled urbanised African community within 'white' South Africa received the backing of those who had once been the staunchest exponents of total segregation.

This reformist thrust within Afrikanerdom was blunted, however, by the powers of the competing faction, calling for considerably more, rather than less, state control over African urbanisation and economic integration. It was the Broederbond, recently man-œuvred into a central policy-making role by Verwoerd, which

---

[46] J. Lazar, 'The Role of SABRA in the Formulation of Apartheid Ideology, 1948–1961', in *The Societies of Southern Africa in the Nineteenth and Twentieth Centuries* (Collected Seminar Papers, Institute of Commonwealth Studies, University of London, 17; 1987).

[47] *The Star*, 21 Apr. 1960.

dominated this power bloc. The 1950s had seen an impressive growth in the size and influence of the Bond, its membership increasing from 3,662 in 260 cells in 1950, to 5,760 in 409 cells by 1960.[48] As the decade advanced, the organisation had become increasingly active in the ideological and cultural activities of Afrikanerdom. The Bond also exercised considerable influence within the public service, provoking frequent allegations that promotion for civil servants depended on their securing Broederbond patronage.[49] Still, before the late 1950s the Broederbond was largely excluded from the sphere of party politics and policy-making.[50] It was Verwoerd's successful bid for leadership of the NP in 1958 that brought the Bond into the forefront of political decision-making, as a *quid pro quo* for its support of Verwoerd in the leadership contest.[51]

Verwoerd's standing in the NP had reached its nadir in 1957. Strongly criticised for his autocratic ways, Verwoerd had indicated his wish to resign his portfolio as Minister of Native Affairs.[52] But in 1958 he rebounded triumphant, with the backing of the Broederbond, and defeated T. Donges's bid to succeed J. Strijdom as Leader of the NP and Prime Minister. Initially, however, Verwoerd's position as Prime Minister was fragile, buffeted by strong opposition from the Cape NP particularly. In order to bolster his power, he therefore rapidly inserted four staunch supporters, all prominent Broeders (N. Diedrichs, A. Hertzog, W. Maree, and D. Uys), into the Cabinet. More secure in the Cabinet, and assured of the loyalty of the Broederbond, Verwoerd then proceeded to expand the Broederbond's powers within the state, as an extension and instrument of his own hold over the course of state policy. Addressing a national meeting of the Broederbond shortly after his election in 1958, Verwoerd announced plainly, 'I did not see it only as my privilege but as my duty to draw the ties close—the ties that always existed between our Afrikaner organisation [the Bond] and our Afrikaner government—through my personal presence.'[53] As Lazar has argued, Verwoerd looked to the Bond

---

[48] *Sunday Times*, 29 Jan. 1978.
[49] See, e.g., *Rand Daily Mail*, 14 Apr. 1953; *Sunday Express*, 12 May 1957.
[50] Lazar, 'Conformity and Conflict', p. 66.
[51] See, e.g., *The Star*, 13 Oct. 1961.
[52] Heard, *General Elections in South Africa*, pp. 71–2.
[53] *Sunday Times*, 29 Jan. 1978.

increasingly . . . as an informal Cabinet . . . the Bond's extensive, well-knit organisational networks, and deep penetration of all Afrikaner institutions, became an indispensable weapon in Verwoerd's armoury, because he was able to bypass the normal political channels whenever he considered it necessary.[54]

Poised at the helm of policy-making, the Broederbond was able to play a key role in marginalising the reformist lobby within Afrikanerdom. By the late 1950s leading Broeders occupied top positions in the DRC, which they used to discredit the position taken by the Cottesloe Consultation and to pressure churchmen into distancing themselves from its recommendations.[55] Overlapping membership of the Broederbond and SABRA allowed Broederbond members to spearhead the offensive against the SABRA visionaries too.[56] The visionaries' calls for reformist urban policies had plunged the 1960 SABRA annual conference into 'an atmosphere of crisis'.[57] These conflicts persisted until the next annual SABRA conference in 1961, when the pro-Verwoerdian faction in the organisation succeeded in trouncing the visionaries as the conference drew to a close by mounting a coup of all the office-bearing positions in the organisation.[58]

By 1960 the SAAU, too, was in the throes of Broederbond infiltration.[59] The Bond's foray into the Afrikaans agricultural community[60] was strongly opposed in some quarters. As an internal Broederbond circular of 1976 admitted, 'committees of organised agriculture had been captured many years ago with great difficulty and sacrifice'.[61] The strength of feeling amongst Afrikaner farmers in the northern Orange Free State, for example, was sufficient to launch an alternative organisation 'to fight the Broederbond secret society and eradicate it from Afrikaner life'.[62] But this move was itself an indication of the power which the Bond had already

---

[54] Lazar, 'Conformity and Conflict', pp. 75, 78.

[55] For more detail, see ibid. 270–5.

[56] *Sunday Times*, 2 Dec. 1962.

[57] *The Star*, 23 Apr. 1960.

[58] *The Friend*, 29 June 1961.

[59] Interview with H. Strydom, on 19 Jan. 1989. See also *Sunday Times*, 15 Jan. 1978.

[60] Note that this discussion is limited by the fact that the state archives covering this period are still closed, and the SAAU claims to have no archival material going back this far.

[61] *Sunday Times*, 14 Jan. 1979.

[62] *Sunday Times*, 16 Dec. 1962.

established within local farmers' organisations. The Broederbond's 'tight grip' on agriculture[63] was also facilitated by its hold over several of the agricultural co-operatives affiliated to, and powerful within, the SAAU.[64] The co-operatives played a key role in assuring farmers' survival, by providing production loans needed by most farmers to buy fertiliser, fuel, and seed. The officials and directors of the co-operatives also allocated loans from the Land Bank, for farm purchases or extensions. (In 1959 £32.5 million was loaned to farmers by the Land Bank, and £320,869 paid out for seed, fuel, etc.)[65] By using their powers to ensure that fellow Broeders secured better loans than non-Broeders, Broederbond members in office-bearing positions in the co-operatives were able to extend their influence and support within the co-operatives and the SAAU at large.[66]

The new-found political ascendancy of the Broederbond had profound implications for the tenor of BAD policy-making. By the late 1950s the three key decision-makers in the Department— Minister de Wet Nel, Deputy Minister Botha, and Secretary Eiselen—were all Broeders and central figures in the dominant faction within SABRA. SABRA's pro-Broederbond leanings were also manifest in the BAD through its research division and the Native Affairs Commission (as discussed in Chapter 3), both dominated by SABRA members. Also, the SAAU's continuing prominence and influence in the BAD gave the Bond another lever within the Department. As a consequence of its infiltration by the Broederbond, the SAAU shifted its position on African urbanisa-tion, to coincide with that taken by the Bond. During the late 1940s and early 1950s the AHI and SAAU had shared a common com-mitment to 'practical' Apartheid (see Chapters 2 and 3). But by 1960, while the AHI remained resolutely 'practical', the SAAU had become increasingly wary of policies which unwittingly increased the size and bargaining power of the urban African proletariat.

This new alliance of interests made its mark within the BAD soon after the Sharpeville disturbances. The SAAU's Liaison Committee, still enjoying a privileged hearing within the BAD, met with leading

[63] *Sunday Times*, 22 May 1960.

[64] Interview with H. Strydom, 19 Jan. 1989.

[65] SAAU, *Report of the General Council to 1960 Annual Congress* (Pretoria, 1960), p. 14.

[66] *Sunday Times*, 14 Jan. 1979.

figures in the Department to draft legislation which would considerably extend the degree of state control over Africans in urban
areas.[67] The Bill which emerged from these discussions, the 'Bantu
in European Areas Bill', was drafted by October 1960 and circulated
confidentially to local authorities, organised commerce and industry, and other interested parties for comment. The contents of this
Bill illustrated plainly that, from the BAD's point of view, the
escalation of African resistance was caused by too little state control,
rather than too much. The threat of further protest was to be
subverted by taking far more drastic steps to curtail the growth of
the urban work-force, and by *weakening* what Verwoerd had earlier
referred to as the 'guarantees, security, and stability' of the urbanised proletariat.

The Bill was far more draconian than anything previously drafted
by the BAD. It accorded the Minister of BAD the power to stipulate
when 'the number of Bantu . . . in an area is in excess of the area's
labour requirements', and provided for the removal of those persons
deemed excessive.[68] The Bill stated specifically that section 10(1)(a),
(b), and (c) rights were no protection against removal: 'any Bantu
born in the area concerned or having unconditional residence
therein may also be removed'.[69]

The Bill also empowered the BAD to take its first steps towards
forcibly curtailing the extent of white dependence on African labour
by authorising

the fixing of labour quotas or labour pools in respect of certain areas or
categories of employment or in respect of individual employers, control of
the movement of labour in accordance with such quotas or from such pools
and the prohibition of employment other than such as determined in
accordance with such quotas or from any source other than such labour
pools.[70]

In swift retaliation to the turbulence generated by the Sharpeville
protests, the BAD had thus initiated a radical departure from the

---

[67] SAAU, *Report of the General Council to 1961 Annual Congress* (Pretoria, 1961),
p. 57, and *Report of the General Council to 1962 Annual Congress* (Pretoria, 1962), p. 53.

[68] BCC BMR 14/1/92, 'Minutes of Finance and General Purposes Committee
Meeting, Item B.A.8', 10 Nov. 1960, p. 8.

[69] Ibid. Also, the BAD's powers to remove Africans deemed 'idle and undesirable'
or 'detrimental to peace and order', irrespective of their 'residential rights', were
increased.

[70] Ibid. 10.

existing legislation governing African residence and employment in the urban areas. Both 'practical' premisses of the previous decade were now under concerted attack.

### Electoral Gains

Another factor which explains the shift in the BAD's approach towards Africans in the urban areas after 1959 was the NP's tightening hold over the white electorate. Electoral support for the NP expanded steadily during the 1950s. After the 1958 election, the NP held 97 seats (as compared with 88 in 1953 and 79 in 1948), having claimed 48.5 per cent of the vote (as compared with 44.5 per cent in 1953 and 39 per cent in 1948).[71] The 1960 Republican referendum, during which the white electorate voted in support of the NP's motion that the country become a republic, gave the NP its first majority of votes: 850,458 voted in favour, 775,878 against, a majority of approximately 52 per cent for the NP. Shortly afterwards the NP won the 1961 general election with a majority of 53 per cent of the vote.[72] The NP was now firmly ensconced at the helm of government, and its policy-makers could afford to be less pragmatic and more aggressive than during its first term of office, which had been the first decisive phase in the making of Apartheid.

### Attack on Local Authorities

The consolidation of the NP's position in government accompanied the expansion of the BAD's powers *vis-à-vis* local authorities, which also contributed towards the shift in the BAD's policies after 1959. As Chapter 8 showed, the NAD's previously diffident attitude to the local authorities began to change as the 1950s drew to a close.[73] The BAD's growing assertiveness was partly a function of its improved administrative capabilities. Throughout the 1950s the NAD had expanded, increasing the resources and expertise necessary for departmental officers to take over some of the responsibilities and powers of the local authorities. Sub-departments proliferated, to the

[71] Heard, *General Elections in South Africa*, pp. 59, 86. These figures are estimates calculated by including uncontested constituencies.
[72] Ibid.
[73] See also S. Bekker and R. Humphries, *From Control to Confusion: The Changing Role of Administration Boards in South Africa* (Pietermaritzburg, 1985), pp. 50–8.

point where, in 1958, the NAD sub-divided into two, the Department of Bantu Administration and Development (BAD) and the Department of Bantu Education. By 1960 their joint white staff numbered 3,000, as compared with the 1,750 employed by the NAD in 1950.[74] The NP's policy of staffing the state bureaucracy with loyal Nationalists as far as possible had borne fruit too, with a greater proportion of positions occupied by Afrikaners. Thus equipped to mount a major offensive against the local authorities, the BAD launched its first move in the wake of the escalation of militant protest in the townships in the late 1950s. In the Department's eyes, the local authorities were either unable or unwilling to maintain order by rigorously enforcing government policy. Durban, it was claimed, was a case in point. The Durban City Council and its administrative arm, the NEAD, had admitted that their authority was completely overthrown during the Cato Manor disturbances (see earlier). The BAD also claimed justification for its attack on local authorities in the wave of protest following the Sharpeville shootings. An official statement found it

significant that the disturbances took place especially in areas where the local authorities are controlled by opponents of government policy, and it is well known that the principles of separate development have not always been applied in the same good spirit as underlies the aims of the government.[75]

The 1960 Bantu in European Areas Bill thus launched a singularly aggressive assault on the powers of local authorities, in a bid to expand direct departmental control over the townships. The powers of influx control were to be wrested from local authorities, and centralised in the BAD itself. In the words of the Bill, 'the Bantu Affairs Commissioner is the officer who must be satisfied that any Native qualifies under one or other of the provisions to remain (in the urban area) for more than 72 hours'.[76]

The Bill also permitted the Department to rob local authorities of all their existing powers 'to make by-laws or regulations in regard to . . . urban Native administration'.[77] This attack was thwarted by

[74] Lazar, 'Conformity and Conflict', p. 124.

[75] BCC BMR 14/1/10, 'Statement of Government Policy following on Recent Riots, 20 May 1960'.

[76] BCC BMR 14/1/92, 'Minutes of Finance and General Purposes Committee Meeting', 10 Nov. 1960, p. 1.

[77] Ibid.

the demise of the Bill. But the significance of the 1960 Bill was as a signpost of the direction of BAD thinking for the forthcoming decade and a half.[78]

In short, then, the BAD's changed approach towards Africans in the urban areas, heralded in the Bantu in European Areas Bill, was orchestrated by the new alliance of Afrikaner interests which dominated the policy-making process. But such policy changes were facilitated by the successful expansion and consolidation of the political powers of the Nationalist government, on the one hand, and of the BAD in its relation to local authorities, on the other.

### Postscript: The Fate of Influx Control after 1961

As had been the case in the previous decade, the BAD policy-makers did not always enjoy their own way. As before, the fate of BAD policies, influx control in particular, lay in the outcome of contests between the BAD, local authorities, urban commerce, industry, agriculture, and the urban African people, in both the policy-making and administrative spheres. A comprehensive assessment of influx control after 1961 is beyond the scope of this book. What follows is a brief selective survey of some of its principal features, seen largely through the lens of the BAD's struggle with the urban business community over the terms of state control of the African labour market.

As the previous discussion has shown, the BAD and organised commerce and industry had passed conflicting verdicts on the failures of the influx control policy of the 1950s, and therefore favoured different strategies for the 1960s. One of the ironies of this next decade was that it saw the simultaneous strengthening of *both* the BAD and its capitalist opponents, which made the continuing struggles between them all the more intense.

The BAD bureaucracy continued to expand throughout the 1960s. By 1968 it comprised no less than seven sub-departments: agriculture and development; housing; departmental administration; labour and identification; community affairs; and land and

---

[78] This attack on the local authorities culminated in the creation of Administration Boards, authorised by the 1971 Bantu Affairs Administration Act. Appointed by and wholly answerable to the BAD, these Boards usurped the rights, functions, and powers of local authorities in respect of 'urban Bantu administration'.

finance. 'Bantu affairs' in 'white' South Africa as well as in the home-lands were wholly in the control of the BAD. As the department grew, so too did its self-sufficiency and autonomy within the state. Other state departments seldom participated in the BAD's decision-making, even in matters of mutual concern. For example, when the BAD's Director of Labour, P. van Rensburg, chaired an inquiry into existing control measures, including the control of African labour, the Department of Labour was not invited to participate in the inquiry. The Department's personnel was also typically more ideologically hard-line and intransigent than had been the case in the 1950s, an index of the breadth of support for the Broederbond and SABRA within the Department.[79] When M. C. Botha took over as Minister of BAD in 1966, with Coetzee as his Deputy, the department entered its ideologically toughest phase. Yet, ironically, the BAD was at its most rigid and uncompromising at exactly the time when economic growth was reaching spectacular new heights, generating enormous urban demands for labour. Between 1963 and 1968 the gross domestic profit at current prices rose by an annual average of 9.3 per cent (compared with an average of 5.2 per cent from 1957 to 1962).[80] The growth of the manufacturing and con-struction sectors, both concentrated in urban areas, was principally responsible for this boom.[81] The BAD was proposing to curb economic integration at exactly the moment that the economic costs of restricting industry's labour supply were increasing dramatically, along with the political bargaining power of organised industry and commerce. The stage was set, therefore, for a bitter battle.

The BAD lost the first round, as opposition from organised commerce and industry, as well as various local authorities, sank the 1960 Bantu in European Areas Bill before it was even gazetted. But the BAD retaliated quickly. During 1961 and 1962 an intensive overhaul of departmental policy was conducted. A conference of chief Bantu Affairs Commissioners was called to evaluate the per-formance of the labour bureaux system, and an interdepartmental

---

[79] There were signs of intra-departmental division, however—particularly over the issue of labour quotas.

[80] Innes, *Anglo American*, p. 188.

[81] Between 1962 and 1970 the combined contribution of manufacturing and construction to the gross domestic profit rose from 24.15% of the total to 28.2%, as compared with the declining contribution over the same period of agriculture and mining (ibid.).

committee, chaired by M. C. Botha (then Deputy Minister of BAD), was appointed to investigate the causes of unemployment and 'idleness' amongst Africans in the urban areas. Vindicated by the findings of the Botha Report, the BAD introduced the 1963 Bantu Laws Amendment Bill, in another attempt to introduce legislation which would both restrict the scale of economic integration and undermine section 10(1) rights. But, once again, organised commerce and industry objected on economic grounds to both clauses. Labour quotas were regarded as an economically arbitrary and destructive measure, particularly since no provision was made to consult with employers over the application of the quota system. And the strategy underpinning the BAD's assault on urban residential rights—the removal of all those who had become 'unemployed perhaps through cyclical business fluctuations'—was condemned as inflicting 'an economic loss to industry and commerce'.[82] These protests were effective. The Johannesburg Chamber of Commerce noted with satisfaction that, 'from a study of the 1964 Bill, which had now passed its second reading, it seems that many of the objections made by the employer bodies during 1963 have now been met'.[83]

Undeterred, the BAD's ideologues tried again to bring employers in line with the ideological dictates of 'homeland-oriented administration'. Van Rensburg's 'Report of the Interdepartmental Committee on Control Measures' (1967) urged once more that unchecked economic integration and section 10 rights were both anomalies within the policy of separate development. Draft legislation (the Bantu Labour Amendment Act) soon followed in 1968. This time the BAD was prepared to bribe organised commerce and industry to support the eradication of section 10(1) rights with the promise of legislation to enlarge prescribed areas.[84] As the FCI reported,

the Transvaal Chamber [of Industries] has, confidentially, been advised that it could probably secure the integration of the Witwatersrand, or at least portions of the Witwatersrand, as a Bantu labour area, *if* it would support

[82] ASSOCOM NEAF, ASSOCOM, 'Special Report to Associate Members', Mar. 1963.
[83] ASSOCOM NEAF, Johannesburg Chamber of Commerce, 'Council Document: Bantu Laws Amendment Bill', Apr. 1964.
[84] The immobility of labour caused by municipally defined prescribed areas remained a source of widespread grievance amongst employers throughout the decade. See later.

the removal of the so-called section 10(1) residential rights of Bantu so that the sole test of a Bantu's right to reside in an urban area would be whether there was work for him in that area.[85]

But the FCI would not budge, and once again the BAD had to weaken its position. Section 10(1) remained on the statute book. But the BAD did succeed in closing one of the loopholes of section 10(1). Introducing the so-called 'call-in card system', the law made it compulsory for migrant workers to return annually to their districts of origin. This precluded the possibility of a migrant notching up the ten or fifteen years of continuous service in a proclaimed area necessary for the acquisition of 10(1)(b) rights.

The powers of industrial and commercial capital to alter the BAD's legislation were limited, however. By the late 1960s the BAD succeeded in trouncing business opposition to a labour quota system for urban manufacturing. The first step was taken by the Physical Planning and Utilization of Resources Act of 1967, which gave the Minister of Planning the authority to restrict the use of land in designated controlled areas for industrial purposes. Local authorities were thus stripped of their powers to regulate the rate of industrial development—and with it, the growth of the industrial African work-force—in their areas of jurisdiction. Then, in 1970, the government's White Paper on the 'Report by the Inter-Departmental Committee on the Decentralisation of Industries' authorised the implementation of labour quotas (initially only on the Witwatersrand). The maximum permissible ratio of white to African industrial workers in the region was to be pegged at 1:2.5 (until 1973) and, thereafter, at 1:2. Any industry exceeding the quota would be compelled to decentralise to a border area or reserve.

Organised commerce and industry also encountered strong resistance in its quest for enlarged prescribed areas to improve the mobility of African labour. The 1960 post-Sharpeville joint statement issued by the FCI, ASSOCOM, and the AHI, amongst others (see earlier in the Chapter), had urged that 'certain main industrial areas should be regarded as a unit and be proclaimed as one labour area, so as to enable a Bantu worker to work in any of the constituent districts without the need to change residence'.[86]

---

[85] ASSOCOM NEAF, FCI Sec. to Members of Non-European Affairs Committee, re 'Brief Notes on the Draft Bantu Labour Amendment Act 1968', 18 Jan. 1968.
[86] *Commercial Opinion*, July 1960, p. 7.

Initially ignored by the BAD, the plea was then renewed two years later. This time, however, commerce and industry were thwarted by the interests of local authorities, an indication that local authorities were not simply at the beck and call of the business community. The BAD was initially sympathetic to the principle of regional labour control, which was included in the first draft of the 1963 Bantu Laws Amendment Bill. But the clause was rapidly retracted, following opposition from local authorities. After the Johannesburg Chamber of Commerce revived the business lobby in 1968, draft legislation in 1969 (the Bantu Labour Amendment Bill) proposed to set up Bantu labour boards, in tandem with local authorities, to administer larger 'labour areas'. But the relevant clause was again dropped following opposition from local authorities, who refused to surrender control over the influx of labour into their areas as long as they retained responsibility for housing workers. It was only when the BAD proposed a wholesale restructuring of the administrative apparatuses of labour control in 1971 (see later) that enlarged prescribed areas became a reality.

By the end of the 1960s, therefore, the BAD's attempts to rewrite the influx control legislation of the 1950s had been only partially successful, following fierce opposition from commerce and industry and/or local authorities. Legal limits on the scale of economic integration were eventually introduced. But section 10(1) remained on the statute books, which therefore perpetuated the contradiction at the heart of the ULPP.

How did BAD policy fare in practice? There were some dramatic successes in the 1960s. The proportion of Union-born Africans in the urban areas declined during the decade.[87] Between 1960 and 1970 the homeland population grew by 977,000, while there was a net decline of 203,000 Africans from the urban areas of 'white' South Africa.[88] Influx control was administered far more rigidly during the 1960s, as was reflected in the increase in the numbers of pass-law contraventions, for example. During 1967 693,661 people were convicted under the pass laws,[89] as compared with 384,497 in 1962. But the reduction in the size of the urban African population

---

[87] Simkins, *Four Essays*, p. 58.

[88] Ibid. 62.

[89] SAIRR, *A Survey of Race Relations in South Africa, 1970* (Johannesburg, 1970), p. 164.

was largely the product of the BAD's forced removals policy, rather than influx control.

Employers also encountered more ideologically zealous BAD officials during the 1960s than had been their experience during the 1950s. This was a partly a result of the expansion and consolidation of the labour bureaux system. But the trend also reflected the greater numbers of Broederbond members and sympathisers within the local authorities themselves.[90] Thus in 1964 the Roodepoort NEAD, for example, pursued a policy of removing two-thirds of the town's African workers.[91]

Ideological rigidity in the application of BAD policy also derived from the expansion of direct departmental control at the administrative level. It was the BAD which administered the Physical Planning Act, for example. In 1968 alone the BAD was thus responsible for prohibiting the building and expansion of factories which would have employed 15,355 African workers. This meant that, for every one job created for Africans that year, 3.1 were vetoed.[92]

The expansion of the BAD's bureaucracy, and the general hardening of attitudes, were insufficient, however, to deter resistance from large numbers of employers and work-seekers. Illegal employment continued on a wide scale, as employers and work-seekers evaded the strictures of the ULPP.[93] As the SAP complained to the Johannesburg NEAD, for example, 'investigations have . . . revealed that large numbers of Bantu from elsewhere are apparently being illegally employed by almost every business in Johannesburg'.[94]

Also, as was the case during the 1950s, the ULPP was thwarted by its contradictory relationship to section 10(1), which remained on the statute book despite the BAD's aggressive campaign against it. And in many cases employers opposed to the ULPP were still aided and abetted by sympathetic local authorities. Indeed, local authorities were themselves amongst the culprits violating the ULPP. For example, the Johannesburg NEAD recruited most of

---

[90] Interview with W. J. P. Carr, 17 Apr. 1984.

[91] *The World*, 13 Mar. 1964.

[92] K Gottschalk, 'Industrial Decentralisation, Jobs and Wages', *South African Labour Bulletin*, 3/5 (1977), 51.

[93] See, e.g., WRAB JMR A78/2/2, Memorandum from Master Builders' Association, 17 Apr. 1967.

[94] WRAB JMR A78/7, Divisional Commissioner, SAP, Johannesburg, to Manager, Johannesburg NEAD, re 'Memorandum on Certain Difficulties being Experienced in Connection with the Pass Laws', 19 Aug. 1965.

its African work-force from Transkei,[95] while the Pretoria NEAD drew all its workers from the Northern and Eastern Transvaal.[96]

Ironically, the BAD's efforts to combat illegal employment compounded the problem still further. As always, the Department's recipe for improved control was to subject the employment process to still more regulations and restrictions. As a result, by 1973 the red tape imposed by the labour bureaux system had become altogether prohibitive to many employers. As the Johannesburg NEAD reported,

because an application [for labour] requires processing at so many offices, it takes an average period of six weeks for a worker to be introduced into [an urban area] . . . from an outside area . . . The inordinate delay in dealing with applications of this nature places the whole system in discredit.[97]

The structural flaw which had bedevilled the adminstration of influx control in the 1950s—the immobility of labour across municipal boundaries—also persisted into the 1960s. Indeed, labour immobility was all the more debilitating to employers as the demand for labour boomed. The BAD finally took action to address the immobility problem in 1971, with the introduction of the Administration Board system. Administration Boards, their boundaries of operation considerably larger than municipal areas, took over the municipal functions of control over African housing and employment. Labour mobility was improved somewhat as a result.

But the Administration Board system was not the perfect instrument of influx control either. When the Riekert Commission reported in 1979 on the performance of labour-control apparatuses to date, it produced a list of failings remarkably similar to those of the 1950s. Administration Board officials still battled against opposition from employers and work-seekers alike, with the result that 'large-scale unlawful employment occurred in prescribed areas'.[98] The contradictions generated by section 10(1) rights had

[95] *The World*, 14 May 1964.

[96] BCC BMR 14/1/19, Agenda of 23rd Ordinary Meeting of Management Committee, 16 Nov. 1970.

[97] WRAB JMR A78/1, vol. 2, Johannesburg NEAD, 'Memorandum on Subjects to be discussed between a Delegation of the Council's Management Committee and . . . the Deputy Minister of Bantu Administration and Education, 16 January 1973'.

[98] Republic of SA, *Report of the Commission of Inquiry into Legislation Affecting the Utilisation of Manpower (Excluding the Legislation Administered by the Departments of Labour and Mines)*, RP 32/1979, para. 4.140.

persisted. Those who qualified for these rights continued to swell the ranks of the legally 'urbanised' community. Workers with rights were still 'job choosy', leaving the unpopular, poorly paid work for the most vulnerable categories of workers.[99] And the competition among the latter for such jobs kept wages low, which in turn reinforced the 'choosiness' of the more secure workers. The result, therefore, was the perpetuation of a cycle of low wages, illegal employment, and urban unemployment which the NAD had set out to combat from the early 1950s. As the Riekert Commission found, the security afforded by section 10(1) rights was associated with 'unemployment among, and depression of the wages of, Black workers to whom authority has been granted to work in a prescribed area where unlawful employment occurs'.[100]

Like the commissions and committees of inquiry before his, Riekert could identify the problem. But, along with his predecessors, he lacked a solution, because he could not find a way out of the contradiction between section 10(1) and the ULPP. Riekert was persuaded that 'the amendment of the existing provisions of section 10 may elicit strong political reactions'.[101] Yet, at the same time, he reiterated the need for the ULPP: 'It is important and in the national interest for employers to be persuaded to make the optimal use of the available labour living on a permanent basis in urban areas.'[102]

In 1982 the clumsily named Orderly Movement and Settlement of Black Persons Bill made a last-ditch effort to remedy the problem by removing section 10. But yet again the strategy failed. Ironically, the state's determined quest to scrap section 10, and abolish the contradiction subverting the ULPP, only succeeded with the demise of influx control in 1986.

---

[99] Ibid., para. 4.206.  [100] Ibid., para. 4.141.  [101] Ibid., para. 4.204.

[102] Ibid., para. 4.214.

# 10
# *Conclusion*

IN contrast to the dominant 'grand plan' treatment of Apartheid, the central theme which has run through this book is the conception of influx control, and Apartheid more generally, as the product of a range of struggles with uneven effects. This concluding chapter draws together the various strands of struggle and accommodation identified in the book, to produce a composite (if abbreviated) picture of the processes whereby influx control, as a central pillar of the Apartheid system, was constructed during the 1950s. The last part of the chapter then summarises the main historiographical and theoretical conclusions of this historical study.

## Struggles between the State and Capital

This book has stressed the key role played by various capitalist groupings in shaping Apartheid. But it has been shown that this impact was not uniform, and cannot be understood without simultaneously taking account of the effects of various forms of African resistance, as well as the course of conflict within the state. For the sake of clarity, these sets of struggles have been examined separately; but their effect must be understood conjointly.

### *Secondary Industry and Commerce*

It was partly the interests of secondary industry and commerce which led the NAD to take a 'practical' stance on the economic integration issue during the 1950s. Employers retained the right to stipulate the number of African workers they required. And Verwoerd hastened to reassure the urban business community that a small surplus of African labour, over and above the number of workers in employment at any one time, would be permissible. However, it would be wrong to paint too pragmatic a picture of the NAD during the first phase of Apartheid. The NAD's responsiveness to the business cause was moderated and moulded by equally fundamental commitments to keeping the size of the urban African presence as small as possible, and meeting white farmers' labour needs. The result was an influx control policy which conflicted in various ways with the interests of urban industry and commerce.

For most urban employers it was the ULPP, designed to restructure prevailing patterns of employment, which was the most threatening aspect of the influx control policy. During the 1950s the majority of industrial and commercial firms were small and labour intensive, recruiting African workers principally for unskilled work. Intent on securing a quiescent and disciplined workforce at the same time as keeping wages as low as possible, most of these firms showed a marked preference for so-called 'raw' migrant workers, newly arrived, or directly recruited, from rural areas. With the ULPP, the NAD was determined to overrule this preference. Until allegedly 'idle' and 'work-shy' city-dwellers had been put to work, the NAD would prohibit employers from drawing migrant workers into the cities. The ULPP thus threatened the majority of firms on several fronts. The size of the existing urban labour reservoir would be cut back considerably. Business people would be compelled to 'make better use' of urban workers who tended to be less vulnerable, more assertive, and more politicised than 'raw' migrant labour. And the overall result would be an increase in unskilled wages, in order to draw the more 'job-choosy' city-dwellers into the notoriously unpopular jobs.

The ULPP posed less of a threat to the larger, more capital-intensive firms, where increasing numbers of Africans were employed to do skilled or semi-skilled work. Urbanised Africans, living permanently with their families in the townships, were widely (although by no means uniformly) regarded as more stable, and offering a better 'quality of labour', than migrant workers. However, the NAD's influx control policy created other inconveniences and frustrations. The NAD's opposition to further African urbanisation restricted the rate at which the supply of 'stable' urbanised labour would expand. Furthermore, despite having little difficulty in meeting their labour needs independently, these firms were now required to submit labour requisition forms to the labour bureaux. Overburdened with red tape, this procedure also took no account of the levels of skill or training required for particular jobs. Labour bureaux treated all work-seekers as homogenous, and simply dispatched those at the head of the job queue.

Organised commerce and industry were therefore dissatisfied with various features of the NAD's influx control policy. Their opposition to the proposed freeze on further African urbanisation, reinforced by similar protests from the Senate and Location Advisory Boards' Congress, forced Verwoerd to extend the ambit of residential rights, although not as generously as his opposition proposed. ASSOCOM and the FCI also disapproved of the curbs on the size of the urban labour reservoir which the ULPP threatened to impose. But, having been reassured by Verwoerd that his department would 'take account of economic realities', they did not oppose the ULPP, resolving to concentrate their energies and powers on ensuring that the policy was loosely applied.

Their efforts were partially successful. The ULPP was weakened by a series of legal and administrative concessions, although some of the latter were subsequently retracted by less pragmatic departmental bureaucrats. However, it was the cumulative powers of individual employers which dealt the more decisive blow to the ULPP. Labour bureaux officials were either unable or unwilling to deter thousands of employers from ignoring the ULPP, and indeed the labour bureaux system at large, by recruiting migrant labour independently. Moreover, those employers who did turn to the labour bureaux to meet their labour needs were usually supplied with migrant labour when they wanted it.

Administratively, therefore, influx control was considerably more closely aligned with business interests than it was intended to be. Indeed, as long as the ULPP was not enforced, influx control unwittingly heightened the very tendency it was designed to overrule—namely, the prevailing preference for so-called 'raw' migrant labour for unskilled work. Section 10(1) of the Natives (Urban Areas) Act added to the vulnerability and insecurity of migrants in search of work, as compared with urbanised Africans whose residential rights afforded them more time, opportunity, and bargaining power in the choice of employment. The majority of industrial and commercial firms, with a predominantly unskilled African work-force, thus developed a vested interest in the influx control legislation, provided it was sufficiently flexibly applied as to render the ULPP a dead letter.

Employers did not inevitably or uniformly get their way, however. In some urban areas the ULPP was upheld by labour bureaux, in spite of complaints from employers. Moreover, the NAD's restrictions on the employment of foreign workers were often uncompromising, particularly in the metropolitan areas. As a result, shortages of unskilled labour were reported in many cities, particularly those on the Witwatersrand. Industrialists complained, too, of the immobility of African labour, created by the labour bureaux system. This problem was particularly frustrating to the growing number of firms expanding or transferring their operations across municipal boundaries. Even with the backing of the NAD, efforts by organised commerce and industry to redefine the administrative boundaries of the labour bureaux were defeated by municipal administrators, who refused to surrender control over African employment in their areas.

During the 1960s conflicts between the (then renamed) BAD and commerce and industry broadened. The South African state's 'institutional self-interest' in the renewed 'vitality of the capitalist economy' forestalled the introduction of policies which inflicted serious damage on industrial or commercial prosperity. But the BAD, its anxieties about a volatile and disaffected urban proletariat stirred anew, was less pragmatic in its attitude to the supply of African labour to the cities. Also, the BAD rejected the co-optive approach towards urban Africans proposed jointly by English- and Afrikaans-speaking business organisations, in the wake of the Sharpeville shootings. The BAD's response to Sharpeville was to call for more, rather than less, state control over urbanised Africans, in a policy designed to reduce, rather than enhance, the rights of urban Africans.

*Capitalist Agriculture*

Organised agriculture was the only capitalist lobby to have enjoyed routine and institutionalised links with the NAD. The NAD invited participation in all departmental matters affecting the agricultural labour supply, from the SAAU's 'Liaison Committee'. Thus, the NAD's plan to institute a national labour bureaux system was first mooted with this Liaison Committee, since the NAD's intention to address the problem of agricultural labour shortages was one of the central objectives of the labour bureaux system. But this is not to say that the architects of NAD policy simply mimicked the SAAU's policy proposals. The SAAU's preparedness to phase out the migrant labour system for urban industries, for example, was not shared by the NAD. Nor was the labour bureaux system designed solely to promote the cause of capitalist agriculture. Taking cognisance simultaneously of the labour needs of urban industry and commerce, the NAD designed the labour bureaux system with an urban bias, in the sense that agricultural labour demands would not have priority over those of urban employers. Still, the NAD's influx control policy took account of farmers' interests in two ways. African farm-workers were prohibited from taking urban employment, except with written permission from their employer and the district labour bureau. Also, by 'optimising' the utilisation of urbanised labour, the NAD hoped to deflect a greater supply of migrant labour from the reserves and urban areas to white farms.

Farmers' labour shortages diminished as the decade advanced, and the labour bureaux system played some role in effecting this change, particularly by increasing the supply of seasonal or casual labour to the white farms. The exodus of farm-workers to town also diminished, although illegal migration was never altogether stamped out. However, partly due to the failure of the ULPP, the regular operation of the labour bureaux system was inadequate to solve the farmers' problems. The NAD, ever-sensitive to the farmers' plight, thus made additional, *ad hoc*, moves to alleviate it. The NAD intervened directly on farmers' behalf, cornering large numbers of foreign work-seekers for farm work, and sending departmental representatives to negotiate with rural chiefs for teams of men to service the needs of nearby white farms. These efforts were especially vigorous before the planting and harvesting seasons. In addition, the so-called 'petty-offenders scheme', essentially a system of forced labour, gave white farmers the right to employ Africans arrested in urban areas for contravening the influx control laws. But the biggest service rendered to white farmers by the NAD (in conjunction with the Department of Prisons) was to put convict labour, often housed in prisons built on or near white farms, at the farmers' disposal. In practice, the degree of success the NAD achieved in meeting farmers' needs had less to do with a 'rational' restructuring of the urban labour market than with the well-established tradition of turning agricultural labour into a penalty for breaking the law.

## Mining

Relatively little has been said about the political powers of mining, because the scope of the labour bureaux system did not encompass the supply of African labour to the mining sector. But it is worth stressing that Verwoerd nevertheless made sure he secured the backing of organised mining capital for the NAD's labour 'canalisation' scheme. Had the influx control system been detrimental to the interests of mining capital, the passage of the 1952 Native Laws Amendment Act might have encountered rougher waters.

### Conflicts within the State

Struggles within the state over its policy objectives and methods were profoundly affected by intra-Afrikaner disputes about the substance of Apartheid. But the state was more than simply an arena for these conflicts. Their impact on the development of Apartheid was mediated by the changing structure and composition of the NAD, and its shifting position in relation to local authorities.

By the late 1940s the issue of how to regulate the flow of African labour into the cities had become the source of deep conflict within the Afrikaner nationalist alliance. This controversy was formulated in terms of the implications of continuing economic integration and African urbanisation for the preservation of white political supremacy. All Afrikaner nationalists shared a firm commitment to white supremacy; they disagreed over the measures necessary to protect it. The internal contradictions and ambiguities in the Sauer Report (1947), endorsed by the NP, indicated that these conflicts had not been resolved within the NP on the eve of its surprise election victory in 1948. Contrary to the conventional wisdom, the new Nationalist government was thrust to power with some of the fundamentals of Apartheid still a source of controversy and uncertainty.

The conflict between the purist and 'practical' positions on Apartheid had a direct bearing on the substance and ideological justification of state policy. Both factions were represented in the NAD (the vanguard of Apartheid policy-making within the state), and exercised varying degrees of influence over its policy. The case for a 'practical' approach to Apartheid, in terms of which the realities of advancing economic integration and African urbanisation were accommodated, resonated well with the priorities of the first generation of Nationalist policy-makers. Uncertain of re-election, they were intent on consolidating and extending their hold on

power. Ambitious programmes of social engineering were, therefore, considered inopportune and impractical.

The impact of the purist position within the NAD during the
1950s was limited. The departmental bureaucracy (which ultimately
became the purists' stronghold) was still small. And the Broederbond (which became the vanguard of the (reworked) purist position
in the 1960s) had yet to capture key positions within the NAD.
Still, purists were not without influence during the first phase of
Apartheid. SABRA, entrenched in the NAD's research division,
succeeded in persuading the Department's policy-makers of the
political dangers of continuing African urbanisation. The NAD thus
deviated from the 'practical' policy programme, in attempting to
curtail any further growth in the numbers of 'detribalised' Africans
in the cities.

These political conflicts were reflected ideologically. Partly in an
attempt to mask the controversy and present a united Afrikaner
nationalist front, the NAD articulated its strategy as a two-stage plan
for the future. Incompatible programmes for Apartheid were ideologically reconciled as two successive stages in a long-term blueprint.

The controversy over the meaning of Apartheid lingered on
throughout the 1950s (and, indeed, into the next decade). Fuelling
an ongoing debate about policy, its effect was also clearly visible
within the administrative sphere, in the vacillating stances by
various departmental bureaucrats on the ULPP. Van Rensburg (Departmental Director of Labour in the late 1950s), for example, was
thoroughly unsympathetic to employers' preferences for migrant
labour, and revoked the concessions enacted by his predecessor
allowing for the ULPP to be waived under certain circumstances.

The shift to the second phase of Apartheid, during which influx
control policy was partially redesigned, was inaugurated in the midst
of conflicts within the state once again, over the appropriate course
for Apartheid (although by now the competing positions had been
partially reformulated, and opposing factions reconstituted). In
some quarters, support was forthcoming for more reformist policies
towards Africans in the urban areas, of the sort favoured by
organised commerce, industry, and mining. But BAD policy-makers
were now more responsive to the views of the majority faction within
SABRA, the Broederbond, and the SAAU. The newly realigned
BAD revised its previous stance on economic integration and
African urbanisation. Curbs on economic integration, previously

rejected as undesirable, were now endorsed; and a removals programme, previously thought unnecessary, was initiated to reduce the size of urban African communities in white areas.

The role of these disputes within Afrikanerdom, in shaping the development of Apartheid, has been overlooked in the literature. Also ignored is the effect on the policy-making process of the changing balance of power between the central and local state. During the early 1950s, when the foundations for the first phase of Apartheid were laid, the NAD was profoundly dependent on the views of municipal administrators (particularly the Rand-based Association of Administrators of Non-European Affairs). Nationalist policy-makers were inexperienced and unskilled in matters of 'urban Native administration', and drew heavily on policy proposals tendered by municipalities, particularly on the Rand. The ULPP, which occupied a central place in the design of the NAD's influx control strategy, was an important case in point.

The relationship between central and local state institutions was also critical in explaining the discrepancies between the policy and the practice of influx control. The NAD depended almost entirely on the municipal NEADs to implement departmental policy. But the NEADs were at the nexus of competing interests and pressures. On the one hand, they were answerable to the NAD. Yet, as employees of elected town or city councils, they were also responsive to the interests of local ratepayers—particularly local industrial or commercial concerns—on the other. The NEADs therefore often favoured a more flexible application of NAD policy than the architects of these policies or the Department's bureaucrats. It was municipal administrators, for example, who regularly waived the ULPP in line with employers' interests—despite the fact that the policy was originally recommended by municipal administrators. Once it became clear that the ULPP could not be imposed without alienating employers and creating local labour shortages, municipal officials running labour bureaux were willing to sacrifice the ULPP. But municipalities did not invariably use their powers in line with the interests of urban capital. For example, the NEADs had a powerful vested interest in retaining direct control over the number of workers accommodated and employed within their areas of jurisdiction. Thus, urban industrialists' calls on the NAD to enlarge the administrative boundaries of the labour bureaux won the backing of Verwoerd, but not of the local authorities.

The application of influx control laws to African women was similarly dominated by municipal decisions. Wary of inciting protest on the issue, local authorities succeeded in pressurising Verwoerd to cede them the authority to determine the women's fate. Most local authorities then pursued far looser controls over African women than the NAD had wanted to institute.

The powers of municipalities rested uncomfortably, however, with the Nationalists' urge to centralise control over Africans in urban areas within the NAD. This strategy was evident in the policy decision enacted in the early 1950s to impose a nationally uniform system of influx control on urban areas (in contradistinction to the previous regime's preparedness to allow local authorities the choice of invoking the influx control laws). But the Nationalists were still too weak to provoke a sustained confrontation with local authorities, and therefore had to base the early formulation of Apartheid policy on the fact of a high degree of municipal autonomy.

It was the NP's improving electoral performance, together with the expansion of the NAD's bureaucracy, which allowed the NAD to chip away at the powers of municipalities. The first such move was to usurp control over the movement and employment of foreign workers; the next encroachment was on municipal powers over the movement of African women. By the end of the 1950s the balance of power between central and local state had begun to shift decisively in favour of the BAD. And this trend was one of the necessary conditions for the policy shift inaugurated in the late 1950s.

### The Impact of 'Struggles from Below'

Collective and individual resistance from African men and women left an indelible mark on the design, legislative promulgation, and administrative implementation of Apartheid generally, and influx control in particular.

Much of the NP's policy platform in the late 1940s was a reaction against the political turbulence of urban African communities. Indeed, the threat of allegedly 'communistic' ideologies—which the NP deemed to include that of the ANC—was one of the principal reasons for the NAD's determination after 1948 to curtail the growth of the urban African proletariat.

Anxiety within the state about the destabilising effects of urban unrest was also an important factor in explaining the transition to Apartheid's second phase. The escalation of African resistance to Apartheid in the late 1950s, which culminated in the Sharpeville shootings, focused national and international attention on the state's policies towards urban Africans, at the same time as refuelling controversy within the state about the political dangers of economic integration and African urbanisation. The policy shifts presaged by the 1960 Bantu in European Areas Bill derived largely from the BAD's view that the unrest reflected shortcomings in state control, and the Bill represented a far more aggressive and ambitious programme for strengthening that control than had been entertained previously.

The legislative effect of collective 'struggles from below' was mixed. The anti-pass protests of the early 1950s had limited results. Resistance in the early 1950s to the state's intentions to extend the influx control system to African women ultimately failed to prevent the enabling law from being passed. Jansen's cautious reprieve early in 1950 was revoked by Verwoerd a few months later. Verwoerd did, however, make one significant, if modest, concession to the broad front of opposition to the new influx control laws. The original section 10(1) in the Native Laws Amendment Act of 1952 was modified to include section 10(1)(b) and (c), which created two narrow, but legal, avenues whereby African urbanisation could continue.

The administrative effects of the mass campaigns against extending influx control to African women were more dramatic. They succeeded in freeing women administratively from the full brunt of the influx control laws for much of the 1950s. Women did not have to carry reference books until the late 1950s; nor were they compelled to register with labour bureaux. Also, in ceding these concessions, Verwoerd handed over direct control over the movement and employment of African women to municipalities. Most municipal administrators, wary of sparking further protests and keen to alleviate shortages of domestic workers, took a less agressive line on influx control for women than for men. Thus, although mass protests failed to hinder the passage of the legislation, the administrative concessions which were won created important loopholes in the NAD's drive to curb women's migration to the urban areas. And, partly for that reason, the proportion of women settling and raising families in urban areas during the 1950s went up—not down, as the NAD had intended.

Women's reprieve was relatively short-lived, however. After 1955 their protests met with the same uncompromising response from the NAD as men's. By the end of the decade the NAD had rescinded its previous concessions. African women were subjected to the Labour Bureaux Regulations, and compelled to carry reference books. Moreover, in order to ensure that these controls were rigorously enforced, the NAD revoked the municipalities' discretionary powers of influx control. Control over African women's movement and employment was now wholly in the hands of the NAD, intent on reversing the failures of its previous drive to curtail African urbanisation.

While collective resistance to influx control thus had limited success, other unorganised and less dramatic forms of resistance were highly effective in subverting the NAD's influx control programme. Despite its formidable powers and draconian laws, the NAD never succeeded in deterring vast numbers of Africans from living and working in the cities illegally. One of the most daunting obstacles to the ULPP during the 1950s and beyond was resistance from migrant and urbanised work-seekers alike (which in turn fed, and was fuelled by, employers' disregard for the labour bureaux system). Urbanised work-seekers had nothing to gain from submitting to the Labour Bureaux Regulations; the ULPP threatened to remove their freedom to refuse 'obnoxious' work until better-paying work became available, or to avoid formal employment in favour of informal economic activities in the townships. And, ironically, the terms of the newly introduced section 10(1)(a), (b), and (c) qualifications (which defined the members of the officially 'urbanised' group) afforded the *legal right* to evade the labour bureaux system. For section 10(1)(a), (b), and (c) qualifiers were permitted to remain in a particular prescribed area, whether or not they were placed in registered employment by labour bureaux. Migrants, too, had compelling reasons to assert their independence from the labour bureaux. The pressures of rural poverty, and the job clustering fostered by migrant associations, led many migrants to take the jobs which urbanised people disdained. But this opportunity was seriously endangered by the NAD's plans to control the allocation of work in terms of the ULPP. The ULPP also threatened to destroy the urban networks built up by migrant associations. Colonising particular places and types of work allowed these associations to maintain cohesion and support amongst migrants from the same clan or district. But the labour bureaux were poised to smash this control. The reach and powers of the labour bureaux expanded during the decade, but they were severely checked by the determined (if often desperate) evasion of the labour bureaux by thousands of African workers. And, as a result, the state remained unable to restructure urban employment practices in the manner intended.

The NAD's parallel drive to limit the numbers of African people inhabiting the urban areas was similarly thwarted by the cumulative effect of informal resistance. Defrauding house tenancy records and repeatedly 'losing' or forging reference books were but two instances of the 'unarticulated, disorganised protest and resistance which the state found most difficult to . . . suppress'.[1]

## Historiographical and Theoretical Conclusions

### The Liberal–Revisionist Debate

This study has shown that the purposes and effects of influx control (and indeed Apartheid more generally) had a complex and hetero-genous relationship to capitalist interests, which simplistic 'either/or' terms of debate between liberals and revisionists cannot capture.

On the one hand, liberals have failed to recognise the sense in which satisfying the industrial and commercial demand for African labour was always one of the principal purposes of the NAD's influx control policy, although the NAD's policy-makers were more prag-matic in this respect during the first phase of Apartheid than in the second. Still, even during the 1960s the state's 'institutional self-interest' in the renewed vitality of the capitalist economy mitigated the introduction of policies which might have inflicted serious economic damage on the country's industries. This 'self-interest' is also one of the reasons why the NAD generally allowed policies which had proven economically disruptive, to be administered rela-tively flexibly, although the degree of flexibility itself varied over time and between different state functionaries.

On the other hand, to date, revisionists have not recognised the point at which the purposes of influx control (as opposed to the way in which it was administered) conflicted with the interest of

[1] Van Onselen, *Chibaro*, p. 227.

manufacturing and commercial capital, in both the 1950s and 1960s. During the 1950s the ULPP was pivotal to the NAD's influx control strategy. Yet, as mentioned earlier, it was starkly at odds with the interests of the majority of industrial and commercial employers, who relied heavily on cheap migrant labour for unskilled work. Nor did the more capital-intensive industries stand to gain much from the ULPP, as it compelled all employers to procure the services of all their African workers through labour bureaux, which took no account of workers' skills and previous experience in allocating work. During the 1960s the BAD's influx control policy then introduced the additional inconvenience of labour quotas, restricting the maximum number of Africans employable in certain industries in particular areas.

This study has shown that the practice of influx control affected commerce and industry in uneven ways, which once again defy the starkly polarised terms of debate between liberals and revisionists. On the one hand, one of the striking features of the 1950s was the extent to which the ULPP was administratively waived or thwarted, succumbing to opposition from employers (along with workers). Indeed, in most areas the ULPP was a dead letter. The extent of the NAD's administrative flexibility in accommodating the labour needs of urban industry and commerce, then, vindicates a revisionist critique of liberal historians. On the other hand, this pragmatism was by no means guaranteed, which produced or exacerbated some of the economic irrationalities of influx control identified by liberal scholars. In some cases, the ULPP was imposed willy-nilly by inflexible state bureaucrats, despite the fact that it aggravated labour shortages in unpopular categories of work. An intransigent attitude to industrialists' interests was particularly marked in the case of foreign workers (who constituted a large proportion of the African work-force in urban areas). Administrative obstacles to employers' interests were encountered within local state institutions too. For example, industrialists' interests in a more mobile work-force were subordinated to municipalities' interests in retaining direct control over the number of Africans employed in their areas of jurisdiction.

Finally the 'either/or' formulation of the liberal–revisionist debate is also belied by the complexity of the notion of capitalist 'interests'. That the NAD's influx control policy had both costs and benefits for industrial capitalists is partly an indication of the divergent nature of their interests. Influx control regulations which denied workers the right to choose their preferred type of work, and which criminalised a person's presence in the urban areas unless he or she was in registered employment, exacerbated the already high labour turnover. For employers lacking the motive or capital to mechanise their operations, this instability of employment was a small price to pay for the ways in which influx control cheapened the price of labour by undermining the bargaining power of illegal workers. For more capital-intensive concerns, however, the enormously high labour turnover was a serious obstacle to improving labour productivity. Also, features of influx control which promoted the immediate interests of many *individual* capitalists had certain long-term costs for the capitalist *class*. Thus, the fact that the practice of influx control depressed the price of unskilled labour was in the individual interests of the urban majority of employers during the 1950s. And it was beneficial to the capitalist class, in so far as industrial concerns continued to expand on the strength of low labour costs. But low wages have had long-term costs for the class. The resultant high labour turnover has retarded labour productivity. Low wages have also inhibited the growth of domestic markets by limiting Africans' purchasing power. And, as organised commerce and industry predicted after the 1957 Alexandra bus boycott, the wage issue has been a burning grievance within an increasingly militant African working class.

## The Nature of the State

This study has underlined the importance of distinguishing analytically between the state's 'institutional self-interest' in accumulation, and its responsiveness to particular dominant class interests at any particular time. For example, throughout the 1950s the state remained acutely sensitive to the interests of white commercial agriculture, one of the key constituencies on which the NP depended heavily for re-election. Until the end of the 1950s, although the NP's prospects of re-election improved, they remained uncertain. Determined to consolidate and extend its power base, the Nationalist government had to make sure not to alienate the support of the agricultural sector. Yet, the overall health of the economy required that agricultural interests could not take precedence over those of manufacturing, by far the greater contributor to the gross national product. From an economic point of view, what the architects of influx control attempted to do was to serve the agricultural cause in ways which did not disrupt the flow of labour to the manufacturing sector.

It has also been shown, however, that the state cannot be understood as simply the guardian of the capitalist system. The analysis of influx control has revealed that the Apartheid state's imperatives were not merely economic. The quest for legitimacy across (white) class lines, coupled with the pursuit of more effective coercive controls, were similarly compelling. Indeed, the state's economic strategies were moulded by the attempt to synthesise economic and political objectives. By 1948 there was an overwhelming consensus among the country's whites that the existing degree of state control over the growth of the urban African population was grossly inadequate. The preservation of white supremacy—again the subject of broad ideological consensus—was seen to be endangered by the sheer size of the African proletariat collecting in the cities, which by the late 1940s had already outnumbered the urban white population. Equally discomforting was the worsening political ferment in the cities. Strengthening the state's hold over the townships, with demonstrable rigour, was thus one of the priorities which motivated the construction of Apartheid.

This study has demonstrated, too, that much about the nature of the state is revealed by delving into its internal institutional mechanisms and divisions. The South African state's strategies in building Apartheid were intimately bound up with, and indeed depended upon, a process of institutional restructuring within the state, which was initiated early in the 1950s and continued into the 1960s. When the NP came to power, the NAD's bureaucracy was small, with limited influence within the state. Also, at this stage, the NAD (along with all other state departments) was dominated by English-speakers with UP sympathies or affiliations. The making of Apartheid went hand in hand with the purging of this so-called 'liberal' element from state bureaucracies, the NAD in particular. Allegedly untrustworthy and uncooperative 'liberals' also dominated many of the local authorities, which exercised considerable control over the urban areas. Relying heavily on the services of the Broederbond, the Nationalist government therefore pursued a vigorous programme of 'Afrikanerisation' within all state institutions, transforming the bureaucracy increasingly into an organ of Afrikaner nationalism generally and the Broederbond in particular. This restructuring was one of the Nationalists' major successes of the 1950s, without which the ambitious social engineering policies of the 1960s would not have been possible.

Another crucial facet in the Nationalists' restructuring of the state was the increasing centralisation of control in central state bureaucracies, especially the NAD, at the expense of local authorities. This in turn necessitated a significant increase in the size of central bureaucracies, to facilitate taking over a range of responsibilities hitherto adopted by local authorities. The proliferation of new bureaucratic structures, such as the labour bureaux system, contributed further to extending the reach and breadth of the NAD's bureaucracy.

Bureaucratic expansion spawned conflict and division within Nationalist ranks, which also made their mark in both the formulation and implementation of Apartheid policy (as surveyed earlier in this chapter). If the construction of Apartheid depended centrally on the restructuring of the state, it was also profoundly shaped by the cleavages and struggles within the state triggered by this restructuring.

In short, the making of Apartheid has exemplified both unifying and fragmenting features of the state. The plethora of state institutions were welded into a single actor through a structural 'self-interest' in promoting capital accumulation, and through the collective interest in consolidating and extending state power. But conflicts within the state emerged over the appropriate mechanisms for pursuing these interests. Indeed, the unevenness in the state's relationship to capitalist interests and powers derived in large measure from cleavages and conflicts within and between state institutions.

An exhaustive understanding of the making of Apartheid has yet to be achieved; but it will depend heavily on probing further the institutional recesses of the state. It is not enough simply to locate the state at the nexus of broader economic, political, and ideological forces (complex and important though this is); it is also necessary to link this exercise to a series of hitherto rather unfashionable questions about the ways in which state institutions enable and constrain the powers of various state actors, in historically specific ways.

# SELECT BIBLIOGRAPHY

## I. Manuscript Sources

Anglo-American Corporation
  Industrial Relations Archive
Associated Chambers of Commerce
  Unsorted Non-European Affairs Files
Brakpan City Council
  Brakpan Municipal Records
  (These records have since been moved to the Central Archive Department)
Central Archives Depot, Pretoria
(The fifty-year rule prevented full use of these records.)
  NTS Vol. 9258 File 4/371; 2229 463/280; 2230 463/280; 7725 166/333;
  2223 430/280; 7651 169/331; 2218 413/280; 9302 1/376; 8585 2/361; 9185
  74/366; 1145 12/162 LD 280 AG106/03
Department of Co-operation and Development Library
  Konferensie van Hoof Bantoesakekommissarisse te Pretoria, 16 tot 18
  November 1961.
Federated Chamber of Industries
  Unsorted Non-European Affairs Files
Killie Campbell Library, University of Natal
  Durban Municipal Records
  S. B. Bourquin Papers
Privately Held Papers
  W. J. P. Carr's Papers
  G. Xorile's Papers
South African Institute of Race Relations Records
  Unsorted South African Institute of Race Relations collection of memo-
  randa in evidence to, and the hearings of, the Native Laws Commission of
  Inquiry
University of South Africa Library
  A. W. G. Champion Papers
  F. J. de Villiers Papers
  Evidence to and Hearings of the Commission for the Socio-economic

Development of the Bantu Areas within the Union of South Africa (Tomlinson Commission)

Ziervogel Papers

University of Witwatersrand, Church of the Province of South Africa Archive

W. and M. Ballinger Papers

J. D. Rheinallt Jones Papers

A. D. Xuma Papers

Microfilms of Evidence to Industrial Legislation Commission of Inquiry, 1951

West Rand Administration Board

Johannesburg Municipal Records

(These records have since been moved to the Intermediate Archive, Johannesburg)

## II. Newspapers, Journals, and Periodicals

*Dagbreek*, 1960–2
*Die Burger*, 1955, 1960.
*Inkululeko*, 1940–50
*New Nation*, 1989.
*Rand Daily Mail*, 1950–63, 1967–8.
*The Friend*, 1955, 1961.
*The Star*, 1954–55, 1958–61, 1963, 1965, 1968
*Die Transvaler*, 1961, 1963
*Die Vaderland*, 1955
*The World*, 1957–70

*Bantu*, 1954–60
*Commercial Opinion*, 1948–64
*Drum*, 1950–63
*The Farmer*, 1950–60
*The Manufacturer*, 1948–60
*NAUNLU*, 1950–60
*National Council of Women News*, 1962
*South African Bureau of Racial Affairs Newsletter*, 1954–60
*Volkshandel*, 1948–60

## III. Interviews Conducted during 1984, 1985, and 1988

Bojong, C. (social worker for Johannesburg NEAD during 1950s)
Bourquin, S. B. (past Manager of Durban NEAD)

Brett, G. (ASSOCOM, Manpower Division)

Carr, W. J. P. (past Manager of Johannesburg NEAD)

Cronje, F. (Department of Co-operation and Development)

de Beer, Z. (Director of Anglo-American Corporation, former United Party MP)

de Villiers, J. C. (past Manager of Johannesburg NEAD)

Duncan, S. (past chairperson of Black Sash)

Godsell, B. (Anglo-American Corporation, Industrial Relations Division)

Knoetze, J. (past Chairman of West Rand Development Board; past Manager of Vanderbijlpark NEAD and Sebokeng NEAD)

Koller, T. W. A. (past Manager of NEAD, Johannesburg)

Lewis, P. (past Johannesburg City Councillor)

Mabin, H. (past Director of ASSOCOM)

Mantata, T. (South African Council of Churches)

Olivier, N. J. (founder member of SABRA, past member of Broederbond)

Oppenheimer, H. (past chairman of Anglo-American Corporation, former United Party MP)

Parsons, R. (Director of ASSOCOM)

Qoboza, P. (past editor of *The World* and employee of Johannesburg municipality during 1950s)

Rees, J. (location superintendent for Johannesburg NEAD during 1950s)

Reynders, H. (Head of National Manpower Commission, past officer of FCI)

Steenhuizen, A. (past Director of Native Labour, Johannesburg NEAD)

Stockenstrom, F. (past Director of AHI)

Strydom, H. (author of important exposé of the Broederbond)

Suzman, H. (Progressive Federal Party MP)

van Zyl, J. (past Director of FCI)

Xorile, G. (past member of Johannesburg Advisory Board)

## IV. Primary Sources

Department of Foreign Affairs, *Dr Malan Explains Apartheid* (1948).

DEPARTMENT OF NATIVE AFFAIRS, 'Native Policy of the Union of South Africa' (NAD Fact Paper no. 9; 1951).

—— 'Progress Report for the Department of Native Affairs during 1949' (NAD Fact Paper no. 10; 1951).

—— 'Progress Report for the Department of Native Affairs during 1950' (NAD Fact Paper no. 11; 1951).

—— 'Memorandum on Availability of Native Labour' (1951).

—— 'Verslag van die Interdepartmentele Kommittee insake Ledige en Nie-Werkende Bantoes in Stedelike Gebiede' ('Botha Report') (1962).

—— 'Verslag van die Interdepartementele Komitee Insake Beheermaat-reëls' ('Van Rensburg Report') (1967).

DURBAN CITY COUNCIL, *Memorandum for Judicial Commission on Native Affairs in Durban* (Durban, 1947).

—— *Mayor's Minute*, 1950–62.

EISELEN, W. M., 'Plan to Rationalise South Africa's Native Labour' (NAD Fact Paper no. 13; 1950).

Institute of Administrators of Non-European Affairs, Record of Proceedings of Annual Conference, 1952–68.

—— Record of Biennial Meeting of Officials, 1966, 1968, 1970.

JOHANNESBURG CITY COUNCIL, *Mayor's Minute*, 1948–66.

—— *Report of the Commission Appointed . . . to Inquire into the Causes . . . of Riots . . . in the Vicinity of Dube Hostel in South-West Native Township . . . 14–15 September 1957 (Centlivres Commission)* (2 Aug. 1958).

REPUBLIC OF SOUTH AFRICA, *House of Assembly Debates*, 1960–65.

—— *Statistical Year Book 1964* (Pretoria, 1964).

—— *Report of the Department of Bantu Affairs and Development for 1958–9.* RP 78/1964.

—— *Report of the Department of Bantu Affairs and Development for 1 Jan. 1961 to 31 Dec. 1961*, RP 72/1962.

—— *Report of the Commission of Inquiry into Legislation Affecting the Utilisation of Manpower (Excluding the Legislation Administered by the Departments of Labour and Mines)*, RP 32/1979.

SOUTH AFRICAN AGRICULTURAL UNION, *Report of the General Council for Submission to Annual Congress*, 1950–64 (Pretoria, 1950–64).

—— 'The South African Agricultural Union, 1904–1954: Brief Outline of its Origin, Growth and Achievements' (n.d.).

—— 'Course for Executive Members of Local Agricultural Organisations: The South African Agricultural Union' (n.d.).

SAUER, P., 'Verslag van die Kleurvraagstuk Kommissie van die Herenigde Nasionale Party' ('Sauer Report') (1947).

TRANSVAAL PROVINCE, *Transvaal Local Government Commission, 1921*, TP 1/1922.

UNION OF SOUTH AFRICA, *Report of the Economic and Wage Commission*, UG 14/1926.

—— *Report of the Native Economic Commission*, UG 22/1932.

—— *Report of the Departmental Committee Appointed to Inquire into and Report upon the Question of Residence of Natives in Urban Areas and Certain Proposed Amendments of the Natives (Urban Areas) Act No. 21 of 1923* (Young–Barrett Report) (1935).

—— *House of Assembly Debates*, 1935–59.

—— *Notes on Conference between Municipalities and Native Affairs Department Held at Pretoria on 28 and 29 September 1937, to Discuss the Provisions of the Native Laws Amendment Act (No. 46 of 1937)*, UG 56/1937.

UNION OF SOUTH AFRICA, *Report of the Native Farm Labour Committee, 1937–9* GP S 3396–1939–102.

—— *Interim Report of the Industrial and Agricultural Requirements Commission*, UG 40/1941.

—— *Report of the Interdepartmental Committee on Social, Health and Economic Conditions of Urban Natives*, GP S 7272, 1942–3.

—— *Review of the Activities of the Department of Native Affairs for the Year 1942–3*, GP S 8618.

—— *Report of Committee on Native Farm Labour*, GP S 5203, 1943–4.

—— *Report of the Commission Appointed to Inquire into the Operation of Bus Services for Non-Europeans on Witwatersrand and in Pretoria, Vereeniging*, UG 31/1944.

—— *Report of the Board of Trade and Industries, no. 282: Investigation into Manufacturing Industries in the Union of South Africa* (Pretoria, 1945).

—— *Report of the Native Laws Commission 1946–8 (Fagan Commission)*, UG 28/1948.

—— *Report of the Department of Native Affairs*, UG 14/1948.

—— *Senate Debates*, 1948–59.

—— *Report of the Wage Board, 1948*, UG 50/1950.

—— *Report of the Commission Appointed to Inquire into Acts of Violence Committed by Natives at Krugersdorp, Newlands, Randfontein and Newclare*, UG 47/1950.

—— *Industrial Classification of the Economically Active Population 1946, Special Report no. 186* (Pretoria, 1950–1).

—— *Report of the Native Laws Commission 1946–8 (Fagan Commission)*, UG 30/1953.

—— *Report of the Native Affairs Commission for the Period 1 January 1948 to 31 December 1952*, UG 36/1954.

—— *Classification and Status of Urban and Rural Areas* (Pretoria, 1953–4).

—— *Population Census, 1946*, vol. 5, UG 41/1954.

—— *34th Industrial Census 1950–1, Special Report no. 201* (Pretoria, 1954–5).

—— *Population Census 1951*, vol. 1, UG 42/1955.

—— *Summary of the Report of the Commission for the Socio-Economic Development of the Bantu Areas within the Union of South Africa (Tomlinson Commission)*, UG 61/1955.

—— *Report of the Department of Native Affairs for the Year 1951/2*, UG 37/1955.

—— *Report of the Department of Native Affairs for the Year 1952/3*, UG 48/1955.

—— *Report of the Department of Native Affairs for the Year 1953/4*, UG 53/1956.

—— *Report of the Commission of Inquiry into Policy Relating to the Protection of Industries*, UG 36/1958.

—— *Report of the Department of Native Affairs for the Years 1954–7*, UG 14/1959.

—— *Memorandum Explaining the Background and Objects of the Promotion of Bantu Self-Government Bill, 1959*, NP 3–1959.

—— *Industrial Census 1956–7, Special Report No. 240* (Pretoria, 1960–1).

—— *Report of the Bantu Affairs Commission for the Period 1 January 1957 to 31 December 1960*, UG 36/1961.

UNITED PARTY, *The Native and Coloured People's Policy of the United Party* (Johannesburg, 1948).

## V. Secondary Sources

*Books and Published Articles*

ADAM, H. and GILIOMEE, H., *Ethnic Power Mobilized: Can South Africa Change?* (New Haven, 1979).

ALLEN, C., and WILLIAMS, G., *Sociology of 'Developing Societies': Sub-Saharan Africa* (London, 1982).

ATTWELL M., *South Africa: Background to the Crisis* (London, 1986).

BALLINGER M., *From Union to Apartheid* (Cape Town and Johannesburg, 1969).

BARKER, W. E., 'South Africa can do without Native Labour', *Journal of Racial Affairs*, 4/4 (1953).

BARNARD, F., *Thirteen Years with Dr H. F. Verwoerd* (Johannesburg, 1967).

BEAVON, K., and ROGERSON C., 'The Council vs. the Common People: The Case of Street Trading in Johannesburg', *Geoforum*, 17/2 (1986).

—— 'The Changing Role of Women in the Urban Informal Sector of Johannesburg', in D. Drakakis-Smith (ed.), *Urbanisation in the Developing World* (London, 1986).

BEKKER, S., and HUMPHRIES, R., *From Control to Confusion: The Changing Role of Administration Boards in South Africa* (Pietermaritzburg, 1985).

BEINART, W., *The Political Economy of Pondoland* (Cambridge, 1982).

—— 'Worker Consciousness, Ethnic Particularism and Nationalism: The Experiences of a South African Migrant, 1930–1960', in S. Marks and S. Trapido (eds.), *The Politics of Race, Class and Nationalism in Twentieth Century South Africa* (London and New York, 1987).

—— and BUNDY, C., *Hidden Struggles in Rural South Africa* (Johannesburg, 1987).

BELL, T., 'Migrant Labour: Theory and Policy', *South African Journal of Economics*, 40/4 (1972).

BERGER, I., 'Solidarity Fragmented: Garment Workers of the Transvaal, 1930–1960', in S. Marks and S. Trapido (eds.), *The Politics of Race, Class and Nationalism in Twentieth Century South Africa* (London and New York, 1987).

BERGER, S., and PIORE, M., *Dualism and Discontinuity in Industrial Societies* (Cambridge, 1980).

BERNSTEIN, H., *For their Triumphs and for their Tears: Women in Apartheid South Africa* (London, 1985).

BLOOM, H., *Transvaal Episode* (Cape Town, 1956; repr. 1986).

—— 'The South African Police: Laws and Powers', *Africa South*, 2/2 (1958).

BOETIE, D., *Familiarity is the Kingdom of the Lost*, ed. B. Simon (London, 1969; repr. 1984).

BONACICH, E., 'A Theory of Ethnic Antagonism: The Split Labour Market', *American Sociological Review*, 37/5 (1972).

BONNER, P., 'Family, Crime and Political Consciousness on the East Rand, 1939–1955', *Journal of Southern African Studies*, 14/3 (1988).

—— and LAMBERT, R., 'Batons and Bare Heads: The Strike at Amato Textiles, February 1958', in S. Marks and S. Trapido (eds.), *The Politics of Race, Class and Nationalism in Twentieth Century South Africa* (London and New York, 1987).

BOTHA, J., *Verwoerd is Dead* (Cape Town, 1967).

BOZZOLI, B., 'Capital and the State in South Africa', *Review of African Political Economy*, 11 (1978).

—— 'Marxism, Feminism and South African Studies', *Journal of Southern African Studies*, 9/2 (1983).

BRANDEL-SYRIER, M., *Black Women in Search of God* (London, 1962).

BUNTING, B., 'The African in Industry', *Africa South*, 4/1 (1959).

—— *The Rise of the South African Reich* (Harmondsworth, 1969).

—— 'The Origins of Apartheid', in A. la Guma (ed.), *Apartheid: A Collection of Writings on South African Racism by South Africans* (London, 1972).

CARTER, G., *The Politics of Inequality: South Africa since 1948* (London, 1958).

—— *Which Way is South Africa Going?* (Bloomington, 1980).

COCK, J., *Maids and Madams* (Johannesburg, 1980).

COMMONWEALTH EMINENT PERSONS' GROUP, *Mission to South Africa: The Commonwealth Report* (Harmondsworth, 1986).

COOK, A., *Akin to Slavery: Prison Labour in South Africa* (London, 1982).

CRONJE, G., *'n Tuiste vir die Nageslag: Die Blywende Oplossing van Suid Afrika se Rassevraagstukke* (Johannesburg, 1945).

—— *Voogdyskap en Apartheid* (Pretoria, 1948).

DAVENPORT, T. R., 'African Townsmen? South African Natives (Urban Areas) Legislation through the Years', *African Affairs* 68/271 (1969).

—— *South Africa: A Modern History* (London, 1977; repr. 1987).

DAVIES, R., *Capital, State and White Labour in South Africa* (London, 1979).

—— KAPLAN, D., MORRIS, M., and O'MEARA, D., 'Class Struggle and the Periodisation of the State in South Africa', *Review of African Political Economy*, 7 (1976).

DELIUS, P., 'Sebatakgomo: Migrant Organisation, the ANC and the Sekhukhuneland Revolt', *Journal of Southern African Studies*, 15/4 (1989).

DE KLERK, M., 'Seasons that will never Return: The Impact of Farm Mechanization on Employment, Incomes and Population Distribution in the Western Transvaal', *Journal of Southern African Studies*, 11/1 (1984).

DE KLERK, W. A., *The Puritans in Africa: A History of Afrikanerdom* (1975; Harmondsworth, 1976).

DE VILLIERS, R., 'The State, Capital and Labour Allocation—The Johannesburg Municipality, 1948–1962', *Africa Perspective*, 12 (1979).

DIKOBE, M., *The Marabi Dance* (London, 1973).

DUNBAR MOODIE, T., *The Rise of Afrikanerdom* (Berkeley, Los Angeles, and London, 1975).

DU TOIT, A., 'Ideological Change, Afrikaner Nationalism and Pragmatic Race Domination in South Africa', in L. Thompson and J. Butler (eds.), *Change in Contemporary South Africa* (California, 1975).

DU TOIT, B., *Ukubamba Amadolo: Workers' Struggles in the South African Textile Industry* (London, 1978).

EDWARDS, I., 'Shebeen Queens: Illicit Liquor and the Social Structure of Drinking Dens in Cato Manor', *Agenda*, 3 (1988).

EISELEN, W. M., 'The Meaning of Apartheid', *Race Relations*, 15/3 (1948).

—— 'Is Separation Practicable?', *Journal of Racial Affairs*, 1/2 (1950).

—— 'The Demand for and the Supply of Bantu Labour', *Bantu*, 5 (1958).

—— 'Harmonious Multi-Community Development', *Optima* (1959).

ELOFF, J. F., 'Die Verandering en Verval van die Gesinslewe van die Stedelike Bantoe', *Journal of Racial Affairs*, 4/3–4 (1953).

ELSTER, J., *Making Sense of Marx* (Cambridge, 1985).

FIRST, R., 'The Bus Boycott', *Africa South*, 1/4 (1957).

—— 'Bethal Case-Book', *Africa South*, 2/3 (1958).

FRANKLIN, N. N., *Economics in South Africa* (Cape Town, 1954).

FREDERIKSON, G., *White Supremacy* (New York and Oxford, 1981).

GAITSKELL, D., KIMBLE, J., UNTERHALTER, E., 'Historiography in the 1970s: A Feminist Perspective', in *Southern African Studies: Retrospect and Prospect* (Proceedings of Conference held at University of Edinburgh, 30 May–1 June 1983).

GENOVESE, E., *Roll Jordan Roll: The World the Slaves Made* (London, 1975).

GERTH, H. H., and WRIGHT MILLS, C. (eds.), *From Max Weber: Essays in Sociology* (London 1948; repr. 1977).

GIDDENS, A., and HELD, D. (eds.), *Classes, Power and Conflict* (London, 1982).

GILIOMEE, H., and SCHLEMMER, L. (eds.), *Up Against the Fences: Poverty, Passes and Privilege in South Africa* (Cape Town and Johannesburg, 1985).

GLASS, Y., *The Black Industrial Worker: A Social Psychological Study* (Johannesburg, 1960).

GOTTSCHALK, K., 'Industrial Decentralisation, Jobs and Wages', *South African Labour Bulletin*, 3/5 (1977).

GREENBERG, S., *Race and State in Capitalist Development* (Johannesburg, 1980).

GRIFFITHS, H. R., and JONES, R. A., *South African Labour Economics* (Johannesburg, 1980).

HARRIS, J. R., and TODARO, M. P., 'Migration, Unemployment and Development: A Two-Sector Analysis', *American Economic Review*, 60/1 (1970).

HARRISON, D., *The White Tribe of Africa* (Berkeley, 1981).

HEARD, K., *General Elections in South Africa, 1943–1970* (Oxford, 1974).

HELD, D. (ed.), *States and Societies* (Oxford, 1983).

—— and KRIEGER, J., 'Accumulation, Legitimation and the State: The Ideas of Claus Offe and Jurgen Habermas', in D. Held (ed.), *States and Societies* (Oxford, 1983).

HELLMAN, E., 'The Importance of Beer-Brewing in an Urban African Yard', *Bantu Studies*, 8/1 (1935).

—— *Rooiyard: A Sociological Survey of an Urban Native Slum Yard* (Cape Town, 1948).

—— (ed.), *Handbook on Race Relations* (Cape Town, 1949).

HEPPLE, A., 'The Fiery Cross of Job Reservation', *Africa South*, 2/3 (1958).

—— *Poverty Wages* (Johannesburg, 1959).

—— 'Unemployment by Race', *Africa South*, 4/2 (1960).

—— *Verwoerd* (Harmondsworth, 1967).

—— *South Africa: Workers under Apartheid* (London, 1969).

HEYMANS, C., and TOTEMEYER, G., *Government by the People?: The Politics of Local Government in South Africa* (Cape Town and Johannesburg, 1988).

HINDSON, D., *Pass Controls and the Urban African Proletariat in South Africa* (Johannesburg, 1987).

HOBART HOUGHTON, D., 'Men of Two Worlds: Some Aspects of

Migratory Labour in South Africa', *South African Journal of Economics*, 28/3 (1960).

—— 'Labour in African Development', in E. A. G. Robinson (ed.), *Economic Development for Africa South of the Sahara* (London, 1964).

—— *The South African Economy* (Cape Town, 1964).

—— and DAGUT, J., *Source Material on the South African Economy, 1960–1970*, iii. 1920–1970 (Oxford, 1963).

HOLLEMAN, J. F., 'Die Bantoehuwelik op die Kruispad', *Journal of Racial Affairs*, 11/2 (1960).

HORRELL, M., *Non-European Policies in the Union and the Measure of their Success* (Johannesburg, 1953).

—— *South Africa's Non-White Workers* (Johannesburg, 1956).

—— *Days of Crisis in South Africa* (Johannesburg, 1960).

—— *The Pass Laws* (Johannesburg, 1960).

—— *Legislation and Race Relations* (Natal, 1971).

HORWITZ, R., *Expand or Explode: Apartheid's Threat to South African Industry* (Cape Town, 1957).

—— *The Political Economy of South Africa* (London, 1967).

HUDDLESTON, T., *Naught for your Comfort* (London, 1956).

HUTT, W., *The Economics of the Colour Bar* (London, 1964).

HUMPHRISS, D., and THOMAS, D., *Benoni, Son of my Sorrow* (Cape Town, 1968).

INNES, D., *Anglo American and the Rise of Modern South Africa* (Johannesburg, 1984).

JOHNSTONE, F., 'White Supremacy and White Prosperity in South Africa', *African Affairs*, 69/275 (1970).

—— *Class, Race and Gold* (London, 1976).

JOSEPH, H., 'Women and Passes', *Africa South*, 2/2 (1958) and 3/3 (1959).

KAHN, E., 'Whither our War-Time Policy', *South African Journal of Economics*, 10/2 (1942).

—— 'The Pass Laws', in E. Hellman (ed.), *Handbook on Race Relations* (Cape Town, 1949).

KANE-BERMAN, J., *Soweto: Black Revolt, White Reaction* (Johannesburg, 1978).

KARIS, T., and CARTER, G., *From Protest to Challenge: Documents of African Politics in South Africa, 1882–1964* (California, 1977), ii, iii.

KATZEN, M. A., *Industry in Greater Durban* (Pietermaritzburg, 1961).

KEPPEL-JONES A., *South Africa: A Short History* (London, 1949; repr. 1975).

KLEU, S. J., 'Industrial Policy' in J. Lombard (ed.), *Economic Policy in South Africa: Selected Essays* (Cape Town, n.d.).

KRIGE, E. J., 'Changing Conditions in Marital Relations and Parental Duties among Urbanized Natives', *Africa*, 9/1 (1936).

KROS, C., *Urban African Women's Organisations, 1953–1956* (Johannesburg, 1980).

KRUGER, D. W., *South African Parties and Policies* (London, 1960).

KUPER, L., 'Rights and Riots in Natal', *Africa South*, 4/2 (1960).

KUZWAYO, E., *Call Me Woman* (London, 1985).

LA GUMA, A. (ed.), *Apartheid: A Collection of Writings on South African Racism by South Africans* (London, 1972).

LANGUAGE, F. J., 'Native Housing in Urban Areas', *Journal of Racial Affairs*, 1/2 (1950).

LAPPING, B., *Apartheid: A History* (London, 1987).

LAZAR, J., 'The Role of SABRA in the Formulation of Apartheid Ideology, 1948–1961', *The Societies of Southern Africa in the Nineteenth and Twentieth Centuries* (Collected Seminar Papers, Institute of Commonwealth Studies, University of London, 17; 1987).

LEGASSICK, M., 'South Africa: Capital Accumulation and Violence', *Economy and Society*, 3/3 (1974).

—— 'Legislation, Ideology and Economy in post-1948 South Africa', *Journal of Southern African Studies*, 1/1 (1974).

LIPTON, M., *Capitalism and Apartheid: South Africa, 1910–1986* (London, 1985).

LITTLE, K., *African Women in Towns: An Aspect of Africa's Social Revolution* (Cambridge, 1973).

LODGE, T., *Black Politics in South Africa since 1945* (London and New York, 1983).

LONGMORE, L., *The Dispossessed: A Study of the Sex-Life of Bantu Women in Urban Areas in and around Johannesburg* (London, 1959).

LONSDALE, J., 'States and Social Processes in Africa: A Historiographical Survey', *African Studies Review*, 24/2–3 (1981).

LUCAS, C. F., 'The Cost to Law and Order', *Africa South*, 2/4 (1958).

LUCKHARDT, K., and WALL B., *Organize or Starve! The History of the South African Congress of Trade Unions* (London, 1980).

LUTHULI, A., *Let my People Go* (London and Glasgow, 1962; repr. 1975).

LUKES, S., *Power: A Radical View* (London, 1977).

MAASDORP, G., and HUMPHREYS, A. S. B., *From Shantytown to Township* (Cape Town, 1975).

MAHABANE, E. E., 'Marital Conditions', *Race Relations*, 14/4 (1947).

MANDELA, N., *The Struggle is my Life* (London, 1978).

MARCUS, T., *Restructuring in Commercial Agriculture in South Africa* (Amsterdam, 1986).

MARKS, S., 'Recent Developments in the Historiography of South Africa', *Research Bulletin, Southern Africa and the World Economy* (Fernand Braudel Centre, 3; 1982).

—— and Rathbone, R. (eds.), *Industrialisation and Social Change in South*

*Africa: African Class Formation, Culture and Consciousness, 1870–1930* (London and New York, 1983).

—— and Trapido, S. (eds.), *The Politics of Race, Class and Nationalism in Twentieth Century South Africa* (London and New York, 1987).

MARQUARD, L., *The People and Policies of South Africa* (Cape Town, 1960).

MATHEWSON, J. E., *The Establishment of an Urban Bantu Township* (Pretoria, 1957).

MAYER, P., and MAYER I., *Townsmen or Tribesmen* (Cape Town, 1961).

MBEKI, G., *The Peasants' Revolt* (Harmondsworth, 1964).

McLEAN, R. C., *How to use Industrial Native Labour Efficiently* (Johannesburg, 1958).

MODISANE, B., *Blame Me on History* (Johannesburg, 1986).

MORRIS, M., 'The Development of Capitalism in South African Agriculture: Class Struggle in the Countryside', *Economy and Society*, 5/3 (1976).

—— 'State Intervention and the Agricultural Labour Supply post-1948', in F. Wilson, A. Kooy, and D. Hendrie (eds.), *Farm Labour in South Africa* (Cape Town, 1977).

MURRAY, M. (ed.), *South African Capitalism and Black Opposition* (Massachusetts, 1982).

MYERS, D. *US Business in South Africa* (London, 1980).

NATTRASS, J., *The South African Economy: Its Growth and Change* (Cape Town, 1981).

NGCOBO, S. B., 'The Urban Bantu Family as a Unit', *Race Relations*, 14/4 (1947).

—— 'The Response of Africans to Industrial Employment', *Race Relations*, 21/1 (1954).

NTANTALA, P., 'Widows of the Reserves', *Africa South*, 2/3 (1958).

NOKWE, D., 'The South African Police: Laws and Powers', *Africa South*, 2/2 (1958).

NORVAL, A. J., *A Quarter of a Century of Industrial Progress in South Africa* (Cape Town, 1962).

O'MEARA, D., 'The 1946 African Mine Workers' Strike in the Political Economy of South Africa', *Journal of Commonwealth and Comparative Politics*, 13/2 (1975).

—— *Volkskapitalisme* (Cambridge, 1983).

—— '"Muldergate" and the Politics of Afrikaner Nationalism', *Work in Progress*, 22 (1983).

OLIVIER, N. J., 'Ons Stedelike Naturellebevolking', *Journal of Racial Affairs*, 10/2–3 (1959).

OWEN, K., *Foreign Africans: Summary of the Report of the Froneman Committee of 1962* (Johannesburg, 1964).

PAUW, B. A., *The Second Generation: A Study of the Family amongst Urbanised Bantu* (Cape Town, 1963).

PELZER, A. N. (ed.), *Verwoerd Speaks* (Johannesburg, 1966).

PIORE, M., *Birds of Passage: Migrant Labour and Industrial Societies* (Cambridge, 1979).

PLATZKY, L., and WALKER, C., *The Surplus People: Forced Removals in South Africa* (Johannesburg, 1985).

PLAUT, M., and INNES, D., 'Class Struggle and the State', *Review of African Political Economy*, 7 (1976).

POSEL, D. B., 'Rethinking the "Race–Class Debate" in South African Historiography', *Social Dynamics*, 9/1 (1983).

—— 'The Meaning of Apartheid before 1948: Conflicts of Interests and Powers within the Afrikaner Nationalist Alliance', *Journal of Southern African Studies*, 14/1 (1987).

—— 'Doing Business with the Pass Laws: Influx Control Policy and the Interests of Manufacturing and Commerce in South Africa in the 1950s', *The Societies of Southern Africa in the Nineteenth and Twentieth Centuries* (Collected Seminar Papers, Institute of Commonwealth Studies, University of London, 17; 1987).

—— '"Providing for the Legitimate Labour Requirements of Employers": Secondary Industry, Commerce and the State during the 1950s', in A. Mabin (ed.), *Organisation and Economic Change* (Southern African Studies, 5; Johannesburg, 1989).

READER, D. H., *The Black Man's Portion: History, Demography and Living Conditions in the Native Locations of East London Cape Province* (Cape Town, 1961).

RHOODIE, N. J., *Apartheid and Racial Partnership in South Africa* (Pretoria, 1969).

RICH, P., 'Ministering to White Man's Needs: The Development of Urban Segregation in South Africa, 1913–1923', *African Studies*, 37/2 (1978).

ROBERTS, M., *Labour in the Farm Economy* (Johannesburg, 1958).

—— *African Farm Labour: Some Conclusions and Reflections* (Johannesburg, 1959).

ROBERTSON, J., *Liberalism in South Africa*, 1948–1963 (Oxford, 1971).

ROBINSON, E. A. G. (ed.), *Economic Development for Africa South of the Sahara* (London, 1964).

ROGERSON, C., 'The Council vs. The Common People: The Case of Street Trading in Johannesburg', *Geoforum*, 17/2 (1986).

ROTBERG, R., *Suffer the Future* (Cambridge and London, 1980).

ROUX, E., *Time Longer than Rope* (Wisconsin, 1948; repr. 1978).

SCHLEMMER, L., and WEBSTER, E. (eds.), *Change, Reform and Economic Growth in South Africa* (Johannesburg, 1978).

SCHOEMAN, B., *Van Malan tot Verwoerd* (Cape Town, 1973).

SIMKINS, C., *Four Essays on the Past, Present, and Possible Future of the Distribution of the Black Population of South Africa* (Cape Town, 1983).

—— 'Household Composition and Structure in South Africa', in S. Burman and P. Reynolds (eds.), *Growing Up in A Divided Society: The Contexts of Childhood in South Africa* (Johannesburg, 1986).

SIMONS, H. J., 'Passes and Police', *Africa South*, 1/1 (1956).

—— *African Women: Their Legal Status* (London, 1968).

—— and SIMONS, R. E., *Class and Colour in South Africa, 1850–1950* (Baltimore, 1969).

SKOCPOL, T., *States and Social Revolutions* (Cambridge, 1979).

SMITH, R. H., 'Some Economic Aspects of Changing Native Policy', *Race Relations*, 11/3–4 (1944).

SNITCHER, F., 'The Eiselen Scheme', *Africa South*, 1/3 (1957).

South African Bureau of Racial Affairs, *Die Naturellevraagstuk: Referate Gelewer op die Eerste Jaarsvergadering van SABRA* (Stellenbosch, 1950).

—— *Integration or Separate Development* (Setellenbosch, 1952).

South African Institute of Race Relations, *Annual Survey of Race Relations in South Africa*, 1946–70 (Johannesburg, 1946–1970).

—— 'A Survey of Urban and Rural Areas', *Race Relations*, 14/2 (1947).

—— *The Economic Development of the 'Reserves'* (Johannesburg, 1959).

—— *African Farm Labour: A Survey* (Johannesburg, 1959).

STADLER, A. W., 'Birds in the Cornfield: Squatter Movements in Johannesburg, 1944–47', *Journal of Southern African Studies*, 6/1 (1979).

—— *The Political Economy of Modern South Africa* (Cape Town and Johannesburg, 1987).

STEENKAMP, W. F. J., 'Bantu Wages in South Africa', *South African Journal of Economics*, 30/2 (1962).

STEYN, A., and RIP, C., 'The Changing Urban Bantu Family', *Journal of Marriage and the Family*, 30/3 (1968).

TRAPIDO, S., 'Political Institutions and Afrikaner Social Structures', *American Political Science Review*, 57/1 (1963).

—— 'African Opposition in South Africa, 1949–1961', in *Collected Papers on Opposition in the New African States* (University of London, 1967–8).

—— 'South Africa in a Comparative Study of Industrialisation', *Journal of Development Studies*, 7/3 (1971).

TROUP, F., *South Africa: An Historical Introduction* (Harmondsworth, 1975).

TUCKER, R. (ed.), *The Marx–Engels Reader* (2nd ed., New York, 1978).

TUROK, B., 'The African on the Farm', *Africa South*, 4/1 (1959).

VAN DEN BERGHE, P., *Race and Racism: A Comparative Perspective* (New York, London, and Sydney, 1967).

VAN DER HORST, S., 'The African Worker in Urban Areas', *Race Relations*, 13/2 (1946).

VAN DER HORST, S., 'Native Urban Employment', *South African Journal of Economics*, 16/3 (1948).

—— 'A Note on Native Labour Turnover and the Structure of the Labour Force in the Cape Peninsula', *South African Journal of Economics*, 25/4 (1957).

—— 'The Economic Implications of Political Democracy, *Optima* (1960).

VAN JAARSVELD, F., *From Van Riebeeck to Vorster, 1652–1974* (Johannesburg, 1975).

VAN ONSELEN, C., *Chibaro* (London, 1976).

VAN RENSBURG, P. S. 'Die Instelling van Arbeidsburo's', *Bantu*, 9 (1954).

—— 'Die Uitskakeling van Bantoearbeid in Stadsgebiede', *Journal of Racial Affairs*, 15/1 (1964).

WALKER, C., *Women and Resistance in South Africa* (London, 1982).

WALSHE, A. P., 'The Changing Content of Apartheid', *Review of Politics*, 25 (1963).

WEBER, M., 'Politics as a Vocation', and 'Bureaucracy', in H. H. Gerth and C. Wright Mills (eds.), *From Max Weber: Essays in Sociology* (London, 1948; repr. 1977).

WELSH, A., 'A Tax on Poverty', *Africa South*, 3/2 (1959).

WELSH, D., 'The Growth of Towns', in M. Wilson and L. Thompson (eds.), *Oxford History of South Africa*, ii (Oxford, 1971).

WILKINS, I., and STRYDOM, H., *The Super-Afrikaners* (London, 1979; repr. 1980).

WILSON, F., 'Farming 1866–1966', in M. Wilson and L. Thompson (eds.), *Oxford History of South Africa*, ii (Oxford, 1971).

—— *Labour in the South African Gold Mines, 1911–1969* (Cambridge, 1972).

—— *Migrant Labour in South Africa* (Johannesburg, 1972).

WILSON, F., KOOY, A., and HENDRIE, D. (eds.), *Farm Labour in South Africa* (Cape Town, 1977).

WILSON, M., and MAFEJE, A., *Langa: A Study of Social Groups in an African Township* (Cape Town, 1963).

—— and THOMPSON L. (eds.), *The Oxford History of South Africa*, ii (Oxford, 1971).

WOLPE, H., 'Capitalism and Cheap Labour-Power in South Africa: From Segregation to Apartheid', *Economy and Society*, 1/4 (1972).

—— 'Towards an Analysis of the South African State', *International Journal of the Sociology of Law*, 7/4 (1980).

—— *Race, Class and the Apartheid State* (London, 1988).

WRIGHT, H. M., *The Burden of the Present: Liberal–Radical Controversy over Southern African History* (Cape Town, 1977).

YUDELMAN, D., 'Industrialisation, Race Relations and Change in South Africa', *African Affairs*, 74/294 (1975).

—— 'State and Capital in Contemporary South Africa', in J. Butler, R.

Elphick, and D. Welsh (eds.), *Democratic Liberalism in South Africa* (Connecticut and Cape Town, 1987).

*Unpublished Articles and Theses*

BEINART, W., 'The Origins of the Indlavini: Male Associations and Migrant Labour in the Transkei' (unpublished mimeo, 1987).

BELL, T. 'Surplus Labour and South African Development', presented to 'Workshop on Unemployment and Labour Reallocation' (Pietermaritzburg, 1977).

BONNER, P., '"Desirable or Undesirable Sotho Women?": Liquor, Prostitution, and the Migration of Sotho Women to the Rand, 1920–1945' (Seminar Paper no. 232; African Studies Institute, University of Witwatersrand, 1988).

BRADFORD, H., 'Getting Away with Slavery: Capitalist Farmers, Foreigners and Forced Labour in the Transvaal, *c*.1920–1950' (paper presented to History Workshop Conference, University of Witwatersrand, 1990).

BUDLENDER, D., 'Mechanisation and Labour on White Farms: A Statistical Analysis' (Carnegie Conference Paper no. 26; University of Cape Town, 1984).

CARR, W. J. P., 'Legislation affecting the Employment of Bantu' (paper delivered to Steel and Engineering Industries Federation of South Africa, 1963).

CLARKE, N., 'From Dependence to Definance: South African State Corporations, 1920–1960' (Ph.D. thesis, Yale University, 1988).

DAVENPORT, T. R. H., 'The Beginnings of Urban Segregation in South Africa: The Natives (Urban Areas) Act of 1923 and its Background' (Occasional Paper no. 15; Institute for Social and Economic Research, Rhodes University, 1971).

DE KLERK, F. J., ''n Evaluering van die Administratiewe Reëlings van Swart Arbeid en die Uitwerking daarvan op Munisipale Terrein' (Ph.D. thesis, Port Elizabeth University, 1980).

EDWARDS, I., 'Living on the "Smell of an Oilrag": African Life in Cato Manor Farm in the late 1940s' (paper presented to workshop on African Life in Durban in the Twentieth Century, University of Natal, Durban, 1983).

EVERATT, D., 'The Origins of Multiracialism' (Seminar Paper no. 270; African Studies Institute, University of Witwatersrand, 1990).

GOLDIN, I., 'Coloured Preference Politics and the Making of Coloured Political Identity in the Western Cape Region of South Africa, with particular reference to the period 1948–1984' (D. Phil. thesis, University of Oxford, 1986).

HINDSON, D., 'The Pass System and the Formation of an Urban African Proletariat' (Ph.D. thesis, University of Sussex, 1983).

HOLLEMAN, J. F., 'The Tightrope Dancers: Report on Seventh Annual IANA Conference' (1958).

HORWOOD, O., 'Some Aspects of Urban African Employment in the Durban Area' (SAIRR Natal region paper, 1958).

HUMPHRIES, R., 'Origins and Subsequent Development of Administration Boards' (MA thesis, Rhodes University, 1983).

KUZWAYO E., 'The Role of the African Woman in Towns' (SAIRR paper), RR 207/1960.

LADLAU, L. K., 'The Cato Manor Riots, 1959–1960' (MA thesis, University of Natal, 1975).

LAZAR, J., 'Conformity and Conflict: Afrikaner Nationalist Politics, 1948–1961' (D.Phil. thesis, University of Oxford, 1987).

LODGE, T., 'Class Conflict, Communal Struggle and Patriotic Unity: The Communist Party of South Africa during the Second World War' (Seminar Paper no. 180; African Studies Institute, University of Witwatersrand, 1985).

MACKENZIE, J., 'African Women and the Urbanisation Process in Durban, c.1920–1949' (paper presented to workshop on African Life in Durban in the Twentieth Century, University of Natal, Durban, 1983).

MAYLAM, P., 'Shackled by Contradiction: The Municipal Response to African Urbanisation in Durban, c.1920–1950' (paper presented to workshop on African Urban Life in Durban in the Twentieth Century, University of Natal, Durban, 1983).

—— 'Twentieth Century Durban: Some Thoughts on its Regional Specificity' (paper presented to History Workshop Conference, University of Witwatersrand, 1984).

MOUAT, J. L., 'The Application of the Pass Laws in the Cape Town City Council Area and Cape Divisional Council Area' (unpublished mimeo for SAIRR, 1961).

M'TIMKULU, G. S., 'African Adjustment to Urbanization' (SAIRR paper), RR 36/1955.

POSEL, D. B., 'The Dimensions of Power' (unpublished mimeo, 1983).

—— 'Interests, Conflicts and Powers: The Relationship between the State and Business in South Africa during the 1950s' (paper presented to conference of Association for Sociology in Southern Africa, 1985).

—— 'Coloured Labour Preference Policy in the Western Cape in the 1950s in the Context of National Policy on African Urbanisation' (paper presented to the conference on 'Western Cape: Roots and Realities', University of Cape Town, 1986).

SAPIRE, H., 'African Political Mobilisation in Brakpan in the 1950s' (Seminar Paper no. 250; African Studies Institute, University of Witwatersrand, 1989).

—— 'African Urbanisation and Struggles against Municipal Control in Brakpan, 1920–1958' (Ph.D. thesis, University of Witwatersrand, 1989).

—— 'Popular Politics and the Rationalization of "Urban Native Administration" in Brakpan, 1943–1948' (paper presented to History Workshop Conference, University of Witwatersrand, 1990).

SEEGERS, A., 'The South African State with Special Reference to the Military' (unpublished mimeo, 1987).

SERFONTEIN, C. H., 'Tuislandgerigte Administrasie van Bantoes in Blankbeheerde Gebiede met verwysing na die Wes-Transvaalse Bantoe-sake Administrasie-Raad', (Ph.D. thesis, Potchefstroom University, 1974).

SIMKINS, C., 'African Urbanisation at the Time of the Last Smuts Government' (paper presented to Economic History Conference, University of Cape Town, 1982).

—— 'African Population, Employment and Incomes on Farms outside the Reserves, 1923–1969' (Carnegie Conference Paper no. 25; University of Cape Town, 1984).

South African Institute of Race Relations, 'The Logic of Economic Integration', RR 76/1952.

—— 'The Economic Development of the Reserves: The Extent to which the Tomlinson Commission's Recommendations are being Implemented' (Fact Paper no. 3; 1959).

STARFIELD, J., '"A Documentary Drama": The Case of Malisela Letsoalo and the Banareng Tribe versus the Union Government' (Seminar Paper no. 229; African Studies Institute, University of Witwatersrand, 1988).

SWILLING, M., and PHILLIPS, M., 'The Power and Limits of the Emergency State' (Seminar Paper no. 258; African Studies Institute, University of Witwatersrand, 1989).

TICHMAN, P., 'Worker Resistance in Durban in 1940s and 1950s' (paper presented to workshop on African Life in Durban in the Twentieth Century, University of Natal, Durban, 1983).

TORR, L., 'Lamont: Durban's "Model Village"?: The Realities of Township Life, 1934–1960' (paper presented to Tenth Biennial Conference of South African Historical Society, University of Cape Town, 1985).

WELLS, J., 'The History of Black Women's Struggle against the Pass Laws in South Africa' (Ph.D. thesis, University of Columbia, 1982).

YAWITCH, J., 'Tightening the Noose: African Women and Influx Control in South Africa, 1960–1980' (Carnegie Conference Paper no. 82; 1984).

# INDEX